Visual Studio® 6 For Dummies®

Cheat Sheet

P9-DMQ-974

Object and Component Naming Conventions

Prefix	Object	Example	Prefix	Object	Example
acd	ActiveDoc	acdMainPage	lin	Line	linDivider
chk	CheckBox	chkBoldface	lst	ListBox	lstNames
cbo	ComboBox	cboDropper	olb	OLEBoundControl	olbInsert
cmd	CommandButton	cmdExit	ole	OLE	oleLinker
cmg	CommandGroup	cmgSelectOne	opt	OptionButton	optGreece
cnt	Container	cntFramed	opg	OptionGroup	opgChooseOne
ctl	Control	ctlSeeThis	pag	Page	pagTurn
edt	EditBox	edtWrite	pgf	PageFrame	pgfRule
frm	Form	frmColors	prj	ProjectHook	prjSuzerine
frs	FormSet	frsTypeIn	sep	Separator	sepZone
grd	Grid	grdGoods	shp	Shape	shpRounded
grc	Column	grcQuantity	spn	Spinner	spnWatch
grh	Header	grhYearsResults	txt	TextBox	txtAddress
hpl	HyperLink	hplURL	tmr	Timer	tmrAnimation
img	Image	imgGraphic	tbr	ToolBar	tbrDropThis
lbl	Label	lblContents			

Shortcut Keys for Editors in Visual Studio Applications

Effect	Shortcut Keys To Press
Display the GoTo Line dialog box	Ctrl+g
Move to the bottom of the current window	Ctrl+Page Down
Move to the top of the current window	Ctrl+Page Up
Move one word left	Ctrl+left arrow
Move one word right	Ctrl+right arrow
Move one character left	Left arrow
Move one character right	Right arrow
Move up one line	Up arrow
Move down one line	Down arrow
Move to the start of the current line or the start of the text on that line	Home
Move to the end of the current line	End
Move to the beginning of the document	Ctrl+Home
Move to the end of the document	Ctrl+end
Move to the next pane in the current window	F6
Move to the previous pane	Shift+F6
Move the insertion cursor to the beginning of the page	Page Up
Move the insertion cursor to the end of the page	Page Down
Scroll up one line	Ctrl+up arrow
Scroll down one line	Ctrl+down arrow

Events Triggered in Internet Explorer

You use the following mouse and keyboard events in your programs to tell Internet Explorer to respond in a certain way to a certain action from the user. The events in the first column react to the user action described in the second column. For details, see Chapter 11.

Mouse Events:

onmouseover	The user moves the mouse pointer onto an object (like a Textbox).
onmouseout	The user moves the mouse pointer away from an object.
onmousedown	The user presses any mouse button.
onmouseup	The user releases any mouse button.
onmousemove	The user moves the mouse pointer within an object.
onclick	The user clicks the left mouse button on an object.
ondblclick	The user double-clicks the left mouse button on an object.

Keyboard Events:

onkeypress	The user presses and releases a key.(If the user holds the key down, multiple onkeypress events are triggered.)
onkeydown	The user presses a key. (Even if the user holds the key down, this event is triggered only once.)
onkeyup	The user releases a key.

Visual Studio® 6 For Dummies®

Cheat Sheet

Themes Available for Visual InterDev and FrontPage

Automotive	Downtown	Nature	Subterranean
Barcode	Expedition	Neon	Sumi Painting
Bars	Fiesta	Network Blitz	Sunflower
Blends	Geared Up Factory	Poetic	Sweets
Blocks	Global Marketing	Polar	Technology
Blueprint	Highway	Postmodern	Tidepool
Bubbles	In Motion	Romanesque	Tilt
Cactus	Industrial	Safari	Topo
Capsules	Kids	Saturday TV Toons	Travel
Checkers	LaVerne	Spiral	Value Added
Citrus Punch	Leaves	Spokes	Waves
Clear Day	Modern Contrast	Straight Edge	World Finance
Construction Zone	Modern Shapes	Street Writing	Zero

File Types and Extensions Used by Visual FoxPro

Extension	File Type	Extension	File Type
.act	Documenting Wizard action diagram	.htm	HTML
.app	Active document or generated application	.idx	Index, or compact index
.cdx	Compound index	.lbt	Label memo
.chm	Compiled HTML Help file	.lbx	Label
.dbc	Database	.log	Coverage log
.dbf	Table	.lst	Documenting Wizard list
.dbg	Debugger configuration	.mem	Variable save
.dct	Database memo	.mnt	Menu memo
.dcx	Database index	.mnx	Menu
.dep	Dependency file (created when you use the Setup Wizard)	.mpr	Generated menu program
		.mpx	Compiled menu program
.dll	Windows dynamic link library	.ocx	ActiveX control
.err	Compilation error	.pjt	Project memo
.esl	Visual FoxPro support library	.pjx	Project
.exe	Executable program	.prg	Program
.fky	Macro	.qpr	Generated query program
.fll	Visual FoxPro dynamic link library	.qpx	Compiled query program
.fmt	Format file	.sct	Form memo
.fpt	Table memo	.scx	Form
.frt	Report memo	.tbk	Memo backup
.frx	Report	.txt	Text
.fxp	Compiled FoxPro program	.vct	Visual class library memo
.h	Header file (for use with Visual FoxPro or C/C++ programs)	.vcx	Visual class library
		.win	Window file
.hlp	WinHelp		

...For Dummies: Bestselling Book Series for Beginners

VISUAL STUDIO® 6
FOR
DUMMIES®

VISUAL STUDIO® 6 FOR DUMMIES®

by Richard Mansfield

IDG Books Worldwide, Inc.
An International Data Group Company

Foster City, CA ♦ Chicago, IL ♦ Indianapolis, IN ♦ New York, NY

Visual Studio® 6 For Dummies®

Published by
IDG Books Worldwide, Inc.
An International Data Group Company
919 E. Hillsdale Blvd.
Suite 400
Foster City, CA 94404
www.idgbooks.com (IDG Books Worldwide Web site)
www.dummies.com (Dummies Press Web site)

Library of Congress Catalog Card No.: 98-89042

ISBN: 0-7645-0374-X

Printed in the United States of America

10 9 8 7 6 5 4 3 2 1

1B/RR/RS/ZY/IN

Distributed in the United States by IDG Books Worldwide, Inc.

Distributed by Macmillan Canada for Canada; by Transworld Publishers Limited in the United Kingdom; by IDG Norge Books for Norway; by IDG Sweden Books for Sweden; by Woodslane Pty. Ltd. for Australia; by Woodslane (NZ) Ltd. for New Zealand; by Addison Wesley Longman Singapore Pte Ltd. for Singapore, Malaysia, Thailand, and Indonesia; by Norma Comunicaciones S.A. for Colombia; by Intersoft for South Africa; by International Thomson Publishing for Germany, Austria and Switzerland; by Distribuidora Cuspide for Argentina; by Livraria Cultura for Brazil; by Ediciencia S.A. for Ecuador; by Ediciones ZETA S.C.R. Ltda. for Peru; by WS Computer Publishing Corporation, Inc., for the Philippines; by Contemporanea de Ediciones for Venezuela; by Express Computer Distributors for the Caribbean and West Indies; by Micronesia Media Distributor, Inc. for Micronesia; by Grupo Editorial Norma S.A. for Guatemala; by Chips Computadoras S.A. de C.V. for Mexico; by Editorial Norma de Panama S.A. for Panama; by Wouters Import for Belgium; by American Bookshops for Finland. Authorized Sales Agent: Anthony Rudkin Associates for the Middle East and North Africa.

For general information on IDG Books Worldwide's books in the U.S., please call our Consumer Customer Service department at 800-762-2974. For reseller information, including discounts and premium sales, please call our Reseller Customer Service department at 800-434-3422.

For information on where to purchase IDG Books Worldwide's books outside the U.S., please contact our International Sales department at 317-596-5530 or fax 317-596-5692.

For information on foreign language translations, please contact our Foreign & Subsidiary Rights department at 650-655-3021 or fax 650-655-3281.

For sales inquiries and special prices for bulk quantities, please contact our Sales department at 650-655-3200 or write to the address above.

For information on using IDG Books Worldwide's books in the classroom or for ordering examination copies, please contact our Educational Sales department at 800-434-2086 or fax 317-596-5499.

For press review copies, author interviews, or other publicity information, please contact our Public Relations department at 650-655-3000 or fax 650-655-3299.

For authorization to photocopy items for corporate, personal, or educational use, please contact Copyright Clearance Center, 222 Rosewood Drive, Danvers, MA 01923, or fax 978-750-4470.

is a trademark under exclusive license to IDG Books Worldwide, Inc., from International Data Group, Inc.

About the Author

Just in case you care about such things, **Richard Mansfield** has written 21 computer books, four of which became bestsellers: *Machine Language for Beginners*, *The Second Book of Machine Language*, *The Visual Guide to Visual Basic*, and *The Visual Basic Power Toolkit* (with Evangelos Petroutsos). His most recent title is *The Visual InterDev Bible* (with Debbie Revette). He used to write two columns and frequent articles in computer magazines, but since 1991 he has focused full-time on writing books. Overall, his books have sold more than 500,000 copies worldwide and have been translated into nine languages.

But that's not the whole story. He's extraordinarily sedentary, preferring to sit and read, write, or program his computers instead of moving around. The old adage holds true for him: When he feels the urge to exercise, he lies down until it passes.

He realizes that sitting around goes against the current American fascination with health, lite food, running, fast walking, leaping about, and other exercises and forms of self-discipline. But his theory is: You don't write books by speed-walking around malls. Besides, after so many years of speed-walking, you fall over dead in front of The Gap. Then what?

ABOUT IDG BOOKS WORLDWIDE

Welcome to the world of IDG Books Worldwide.

IDG Books Worldwide, Inc., is a subsidiary of International Data Group, the world's largest publisher of computer-related information and the leading global provider of information services on information technology. IDG was founded more than 30 years ago by Patrick J. McGovern and now employs more than 9,000 people worldwide. IDG publishes more than 290 computer publications in over 75 countries. More than 90 million people read one or more IDG publications each month.

Launched in 1990, IDG Books Worldwide is today the #1 publisher of best-selling computer books in the United States. We are proud to have received eight awards from the Computer Press Association in recognition of editorial excellence and three from Computer Currents' First Annual Readers' Choice Awards. Our best-selling *...For Dummies*® series has more than 50 million copies in print with translations in 31 languages. IDG Books Worldwide, through a joint venture with IDG's Hi-Tech Beijing, became the first U.S. publisher to publish a computer book in the People's Republic of China. In record time, IDG Books Worldwide has become the first choice for millions of readers around the world who want to learn how to better manage their businesses.

Our mission is simple: Every one of our books is designed to bring extra value and skill-building instructions to the reader. Our books are written by experts who understand and care about our readers. The knowledge base of our editorial staff comes from years of experience in publishing, education, and journalism — experience we use to produce books to carry us into the new millennium. In short, we care about books, so we attract the best people. We devote special attention to details such as audience, interior design, use of icons, and illustrations. And because we use an efficient process of authoring, editing, and desktop publishing our books electronically, we can spend more time ensuring superior content and less time on the technicalities of making books.

You can count on our commitment to deliver high-quality books at competitive prices on topics you want to read about. At IDG Books Worldwide, we continue in the IDG tradition of delivering quality for more than 30 years. You'll find no better book on a subject than one from IDG Books Worldwide.

John Kilcullen
Chairman and CEO
IDG Books Worldwide, Inc.

Steven Berkowitz
President and Publisher
IDG Books Worldwide, Inc.

Eighth Annual Computer Press Awards ➢1992

Ninth Annual Computer Press Awards ➢1993

Tenth Annual Computer Press Awards ➢1994

Eleventh Annual Computer Press Awards ➢1995

IDG is the world's leading IT media, research and exposition company. Founded, in 1964, IDG had 1997 revenues of $2.05 billion and has more than 9,000 employees worldwide. IDG offers the widest range of media options that reach IT buyers in 75 countries representing 95% of worldwide IT spending. IDG's diverse product and services portfolio spans six key areas including print publishing, online publishing, expositions and conferences, market research, education and training, and global marketing services. More than 90 million people read one or more of IDG's 290 magazines and newspapers, including IDG's leading global brands — Computerworld, PC World, Network World, Macworld and the Channel World family of publications. IDG Books Worldwide is one of the fastest-growing computer book publishers in the world, with more than 700 titles in 36 languages. The "...For Dummies®" series alone has more than 50 million copies in print. IDG offers online users the largest network of technology-specific Web sites around the world through IDG.net (http://www.idg.net), which comprises more than 225 targeted Web sites in 55 countries worldwide. International Data Corporation (IDC) is the world's largest provider of information technology data, analysis and consulting, with research centers in over 41 countries and more than 400 research analysts worldwide. IDG World Expo is a leading producer of more than 168 globally branded conferences and expositions in 35 countries including E3 (Electronic Entertainment Expo), Macworld Expo, ComNet, Windows World Expo, ICE (Internet Commerce Expo), Agenda, DEMO, and Spotlight. IDG's training subsidiary, ExecuTrain, is the world's largest computer training company, with more than 230 locations worldwide and 785 training courses. IDG Marketing Services helps industry-leading IT companies build international brand recognition by developing global integrated marketing programs via IDG's print, online and exposition products worldwide. Further information about the company can be found at www.idg.com.   10/8/98

Dedication

This book is dedicated to my friends Jim Coward, Larry O'Connor, and David Lee Roach.

Author's Acknowledgments

Sometimes, if you're lucky, you get a really good editor. A book is always stronger when an author can work in partnership with someone who knows his stuff. I was fortunate to have Ryan Rader as the primary editor of this book. His many thoughtful suggestions strengthened the organization of the chapters and improved the writing. (He also knows what a *gerund* is.)

The technical accuracy of the book was improved by Allen Wyatt and Greg Guntle, who provided careful scrutiny and double-checking of all the examples and steps in the book.

Specialists in ambiguity-detection, copy editors Constance Carlisle, Tina Sims, and Billie Williams deserve credit for blowing the whistle on murky pronoun references, advising clarification of oblique patches in the book, and suggesting that I stay away from words like *oblique*. And, throughout the entire process of publishing this book, none of these fine people became hysterical. As far as I know.

Publisher's Acknowledgments

We're proud of this book; please register your comments through our IDG Books Worldwide Online Registration Form located at http://my2cents.dummies.com.

Some of the people who helped bring this book to market include the following:

Acquisitions, Editorial, and Media Development

Project Editor: Ryan Rader

Acquisitions Editor: Sherri Morningstar

Copy Editors: Constance Carlisle, Tina Sims, Billie A. Williams

Technical Editors: Allen Wyatt, Greg Guntle

Media Development Editor: Marita Ellixson

Associate Permissions Editor: Carmen Krikorian

Editorial Manager: Kelly Ewing

Media Development Manager: Heather Heath Dismore

Editorial Assistant: Paul E. Kuzmic

Production

Project Coordinator: E. Shawn Aylsworth

Layout and Graphics: Lou Boudreau, Valery Bourke, Linda M. Boyer, Angela F. Hunckler, Jane E. Martin, Brent Savage, Kate Snell

Proofreaders: Christine Berman, Vickie Broyles, Michelle Croninger, Betty Kish, Nancy Price, Janet M. Withers

Indexer: Sharon Hilgenberg

General and Administrative

IDG Books Worldwide, Inc.: John Kilcullen, CEO; Steven Berkowitz, President and Publisher

IDG Books Technology Publishing: Brenda McLaughlin, Senior Vice President and Group Publisher

Dummies Technology Press and Dummies Editorial: Diane Graves Steele, Vice President and Associate Publisher; Mary Bednarek, Director of Acquisitions and Product Development; Kristin A. Cocks, Editorial Director

Dummies Trade Press: Kathleen A. Welton, Vice President and Publisher; Kevin Thornton, Acquisitions Manager

IDG Books Production for Dummies Press: Michael R. Britton, Vice President of Production and Creative Services; Cindy L. Phipps, Manager of Project Coordination, Production Proofreading, and Indexing; Kathie S. Schutte, Supervisor of Page Layout; Shelley Lea, Supervisor of Graphics and Design; Debbie J. Gates, Production Systems Specialist; Robert Springer, Supervisor of Proofreading; Debbie Stailey, Special Projects Coordinator; Tony Augsburger, Supervisor of Reprints and Bluelines

Dummies Packaging and Book Design: Robin Seaman, Creative Director; Kavish + Kavish, Cover Design

◆

The publisher would like to give special thanks to Patrick J. McGovern, without whom this book would not have been possible.

◆

Contents at a Glance

Cartoons at a Glance

By Rich Tennant

page 7

page 77

page 185

page 235

page 331

page 373

page 413

Fax: 978-546-7747 • E-mail: the5wave@tiac.net

Table of Contents

Part III: Jazzing Up Your Web Site with Multimedia (Lights! Camera! Action!) 185

Introduction

. . . .

*W*elcome to the world of Windows programming and Web site creation in *Visual Studio 6 For Dummies*. Microsoft has put all its best cutting-edge tools into this powerhouse package. And this book shows you how to use these great tools.

Visual Studio 6 is both powerful and diverse. If you want to do *anything* with Internet site development or creating Windows programs, you can do it with Visual Studio 6. But, best of all, many of the Visual Studio 6 features are designed to be easy to use. The tools include hundreds of shortcuts.

For example, even if you've had no experience at all in creating a Web page, you can find out how to build one in about three minutes. (Seriously! See Chapter 3.)

Want to build a complete Web site? That may take longer. How much longer depends on what you want the Web site to do and how many pages are involved. But if you can click a mouse, you can create Web pages and Windows applications. Visual Studio 6 is filled with great *visual* aids — pre-built components, templates, professionally designed themes, and wizards.

About This Book

Because Visual Studio 6 is so huge, you can easily overlook the many shortcuts it contains. I've been on the beta program for nearly a year during the development of Visual Studio 6. I know Visual Studio 6 well. My main job in *Visual Studio 6 For Dummies* is to tell you when to use a simpler, better way to accomplish a job. Otherwise, you can spend days hand-programming something that's already been built, something that you can create by clicking a simple menu option.

Also, unlike other books about Visual Studio 6 and its major applications (Visual InterDev, Visual J++, Visual Basic, Visual FoxPro, FrontPage, and Visual C++), this book is written in plain, clear English. You can find sophisticated tasks made easy: The book is filled with step-by-step examples that you can follow, even if you've never written a line of programming or designed anything.

Saying that this book is ...*For Dummies* is a bit misleading because I know you're not dumb, and Visual Studio 6 requires some brains and practice to master (but you can handle it). To make this book as valuable for you as possible without writing a six-volume life's-work on all the Visual Studio 6 features and functions, I geared this book toward familiarizing you with the Visual Studio 6 tools as you use them to create Windows or Web applications.

This book obviously can't cover every feature of all the Visual Studio 6 applications. Instead, as you work through the many step-by-step examples in this book, you become familiar with the most useful features of Visual Studio 6 and many of the shortcuts and time-saving tricks, some of which can take years to discover on your own.

Whether you want to create stunning Web sites or impressive Windows applications, this book tells you how to get where you want to go. The following are just a few of the useful tasks that you'll be able to accomplish after reading this book:

- ✔ Building a professional-looking, interactive Web site.

- ✔ Writing effective script programming (and being smart enough to know when to let Visual Studio 6 write script for you).

- ✔ Understanding how to best use the common interface found in all Visual Studio 6 applications.

- ✔ Designing your own reusable components with Visual Basic Wizards.

- ✔ Killing bugs in Windows applications or Web sites.

- ✔ Creating dazzling, state-of-the-art special effects with multimedia and animation.

Many people think that computers are hard to use. And that creating things by communicating with a computer (otherwise known as *programming*) is even harder. It doesn't have to be. In fact, many common programming jobs have already been programmed so that you don't have to do the programming. If you're smart, you don't reinvent the wheel. All you need to know is where to find the components, scriptlets, Wizards, and other pre-built solutions. Then drop them into your Web page or Windows application. And if you do want to program, Visual Basic and Visual InterDev make the job both easy and very enjoyable.

This book tells you if a particular wheel has already been invented. It also shows you how to save time by modifying existing components to fit your needs, instead of building new components from scratch. But if you're creating something totally original (congratulations!), this book gives you many step-by-step recipes for creating things from the ground up.

How This Book Is Organized

This book is divided into seven parts, with several chapters in each part. But just because the book is organized doesn't mean you have to be. You don't have to read the book in sequence from Chapter 1 to the end, just like you don't have to read a cookbook in sequence.

If you want to create a component, go right to Chapter 13. You're not expected to know what's in Chapter 8 before you can get results in Chapter 13. Similarly, within each chapter, you can scan the headings and jump right to the section covering the task that you want to accomplish. No need to read each chapter from start to finish.

The following sections give you a brief description of each of the book's seven main parts.

Part I: Getting to Know Visual Studio 6

This part introduces the various applications that make up Visual Studio 6 and explains their purposes. You find out that Microsoft has been trying to make all its major applications — languages, database managers, and Internet tools — share a common look and feel, which has been a largely successful endeavor. In Chapter 3, you jump right in and create your first Web page in just minutes.

Part II: Building a Web Site

You can use Visual Studio 6 to create and manage databases, Web sites, or Windows applications (and to accomplish a few other, perhaps less towering, tasks such as creating reusable pieces of applications called *components*). If you want to quickly create an Internet Web site that looks great and runs great, this section shows you how. I show you that Visual Studio 6 provides shortcuts, themes, and helpful templates, such as the Site Designer that helps you plan the hyperlinks that tie your Web pages together in a logical way.

Part III: Jazzing Up Your Web Site with Multimedia (Lights! Camera! Action!)

A Web site is a great way to communicate with people in your company (on an intranet) or with people anywhere in the world (on the Internet). But you can always goose up the communication with what theater people call *dazzle*. This part isn't for the faint of heart. If you confuse computer programming with secret, solemn ceremonies or religious rites (with you as the priest), you won't like this part because it's all about making your Web site jump with animation and special effects. Ordinary people love these tricks. Stuffy people sniff and walk away.

Part IV: The Basics of Internet Programming

In this part, you can compare JavaScript with VBScript to see which Internet programming language you prefer. You also find out how to connect scripts to events. You see how easily you can make your Web pages respond to visitors — or make them just calculate information that you need, such as checking a visitor's information after she fills out an order form to buy $1 million worth of your product. Finally, you try your hand at debugging — tracking down those pesky errors in what you thought was brilliant, perfect programming code.

Part V: The Database Connection

More and more, Windows applications and Web sites need to display catalogs, order forms, delivery status, or other information that's stored in databases. Attaching a database to something is called *database connectivity*, which used to be a real drag. In this part, you discover how very easy dealing with databases has become. Now database connectivity is just a matter of dragging and dropping.

Part VI: Managing Your Web Projects with Visual Studio 6

Here's where you find out how to take care of a Web site that you've already built. You reorganize and update a site, and also deploy the site when it's perfect and you're ready to send it out into the World Wide Web for all to see and enjoy.

Part VII: The Part of Tens

This part contains only one chapter, but you don't want to miss it. This Part of Tens chapter includes useful and cool information — ten important items that didn't fit into the other chapters of the book. You definitely want to try out some of these pointers.

Conventions Used in This Book

This book is filled with step-by-step lists that function like recipes to help you cook up a finished product. Each step starts off with a **boldface** sentence or two telling you what *you* should do. Directly after the bold step, you see a sentence or two, not in boldface, telling you what happens as a result of the bold action — a menu opens, a dialog box pops up, a Wizard appears, you win the lottery, whatever.

A special symbol shows you how to navigate menus. When you see "Choose File⇨Save," you should click the File menu and then click the Save option in the File menu.

When you need to deal with programming code, you see it in a special monospaced typeface, like this:

```
function movep()
```

Note that every line of code that you see in this book is also included on the CD that accompanies the book. Take advantage of this handy electronic version of the code by cutting and pasting source code examples instead of typing them by hand. (The On the CD icon draws your attention to longer code examples, but even single-line programming examples are included on the CD. See "Icons Used in This Book," later in this Introduction.)

The Visual Studio 6 dialog boxes are packed with buttons, check boxes, text boxes, list boxes, option buttons, and other features, all with descriptive names that can be long at times. To keep this book's text easy to read and to make the names of these features stand out from the surrounding sentences, this book capitalizes the first letter in each word of these names (even though you may see lowercase letters in the name on your Visual Studio 6 screen). This capitalization convention changes phrases such as "Clear the text in the Choose a title for your FrontPage web text box" into "Clear the text in the Choose A Title For Your FrontPage Web text box," which helps you avoid having to reread sentences containing complicated names.

What You Need to Get Started

To use this book to the fullest, you need a couple of things. Of course, you want a copy of Visual Studio 6. Visual Studio 6 is sold in two versions: Professional and Enterprise. This book assumes that you have the Professional Version. (See Chapter 1 for a description of the differences.)

However, you can get by with owning only Visual Basic and Visual InterDev, because the book focuses on them instead of focusing on the alternative languages (Java and C) included in Visual Studio 6.

Why focus on Visual Basic? It's the world's most popular programming language by far — and with good reason. Visual Basic can do everything that the other languages can do and is often far easier to use. And, to me, Visual Basic is *always* a lot more fun.

Icons Used in This Book

Notice the eye-catching little icons in the margins of this book. These tiny pictures are placed next to a paragraph to draw your attention to items that you may — or may not — want to read immediately. Here are the icons and their meanings:

This icon points you to shortcuts and insights that save you time and trouble.

This icon highlights nerdy technical discussions that you can skip if you want to.

This icon signals you to programming code that's included on the book's CD.

This icon aims to steer you away from dangerous situations.

This icon urges you not to forget an important piece of information.

Part I
Getting to Know
Visual Studio 6

The 5th Wave   By Rich Tennant

I HAVEN'T LOCATED THE PROBLEM YET.

In this part . . .

Creating Web pages doesn't have to be hard to do. Same with creating Windows applications. If you've tried before but were baffled by computerese, hard-to-understand books, or bewildering classes at school, Part I of this book will show you how Visual Studio 6 can help.

In Visual Studio 6, Microsoft has assembled programming languages and Web-page tools that are now very easy to use. The Visual Studio 6 tools are filled with shortcuts — pre-built components, templates, professionally designed themes, and wizards. Using these helpful tools, you just *customize* your creations rather than starting from scratch. This part shows you how.

So fire up Visual Studio, sit down with your favorite music and munchies, and start having fun. (The big secret that programmers try to keep from their bosses is that creating computer programs and Web pages can be very fun!)

Chapter 1

How Visual Studio 6 Works

In This Chapter

▶ Understanding Visual Studio 6's major applications

▶ Integrating the Visual Studio 6 components

▶ How Visual Studio 6 applications organize their documents

▶ Explaining the two versions of Visual Studio 6

▶ Working with RAD languages and applications

▶ Creating cascading style sheets easily

▶ Adding a cascading style sheet to Web pages

This chapter surveys the main features of Visual Studio 6, but includes only two hands-on examples. They're included just to demonstrate Visual Studio's power and ease of use. The rest of the book is packed with examples for you to try.

If you want to see how to do something simple, like start a new Visual InterDev project, you can find the answer in this book and be up and running before you know it. If you want to do something sophisticated — like add spectacular visual effects; design or deploy a Web site; or attach a database to a Web site or Windows application — again you can find clear, easy to follow steps.

I can't take the credit for how easy this book makes programming and developing Web sites, custom controls, databases, Windows applications, and other practical, cutting-edge computing. A good deal of the credit goes to Microsoft for its efforts, mostly successful, to make Visual Studio 6 a powerful, yet often effortlessly efficient, set of tools. Imagine adding a database to a Web page in seven simple steps.

This chapter introduces you to Visual InterDev 6, Microsoft's powerhouse package of cutting-edge tools. Microsoft really has included everything but the kitchen sink — all the newest technologies, application programming languages, and Internet site designers. In this chapter, you take a helicopter ride over the landscape, to get an overall idea of what's what and how the various parts of Visual Studio 6 parts work together. At the end of the chapter, you try a couple of hands-on examples to see how easily the Visual Studio 6 tools can help you accomplish even some pretty advanced tricks.

A Motley Crew of Tools

Visual Studio 6 is a most unusual product. For one thing, it's a collection of major applications and utilities, but some of them may seem redundant. Why include Microsoft's three major languages: Visual Basic, Visual J++, and Visual C++? Do you know anyone who writes programs in all three languages?

And some of the applications in Visual Studio 6 may seem to be rather strange bedfellows. What does Visual C++ have to do with FrontPage or Visual FoxPro? Perhaps not a whole lot at first glance.

Finally, you have Visual InterDev, the powerful Microsoft Web development application.

Here's a list of the Visual Studio 6 Professional Edition lineup:

- Visual C++
- Visual Basic
- Visual J++
- Visual FoxPro
- Visual InterDev
- FrontPage

Five powerful applications for developers, plus FrontPage, a Web page designer that's powerful in a different way. FrontPage is useful to writers, artists, and the boss — people who probably know little about programming or project management. With FrontPage's many wizards and tools, these nonprogrammers can put together excellent Web pages with no assistance.

Is Visual Studio 6 designed for creating Web sites or distributed applications? Yes. With Visual Studio 6, you can do it all. *Distributed application* has several meanings. For one thing, it means that a project is not located in one folder on a single hard drive. A distributed application can be scattered physically on various hard drives, or even scattered geographically — a graphic designer may be in Tucson and a programmer at the home office in San Jose, but both are working on the same Web site or Windows application. (Microsoft calls this situation a *distributed project model*.) Also, a distributed application can be composed of several separate objects — perhaps a spellchecker on one server, the main application on a different server, and an attached database on yet another hard drive. In addition to spreading the storage load, distributing applications can also divide the processing load among more than a single CPU. (A CPU is the microprocessor that's at the heart of a computer, and does most of the calculations, such as a Pentium II chip.) Distributed applications work a bit like parallel processing, and can increase speed.

One way to think of Visual Studio 6 is that it combines two categories of tools; what Microsoft calls its *development tools* are combined with its Internet technologies. In general, the development tools are Visual Basic, Visual C++, Visual J++, and Visual FoxPro. The Internet tools are Visual InterDev and FrontPage.

In other words, you can use Visual Studio 6 to build many different kinds of things, including components (Java applets or ActiveX controls), databases, Windows applications, or Web sites. And you can usually blend and combine those items, mixing and matching as you want, within applications or Web pages. You can even combine Visual Basic programming with a DHTML page — avoiding the usual restrictions that limit Web page programming to scripting.

Integration All Over the Place

Distribution generally means dividing things into pieces and then separating them. But, in other ways, Visual Studio 6 represents a move in the opposite direction. In Visual Studio 6, integration means bringing pieces together and blending them. And a key feature of Visual Studio 6 is integration.

You can combine scripting, objects, and HTML source code. You can even combine two kinds of scripting: VBScript and JScript. And, when such things are combined, they can usually be debugged seamlessly. What Microsoft calls *end-to-end debugging* means that you can test across applications running simultaneously, and also test applications that are running on a client and a server at the same time.

Also, the Visual Studio 6 editors and programming tools are integrated in two major ways:

✔ **Internal integration:** Visual InterDev is a good example of the internal integration of Visual Studio 6. An IDE (Integrated Design Environment) such as Visual InterDev includes features supporting various kinds of seemingly unrelated objects. You can freely mix and match HTML, script, and components produced in Visual J++, Visual Basic, Visual FoxPro, or Visual C++.

✔ **External integration:** Visual Studio 6 achieves external integration by making all the Visual Studio 6 application's IDEs similar — similar menus, toolbars, Property windows, editing features, debugging tools, wizards, utilities, and other elements. This way, you can move from one Visual Studio 6 tool to another and feel comfortable. Your learning curve is reduced because you're in a familiar environment. In fact, Visual J++ and Visual InterDev actually *share* a single IDE, as you can see in Figure 1-1. After you start either one of these applications, you see a New Project dialog box that includes options for starting a Visual J++ or a Visual InterDev project in its left pane. You can't get much more integrated than that!

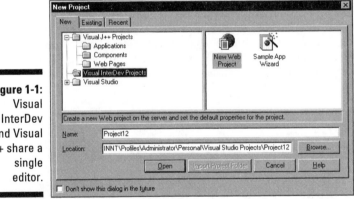

Figure 1-1:
Visual
InterDev
and Visual
J++ share a
single
editor.

All this and Visual Studio 6's applications are Year 2000-compliant. Hopefully, your electric utility company is using Visual Studio 6; other electric companies may have problems when New Year's Day 2000 arrives.

Understanding Visual Studio 6's Organization

It's paradoxical, isn't it? Even though Visual Studio 6 embraces *distributed* computing, it also emphasizes *integration*.

Distribution features include:

- ✔ **Distributed applications:** Parts of a project can be stored in different hard drives — in some cases, the parts may be halfway around the world.

- ✔ **Distributed workforce:** Various pieces of a Windows application or a Web site are worked on by various people located here and there.

- ✔ **Mixing and matching objects:** Objects and various programming languages are freely (and easily) mixed even on the same Web page or in the same project.

Integration features include:

- ✔ **Visual FoxPro**: The database development environment looks more and more like Visual Basic, the world's most popular Windows application development environment.

- ✔ **Visual J++**: Actually shares an editor and integrated design environment with Visual InterDev.

- ✔ **All Visual Studio 6 applications**: Are converging on a single IDE look and feel.

- ✔ **All Visual Studio 6 applications**: Share some utilities, components, add-ons, and wizards.

I guess that when you've got integration at the same time as distribution, the overall result is merely reorganization and change. Programming, Web site development, and application development are changing — getting easier to do in some ways, less monolithic, and less application-specific. That's a form of integration. But don't forget that a single project can be worked on, or executed, simultaneously in various spots around the world. That's a form of distribution.

However, one aspect of the new integration that you can appreciate is that, more and more, the various kinds of Visual Studio 6 applications look the same, have similar features, and are organized in similar ways. For example, most of the Visual Studio applications include Project Explorer windows that mimic the familiar Windows Explorer utility — giving you an overall view of the various folders, subfolders, and files that, collectively, make up the current project or projects.

Worlds within worlds

Some Visual Studio 6 applications can also now hold more than one project at a time. For example, you used to work on a single application (program) at a time in Visual Basic. However, now you can work on two or more programs at a time. This is an important side-effect of distributed programming. How? Read on.

To understand how this multiple-project technique works, consider that each Visual Studio 6 application specializes in generating its own particular product. Visual FoxPro produces databases. The languages (Visual Basic, Visual C++, and Visual J++) produce traditional Windows applications and also reusable objects called *applets, controls*, or *components*. FrontPage and Visual InterDev produce Web pages and Web sites.

However, Visual Studio 6 applications can now contain more than just a single product. The Visual Studio applications have bigger *containers* now for their products so that you can work on more than a single product at the same time.

Consider this example: Visual InterDev creates Web site pages, but a Visual InterDev project can include a variety of support files (graphics, scriptlet pages, databases, components, and so on). Collectively, all the elements in a Visual InterDev Web site are called a *solution* in Visual InterDev. This *solution* is an abstract container that can include many elements that can be worked on at the same time in the Visual InterDev integrated design environment.

Another example: Visual Basic's product is applications or components. But to test a component, you need to simultaneously work with that component and a container application that hosts the component. Therefore, with Version 5, Visual Basic introduced a more abstract category than the traditional *application*. It now includes a concept called a *project,* which can contain more than one application or component at the same time in the Visual Basic integrated design environment.

Similarly, Visual FoxPro's product is databases. However, Visual FoxPro has a container concept larger than a database. (You used to be able to work on only a single database at a time.) On the highest level, you have the Visual FoxPro project, which can include a variety of support files and can contain more than one database at the same time.

The new, expanded container features in Microsoft's major software — whether called *projects* or *solutions* or whatever — are not mere coincidence. Nor is this change a whim on Microsoft's part. You have to get used to the idea that an application may be divided into many pieces (components or objects) and that those pieces need not necessarily be located together physically on a single hard drive or a single local area network. The files that make up a project may not even be located in the same country. A project composed of various reusable objects, not necessarily stored together, is a definition of the *distributed applications* concept. And that concept, if not *the* wave of the future of computing, is at least *a* wave among several.

The Two Versions of Visual Studio 6

Visual Studio 6 comes in two versions: Professional and Enterprise. The
Professional version includes all the applications (Visual Basic, Visual J++,
Visual InterDev, and the others), but it doesn't include a number of highly
sophisticated utilities, such as the Oracle Server Database Designer and
Visual SourceSafe. This book focuses on the major applications and utilities
included in the Professional version. The Enterprise version includes every
major technology that Microsoft offers. The Professional version is priced at
$1,079, but if you already own any of the Visual Studio 6 applications (Visual
FoxPro, Visual Basic, and so on), or you own some miscellaneous developer
products from Borland or others, you can get the upgrade version of Visual
Studio 6 Professional for a suggested price of $549. The Enterprise edition of
Visual Studio 6 is priced at $1,619, with an upgrade price of $1,079.

Visual Studio 6 Is RAD Hot

RAD (rapid application development) is a goal that nearly everyone agrees
on: Build efficient and sturdy applications, but build them quickly and easily.
Visual Studio 6 includes all the latest versions of Microsoft's best technologies for developers and programmers. You may find that the Visual Studio 6
programs and utilities are filled with wizards, drag and drop techniques, pre-
built components, add-ins, and other shortcuts.

Chapter 2 demonstrates the many aspects of RAD — and indeed you can
find RAD techniques exploited all through this book because RAD is used
throughout the Visual Studio 6 suite of applications.

But the following sections give you a taste of how easily you can create
programming components or Web pages that used to take programmers
days to accomplish, if they could do it at all. Wizards, special utilities, and
other helpers abound in Visual Studio 6.

Creating a cascading style sheet the RAD way

Say you want to create a CSS (cascading style sheet) and apply it to your
Web site. (You use cascading style sheets to enforce a consistent look for
the headlines, background colors and other elements throughout your
entire Web site. See Chapter 7 for more explanation of cascading style
sheets.) Visual InterDev includes a special utility called the CSS Editor. It
makes creating CSSs a snap.

Imagine that you're creating a Web site to promote asparagus. Obviously all headlines should be green in this Web site! The easiest way to accomplish this uniformity is to make a CSS that forces all headlines to be light green. To create a CSS using the Visual InterDev CSS Editor, follow these steps:

1. **Start Visual InterDev by clicking its icon on your desktop.**

   Depending on how you've specified the Visual InterDev start-up options, you may or may not see the New Project dialog box. If you don't see this dialog box, choose File➪New Project.

2. **Click the Recent tab in the dialog box.**

   You see a list of recent Visual InterDev projects. If you don't (because you're just starting out with Visual InterDev and have never made a project), click the New tab in the New Project dialog box and then click Visual InterDev Projects in the left pane and double-click New Web project in the right pane. The Web Project Wizard opens. Follow the steps in Chapter 4 in the section "Building the Web project." After you're through following those steps, you have a brand new Web project to work with. So you can skip to Step 4 below.

3. **Double-click any one of your recent Visual InterDev projects.**

   The New Project dialog box closes and the project you selected opens.

4. **Choose File➪New File.**

   The Visual InterDev New File dialog box opens, as shown in Figure 1-2.

5. **Click Visual InterDev in the left pane.**

   The right pane displays the templates and editors you can start with when creating a new page in Visual InterDev.

6. **Double-click the Style Sheet icon.**

   The Style Sheet Editor appears, as shown in Figure 1-3.

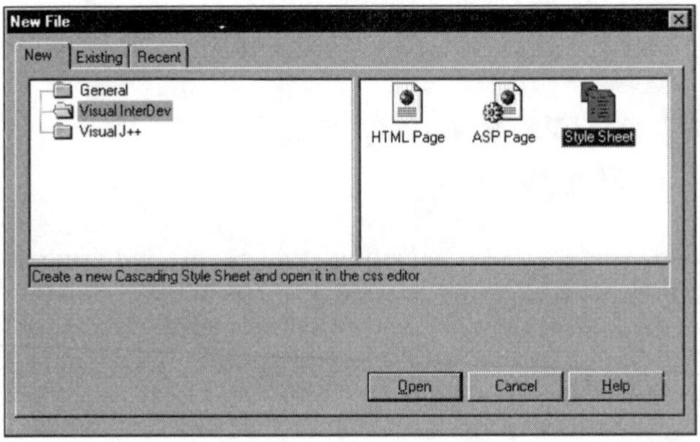

Figure 1-2: The New File dialog box.

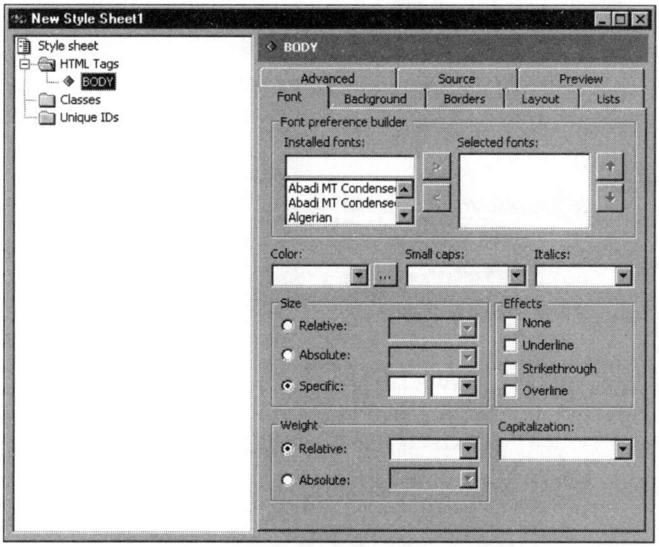

Figure 1-3:
The Style
Sheet Editor
makes
creating a
cascading
style sheet
easy.

7. **Right-click the word BODY in the left pane of the Style Sheet Editor and then click Insert HTML Tag in the context menu that appears.**

   The Insert New HTML Tag dialog box appears. This dialog box enables you to modify the characteristics of most HTML elements.

8. **Search the HTML Tag drop-down list box and select H1.**

   H1 is Heading 1, the largest headline format in Internet pages.

9. **Click the OK button.**

   The Insert New HTML Tag dialog box closes, and the H1 entry appears underneath the BODY entry on the left pane of the Style Sheet Editor.

   H1 is selected (white lettering against a blue background). Also, at the top of the right side of the Style Sheet Editor you see BODY H1. Both these cues tell you that any adjustments you make to the Font is applied to H1 headlines.

10. **Click the button with three dots (...) next to the Color text box.**

    The standard Windows Color Picker dialog box appears. From this dialog box, you can choose the color for the H1 elements.

11. **Pick a dusty green color that looks like asparagus and then click the OK button.**

    The Color Picker dialog box closes and YellowGreen appears in the Color text box in the Style Sheet Editor.

12. **Repeat Steps 7–11 until you've turned H2, H3, and H4 — all the usual headline styles — into asparagus green.**

   H1 through H4 are listed under the BODY label in the left pane; they've all been redefined and turned dusty green, as shown in Figure 1-4.

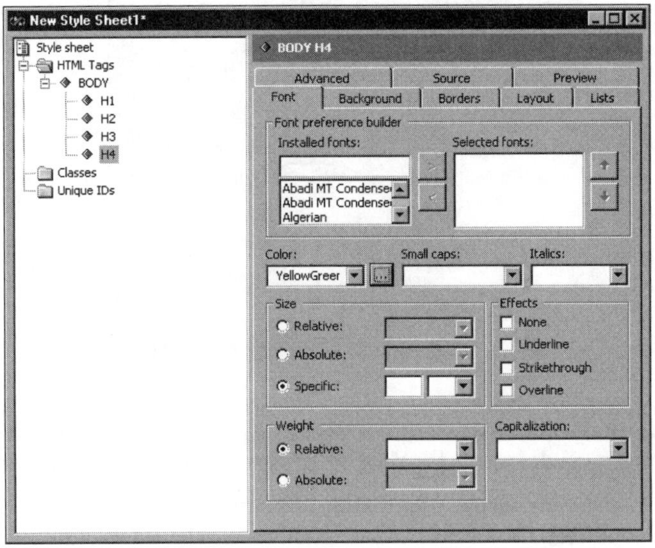

Figure 1-4:
The tags in the left pane — H1, H2, H3, and H4 — have all been redefined in this style sheet you've built.

13. **Click the Preview tab on the Style Sheet Editor.**

   A sample page is displayed showing many HTML elements, including headlines, as you can see in Figure 1-5.

   The Preview tab of the Style Sheet Editor has a nice feature: You can look at *any* HTML page, on your local hard drive or anywhere on the Internet. All you have to do is click the button with three dots (...) next to the HTML page to preview the style sheet with the text box shown in Figure 1-5. After you click the ... button, the Select Preview Page dialog box opens, as shown in Figure 1-6. You can see how your style sheet affects any Web page by specifying an Internet address (URL) in this dialog box. Note that all displayable pages in your current Visual InterDev Web project are also available for clicking in the URL drop-down list, as shown in Figure 1-6.

   Try typing **http://Microsoft.com** or some other Web page address into the URL text box. Click the OK button. The dialog box closes and, if your machine is connected to the Internet, you see the Web page, with your style sheet's customizations, as shown in Figure 1-7.

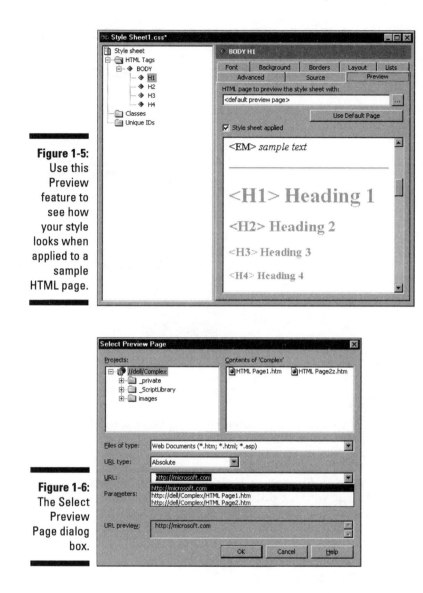

Figure 1-5:
Use this
Preview
feature to
see how
your style
looks when
applied to a
sample
HTML page.

Figure 1-6:
The Select
Preview
Page dialog
box.

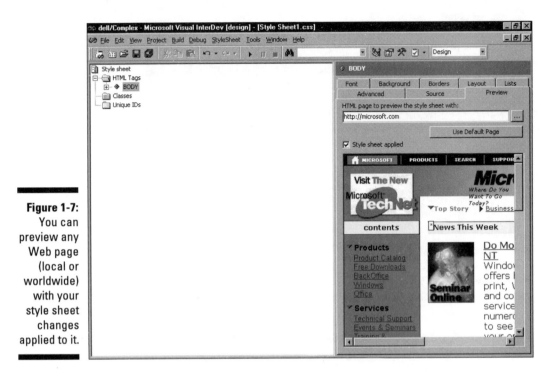

Figure 1-7:
You can
preview any
Web page
(local or
worldwide)
with your
style sheet
changes
applied to it.

14. **Close the Style Sheet Editor.**

    The Microsoft Development Environment dialog box opens, asking
    whether you want to save the changes to your Style Sheet1.CSS.

15. **Click the Yes button.**

    The dialog box closes, Style Sheet 1.Css is stored on the hard drive, and
    it's also listed along with the other files in the Project Explorer. (If the
    Project Explorer isn't visible, choose View⇨Project Explorer from the
    Visual InterDev menu bar.)

Adding a cascading style sheet to a Web page

When you've created several cascading style sheets and saved them to your
hard drive as part of a project, you can choose among those style sheets to
add one to your Web page. (If you haven't created a cascading style sheet,
follow the steps in the preceding section, "Creating a cascading style sheet
the RAD way.")

What would be the very simplest and easiest way to add a cascading style sheet to a Web page in your Visual InterDev project? Drag and drop it, right?

As you probably guessed, adding a style sheet to a Web page is simplicity itself in Visual InterDev. It's effortless. Follow these steps to add a style sheet to a Web page:

1. **Choose File⇨New File from the Visual InterDev menu bar.**

   The New File dialog box opens. (For an example of the New File dialog box, refer to Figure 1-2.)

2. **Double-click HTML page in the right pane of the New File dialog box.**

   The dialog box closes and a new, blank Web page is displayed in its editor, as shown in Figure 1-8.

3. **Click the Source tab at the bottom of the Web page editor.**

   The default source code for a new, blank Web page is displayed.

4. **Drag your mouse across all the default source code to select it and then press the Del key.**

   The editor is now clean and empty of any programming.

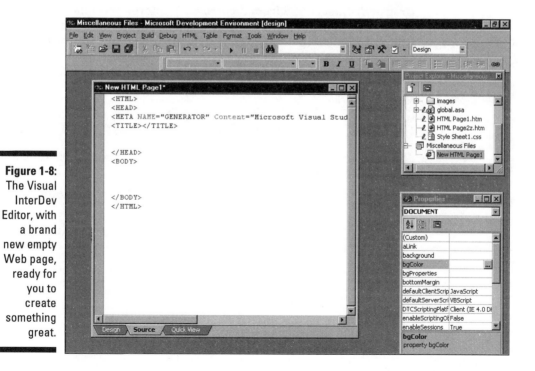

Figure 1-8:
The Visual InterDev Editor, with a brand new empty Web page, ready for you to create something great.

5. **Type the following source code into the source page:**

```
<HTML>
<HEAD>
</HEAD>
<BODY>
<H1>HEADLINE LEVEL 1</H1>
<H2>HEADLINE LEVEL 2</H2>
<H3>HEADLINE LEVEL 3</H3>
<H4>HEADLINE LEVEL 4</H4>
</BODY>
</HTML>
```

You've now created four headlines.

6. **Click the Quick View tab at the bottom of the editor.**

You see the four headlines you created. (If your machine is not on the Internet, depending on your settings, you'll perhaps be connected to the Internet before the Quick View appears.)

7. **Click the Source tab at the bottom of the editor.**

You're returned to the programming view of this Web page.

8. **Drag Style Sheet1.CSS from the Project Explorer Miscellaneous drop-down list and drop it in your source code, right next to (just after) the first <HEAD> tag (not the ending </HEAD> tag that includes a slash).**

The Cascading Style Sheet is now a part of your Web page. Visual InterDev automatically inserts the following source code that accomplishes this attaching:

```
<LINK rel="stylesheet" type="text/css" href="Style
        Sheet1.css">
```

(If the Project Explorer isn't visible, choose View⇨Project Explorer from the Visual InterDev menu bar.)

9. **Test the style sheet by clicking the Quick View tab at the bottom of the editor.**

All the headlines turn asparagus green, just as you'd hoped (if they didn't, don't despair, see the following tip). The result is shown in Figure 1-9.

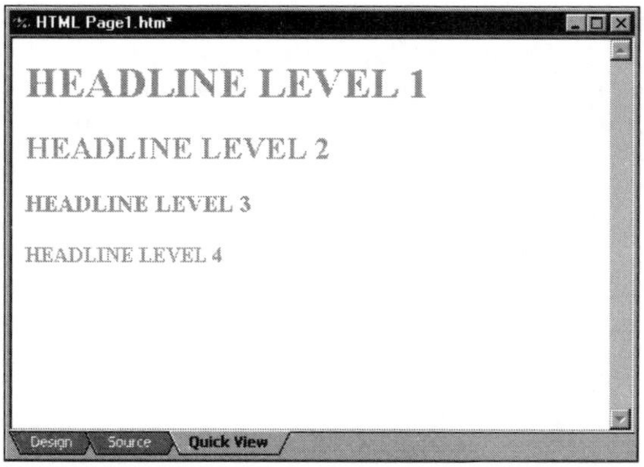

HEADLINE LEVEL 1

HEADLINE LEVEL 2

HEADLINE LEVEL 3

HEADLINE LEVEL 4

Figure 1-9:
Success!
You've
turned
each of
these
headlines
green.

If things don't work as planned

Did your headlines turn green in the previous example? If not, you have an easy solution. Choose View⇨View in Browser on the Visual InterDev menu bar. After the Internet Explorer browser is up and running, it loads your page and shows you the asparagus green that you've been waiting for. Why did this happen? Some Web page effects don't immediately show up when you click the Visual InterDev Quick View tab (or FrontPage's equivalent, the Preview tab). The engine that drives the browser has to be running. (Note that depending on how your internet connection options are set up in Windows or NT, clicking the Quick View or Preview tab can automatically load the browser and even cause your machine to be connected to the Internet.)

Some effects won't show up at all in the Quick View or Preview windows (such things as Server-side script programming and design-time controls). Anywhere in this book that an example won't work in Quick View or Preview, I'll tell you. But if you're working on a Web page of your own and you're not getting the results you expect, always try two techniques:

✔ Choose View⇨View in Browser in Visual InterDev or File⇨Preview in Browser in FrontPage.

✔ Some effects require that you save the files you've been editing to the hard drive. If you change a headline's color, for example, in a style sheet, you won't see the effect until you save that style sheet to the hard drive. (Quick View, Preview, or even View in Browser all load the style sheet from the hard drive. If you've only made changes to the style sheet in the Style Sheet Editor onscreen, but haven't saved the style sheet file — your changes won't be in the older version of the file on the hard drive.)

Therefore, if you're not seeing the effect that you expect, choose File⇨Save All in the FrontPage Editor, or choose File⇨Save All in Visual InterDev. Then click the Quick View or Preview tabs, or press F5 in Internet Explorer to force it to reload the page you're testing.

Chapter 2

Using the Visual Studio 6 Interface

Sometimes, in a pinch, I've pounded a nail into a wall with the handle of a screwdriver. I couldn't find the hammer. And I've sometimes tightened a screw with a dime. But using the right tool for each job is always easier and faster — not to mention safer.

Microsoft provides you with a very complete toolbox in Visual Studio 6. You can find everything you need to create distributed applications and Web sites. Yet, like a good tool set, you also have a family resemblance. The various tools are easy to locate and have the same basic balance and feel. They *look* alike and, as much as possible, they behave alike, too.

Ideally, if you find out how to use one Microsoft application, you're able to switch to a different Microsoft application, easily. You find a familiar environment with familiar menus, toolbars, and, overall, a sense of comfort that you're not picking up a whole new kind of tool. With the various applications in Visual Studio 6, Microsoft has largely succeeded in achieving that goal. When you switch among the six major Visual Studio 6 applications, you nevertheless always find yourself in a familiar environment.

Welcome to the Integrated Design Environment

Understanding the Visual Studio 6 user-interface is the first step in creating a Web site. But you may think that speaking of *the* Visual Studio 6 interface doesn't make sense. After all, six applications (Visual Basic, FrontPage, Visual InterDev, Visual FoxPro, Visual C++ and Visual J++) make up Visual Studio 6. So you must see six user interfaces, right?

Microsoft has tried hard to create the same interface for each of the six applications in Visual Studio 6. In most Microsoft applications, including Visual Studio 6, this interface is called the *integrated design environment* or *IDE*. Of course, making every tool look like every other tool isn't always possible. Menu items, windows, and other items must differ to an extent. But the idea is to make the applications as similar as possible. That way, after you're comfortable with one of the applications, you can quickly adjust to any of the others.

How similar are these six applications? One way to get a feel for the similarity of the interfaces is to fire up each application. When you first run Visual Studio 6 applications, they have a tendency to pop up a dialog box that most of the applications call the New Project dialog box. The New Project dialog box differs from application to application, though. And you notice differences in the steps that you must take to make the dialog box close.

Chapter 5 focuses on the details of the Visual InterDev Editor and Chapter 6 focuses on the details of the FrontPage Editor. In this chapter, the common features of all Visual Studio 6 applications is the topic. For an in-depth discussion of the major Visual Studio 6 IDE features such as docking, the multiple document interface, and so on, see the section "Getting to Know the Common Integrated Design Environment," later in this chapter.

Running Visual Studio 6 Components

The Visual InterDev interface is similar to most interfaces in Visual Studio 6. So start up Visual InterDev to see how the interface looks when you first open most Visual Studio 6 applications. Follow these steps to run Visual InterDev and check out its interface:

1. **Click the Visual InterDev icon on your desktop (if you put it there). Or use the taskbar and click Start➪Programs➪Microsoft Visual Studio 6.0➪Microsoft Visual InterDev 6.0.**

   Visual InterDev opens and its interface appears (which may look like the interface in Figure 2-1).

2. **Compare your Visual InterDev Editor interface to the one shown in Figure 2-1.**

   If your editor isn't arranged as you like it, you can resize and rearrange its elements to suit your tastes.

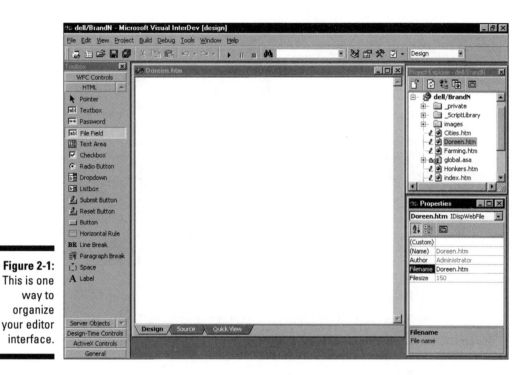

Figure 2-1:
This is one
way to
organize
your editor
interface.

3. **Try rearranging the elements of your Visual InterDev interface to match Figure 2-1. Drag each window to position it as shown and then drag the sides of each window so that they're about the shape shown.**

When you first run a Visual Studio 6 application, you may first see a New Project dialog box, such as the one shown in Figure 2-2. Seeing this introductory dialog box every time you open an application can get a little annoying after you've used Visual Studio 6 for a while. The following sections show you how to get rid of this dialog box if you find it a nuisance. (Some people don't like dealing with this dialog box each time they start a Visual Studio 6 application. They'd rather use the applications' menus to specify their wishes.)

Avoiding the New Project dialog box in Visual InterDev

To prevent the New Project dialog box from appearing every time you run Visual InterDev, follow these steps:

1. **Choose Tools⇨Options.**

   The Options dialog box opens.

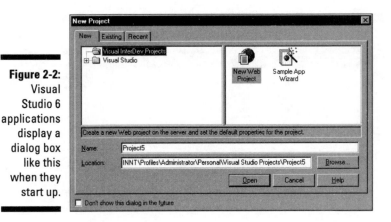

Figure 2-2:
Visual
Studio 6
applications
display a
dialog box
like this
when they
start up.

2. **Click General under the Environment list in the left pane of the Options dialog box.**

3. **Locate the On Startup section in the Options dialog box.**

4. **Select the Show Empty Environment option.**

5. **If you want to automatically load the project that you previously worked on, click Load last solution.**

6. **Click the OK button to close the dialog box and make your changes official.**

To just avoid the New Project dialog box without taking the preceding steps to set your options for opening projects, you can click the Don't show this dialog in the Future check box, located at the bottom of the New Project dialog box. The process of suppressing the New Project dialog in other Visual Studio 6 applications is just as easy. Follow these steps to run Visual Basic:

1. **Run Visual Basic by clicking its icon on your desktop, or use the Start menu: Choose Start⇨Programs⇨Microsoft Visual Studio 6.0⇨ Microsoft Visual Basic 6.0.**

2. **Click the Don't Show this dialog in the future check box, as shown in Figure 2-3.**

Note: Visual J++ melds itself into the Visual InterDev Editor (see Figure 2-4). So, if you turn off the New Project dialog check box for Visual InterDev, you also turn it off for Visual J++ at the same time.

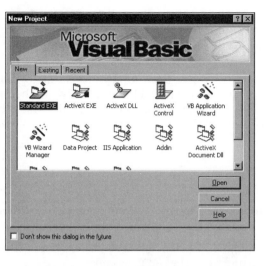

Figure 2-3:
The Visual
Basic New
Project
dialog box
is similar,
but not
identical, to
the Visual
InterDev
dialog box
shown in
Figure 2-2.

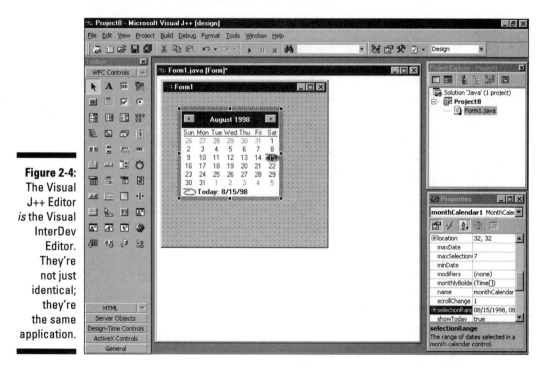

Figure 2-4:
The Visual
J++ Editor
is the Visual
InterDev
Editor.
They're
not just
identical;
they're
the same
application.

Avoiding the New Project dialog box in Visual Basic: The Long version

If you don't want to suppress Visual Basic's New Project dialog box by selecting the check box on the New Project dialog box described in the preceding section of this chapter, you can instead use the Visual Basic Options dialog box. To turn off the New Project dialog box in Visual Basic, follow these steps:

1. **Choose Tools⇨Options.**

   The Options dialog box opens.

2. **Click the Environment tab in the Options dialog box, shown in Figure 2-5.**

   The Environment page of the dialog box opens, with many options for templates and starting projects and programs.

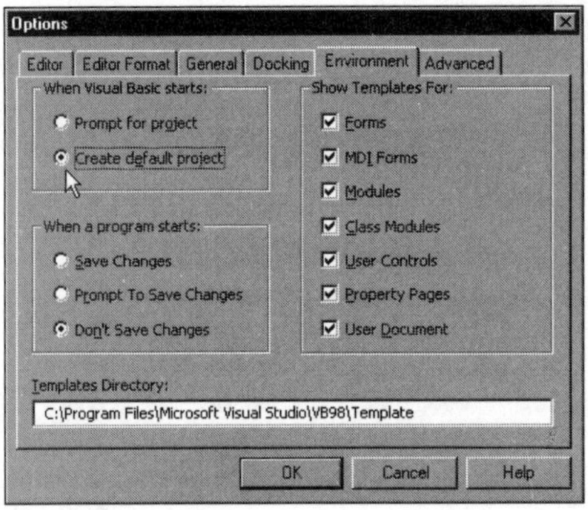

Figure 2-5:
Visual
Basic's
Options
dialog box
differs from
Visual
InterDev's
Options
dialog box.

3. **In the When Visual Basic starts section, select the Create default project option.**

4. **Click the OK button.**

Avoiding the Getting Started dialog box in FrontPage

FrontPage is often a maverick. It may have the same features as other Visual Studio 6 applications, but FrontPage names those features differently or organizes them in some unusual way. For example, the New Project dialog box goes by a different name in FrontPage. It's called the Getting Started dialog box. But, a rose by any other name will smell as sweet. You can get rid of this dialog box in two ways. The easy way is to choose the Always Open Last Web option on the FrontPage Getting Started dialog box, as shown in Figure 2-6. Then the dialog box no longer appears when you open FrontPage.

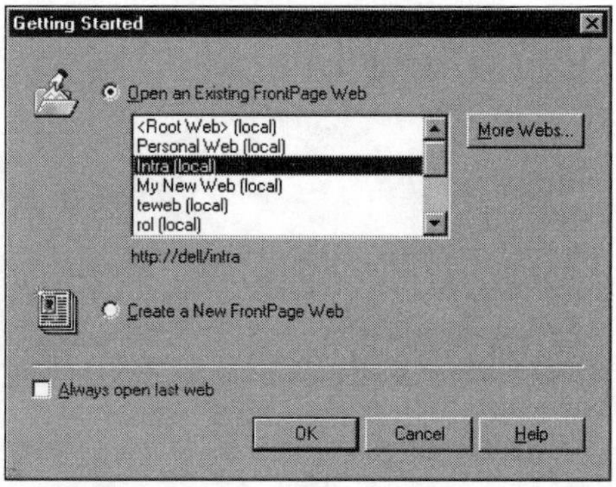

Figure 2-6: The FrontPage Getting Started dialog box.

The second way to get rid of the Getting Started dialog box is a little more difficult. If you want to avoid the Getting Started dialog box (or toggle it so that it shows up again each time you run FrontPage), follow these steps:

1. **If you're currently in the FrontPage Editor, choose Tools⇨Show FrontPage Explorer.**

   The FrontPage *Explorer* (not the FrontPage *Editor)* opens.

2. **Choose Tools⇨Options.**

   The Options dialog box opens.

3. **Click the General tab.**

4. **Click the Show Getting Started dialog check box.**

5. **Click the OK button.**

Turning off the Welcome To dialog box in Visual FoxPro

Visual FoxPro (alone among the Visual Studio 6 applications) displays a dramatic graphic list of choices when you first run it, as shown in Figure 2-7. This list enables you to organize components, create a new application, or open an existing project. If you don't want to see this screen each time you run Visual FoxPro, click the check box in the lower-left corner of the graphic, Don't display this Welcome screen again.

Figure 2-7:
The Visual
FoxPro
flashy
splash
screen.

Getting to Know the Languages, the Database Manager, and the Designers

With two exceptions (FrontPage and Visual J++), you start each Visual Studio 6 component as a separate application. They're part of Visual Studio 6, but they run as separate programs just like running a word processor at the same time you're running Internet Explorer.

FrontPage is an exception because it contains two separate windows: the FrontPage Explorer and the FrontPage Editor. Therefore, this is not strictly speaking what's usually called an *integrated* design environment. Visual J++ is an exception because it shares its window with Visual InterDev. Perhaps you can say that Visual J++ and Visual InterDev are *super-integrated*.

If you want to create a component, such as a custom text box, you run one of the languages — Visual C++, Visual Basic, or Visual J++ — and get to work. If you want to create or edit a database, start Visual FoxPro, the Visual Studio 6 database manager application. If you want to create or edit Web pages, run Visual InterDev or FrontPage. These applications can be called *designers,* though they do include some language features for HTML, VBScript, and JScript.

Microsoft has tried for years to make life easier for people who use its applications. Microsoft conducts focus groups, hires consultants, and generally tries to smooth the way for users. But life isn't perfect. Consider the common task of searching. The shortcut key for searching through text is F3 in Word for Windows, but Ctrl+F in Internet Explorer and all the Visual Studio 6 applications. As you can see in this chapter, the Visual Studio 6 suite of applications have similar interfaces. But they aren't yet as similar as they should be (and likely will be) in the future. An option that appears in the View menu in one application can easily appear in the Tools menu in another application.

Getting to Know the Common Integrated Design Environment

Getting used to the Visual Studio 6 Editor, or IDE as it's sometimes called, is a good idea. IDE stands for Integrated Design Environment. That means that even though an IDE looks something like a word processor, you can do lots of things with it beyond typing in programming. It's called an IDE because it includes a variety of tools within a single environment. The environment is *integrated* in the sense that the different tools are designed to work harmoniously together. In most IDEs you can find a text editor; a debugging utility; sets of templates and predesigned layouts; a toolbox containing components you can add to your projects; and various other features.

If you want to see two applications in Visual Studio 6 that are *really* integrated, run Visual InterDev. If you installed Visual J++ during the Visual Studio 6 setup process, you see both Visual InterDev and Visual J++ options available in the New Project dialog box. Did you run Visual InterDev or Visual J++?

Until you actually select something from the New Project dialog box, the title bar on the IDE says Microsoft Development Environment. Only after you select a Visual InterDev or Visual J++ project does the title bar change to say Microsoft Visual InterDev or Microsoft Visual J++.

You can bring up a New Project dialog box any time. Just choose File⇨New Project (or press Ctrl+N). You can jump back and forth between Visual J++ and Visual InterDev quickly this way, just by choosing projects that were constructed by one or the other application.

Pull that window up to the dock!

One feature you can find in most Visual Studio 6 applications is *docking*. You have two kinds of windows: the main application window (called the *parent*) and the smaller windows inside the main window like Toolboxes, document editors, or Properties windows. The smaller windows are called *child* windows. When you drag a child close to the frame of the parent window, the frame can act like a magnet and snap the child window to the main frame. You can pull the child window off, but a little tugging takes place before it comes free. This magnet-like behavior is called *docking*.

Technically, a window is docked when it's attached to any other window. Mostly, a child docks with the main window, but some child windows can also dock to each other, such as the Project Explorer and Properties Window in Visual InterDev or Visual Basic. If a window is not dockable, it can be moved anywhere, and it will stay put.

All the Visual Studio 6 applications feature docking, with two exceptions. Visual FoxPro and FrontPage don't yet have a docking feature. Chances are, they'll add this selective docking option in their next versions. They'll probably also add the ability to switch between SDI and MDI window styles as well. Those two options (SDI and MDI), and docking, are important features — some people love docking, some hate it. You want as much control over customizing docking behavior as you can get.

SDI means Single Document Interface. In SDI mode, all windows float free. No window can be docked to a container window. MDI mode means Multiple Document Interface. That's the familiar large container window with several child windows contained within it. In some Visual Studio 6 applications, you can choose between SDI and MDI modes (see the next section "Turning docking on and off, the crude way"). For further examples of MDI versus SDI, see the section "Understanding the difference between Multiple- and Single-Document Interfaces" later in this chapter.

Turning docking on and off, the crude way

One way to get rid of docking is to switch to the SDI mode. Stopping the docking behavior by switching to SDI mode is a bit like paving your yard to get rid of dandelions in the grass. It's overkill. But in some applications, the SDI mode is the only way to prevent docking.

In Visual InterDev, you can switch between MDI mode and SDI mode. Follow these steps:

1. **Choose Tools⇨Options.**

   The Options dialog box opens.

2. **Select General under the Environment option in the list on the left side of the Options dialog box.**

3. **Click SDI Environment to select it, or to deselect it.**

4. **Click the OK button.**

Visual Basic, Visual InterDev, and Visual C++ have the most advanced docking options of all Visual Studio 6 applications. They boast the most flexibility, and include the most child windows that have a docking capability.

Adjusting docking individually in Visual Basic

You can individually assign dockability to each of the primary child windows in Visual Basic. To adjust Visual Basic's docking, follow these steps:

1. **Choose Tools⇨Options.**

   The Options dialog box opens, as shown in Figure 2-8.

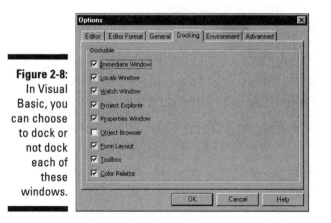

Figure 2-8: In Visual Basic, you can choose to dock or not dock each of these windows.

2. **Click the Docking tab.**

   The Docking page appears with many check boxes for the windows that you can make dockable.

3. **Check the check boxes for the child windows that you want to make dockable.**

4. **Click the OK button.**

Adjusting docking individually in Visual C++

To adjust Visual C++ docking, follow these steps:

1. **Choose Tools⇨Options.**

   The Options dialog box opens.

2. **Click the arrows at the top right of the dialog box until the Workspace tab appears.**

   Too many tabs are in this dialog box for you to see them all at once. So as you click the arrows, the tabs scroll past and you can see them all.

3. **Click the Workspace tab.**

   The Workspace page appears with several options that you can adjust involving the status bar, menus, and docking.

4. **Select which child windows you want to make dockable in the Docking Views list.**

5. **Click the OK button.**

An even quicker way exists to adjust the docking behavior of the child windows in Visual Basic, Visual C++, Visual J++, and Visual InterDev. Just right-click the child window and then select (or deselect) the Dockable option from the menu that appears. Note that in Visual Basic, you right-click *inside* a window to display its context menu. If you click the title bar of a window, a different menu is displayed. However — and this is yet another one of those annoying little inconsistencies of behavior among Visual Studio 6 applications — to adjust docking for Visual InterDev's Properties window, you *must* right-click its title bar! My advice: Try right-clicking everything until you see the Dockable option.

Understanding the difference between Multiple- and Single-Document Interfaces

One of the main features of the Visual Studio 6 IDE is called *MDI* for Multiple-Document Interface. MDI means you have one big window, with various child windows inside it. You can move the children around.

When you're using an MDI, the child windows aren't supposed to float outside the parent (application) window. If you open several documents at the same time, in Word for Windows, that's an MDI. However, if you move Word itself, all the child document windows move with it — as if they're attached to it. By contrast, Visual InterDev/Visual J++ windows can be dragged outside the main window, even in MDI mode, as you can see in Figure 2-9. In Visual InterDev, only the editor window can't be dragged outside of the parent window.

If you want to move a window, but don't want it to dock, just hold down the Ctrl key while you're dragging it. It won't attach itself to anything.

If you choose SDI environment, all windows float free on the desktop. The child windows need not remain within a main container window. Docking is not possible because you have no main, gray, background container parent window. In Figure 2-10, every window is on the main Windows desktop. Each window is self-contained and free. No docking.

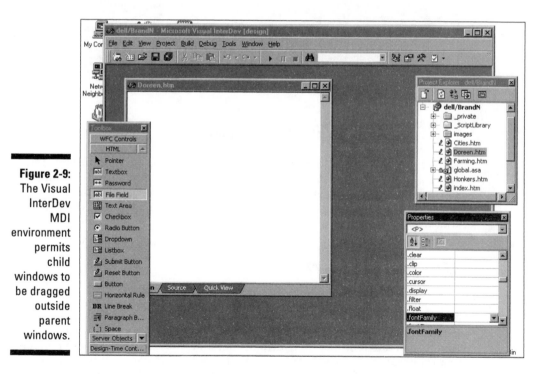

Figure 2-9:
The Visual InterDev MDI environment permits child windows to be dragged outside parent windows.

Figure 2-10:
All windows
are
independent
in the SDI
style
environment.

RAD Hot and Ready to Go

One of the best things to happen to people who work with computers is the concept of *RAD*, Rapid Application Development. Whether you're a graphic designer putting together a Web site's user interface or a programmer writing the code that makes an application work, you'll appreciate the tools that RAD offers.

What's Visual?

Visual is another way of defining RAD. Consider the names: Visual J++, Visual FoxPro, and all the other visual tools that are brought together into Visual Studio 6. *Visual* means several things that collectively boost programming and design efficiency by an enormous amount. Also, as anyone who remembers the transition from DOS computing to Windows can testify, a visual environment is a lot more fun to work with. Some of the efficiencies in a RAD application are: You can see what a visitor to your site would see; you can drag and drop components into your pages; you can *draw* (instead of program) Web page items, such as tables. In other words, you get to work with visible objects rather than having to type in obscure text commands or write computer programming code to make things happen.

Changing a background

You may find many jobs are surprisingly easy to accomplish using Visual Studio 6 applications. For example, changing the background behind a Web page is a snap in FrontPage. To see how WYSIWYG helps you to efficiently accomplish this task, follow these steps:

1. **Start FrontPage running.**

2. **If you're in the FrontPage Explorer, choose Tools⇨Show FrontPage Editor.**

   The FrontPage Editor comes into view.

3. **In the FrontPage Editor, choose File⇨New.**

   The New dialog box opens, showing a list of 27 templates that you can choose for your new page.

4. **Double-click Normal Page in the list.**

   A new, blank page appears in the FrontPage Editor and the dialog box closes.

5. **Click the Normal tab on the bottom of the FrontPage Editor window.**

   You see a blank, empty page. If you see colors, buttons, a background, or other elements, choose Format⇨Theme and click the This Page Does Not Use Themes option button. (Anything other than a blank page means that you're working with a project that has a Theme associated with it. See Chapter 7; it's all about Themes.)

6. **Choose Format⇨Background**

   The Page Properties dialog box opens with the Background page displayed.

7. **Click the Specify Background and Colors option button.**

8. **Click the Browse button.**

   A Select Background Image dialog box opens.

9. **Click the Select A File On Your Computer button in the Select Background Image dialog box. (The button has a file/magnifying glass icon on it and is located in the lower right of the Select Background Image dialog.)**

   The classic Windows Select File dialog box opens.

10. **Choose a .Gif or .Jpg graphic file on your hard drive.**

11. **Click the OK buttons twice to close all the dialogs.**

You now see that whatever background image you've chosen is added to the Web page. The key word here is *see*. What you're seeing is what anyone visiting this Web page can see in a browser. (Take a look at Figure 2-11.) (Technically, FrontPage shows you what *most* visitors *probably* see. Some final formatting decisions are left up to the visitor's browser. For example, a large headline <H1> tag can be displayed slightly differently in different browsers.)

Now, click the HTML tab on the bottom of the window. You see something similar to the HTML source code programming shown in Figure 2-12.

Before the RAD applications, you often couldn't easily see the results of your work. If you typed in a new line, or changed an existing line of HTML, you then had to save the file to your hard drive. Next you had to load that file into your browser (such as Internet Explorer). After all that, you could see the effects of your work.

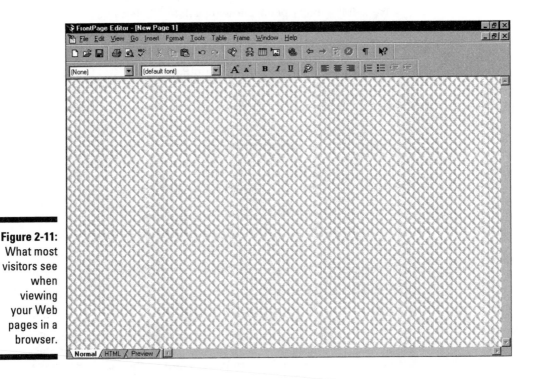

Figure 2-11:
What most
visitors see
when
viewing
your Web
pages in a
browser.

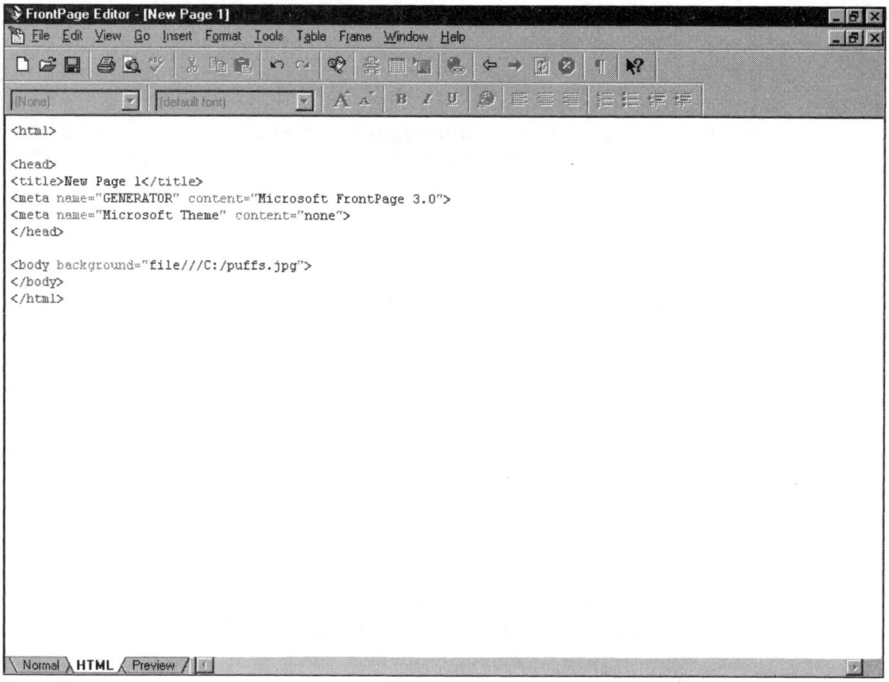

Figure 2-12:
The programming underneath defines the visible surface shown in Figure 2-11.

This clumsy back and forth process wastes time. That process was necessary in the previous version of Visual InterDev. However, with Visual InterDev 6 in Visual Studio 6, the clumsiness is history. Visual InterDev has gone RAD like FrontPage. Switching between code view and preview is now as simple as clicking a tab on the bottom of the editor window.

Many of the Microsoft applications are now RAD, even the Visual FoxPro database application and C++, the most complex, you may even say *austere,* of computer languages.

Components: Your Rapid Development Toolbox

In the early days of Windows's popularity (back at the start of this decade), creating applications took forever. Why? Because writing programs for a Graphical User Interface (GUI) is exceedingly complex. All over the world, programmers were gasping as they struggled to create check boxes, movable windows, buttons that seem to move in a little when clicked, and all the other elements of a GUI that are now taken for granted.

Rather suddenly in 1991, the way people worked when writing computer programs went through a big change. The idea was to create only one official check box; then everybody could just reuse that check box when they wrote a new application. Instead of each application containing special programming code to display and manage user interaction with a check box, the programmer could simply drag and drop a pre-built check box component into his new application! Custom-writing a check box in a language such as C can take many weeks. Dragging and dropping a check box component takes only a few seconds.

This new idea — using standardized components — first appeared in Visual Basic in 1991, and computer programming hasn't been the same since. This standardization also brought great benefits to users. No longer did users have to figure out how to use different ways to accomplish common tasks such as saving a file or scrolling text. Each application, no matter which manufacturer created it, had the same printer setup dialog, the same scroll bars, the same components.

Visual Basic also introduced the idea of the Toolbox, a window that contained all the components that could be dropped into a program. To see how easily you can use components, the following sections show you how to build and customize a text box. The user can type messages into it and, by clicking a button, the user can clear the text box to start over. Even if you've never programmed in your life, you'll be able to do this in a few minutes!

Creating a text box the easy way

To put a text box into a Visual Basic program, follow these steps:

1. **Run Visual Basic 6.**

2. **Double-click the Standard EXE icon in the New Project dialog box.**

   If this New Project dialog box doesn't open when you start Visual Basic, choose File⇨New Project to open it. You see a blank form, as shown in Figure 2-13.

3. **Double-click the text box component in the Toolbox.**

   The text box appears on Form1, as shown in Figure 2-14.

   If the Toolbox isn't visible, choose View⇨Toolbox.

4. **Stretch the text box so that it nearly fills the Form, except on the bottom, as shown in Figure 2-14. Leave some space for the button you add in the following section "Resizing a component."**

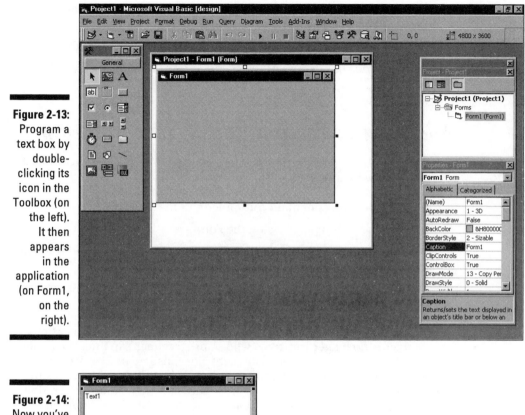

Figure 2-13:
Program a
text box by
double-
clicking its
icon in the
Toolbox (on
the left).
It then
appears
in the
application
(on Form1,
on the
right).

Figure 2-14:
Now you've
got a text
box on your
program's
user
interface.

Resizing a component

To stretch a component to make it larger, smaller, or a different shape,
follow these steps:

1. **Click the text box component in Form1.**

   This action selects the text box, adding drag handles to it at each of its
   four corners and four sides. (The drag handles are the small rectangles
   that you see surrounding the text box in Figure 2-14.)

2. **Move your mouse pointer until it changes into a double-headed arrow when you place it onto one of the drag handles.**

3. **Hold down the left mouse button as you move the mouse (drag).**

4. **Pull the sides or corners of the text box until it's the size and shape you want.**

Adding a command button to a program

Now you want to create a button that, when clicked, clears any text from the text box. Follow these steps:

1. **Double-click the command button icon in the Toolbox.**

   A command button appears on the Form.

2. **Drag the command button across Form1 until you've moved it down to the lower right of the Form.**

3. **Then drag the command button to make it a little wider and narrower than its default shape.**

Now that everyone is using standard components in the RAD applications, a programmer is no longer free to go wild. A programmer can't make a really eccentric text box, for example, with eight sides instead of four. Well, if you're clever enough, you *can* build an octagonal text box, by hand, using special programming to get down to the innards of the Windows operating system. You can design pretty much any look you want, if you know enough about programming. But even if an octagonal text box perhaps looks good to the inhabitants of Dune, on our planet we expect text-entry components to be rectangular. Standards have been set, and designs are generally agreed on, for many computer components.

In spite of the general standards, though, you can nevertheless customize many of the less fundamental qualities of a RAD component. You can usually adjust its color, its size, its position, the typeface used in it, and many other properties. How hard is this customization? You guessed it: it's very, very simple. You just make your changes in a Properties window.

Changing a font

You've added components to a window (or the *Form* as a window is called in Visual Basic). Now you can customize these components. All RAD environments include Properties windows where you can adjust the *qualities* or *characteristics* (officially called the *properties*) of the components.

Say that you want to make the typeface in the text box 10 pt. Times New Roman. Follow these steps:

1. **Right-click the text box.**

   A context menu appears.

2. **Click Properties in the context menu.**

   The Properties Window is displayed.

3. **Scroll the Properties window until you see Font, as shown in Figure 2-15.**

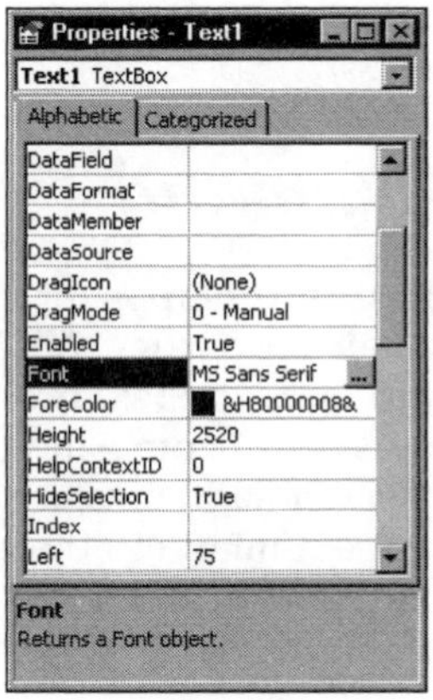

Figure 2-15: You adjust the qualities of a component in the Properties window.

4. **Double-click the Font entry in the Properties window. (Or you can single-click the three-dot icon ... next to the word Font.)**

   The standard Windows font dialog appears.

5. **Choose Times New Roman as the Font and 10pt. as the size. Click the OK button to close the font dialog.**

   Notice that the sample text in the text box has changed to reflect your selections. Another example of RAD WYSIWYG.

Changing a color

Follow these steps to change the Form's color to blue:

1. **Right-click the Form.**

   Its context menu appears.

2. **Click Properties in the context menu.**

   The Properties window appears.

3. **Scroll the Properties window until you see the BackColor.**

4. **Double-click the BackColor entry in the Properties window.**

   A drop-down list of colors appears.

5. **Click the Palette button.**

   A dialog box opens with various colors displayed.

6. **Click a shade of blue to select it.**

   The button now turns blue automatically and the color palette dialog box closes. The Form is now blue.

Adding a programming command

The preceding sections show you how to adjust the component's size and position on the Form and how to customize their properties. All that remains to do is tell the command button how to clear the text box when the user clicks the button. This process is quite easy. A "" command in Visual Basic clears any text from the text box. The "" command means empty string (no characters). Follow these steps to add that command to the command button:

1. **Double-click the command button.**

   You drop down into the code area, as shown in Figure 2-16.

2. **Type in the words** Text1.Text = **The** "" **command between the** Private Sub **and** End Sub **commands, as shown in Figure 2-16.**

   This programming, Text1.Text = "" says that the contents (its Text property) of Text1 (the text box's name) should be cleared any time this command button is clicked.

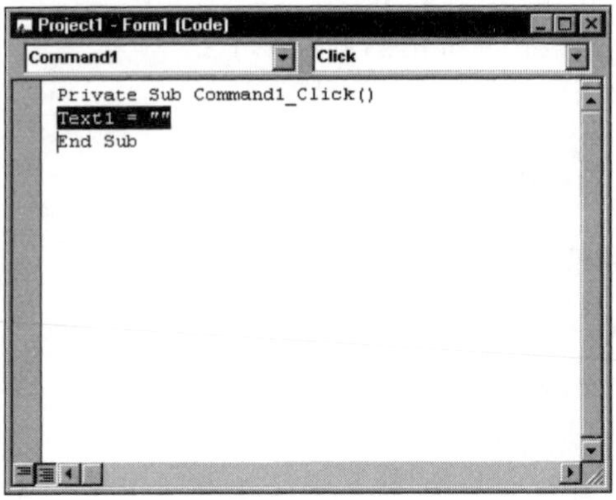

Figure 2-16:
Commands you want a component to follow are put into this special Code window.

```
Project1 - Form1 (Code)
Command1                    Click
    Private Sub Command1_Click()
    Text1 = ""
    End Sub
```

3. **You're done, so click the x in the upper right of the code window to close it.**

Testing your work

All RAD applications in Visual Studio 6 boast that you can quickly check your changes and see the results of your work. The three languages — Visual Basic, Visual C++ and Visual J++ — each have three ways you can start running the current program to test it:

- ✔ **Press F5.**
- ✔ **Click the triangle icon on the standard toolbar in Visual Basic or Visual J++. (Click the document with a down arrow icon on the Build toolbar in Visual C++.)**
- ✔ **Choose Run⇨Start in Visual Basic, choose Debug⇨Start in Visual J++, or choose Build⇨Start Debug⇨Go in Visual C++.**

To test the Text1 = "" behavior you've programmed into the command button in Visual Basic, follow these steps:

1. **Press F5 (the easiest way to start a program running).**

   The Form appears as if it were a real, running Windows program, and you see the default text *Text1* in the text box.

2. **Click the command button.**

   The text disappears from the text box.

3. **To stop the running program, click the x in the upper right of the window, or click the blue square icon on the Visual Basic standard toolbar.**

Testing in Visual InterDev, Visual FoxPro, and FrontPage

In Visual InterDev, FrontPage, or Internet Explorer, pressing F5 refreshes (reloads) the currently loaded Web page. If, for example, the page contains a running clock, the time is updated by a refresh.

You can see the effect of changes to a Visual FoxPro database by merely looking at that database. However, Visual FoxPro does have *executable* (programming that can be run) features. To start a Visual FoxPro program, choose Program⇨Do or press Ctrl+D.

You test a Web page in Visual InterDev by clicking the Quick View tab on the bottom of the Editor window. You test a Web page in FrontPage by clicking the Preview tab on the bottom of the Editor window.

A few kinds of programming you may do in Visual InterDev or FrontPage — namely inserting specialized kinds of components or programming — can't be tested using the Quick View or Preview features. In those cases, you must test the Web page by loading the page into Internet Explorer or some other browser. However, you have a shortcut even for this testing approach. In Visual InterDev, choose View⇨View In Browser or in the FrontPage Editor, choose File⇨Preview in Browser.

Off to See the Wizards2

Many design and programming tasks can be simplified by dropping components such as text boxes into a Web page or a program. But you can make good use of another tool that makes life easier for designers and programmers: Wizards.

A Wizard is a set of dialog boxes built into an application such as FrontPage. When you choose to do a task that has a Wizard, it can lead you through the task, step-by-step. Wizards ask questions, such as how big do you want this picture? Or how often do you want this reminder displayed to the user?

Even if you think you've never worked with a Wizard, you probably have. You can tell that a Wizard is in operation if you're looking at a dialog box that has three buttons on the bottom: Back, Next, and Finish. Any time you install a Windows application, you're working with a *Setup Wizard*.

As you answer its series of questions, the Wizard is writing the programming code for you that accomplishes what you're trying to do. (Most Wizards write code, but some, like a Setup Wizard, do other jobs such as deciding which files to save to your hard drive.)

Wizards can be invoked in various places. Often you can find them on the Project, Insert, or Tools menus. Visual FoxPro is the grand champion in Visual Studio 6 for the sheer number of Wizards it contains. Visual FoxPro boasts 14 Wizards on its Tools⇨Wizards menu, including Report, Web Publishing, Database, Query, and even Pivot Table. In other Visual Studio 6 applications, Wizards are spread across several menus, including Tools and Project menus.

To get an idea how Wizards step you through a process, try creating a Form in FrontPage. Forms are used in Internet sites to gather information or otherwise interact with the user. To create a form in FrontPage, follow these steps:

1. **Start FrontPage running.**

2. **Click the Cancel button if the New FrontPage Web dialog box opens in the FrontPage Explorer.**

   The dialog box closes.

3. **Switch to the FrontPage Editor.**

   If you're in the FrontPage Explorer, choose Tools⇨Show FrontPage Editor.

4. **Click File⇨New in the FrontPage Editor.**

   The New dialog box opens with a list of predefined Wizards and templates.

5. **Double-click Form Page Wizard in the New dialog.**

   The New dialog box closes and you see the Form Page Wizard's first dialog, as shown in Figure 2-17. Wizards often begin with a dialog box that explains their purpose.

6. **Click Next and type in** User Information **as the Title.**

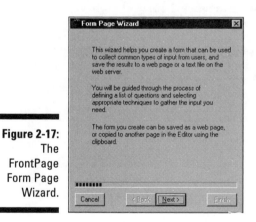

Figure 2-17:
The
FrontPage
Form Page
Wizard.

7. **Click Next and then click Add.**

   A list of categories of input appears.

8. **Click Personal Information in the Select the type of input to collect for this question list box.**

9. **Click Next and use the defaults shown in Figure 2-18.**

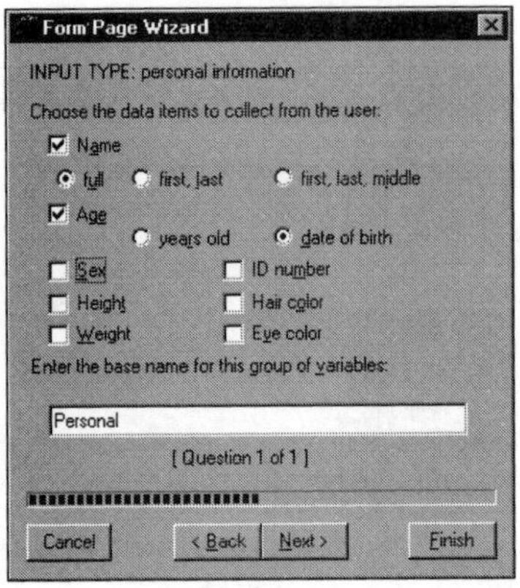

Figure 2-18:
The information you want to collect about visitors to your Web site.

10. **Click Next twice to get to the Presentation Options. Leave these options set to the default as normal paragraphs.**

11. **Click Next and select the save results to a text file option.**

12. **Click Next and then click Finish to let the Wizard do its final work. You can see the results shown in Figure 2-19.**

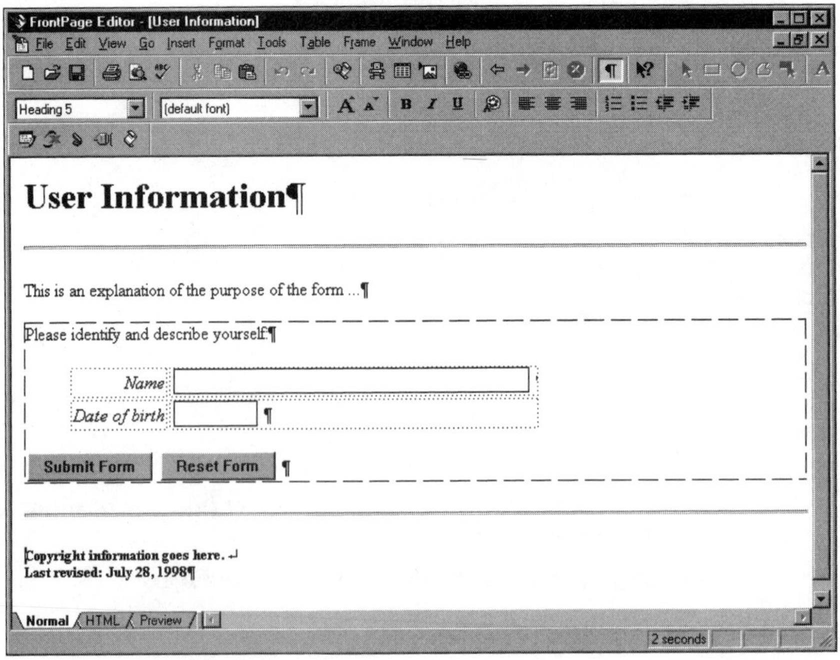

Figure 2-19:
The Wizard has produced this form.

Now you've defined how you want your form to work. Did you do any programming? No, you just answered the Wizard's queries and it did the hard part. At this point, you probably want to make some changes, such as typing in your company's copyright information and erasing Copyright information goes here. You may also want to replace This is an explanation of the purpose of the form with an actual explanation.

To see how this form looks to the user when it loads into a browser, click the Preview button at the bottom of the FrontPage edit window.

To see how much work the Wizard had to do to create this form, click the HTML tab. You see the following source code. If you didn't have the Wizard's assistance, you'd have to type all this HTML programming in yourself. Worse, you'd have to know all the HTML rules that are involved when creating a form; input and submit buttons; and all the rest. Better to let the Wizard do it.

```
<html>

<head>
<meta HTTP-EQUIV="Content-Type" CONTENT="text/html; iso-
         8859-1">
<meta name="GENERATOR" content="Microsoft FrontPage 3.0">
<title>User Information</title>
</head>

<body>

<h1>User Information</h1>

<hr>

<p>This is an explanation of the purpose of the form
         ...</p>

<form METHOD="POST" ACTION="--WEBBOT-SELF--">
<!--webbot bot="SaveResults" startspan U-
         File="formrslt.txt" S-Format="TEXT/TSV"
B-Label-Fields="TRUE" --><!--webbot bot="SaveResults"
         endspan --><p>Please identify and
describe yourself:</p>
<blockquote>
  <table>
   <tr>
    <td ALIGN="right"><em>Name</em></td>
```

(continued)

(continued)

```
        <td><input TYPE="TEXT" NAME="Personal_FullName"
            SIZE="35"> </td>
    </tr>
    <tr>
    <td ALIGN="right"><em>Date of birth</em></td>
    <td><input TYPE="TEXT" NAME="Personal_DateOfBirth"
            SIZE="8"> </td>
    </tr>
    </table>
  </blockquote>
 <p><input TYPE="SUBMIT" VALUE="Submit Form"> <input
            TYPE="RESET" VALUE="Reset Form"> </p>
</form>

<hr>

<h5>Copyright information goes here.<br>
Last revised: <!--webbot bot="TimeStamp" S-Type="EDITED" S-
            Format="%B %d, %Y" --></h5>
</body>
</html>
```

If you look closely at the preceding HTML source code, you may wonder what the heck a *Webbot* is. The Wizard slipped a couple of them into this Form's source code. Pay no attention to the man behind the curtain! One of the great things about Wizards and such is that you need not know how they do their magic. You can just make use of the results of that magic. Nevertheless, you get into Webbots in Chapter 10. You can slip them into your Web pages, too, if you want.

Of course, you have many more Wizards and other RAD tools to explore throughout this book. RAD has greatly decreased the expertise, as well as the amount of time, needed to create Windows programs and Internet sites. (Also, as a side effect, RAD has greatly increased the number of programmers and site designers.) Wizards, components, and other RAD tools are your best friends when you want to create something great, but get it done quickly and easily. And creating great distributed applications and Web pages is the topic of this book.

Chapter 3

Creating Your First Web Page Using Visual Studio 6

*N*o point in pussyfooting around. You want to create a Web page? This is your chapter.

You have two basic approaches for creating a Web page. You can think things through and plan a Web page before even turning on the computer. Or you can fire up Visual InterDev or FrontPage and jump right in. In this chapter, you try a little planning. If you're one of those who prefer to plunge in, skip to the section "It All Starts in the Home Page" later in this chapter.

Home Page, Sweet Home Page

When people visit your Web site, they see your *home page* first. This page is also the *only* page at your site that people see if it's a bad, uninformative, ugly piece of work. Visitors know how to surf. They click away fast if you don't make them happy. Some of your visitors have the attention span of a hummingbird. So how do you make your home page attract even the most hyper mouse-clicker? You put some careful forethought into specific aspects of your home page as you plan it.

Planning a home page

If you want to make a good first impression, consider the following points when planning your home page:

- It's the entrance to your site, and first impressions count. Make your home page beautiful. Does your home page make a visitor want to stay around to see the rest of your site?

- Include some way for the visitor to jump to other pages in your site from your home page. Is the navigation method easy to understand? You can use buttons or a text-style table of contents, but make whatever navigation method you use clear to the visitor. If a button's caption can't fully describe its purpose, add a label next to the button.

- Describe the overall purpose of your site in the home page. Have you accurately described it in text and symbolized it in graphics?

- What look and feel do you want? A candy store's home page must look different from a bank's.

- Is the text easy to read? (Make the text dark and the background light, so that the page is more readable. The Velvet Elvis painting effect — light-colored text against a black background — is tiring to read. Plus, it's a style that some people don't find very attractive.)

- Are you using too many graphics, or are you using large, high-resolution graphics — causing the page to load very slowly into a browser? Consider replacing slow graphics with compressed .Jpg graphics that load faster.

- Is the page up-to-date? You don't want visitors to see text describing your 1987 product line.

- Are the page elements consistent? Do all the buttons look the same, except for their captions? Using the Visual Studio 6 professionally designed Themes can help you keep the visual elements harmonious across your entire Web site. See Chapter 7 for everything you'll ever want to know about using Themes.

- Make the top of your home page the best it can be.

Currently, most people are using 800 x 600 or, worse, 640 x 480 resolution in their Windows computer. In practical terms, this means that these visitors are only going to see five or fewer inches of your Web pages. Therefore, assume that many people see only the very top of your home page, so put the most important information (and best looking graphics) right up there at the top of your home page. Just as the home page is the first impression they get of your Web site, the top of the home page is the first impression of your home page as a whole. Also, don't force them to scroll forever. Limit the size of your home page to two or three visible pages when someone is scrolling down the page using 800 x 600 resolution.

Deciding what type of home page you're creating

Here's another checklist for you. Stop for a minute and think about the overall *type* of home page you're creating.

Of the following general types of home pages, which type is closest to yours?

- ✔ **Corporate Image:** You want to provide a site where your business gets publicity and a chance to explain its goals and products.

- ✔ **Customer Support:** You're offering answers to customer questions ranging from "Where the heck is my merchandise?" to "How do I turn it off? It's been running for days now!"

- ✔ **Reference:** Out of kindness, you provide your list of every stamp ever issued from the Republic of Belize. You don't get a stampede of visitors, but you're making the world a richer, more informed place. Reviewers call your site "maddening."

- ✔ **Personal Page:** This can be anything. Maybe you're just having fun or you want to display the family album. Many Internet service providers offer a certain amount of storage space free, where you can set up your own Web site. And some personal pages evolve into a business. You never know. Each of the various kinds of sites requires different techniques. Knowing what look you're after, and the purpose of your site, can help you get the results you're after.

Note: You can find lots of good ideas to spark your imagination at Microsoft's Site Builder Network. Enter this address in your browser:

```
http://www.microsoft.com/sitebuilder/siteinfo/newtosite.asp
```

Building a Home Page

FrontPage is an easier application to use than Visual InterDev when working on an individual Web page. (Visual InterDev has better tools for organizing a large, complicated *site,* but FrontPage is often best when you want to build, or tweak, a single *page.*) In this section, you use a FrontPage template to create a home page with an attractive layout. Then you modify the template to customize it to your particular needs. Finally, you manipulate the graphics in the page, including finding out how to access the extensive Microsoft collection of high-quality clip art. (It's free.)

Choosing a template for your first home page

You can create a plain vanilla home page, or you can divide it into zones (sidebars, columns, frames, and other kinds of subdivisions). Most professional Web pages are subdivided, just as most newspapers and magazines divide their pages into logical areas (table of contents, heading, related stories grouped into a section of their own). You can use FrontPage's set of templates to easily divide your home page into several sections.

To see how to create a home page divided into a table of contents list on the left, plus a larger section containing the body text on the right, follow these steps:

1. **Start FrontPage by clicking the FrontPage icon on your desktop.**

   Depending on how you have FrontPage set up, you may or may not see a Getting Started dialog box.

2. **Click Cancel if the Getting Started dialog box asks whether you want to create a new FrontPage Web.**

   The Getting Started dialog box closes.

3. **Choose Tools⇨Show FrontPage Editor.**

   The FrontPage Editor appears, containing a blank, empty page.

4. **In the FrontPage Editor, choose File⇨New.**

   You see the New dialog box shown in Figure 3-1.

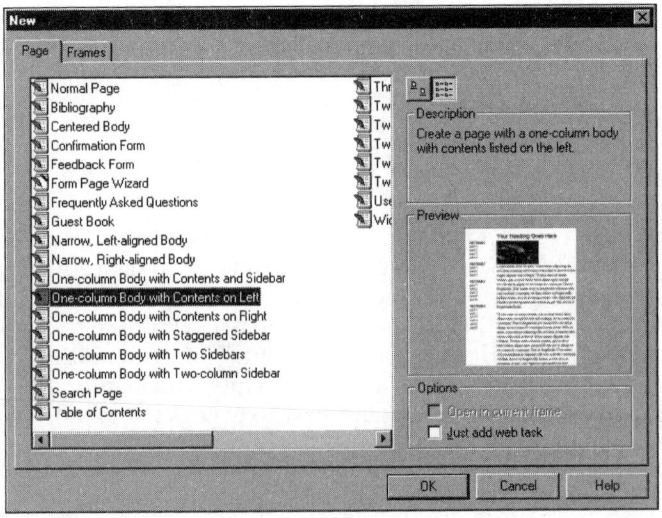

Figure 3-1: In the New dialog box, you can choose a Template and see a Preview of the selected page.

5. **Double-click the One Column Body with Contents on Left template in the list box on the left.**

   The New dialog box closes and you can see the template that you selected in the FrontPage Editor. You've chosen a nice-looking template from FrontPage's generous list of predesigned pages.

   Click the HTML tab at the bottom of the FrontPage Editor and take a look at all the HTML programming code you *don't* have to write when you use a template!

   Templates are obviously a valuable shortcut. You know you want this look, but you certainly don't want to bother creating it with commands like this:

```
<table border="0" cellpadding="0" cellspacing="8"
       width="98%">
```

Modifying a template

If you choose an organized, nice-looking template for your home page (as shown in the previous section), you need to customize it to give your page its own personality.

When you're ready to modify the template page to display your home page, all you have to do is type over the text and, perhaps, change the graphic. You can ignore all the programming between the 〈 〉 symbols. It creates the structure of the page, and you want to retain that.

1. **Click the Normal tab in the FrontPage Editor.**

   Use Normal view when personalizing a template. Normal view is the easiest way to edit the text and graphics on a page, without being bothered by having to work around all the HTML programming code. In Normal View, the code is invisible.

2. **Drag your mouse to highlight the text that you want to replace.**

   For this example, highlight the heading text "Your Heading Goes Here," as shown in Figure 3-2.

3. **Type in the text that you want to use instead of the placeholder text on your home page.**

   Perhaps you want the heading of your page to be the name of your business or "Complete Guide to Belize Philately." Note that when you highlight text and then begin typing, the text that you type replaces the highlighted text.

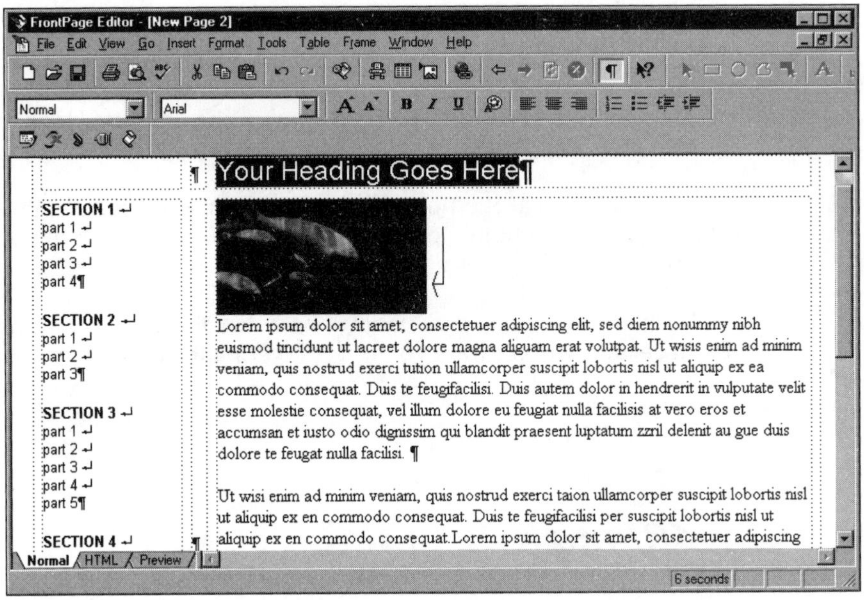

Figure 3-2: Highlight the placeholder text that you want to replace with your own text.

4. **Repeat Steps 2 and 3 to highlight and then replace any placeholder text that you want to replace on your home page.**

   For example, you can fill in the contents section on the left side of your home page.

5. **Replace the "greeking" in the body text (all that nonsense text like *quis nostrud exerci tution ullam*) with a description of your own.**

   Designers use greeking to visually stand in for normal text. The greeking just shows how the page looks after the real text is filled in by writers. And it isn't even real Greek; it's closer to Latin, actually. Latin mumbled after a three-day feast.

6. **Click the Preview tab at the bottom of the Editor window any time you want to see the results of your editing.**

   You see what a visitor to your site sees, as shown in Figure 3-3.

When you're attempting to replace text by highlighting it, be careful to highlight only the text that you want to replace. If you highlight more than the exact text, you could remove some of the formatting code as well. However, if you goof up, press Ctrl+Z to restore the text and formatting that was accidentally deleted. Ctrl+Z is the nearly universal Whoops! key combination. Press it in most Windows applications and whatever you just did is undone.

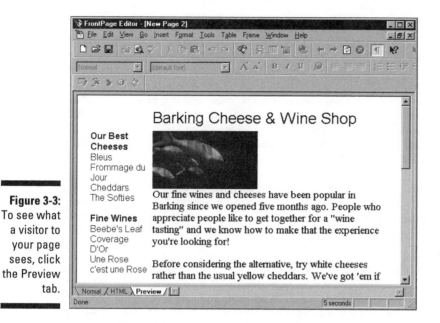

Figure 3-3:
To see what
a visitor to
your page
sees, click
the Preview
tab.

Understanding the text symbols

You've probably noticed those broken arrow symbols and paragraph symbols. The broken arrow means move down one line and is coded in HTML as <BR>. The paragraph symbol means move down two lines (to separate paragraphs) and is coded in HTML with <P> at the start of a paragraph and </P> at the end of a paragraph.

Notice two things when you're editing an existing page in Normal View:

✔ When you press the Enter key, a paragraph symbol is inserted and a blank line separates the paragraphs.

✔ If you keep typing and get to the end of a zone, the text automatically wraps around to the next line, just as it does in a word processor. However, sometimes you want to force (insist) that a line breaks at a particular character in the line. You don't want a separate paragraph with a blank line between the paragraphs. You just want to move down to the next line at a particular character in your text (you don't want line wrapping on this line). You can't do that in Normal View. Pressing the Enter key inserts a blank line. To see how to insert a forced line break in your text, look at the next section.

Forcing a line to break

Ordinarily, you want the browser to determine where to break text. In other words, if the user has stretched the browser wide, you want to enable the browser to display your text as a long line. If the user resizes the browser window, making it narrow, you want to enable the browser to redisplay your text, breaking the lines where appropriate to the new, narrow window. However, you may want to force a break — to force the next word to be on the next line. For instance, you want each of the items in the table of contents list on its own line.

In Normal View, a forced line break is illustrated by the broken arrow. If you want to force a line break when typing in Normal View, hold down Shift while pressing the Enter key.

Replacing a graphic

Some of FrontPage's templates include a graphic. In the example template that I show you earlier in this chapter ("One Column Body with Contents on Left"), you see a picture of fish. Fish aren't a good illustration for a wine and cheese shop. In fact, fish aren't a good image for most Web pages. Follow these steps to replace the fish graphic with a different one:

1. **In Normal View, click the picture to select the fish picture.**

   The picture displays *drag-handles* (small rectangles on its sides). These rectangles tell you the graphic has been selected.

2. **Choose Insert⇨Image in the FrontPage Editor.**

   The Image dialog box opens. In this dialog box, you can replace the selected graphic with one from your hard drive. You browse your hard drive by clicking the hard drive button (which has a picture of a folder and a magnifying glass) in the lower right part of the Image dialog box, as shown in Figure 3-4.

   Suppose that you've paid an artist to create a special logo for your cheese store. You asked the artist to make the logo look metallic and narrow, as shown in Figure 3-5. (Your home page sells cheese, not art. So you can get away with using narrow metallic lettering.) You received a .Jpg or .Gif image file of the logo from the artist and saved it to your hard drive.

3. **Click the hard drive icon shown in Figure 3-4 and find the .Jpg or .Gif image file on your hard drive. Double-click its filename.**

   Navigate through the folders in the main window of the Image dialog box until you find the image file that you're looking for. Files ending in .Jpg or .Gif are the only two kinds of graphics file types that Web browsers can display.

After you double-click the image's filename, the Image dialog box closes and the new image replaces the old one on your page.

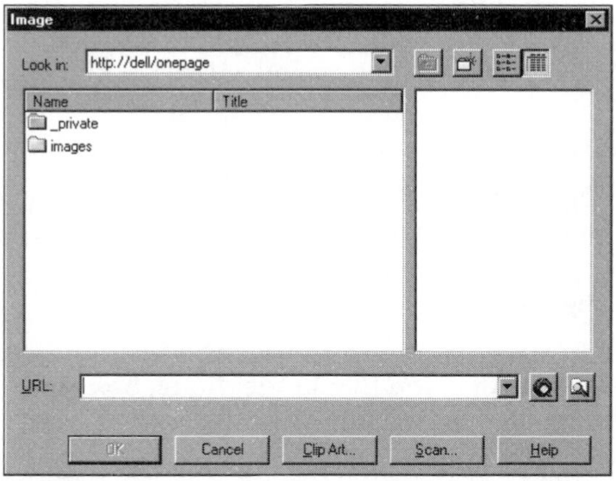

Figure 3-4:
Use the
Image
dialog box
to replace
the
selected
graphic
with one
from your
hard drive.

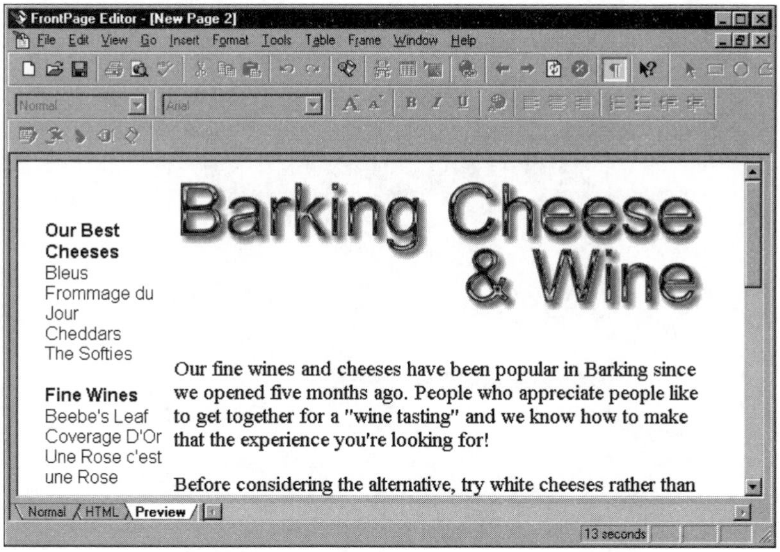

Figure 3-5:
Replacing
the picture
of the fish
with a
custom logo
takes only
a few
seconds.
Creating
the logo
graphic
itself can
take a little
longer.

Inserting clip art from FrontPage

If you prefer to use clip art (cartoons and sketchy drawings) instead of a photo or a logo, FrontPage offers a nice collection of clip art from Microsoft. In addition to cartoons, you have some great graphics to put onto buttons or use as icons. To add clip art to a Web page, follow these steps:

1. **Switch to Normal View in the FrontPage Editor.**

   Click the Normal tab at the bottom of the FrontPage Editor window.

2. **Move your mouse cursor to the location within the page where you want to insert some clip art. Click the mouse to define the location.**

   The blinking insertion cursor shows you where the clip art is placed on the page.

3. **Choose Insert⇨Clipart.**

   The Microsoft Clip Gallery 3.0 dialog box opens, as shown in Figure 3-6. You have about 200 clip art images on your hard drive, thanks to FrontPage. And if that's not enough, you can find more clip art on the Internet. (See the section "Locating clip art on the Internet," later in this chapter.)

4. **Find a clip art image that you like in the dialog box and double-click it.**

   The selected clip art image is inserted into your Web page where you last clicked the mouse cursor.

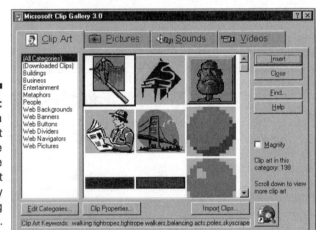

Figure 3-6: Choose a clip art image from the Microsoft Clip Gallery 3.0 dialog box.

Locating clip art on the Internet

If you want a really huge selection of free drawings from which to choose, visit the Clip Gallery Live at the Microsoft site. You can find many categories — well organized into many subcategories — from which to choose. For example, the Food & Wine category includes 732 drawings, divided into these categories: Fruits, Wine Bottles, Wine Glasses, Grapes, Wines, Stemware, Dining, Food, Drinks, and Goblets.

To insert clip art from the collection at the Microsoft Web site, follow these steps:

1. **Switch to Normal View in FrontPage Editor.**

   Click the Normal tab at the bottom of the FrontPage Editor window.

2. **Move your mouse cursor to the location within the page where you want to insert the clip art. Click the mouse to define the location.**

   The blinking insertion cursor shows you where the clip art is placed on the page.

3. **Choose Insert⇨Clipart.**

   The Microsoft Clip Gallery 3.0 dialog box opens.

4. **Click the Connect to Web button (a picture of the earth) in the lower-right corner of the Clip Gallery dialog box. (Refer to Figure 3-6.)**

5. **Click the OK button if you see a message box asking whether you "have access to the Web."**

   Note that you must have an Internet connection to answer that question with an OK.

   Your browser navigates the Internet and then displays the Clip Gallery Live site, shown in Figure 3-7, at the following address:

   `http://www.microsoft.com/clipgallerylive/default.asp`

   If you've never visited the Clip Gallery Live before, you have to click an OK button, accepting a license agreement.

   Note the Browse Clips by Category list box on the left of the Clip Gallery Live page in Figure 3-7. At this site, you can choose from hundreds of well-drawn clip art images, including a collection of the following additional graphics elements: backgrounds, banners, bullets, buttons, dividers (stylized lines), and pictures.

6. **In the Browse Clips by Category list box, click the category that you're interested in.**

   You see a group of drawings relating to the category of your interest. Naturally, for the example page, I selected Food & Dining as the category, as shown in Figure 3-8.

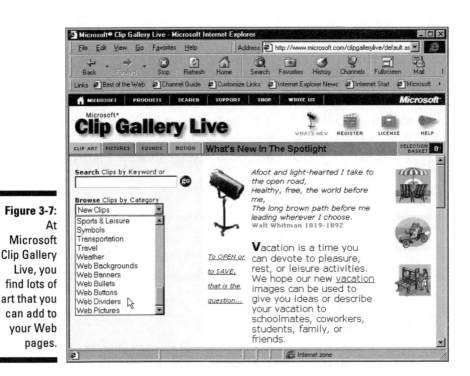

7. **When you find the drawing you're after, click the red arrow icon beneath the drawing to download it.**

   A File Download dialog box opens, asking whether you want to open or save the drawing.

8. **Choose Open.**

   The drawing is added to your Clip Gallery in a new category named Downloaded Clips. The dialog box closes.

9. **Double-click the downloaded graphic in your Clip Gallery to insert it into the Web page you're working on in FrontPage.**

Here are some tips to make things easier if you visit Clip Gallery Live:

✔ Note in Figure 3-8 that you can click the Previous or More icons just above the clip art illustrations. These choices enable you to cycle through all the art in any category.

✔ Click any drawing to see a preview of it, enlarged in the left pane.

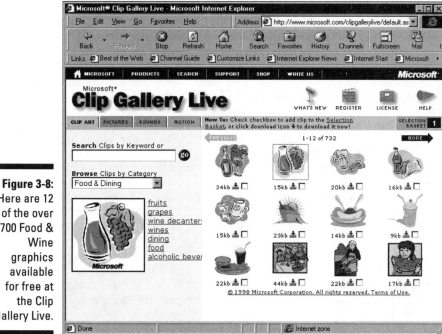

Figure 3-8:
Here are 12
of the over
700 Food &
Wine
graphics
available
for free at
the Clip
Gallery Live.

✔ Click as many check boxes (found underneath each drawing) as you wish. Each choice is added to your Selection Basket shown in the upper right, just under the Help feature. Try clicking the basket to see what happens.

✔ When you're finally ready to download, all the clips you've selected are added to your personal Clip Gallery dialog box.

✔ When you're ready to download a drawing, click the red arrow icon underneath one of the drawings.

If you decide to use any of the bullets or buttons available at the Clip Gallery Live, check out the Backgrounds, as well. Some of the bullets and buttons are designed to go with some of the Backgrounds.

Using Properties to Fix Parts of Your Web Page

You can find several great features in RAD (Rapid Application Development) applications like those that make up Visual Studio 6. One of the best features is that you can often easily adjust something's characteristics by just right-clicking it and then choosing Properties. This process works with most major elements of a Web page when you're in Normal view in FrontPage.

When you right-click an element of your page and choose Properties from the shortcut menu, a Properties dialog box opens, giving you options to adjust a cell, table, form, paragraph, image, font, and even the entire page. The options in the Properties dialog box enable you to quickly turn an unappealing (or just plain ugly) page into a well-organized, eye-pleasing page. Without the Visual Studio 6 Properties shortcuts, you'd have to get down and dirty and type in HTML code to make such major changes. With Properties, you don't have to understand the HTML code or syntax.

Figure 3-9 shows a Web page that has some major cosmetic problems — mainly with the alignment of its graphics and the unsightly white space. When you insert a graphic into a Web page, FrontPage initially leaves extra chunks of white space surrounding the graphic. The HTML language has a number of flaws. One flaw is that, by default, a graphic divides any surrounding text just as if the graphic were a new paragraph. If the graphic is the same width as the text into which it's inserted, the Web page looks fine. But graphics often aren't as wide as the text, as you can see in Figure 3-9.

Figure 3-9:
By default,
graphics
dropped
into text
create
large, ugly
slabs of
white space
around the
graphic.

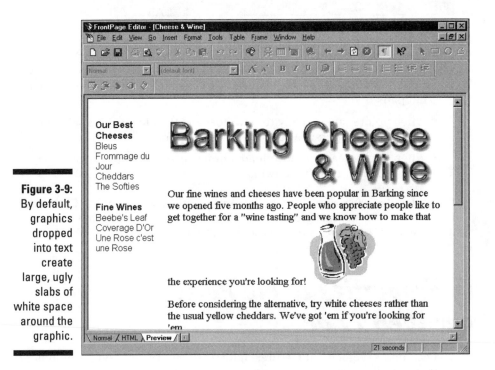

The following sections show you several ways to improve an unattractive Web page by using the FrontPage Properties options.

Flowing text around a graphic

To fix the awkward spacing that appears around a graphic after you first place it, you want to make the text flow around the graphic and fill in the white space. Follow these steps to use a graphic's Properties dialog box to adjust the way the text flows:

1. **Right-click the graphic in the FrontPage Editor, and choose Image Properties from the context menu that appears.**

   You can easily adjust the qualities of the items in a Web page by right-clicking them and then choosing Properties. (Make sure that the Normal tab is selected at the bottom of the Editor window.)

   The Image Properties dialog box opens, displaying three pages you can select by clicking their tabs. (See Figure 3-10.)

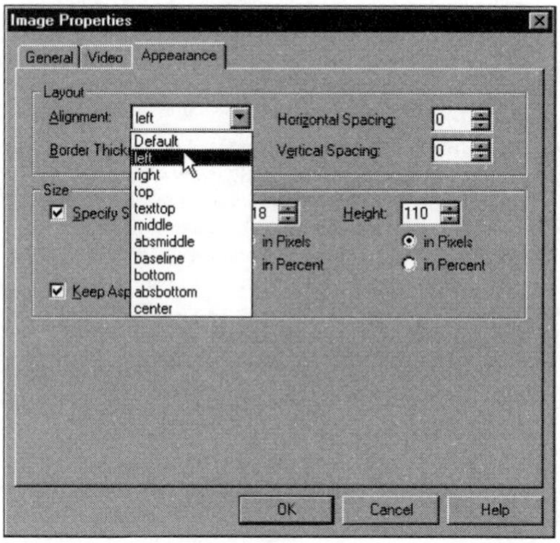

Figure 3-10:
The Image Properties dialog box.

2. **Click the Appearance tab in the Image Properties dialog box.**

   The Appearance page appears.

3. **Click the Alignment drop-down list box.**

4. **Choose Left or Right in the list box, depending on where you want the image placed in the page (and, as a result, how you want the text to then wrap around the image).**

5. **Click the OK button to apply the effect.**

   The Image Properties dialog box closes.

6. **Click the Preview tab to see how the text wraps, as shown in Figure 3-11.**

   In general, a Web page looks much better if you force the text to wrap around embedded graphics. Compare the page in Figure 3-11 to the page in Figure 3-9.

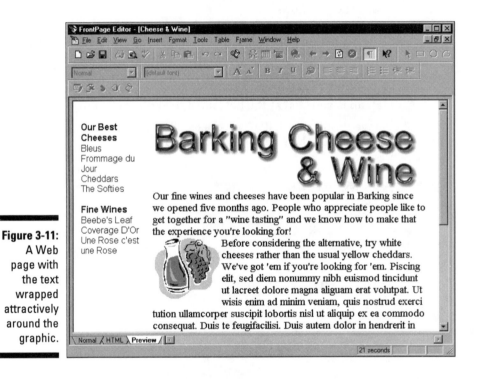

Figure 3-11: A Web page with the text wrapped attractively around the graphic.

Resizing an image

In many situations, using a Properties dialog box is the quickest way to make changes to an item in a Web page. Other times, you'll find even simpler shortcuts. If you want to change the size of an image, click it. The eight drag handles appear. Drag one of the *corner* handles to make the graphic larger or smaller. It's good that you don't have to use a Properties dialog box in this case because you want to be able to see what your resizing looks like (as opposed to guessing what numbers you should type in to describe the size).

I suggest that you drag a corner handle. If, instead, you drag one of the side handles, you distort the picture by making it fatter or skinnier than the artist intended.

The physics of Web page design

Skip this tip if you're not seriously into the physics of Web page design. Graphics in a Web page are *absolute*. They're a particular size and they stay that size even if the viewer stretches her browser to make it wider, for example. Text, by contrast, is usually *relative* in a Web page. The lines of text grow longer if the viewer stretches the browser. There's a good reason for this difference: Graphics begin to look quite bizarre if the ratio between their width and height (their *aspect ratio*) is changed. That change causes a fun-house mirror effect. Text, though, doesn't suffer from this problem because it remains as readable whether you stretch a line or not. Stretching text just adds more words to that line; it doesn't distort the characters.

Repositioning an image in text

Because of restrictions imposed by HTML, you can't just drag an image around on a Web page. Your choices of position for an image are limited when an image is located within a block of text. Follow the steps listed in the section "Flowing Text Around a Graphic," earlier in this chapter to see the options permitted when using the HTML alignment property. You can choose Left, Right, Top, Texttop, Middle, Absmiddle, Baseline, Bottom, Absbottom, or center. In nearly all situations, you want to choose only Left or Right because they're the only alignments that permit text wraparound.

Adjusting text properties with the Properties dialog box

You can usually adjust text as much as you need to by using the Format Toolbar. But if you want to go further, you have a set of a few additional adjustments available in the Font Properties dialog box. Follow these steps to dazzle your visitors with superscript text and other special text formats:

1. **Look at your Web page in the FrontPage Editor with the Normal tab selected (at the bottom of the Editor window).**

2. **Select a letter, word, paragraph, or whatever amount of text you want to change.**

   Select text by dragging your mouse across the text to highlight it.

3. **Right-click the selected text, and choose Font Properties from the context menu that appears.**

The Font Properties dialog box shown in Figure 3-12 appears. In the Font Properties dialog box, you can make some special adjustments.

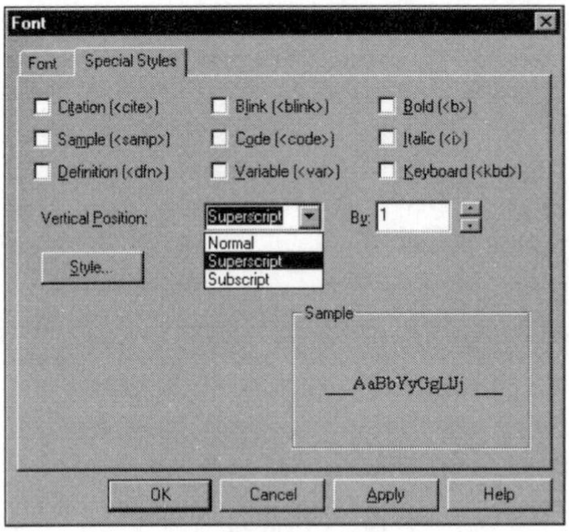

Figure 3-12:
The Font
Properties
dialog box.

Of the various options in the Font Properties dialog box, most options are seldom-used HTML codes. For example, the citation typeface is supposed to be used for footnotes. The only options you're likely to be interested in on this Special Styles dialog page are the Superscript or Subscript features.

4. **Click the Font tab in the Font dialog box.**

The Font page gives you the option to add underlining to your text.

5. **Click the OK button to close the dialog box and apply the new style.**

As often happens in FrontPage and other Visual Studio 6 applications, you have more than one way to get a job done. You can adjust text size in two ways — with the FrontPage Format Toolbar or with the Font Properties dialog box. To use the toolbar, follow these steps:

1. **Look at your Web page in the FrontPage Editor with the Normal tab selected (at the bottom of the Editor window).**

2. **Select a letter, word, paragraph, or whatever amount of text you want to change.**

Select text by dragging your mouse across the text to highlight it.

3. **Click the drop-down list on the left of the Format Toolbar to see all the standard HTML font styles.**

   If the Format Toolbar isn't visible, choose View⇨Format Toolbar.

4. **Click the fonts drop-down list box (which is the second list box from the left on the Format Toolbar) to specify a particular font.**

   If the viewer doesn't have the font you choose on his or her computer, the browser tries to match your specified font as closely as possible from those available. This is one good reason for sticking with fairly common fonts such as Times New Roman, Lucinda, or Arial.

5. **The two A icons next to the drop-down list boxes increase or decrease the font size.**

6. **Check out the many other options that are available on the Format Toolbar.**

Coloring the Background

A plain white background is good for books, but not so hot in a Web page. If you don't want to go whole hog and add a texture (see Chapter 7), you can at least change the background from white to some light color.

The color should be very light because you don't want to make the text hard to read. And you don't want to be one of those people who believe in the Elvis-on-black-velvet theory of design. For most purposes, you're better off to not use light-colored lettering on a dark-colored background.

To add a light color to the background of a page, follow these steps:

1. **Follow Steps 1 through 5 in the section titled "Choosing a template for your first home page" earlier in this chapter.**

   You see a sample Web page loaded into the FrontPage Editor.

2. **Choose Format⇨Theme.**

   The Choose Theme dialog box opens.

3. **Click the option button labeled This Page Does Not Use Themes.**

4. **Click the OK button.**

   The Choose Theme dialog box closes and your page now has no background.

5. **Look at your Web page in the FrontPage Editor with the Normal tab selected (at the bottom of the Editor window).**

6. **Right-click anywhere on your Web page and choose Page Properties from the context menu that appears.**

   The Page Properties dialog box opens with five tabs, offering many ways to modify the current page.

7. **In the Page Properties dialog box, click the Background tab.**

   You see the Page Properties dialog box, shown in Figure 3-13.

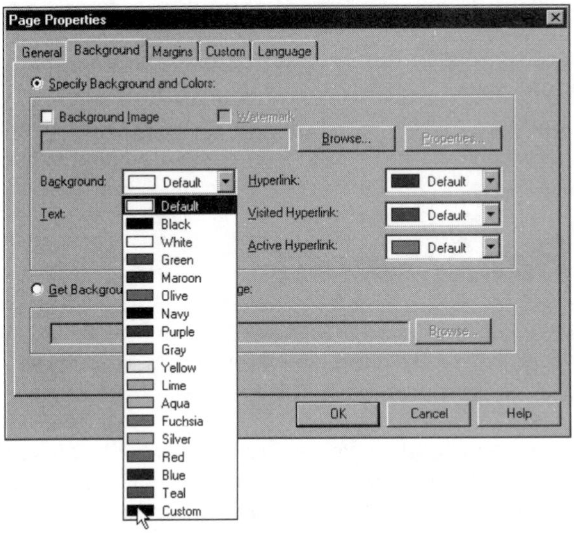

Figure 3-13: Select a background color for your Web page using this dialog box.

Unfortunately, the default colors in the drop-down list box are almost all bad choices. (They're the traditional old 16 basic Windows colors, not chosen for their suitability for Web pages.)

8. **Click the Custom option at the bottom of the Background drop-down list box.**

   The Color dialog box opens. In this dialog box, you can define a light color for your background. In the thin pane on the far right side of the dialog box, drag the pointer up to lighten the shade of any color. You can use this method to create a pastel shade that works well as a background for a Web page.

9. **Click the OK button twice to close both dialog boxes.**

10. **Click the FrontPage Editor Preview tab to see the results.**

    If you have some clip art in your page with transparent areas (as you can see in Figure 3-14), the clip art looks good against the new background because the transparent areas allow a background color or texture to show through. However, logos don't have that capability, so the Barking Cheese & Wine logo overshadows the background. (Also, not all clip art includes transparent areas either.)

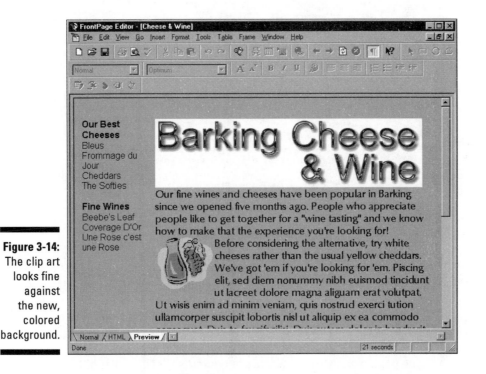

Figure 3-14:
The clip art
looks fine
against
the new,
colored
background.

To make the background under the "Barking Cheese and Wine" logo match your new color, you have to ask whoever created the logo to change the white to your new, custom color. You want the result shown in Figure 3-15.

You can make someone who is on a different computer a copy of a custom color by displaying the custom color on screen and then pressing the Print Scrn key. Next choose Start⇨Programs⇨Accessories⇨Paint. Then choose Edit⇨Paste in Paint and use File⇨Save to save this screen capture (which shows the special color) to your hard drive. You can then give the logo designer a copy of the color by giving him a copy of this file. This technique assumes that you've set your video settings higher than 256 colors. (Right-click your desktop and choose Properties. Click the Settings tab. Change the drop-down list under Color Palette so that it says 65536 or True Color. Click the OK button.)

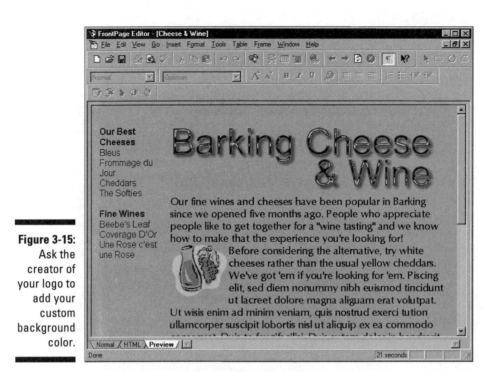

Adding Hyperlinks to Your Web Page

A home page usually offers a table of contents. This is a list of the topics that the viewer can see within the Web site. The Web pages shown in earlier sections of this chapter, such as the Web page in Figure 3-15, have a table of contents in the left zone of the page.

However, visitors may want to *use* this table of contents to get to other locations in the Web site. That means that you have to create separate pages for both major items in the table of contents: Our Best Cheeses and Fine Wines.

As soon as you've created the other pages, you can easily change the phrases "Our Best Cheeses" and "Fine Wines" into hyperlinks. Users can click on one of those phrases to load the new page into their browser.

To change text into a hyperlink, follow these steps:

1. **Look at your Web page in the FrontPage Editor with the Normal tab selected (at the bottom of the Editor window).**

2. **Select the text that you want to transform into a hyperlink by dragging your mouse over the text to highlight it.**

   On the Barking Cheese & Wine page, you highlight the words "Our Best Cheeses."

3. Choose Insert⇨Hyperlink.

The Create Hyperlink dialog box shown in Figure 3-16 opens.

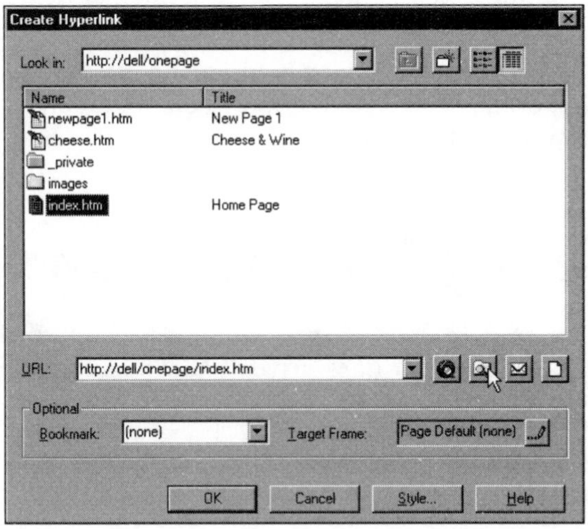

Figure 3-16:
Select a file
in this
dialog box
as the
target of
a new
hyperlink.

4. Double-click the target file that will be displayed in a browser when your new hyperlink is clicked.

The hyperlink is created when you double-click the filename, and the Create Hyperlink dialog box closes.

The filename you select must be a Web page file: In most cases, the filename ends with an .Htm, short for *HTML*, the traditional Web page language. If your target file is not displayed in the dialog box, you can browse for it by clicking the icon with the mouse arrow on it, as shown in Figure 3-16.

5. If you don't yet have a Web page built for this hyperlink, you can build it by clicking the blank page button, shown on the far right in Figure 3-16.

As soon as you've created your hyperlink, the text you highlighted changes. By default, it changes to blue and is underlined. These changes cue visitors that they can navigate your site by clicking the hyperlink. One more visual cue is also offered: When the mouse pointer is moved over a hyperlink, it changes the FrontPage Editor Preview tab to see these effects. Try moving your mouse pointer onto your new hyperlinks and watch it change into a hand.

If you click the HTML tab, you notice that FrontPage has changed your text from:

```
<font size="2" face="Arial"><strong>Our
    Best Cheeses</strong></font>
```

To:

```
<a href="bestchee.htm"><font size="2"
          face="Arial"><strong>Our
   Best Cheeses</strong></font></a>
```

The a and href commands are HTML programming code that define text as a hyperlink. If the hyperlink is clicked, the href command tells the browser where to find the new target page to load .

Safety First: Saving Your Web Page

After you've spent the time to create a great home page, you don't want to lose it. You want to save it to your hard drive so that you can later incorporate it into a Web site. Follow these steps to save your Web page:

1. **Choose File⇨Save in the FrontPage Editor menu bar.**

   You see the typical Windows Save As dialog box.

2. **Type in the name that you want to give to this Web page.**

3. **Click the OK button.**

   The Save As dialog box closes and your page is saved.

Note that if you've embedded a graphic (or other embedded object such as a video clip), you next see the Save Embedded Files dialog box. This dialog box enables you to specify where to save any embedded objects such as graphics, sounds, or video clips.

The Save Embedded Files dialog box, is displayed when you save a Web page into which you have inserted graphics, sounds, or videos. In this dialog box, you specify whether you want the embedded object stored with the current FrontPage Web; or, if no Web is currently active, you can save the embedded object to your hard drive. (A *FrontPage Web* just means a collection of files that FrontPage is managing as a Web site.) If you save the embedded object to your hard drive, the hyperlink points to that location.

When you insert an image into a Web page, that image doesn't become part of the Web page itself. The image is not merged into the .HTM file holding your Web page when it's saved to disk. Instead, the address of the image file (a .Gif or .Jpg type file) is inserted into the HTML code. (Graphics are notoriously bulky and inserting them into the actual Web page is wasteful. For example, if you use the same graphic for ten buttons on a page, why not just load a single graphic ten times rather than bulk up the .Htm file with ten repeated copies?)

Part II
Building a Web Site

The 5th Wave — By Rich Tennant

"That's right, Daddy will double your allowance if you build a Web site for his company."

In this part . . .

*I*f you want to quickly create an Internet Web site that looks great and runs great, Part II shows you how. As usual, you'll find that Visual Studio 6 includes lots of shortcuts and helpful templates. You'll get to know the Site Designer, which helps you define the hyperlinks that tie your Web pages together into an organized site. No programming required. Just drag and drop, and Visual Studio creates the programming for you. What could be easier?

And to help you create a great-looking Web site, you also find a set of 54 themes designed by some of the best visual artists in the business. Many of them are stunning. So, if by some chance you're not a first-rate visual artist, this part shows you how to borrow these themes. A pro design can make the difference between a tiresome site and an awesome site.

Chapter 4

Site Building Basics

Creating a Web site may seem formidable, but if you use the tools available in Visual Studio 6, you can do it step by step. You may be surprised how easy Visual Studio 6 makes the job of planning and constructing even a complex Web site.

First you drag and drop to visually organize the pages in the site. Then you employ the services of the Navigation Bar component to construct links between those pages. And even if you later reorganize your site — and you will — the Navigation Bar reorganizes the links behind the scenes for you.

Creating a New Web

In this chapter, you construct an entire Web site. You include a home page, and several secondary pages — all linked together with hyperlinks to enable visitors to navigate easily through the Web.

A Web site is a collection of Web pages. The pages, though, are not randomly scattered about. Instead, they're *linked* to each other with hyperlinks. The user can click these links to get to other pages in the site. This process of maneuvering around a site by using links is called *navigating the site*.

When creating a site, your job is to make the navigation process easy to understand. Some organization is necessary so that users can quickly get to the pages they're interested in.

Badly designed sites are like the links of a chain — a visitor has to go through each link in turn to get to the next link. Well-designed sites look like wheels, with a hub in the center surrounded by spokes leading in all directions to the second- or third-level pages. But first things first.

Before you can start thinking about avoiding chains and designing wheels, you have to first create a brand-new project in Visual InterDev.

Why Visual InterDev?

Why use Visual InterDev to build the site? You *can* use FrontPage to create a new distributed application or Internet Web site (called a *Web* in FrontPage and an *application, solution,* or *project* in Visual InterDev). However, the site design features in Visual InterDev are better. FrontPage has much to offer when working on individual *pages,* but Visual InterDev offers better tools for creating and designing a larger structure, such as a collection of related pages.

Visual InterDev has various Wizards and tools, similar to its Site Designer utility, that make the job of building a Web much easier.

Building a Web project

The Visual InterDev Web Project wizard steps you through the process of creating a new Web site — and the Wizard takes care of the details of setting up the necessary support files and folders on the hard drive.

Usually, you set up a Web project on a server. Then after the project files and folders are in place, all the people who want to work on the Web can also run the Visual InterDev Web Project wizard on their local workstation. When run on a workstation, the wizard builds the required local folders and files on each person's individual system. This creates local versions of the main (master) project.

To create a new Web project on a server, follow these steps:

1. **Start Visual InterDev by clicking its icon on your desktop.**

   Depending on how you've specified the Visual InterDev start-up options, you may or may not see the New Project dialog box. If you don't see this dialog box, choose File⇨New.

2. **Click the New tab.**

3. **Click Visual InterDev Projects in the left pane.**

4. **Type in whatever name you want to give your project in the Name text box in the New Project dialog box.**

5. **Leave the folder names and path alone in the Location text box.**

   Because this is an exercise, you can use the default location. But when you're creating a new project for an actual, real-world Web site, you want to locate the project in a folder that describes the site, such as AjaxCorp or QuikPool.

6. **Double-click the New Web Project icon in the right pane.**

   The Web Project Wizard starts running, and its first dialog box opens, as shown in Figure 4-1. In its first dialog box, the wizard wants to know the name of your server. If you're not on a network, use the name of your computer.

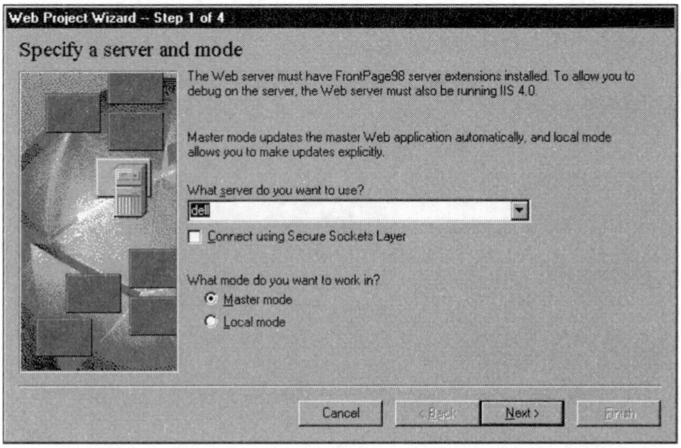

Figure 4-1:
The first
dialog box
of the Web
Project
Wizard.

7. **Leave the Master Mode option button selected.**

8. **Click Next.**

   The Web server is contacted and the second dialog box in this wizard opens. By default, the Create A New Web Application option button is selected. Leave it selected, as shown in Figure 4-2.

9. **Click Next.**

   The third Web Project Wizard dialog box opens, in which you can add a layout or theme to your new site. Leave the default <none> option selected in the list box so that the Preview window displays No theme/ layout applied, as shown in Figure 4-3.

   Refer to Chapter 7 for all the details about themes, templates, and layouts.

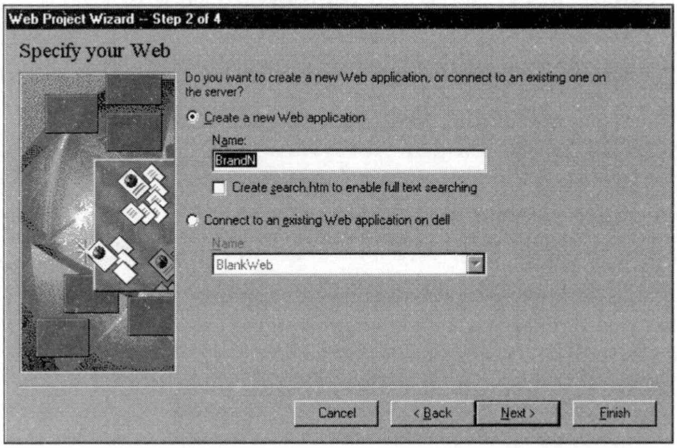

Figure 4-2:
After your
server has
been
contacted
by the
wizard, you
can either
connect to
an existing
Web
project or
start a new
one.

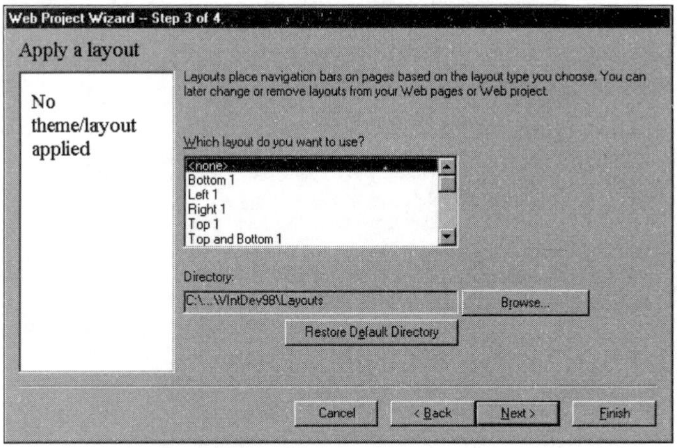

Figure 4-3:
You add a
layout or
theme to
your site in
this dialog
box.

10. **Click Next to get to the final dialog box in this Web Project Wizard.**

    The fourth Web Project Wizard dialog box asks you to choose a theme from its list box.

11. **Leave the default No theme/layout applied and click Next.**

    The left pane of the dialog box displays your choice (No theme/layout applied), and the Finish button becomes enabled, as shown in Figure 4-4.

    You can always add a Theme or Layout later, after you build the Web project.

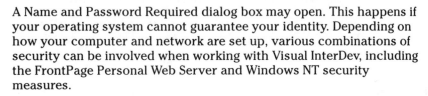

Figure 4-4:
This dialog
box shows
that you
want no
theme
applied to
your site.

12. Click Finish and your site is built (if you have permission).

A Name and Password Required dialog box may open. This happens if your operating system cannot guarantee your identity. Depending on how your computer and network are set up, various combinations of security can be involved when working with Visual InterDev, including the FrontPage Personal Web Server and Windows NT security measures.

Networks can contain sensitive information, so they're usually protected from unauthorized access (people like you!). When you're creating a new Web project on a server, you're dealing with a network. (Your computer is called a workstation, and usually several, or many, workstations are connected to a network *server* machine.)

When creating a new Web project, if you're asked for a password and have problems providing one at this point, you've got the dreaded *permissions problem*. This problem means that you can't create the new Web project until you have permission to do so. The intricacies (and secrets) of network security are beyond the scope of this book. But here are several steps you can try that may get you past this barrier:

- ✔ Type in the name of your NT domain, a backslash, and then your User ID. For example, if your domain is named Arcs and your User ID is Pasta, you type **Arcs\Pasta** into the User Name text box in the Name and Password Required dialog box. Then type in your network password in the Password text box. Click the OK button.

- ✔ If that doesn't work, change the User Name text box to remove the domain name, leaving only your User ID. For example, Pasta. Use your ordinary network password.

✔ And if that doesn't work, try using your User ID (no domain name) and use the same password you use when working with FrontPage. (It can be different from your network password.)

✔ If that doesn't work, shut down Visual InterDev. Start FrontPage. (This program also starts the FrontPage Personal Web Server.) Then restart Visual InterDev and try again going through Steps 1 to 12 as described earlier in this section to create a new Web project.

✔ If even that fails, you may as well go home and go to sleep. Or you can contact your network administrator and beg for permission to do your job.

Visual InterDev automatically adds files

By default, Visual InterDev adds various files to a new project. Whether or not some of them are added depends on what you've selected in the Options dialog box, and also whether or not you chose to add a layout or theme to your project when building the project with the New Project Wizard.

Figure 4-5 shows a typical new project in Visual InterDev. So far, no ordinary .Htm Web page files exist in the project, merely a set of default files and folders.

Figure 4-5:
You see a set of default files and folders after creating a new Web project in Visual InterDev.

However, here is a description of the folders and files commonly added to new Web projects in Visual InterDev:

✔ **The Global.Asa file:** Is where you can put scripts (programming) that tell the Web site what to do when it's first loaded into a browser (initialization) or when it's shut down. Global.Asa is a bit similar to AUTOEXEC.BAT in DOS or the Startup folder in Windows. When your Web first executes, programming found in this file is executed if it follows certain rules. Likewise, when a user leaves your site, other programming can be executed. For details on writing scripts to use during your site's startup or shutdown, double-click the Global.Asa file and you see the following instructions:

```
<SCRIPT LANGUAGE='VBScript' RUNAT='Server'>

'You can add special event handlers in this file that
          will get run automatically when
'special Active Server Pages events occur. To create
          these handlers, just create a
'subroutine with a name from the list below that
          corresponds to the event you want to
'use. For example, to create an event handler for
          Session_OnStart, you would put the
'following code into this file (without the comments):

'Sub Session_OnStart
'**Put your code here **
'End Sub

'EventName                Description
'Session_OnStart          Runs the first time a user
          runs any page in your application
'Session_OnEnd            Runs when a user's session
          times out or quits your application
'Application_OnStart      Runs once when the first page
          of your application is run for the first time
          by any user
'Application_OnEnd        Runs once when the web server
          shuts down

</SCRIPT>
```

✔ **The Private folder:** Holds management tools used by the FrontPage Server Extensions to manage a Web application. It's empty in a new Web.

✔ **The Script Library folder:** Includes all the instructions for the *design-time components*. (See Chapter 15.) Don't change any of these files. They're the support files that make all the components you can see displayed if you click the Design-time Components tab on the Visual InterDev Toolbox.

✔ **The Images folder:** Where you can store graphics files that are used in your Web site.

Sketching Your Ideas with the Site Designer

Visual InterDev includes an excellent tool for creating a prototype of a new Web site. After you've created the bare bones site as described earlier in this chapter, in the section titled "Building a Web project," you're ready to fire up the Site Designer.

Why do you need to create a prototype? A site is composed of pages, but they're not just scattered around randomly. They're associated with each other in a formal hierarchy. That's the design of the site. And the fact that you have a utility called the Site Designer hints that there is something, after all, to design in the first place. You create a prototype of a Web site for the same reason that you use a blueprint when building a house — to make sure that all the parts are included, and that they're connected together logically. You want a workable, useful, easily navigable Web site, not just a random accumulation of pages, clustered together with no more organization than barnacles on a boat.

You want your site to be easy to understand and easy to navigate by people who have no idea what structure underlies the site. These visitors arrive at your Web page and should be able to almost intuitively grasp the plan of your site. Visitors should be able to get where they want to go within your site — to get to the information they want — with as little effort as possible. To ensure that your site is intuitive for visitors, you need to plan and develop a prototype of your site before building it.

The Site Designer greatly simplifies the process of sketching and building the relationships between the pages in your site. You create a *visual* prototype of your Web application by using site diagrams. The Site Designer enables you to simultaneously add Web pages to (or remove pages from) your site and also build the navigational links between those pages.

And there's more: As soon as you choose to save the diagram, the Site Designer transforms the plans in your diagram into reality. The Site Designer creates the pages you define and updates the links in those pages. Given that Visual InterDev is supposed to be a Visual Studio 6 Rapid Application Development (RAD) tool, you won't be surprised to find out that you drag and drop files to build your site. It doesn't get much easier than that!

Starting Site Designer

To start running Site Designer, follow these steps:

1. **Choose P̲roject⇨Add I̲tem.**

   You see the Add Item dialog box shown in Figure 4-6.

2. **Double-click the Site Diagram icon in the right pane of the Add Item dialog box.**

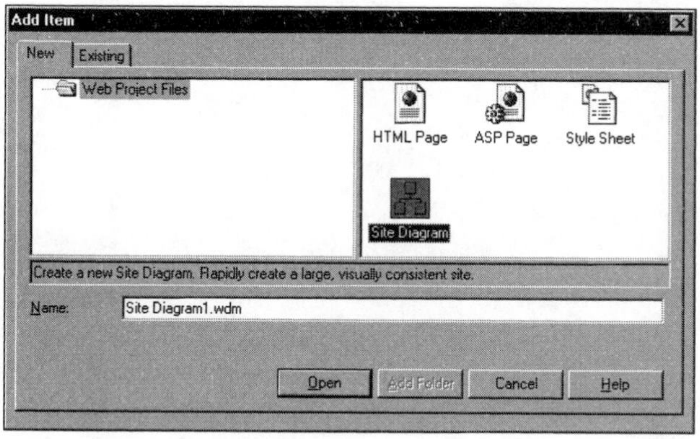

Figure 4-6:
A site
diagram,
and Site
Designer
itself, are
both
activated by
double-
clicking
this site
diagram
icon.

Four things now happen:

- The Add Item dialog box closes.
- A new file (Site Diagram1.Wdm) is added to your Project Explorer.
- The Site Diagram window opens, with a home page already in it, as shown in Figure 4-7.
- The Site Diagram Toolbar appears, as shown in Figure 4-7.

Now your tools are all in place, and you're ready to begin prototyping your site. But, before you start to build the prototype, take a look at the various buttons on the Site Designer Toolbar, as shown in Figure 4-8. The features accessed by these buttons are explained throughout this chapter.

Adding new child pages to your site

A child page is similar to a subfolder in Windows Explorer. You know the idea: A child page is contained within a parent page in the same sense that a Windows folder contains more folders.

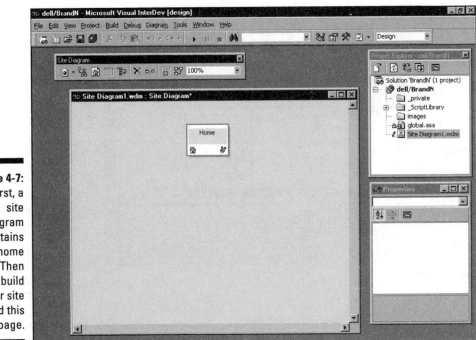

Figure 4-7:
At first, a site diagram contains only a home page. Then you build your site around this home page.

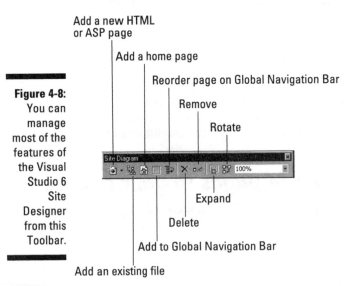

Add a new HTML or ASP page

Add a home page

Reorder page on Global Navigation Bar

Remove

Rotate

Figure 4-8:
You can manage most of the features of the Visual Studio 6 Site Designer from this Toolbar.

Expand

Delete

Add to Global Navigation Bar

Add an existing file

You have five ways to add a subsidiary (child) page in the Site Designer:

- ✔ **Click the New HTML Page icon on the far left of the Site Diagram Toolbar.**
- ✔ **Press the Ins key.**
- ✔ **Press Ctrl+Shift+H.**
- ✔ **Choose Diagram⇨New HTML Page.**
- ✔ **Right-click the background of the Site Designer and choose New HTML Page from the context menu.**

Follow these steps to create two child pages, each *within* a parent page:

1. **Use one of the five methods for adding a subsidiary page in Site Designer.**

   I prefer to press the Ins key to add the page. A child page is added to the home page in your site diagram, as shown in Figure 4-9.

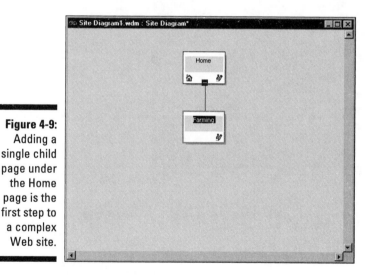

Figure 4-9: Adding a single child page under the Home page is the first step to a complex Web site.

2. **Drag your mouse pointer across the default name Page1 in the new child to select it.**

   By default, Site Designer provides serial names: Page1, Page2, and so on. The name is highlighted when you drag across it.

3. **Type in** Farming **as a new name.**

4. Press Ins again to add a second page.

Because Farming was the active page (the page surrounded by a red frame), the new page becomes its child. When you add a page, it always becomes the child of the currently active page. The new page in this step doesn't become a child of the Home page because the page named Farming in Figure 4-9 remained selected.

5. Rename the new page Seeds.

At this point, you have three pages: the Home page, its child that you named Farming, and Farming's child, Seeds, as shown in Figure 4-10. The seeds page is linked to the farming page, and the farming page is linked to the home page.

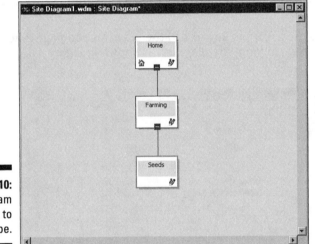

Figure 4-10:
A diagram
begins to
take shape.

Deleting pages from a site diagram

To delete a page from a site diagram, follow these steps in the Site Designer:

1. Click the page that you want to delete to select it.

A red frame surrounds the selected page.

2. Press the Delete key (or click the Delete button on the Site Designer Toolbar).

The Delete Pages dialog box opens, asking if you want to remove the selected pages from all navigation bars in the site, or delete the pages from the entire Web project. If you choose the first option, you can't create links to or from the pages, but the pages still exist in the Web project. (Therefore you can later decide to add them back to the site diagram in the future by dragging them from the Project Explorer.) The second option entirely deletes the pages from the Web site, never to be seen again.

3. **Click the OK button.**

   The default (removing the selected pages from all navigation bars in the site) takes effect.

   The dialog box closes and the pages that you deleted are removed from the site diagram.

Reorganizing a site diagram

Suppose that you've decided to change the name of your page from Seeds to Cities. You also want to make the page a child of your home page rather than a child of the second-level page, Farming. In the Site Designer, follow these steps:

1. **Click or drag over the name Seeds to highlight it.**

   The name of this page is now ready to be edited.

2. **Type in Cities.**

3. **Click the background of the site diagram to set (make the change) the new name.**

   The red frame disappears from around the page, and the new name takes effect.

4. **Drag the newly named Cities page near, and just under, the home page until you see a dashed line appear, showing an attachment between the Cities page and the home page, as shown in Figure 4-11.**

5. **Drop the Cities page when you see the relationship line, as shown in Figure 4-11.**

   The Cities page becomes a child of the home page.

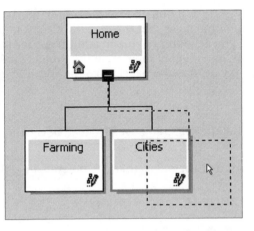

Figure 4-11:
When a link
relation-
ship is
established
between
two pages,
you see this
dashed line
between
them.

Making your design official

After you create a site diagram, add pages, and reorganize those pages, your site still isn't quite finished. If you look at the Project Explorer, you see the site diagram, but the pages that you diagrammed don't appear because you haven't taken the steps to officially create them. The pages don't yet exist; they're merely prototypes. They become official, existing pages when you commit them to the hard drive.

To make the actual pages, or *files,* of your site, choose File⇨Save All. Now your pages are saved and official. You can see your pages as .Htm files added to those already in the Project Explorer window. The Index.Htm file is the home page.

Creating a second tree

A site diagram can have more than one *tree.* (A tree is a set of connected pages.) (The Windows Explorer displays a tree diagram in its left pane. A tree diagram is hierarchical. In Windows Explorer, you see hard drives, then folders on the drives, then any subfolders, and finally the files. In the case of a site diagram, the relationships between parent and child pages form a tree diagram.)

You may want to work on more than one tree in your diagram. Having separate pieces (trees) may simplify the job of building the various parts of your Web site. This is particularly true if you're building a really large site with many pages. You may create a customer service tree, a billing tree, a catalog tree, and an inventory tree. Working on separate trees is similar to the process of simultaneously working on several sections of a jigsaw puzzle. However, at the end, when you're ready to finish your site, you connect all the trees together into the single, large, complete Web site.

To create a second tree in your site diagram, follow these steps:

1. **Click the blank background in the Site Designer.**

   This step deselects all the pages in the diagram. (None of them now has a red frame.)

2. **Right-click the background of the Site Designer and select New HTML page from the context menu that appears.**

   The new page appears but is not connected to the existing tree, as shown in Figure 4-12. When you first add a floating page (one that's not attached to an existing tree diagram), Site Designer places it on top of existing pages.

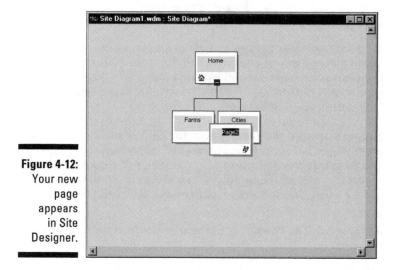

Figure 4-12:
Your new
page
appears
in Site
Designer.

3. **Drag the new page over to the side, so that it's not connected to the existing pages. Be sure to drag it until the dashed connecting line breaks.**

4. **Press Ins a couple of times to add two more pages beneath the new page.**

   You can see two trees now, as shown in Figure 4-13. You can use these steps to create as many tree diagrams as you like. You can always connect them together later by just dragging the entire tree.

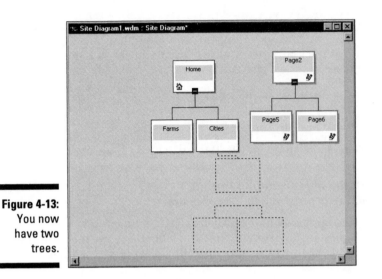

Figure 4-13:
You now
have two
trees.

Mass dragging and deletion

You can move or delete groups of pages as well as single pages. For example, if you create more than one tree structure for your Web site, you can drag one or more trees to make them children of a particular page. The following steps show you how to use Site Designer to move a tree structure to be the child of another page in the site:

1. **Drag your mouse around the three pages in the tree on the right. You want to select pages 2, 5, and 6, as shown in Figure 4-13. To drag-select, press your left mouse button in the upper-left corner of the objects you want selected. Then hold down the mouse button as you drag the mouse down to the lower-right corner. Release the mouse button.**

   All the borders around all the pages in the tree turn red, indicating that they are all selected.

   You can also select a group by clicking the first page in the group and then holding down the Ctrl key while clicking all the rest of the pages that you want to add to the selected group.

2. **Drag the entire highlighted tree down below the Cities page, until the attachment dashed line appears, showing that the tree will become a child of the Cities page.**

3. **Drop the tree.**

   The new child tree appears beneath the Cities page.

Resizing the diagram

When you create and rearrange pages on your site diagram, you often find that you've populated your site diagram with so many pages that you can't see all of them on-screen. You can use the scroll bars to move your view around the diagram, or you can resize the diagram by following these steps:

1. **Right-click the background of the site diagram.**

   The context menu appears.

2. **Click Zoom⇨Fit.**

   The Fit menu selection sizes your site diagram to perfectly fit on your screen. If you want to make your site diagram bigger or smaller, choose one of the other sizing options on the menu, from 10 percent to 200 percent.

Importing existing pages

The Site Designer enables you to easily create and organize new Web pages in a site diagram. What about that great page that Matt has been working on at home? What about that perfect order form from the other Web site? Can you import existing Web pages into a site diagram? Yes.

To import an existing file into a site diagram, follow these steps:

1. **Right-click the name of the project in the Project Explorer. (The project name is in boldface.)**

   A context menu pops out for the current project.

2. **Choose Add⇨HTML Page from the context menu.**

   The Add Item dialog box opens.

3. **Click the Existing tab in the Add Item dialog box.**

   A drive list box opens, enabling you to explore the hard drive and locate the .Htm file (or other kind of file) on the hard drive.

4. **Use the Add Item dialog box to locate the file you want to add to the current project.**

5. **Double-click the filename of the file you want to add.**

   The dialog box closes, and the file now appears in the Project Explorer.

6. **Drag the new file from the Project Explorer into the site diagram.**

7. **Drop the new file into the site diagram wherever you want to place it.**

   The new file becomes part of the site diagram.

Employing the Navigation Bar

Now it's time to reveal the secret of the Site Designer. A design-time component in Visual InterDev creates links between the pages in your site diagram — based on the parent and child relationships you specify in the diagram. And even if you reorganize the site, the Navigation Bar keeps the link relationships straight for you.

A design-time component is inserted into a Web page. Then it creates the HTML source code that does a job for you. Most design-time components help you connect to a database, so you can find them discussed in detail in Chapter 15.

The Navigation Bar's official name is PageNavBar. It displays a set of hyperlinks so that a visitor can click them and thereby move from page to page within your site. The links can be either text or buttons.

Your Web site server (or Internet service provider) must have the FrontPage server extensions installed on the server for the PageNavBar to work.

Adding a PageNavBar component to a site diagram

To add a PageNavBar to a site diagram, follow these steps:

1. **Follow the steps in the "Starting Site Designer" and "Adding new child pages to your site" sections, earlier in this chapter, so you have a site diagram to work with.**

   A Site Diagram window appears with a Home page and two child pages showing in it.

2. **Double-click the Home page in the Site Diagram window.**

   If you haven't saved your most recent work, a dialog box opens, asking whether you want to save it. Click the Yes button.

   A Visual InterDev Editor window opens with Index.Htm loaded in it. Index.Htm is the filename of the home page.

3. **Click the Source tab on the editor.**

   You see the HTML source code for the home page.

4. **Click between the <BODY> and </BODY> HTML elements.**

   The blinking insertion line appears, showing where the next component will be inserted, or where the next typing will appear.

5. **Click the Design Time Controls tab in the Visual InterDev Toolbox.**

   The set of DTCs appears on the Toolbox. If the Toolbox isn't visible in Visual InterDev, choose View⇨Toolbox.

6. **Drag the PageNavBar component from the Toolbox onto the Index.Htm page in the Editor window.**

7. **Right-click the PageNavBar icon in the editor and then select Properties from the context menu.**

   The PageNavBar Properties dialog box opens, as shown in Figure 4-14. By default, the PageNavBar component displays child links, but you can modify its behavior.

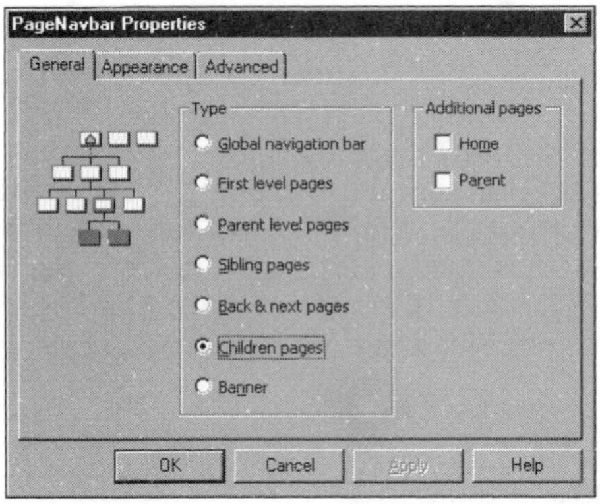

Figure 4-14:
The
PageNavBar
Properties
dialog box.

As Figure 4-14 demonstrates, a new PageNavBar by default displays child links (children pages) only. However, you may want to click the Additional Pages check boxes. You may want to offer your visitor a way to get back to the home page from any other page. If you check the Home check box, a link to the home page is provided on the navigation bar in each page in the site. You may also want to offer a link to a parent page. Providing a way to go from each child page to its parent page enables a visitor to backtrack through the site.

Choosing the Global Navigation Bar option in the PageNavbar Properties dialog box enables you to add any page (and as many pages as you want) to the navigation links. To specify each page that you want to add, close the PageNavBar Properties dialog box and go back to the Site Diagram Editor. Click the page you want to add (its frame turns red). Choose Diagram⇨Add To Global Navigation Bar.

Don't choose the Add to Global Navigation Bar option (from the site diagram Toolbar or the Diagram menu) thinking that you're making this page available as a hyperlink. The design of your site is *automatically* reproduced by the PageNavBar component. You don't need to individually add your various pages to it. You use the Add to Global Navigation Bar option to force the PageNavBar component to always provide a link to a page or pages. Normally, the PageNavBar displays a link to a page only if the page is currently in the categories you specified by selecting option buttons in the PageNavBar Properties pages (as shown in Figure 4-14).

Selecting the appearance of your hyperlinks

The PageNavBar Properties dialog box includes an Appearance tab.

Click the Appearance tab (shown in Figure 4-15), and you can define the orientation of the set of links (Horizontal or Vertical). You can also choose from three styles of links: Buttons, Text (similar to a table of contents), or HTML. The HTML option enables you to edit source code to add a link, like this: `<a href=#URL#>#LABEL#</a>`. You replace #URL# and #LABEL# with an address for the target of your link and a label that describes the link.

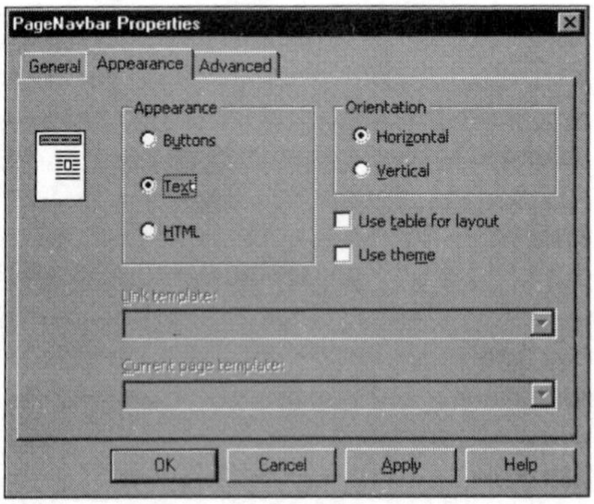

Figure 4-15:
Specify the appearance and orientation of your hyperlinks in this dialog box.

Viewing your hyperlinks

To see a component in action, you have to load its page into Internet Explorer or another browser. You can't see the PageNavBar in the Visual InterDev Quick View, which is often the case with the other components, too, such as FrontPage Webbots and the Visual InterDev design-time controls.

To see the current PageNavBar, follow these steps:

1. **Double-click the Home page in the Site Designer.**

   The home page is displayed in a Visual InterDev Editor window.

2. **Choose View➪View In Browser from Visual InterDev's menu bar.**

   The home page (Index.Htm) is loaded into your browser, and you can see the hyperlinks.

You may have noticed that the Site Designer adds tiny icons in the lower corner of some pages in a site diagram. These icons (shown in Figure 4-16) cue you about special qualities of a page. The icon that looks like a tiny house signals you that the page is the home page. The icon that looks like a pencil signals that this is a modified page (meaning that the page hasn't yet been saved to the hard drive, but has been changed). The globe icon represents an external page (one that isn't located with the other pages in the site on the hard drive). The icon that looks like a miniature page means a global navigation page (a page that has been forced onto a PageNavBar as described at the end of the section titled "Adding a PageNavBar component to a site diagram").

Figure 4-16:
When
added to a
page in
a site
diagram,
these
symbols tell
you what a
page is or
does.

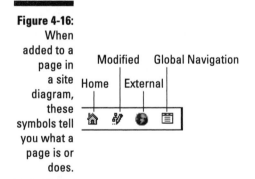

Printing a site diagram

Visual InterDev offers two special menu options if you decide you want to print the site diagram on paper. Before sending the site to the printer, choose Diagram➪View Page Breaks. This feature adds a blue line in your site diagram, showing you where the printer ends one page and begins another.

If some page breaks cut through page symbols or are otherwise annoying, fix the problem by right-clicking on the blank background of the site diagram and then choosing Zoom from the context menu. Adjust the Zoom level until the page breaks aren't annoying.

Another factor to consider when printing a site diagram is that if you add or remove pages from the diagram, the page breaks may well have become different since you last used the View Page Breaks feature. In other words, the current blue lines may not accurately represent page breaks. To update the Page Break View, choose Diagram⇨Recalculate Page Breaks.

Chapter 5

Using the Visual InterDev Editor

*I*n a way, this chapter and Chapter 6 are a pair. But you may want to look through only one of them. This chapter introduces Visual InterDev Editor and explains its primary tools and how you put them to work. Chapter 6 introduces the FrontPage Editor and puts *it* through its paces.

Most people choose one of these editors and stick with it as their primary tool for working on distributed applications and Web sites. If you already know which editor you prefer, take a look at its chapter. (You can find tips and techniques that you probably didn't know about.) If you don't know whether to use FrontPage or Visual InterDev, look at the introductory section in Chapter 6.

Of course, you could be multitalented, or maybe you run a small business (which, of course, usually requires you to be multitalented). If so, you probably want to use Visual InterDev for organizing, maintaining, and writing script programming for a Web site. And you can switch hats and tools, using FrontPage when working with the text and graphics within individual Web pages.

In general, Visual InterDev is the more complicated, sophisticated tool. It's your best choice when working on complicated, sophisticated applications and programming. FrontPage is more user-friendly, containing many high-efficiency features such as pre-built Webbots, Wizards, and point-and-click dialog and property boxes. People who haven't studied computer science or programming may want to rely on FrontPage's many helpful assistants.

The Visual InterDev Editor is an *IDE* (Integrated Design Environment), which is just a fancy acronym meaning that the editor does a lot of things beyond simply offering you a place to type programming code. In this chapter, you see just how many things you can do with the Visual InterDev Editor.

To get a feel for the powerful capabilities of the Visual InterDev Editor, read on. If you know that you want to work exclusively with FrontPage, skip to Chapter 6.

Understanding The Visual Studio Design Environment

You can display (or hide) many windows and toolbars while working in the Visual InterDev IDE. In this section, you see how to use the three views available in the main editing window. You also find out how to customize your workspace by arranging secondary windows, such as the Toolbox and Project Explorer windows, to suit your working style.

Like FrontPage, Visual InterDev offers you three ways to look at a Web page while you're working on the page in the main editing window. The main editing window is where you create and modify a Web page. Each Web page has its own Editor window, and that window provides three views of the page (selected by clicking one of the three tabs at the bottom of the Editor window).

The first of the three main editor views is Design View. In Design View, you can add images and type in text. You can also add components such as text boxes or Command buttons. (A *component* is an object that you can plug into a Web page or Windows application. They're sometimes also called *controls*.)

The second view is called Source View, which shows you the down and dirty source code that tells a browser what to display. Fortunately, nonprogrammers rarely need this view. You can create excellent, powerfully designed Web pages in Visual Studio without writing a single word of programming.

The third view is called Quick View and shows you what your page looks like when loaded in a browser such as Internet Explorer. *Usually.* Some components and source code that run on a server can't be viewed in Quick View. When this happens, I tell you. You need to actually load your page into Internet Explorer to get the fully working Web page. You choose View⇨View in Browser. Luckily, most of the time you can just click the Quick View tab and see everything perfectly.

Seeing the three views in an Editor window

To see how the main Editor window works, follow these steps:

1. **Start Visual InterDev by clicking its icon on your desktop.**

   You can use an existing project or start a new one. It doesn't matter.

2. **Choose File➪New File.**

   The New File dialog box opens.

3. **Click Visual InterDev in the left pane and then double-click HTML page in the right pane.**

   A new, empty page appears in Visual InterDev.

4. **Click the Source View tab at the bottom of your new page.**

   You see a few lines of HTML, as shown in Figure 5-1.

5. **Click the Design View tab.**

   In this view, you can add components from the Toolbox.

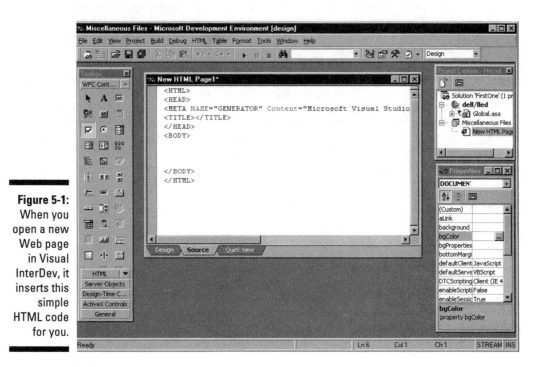

Figure 5-1:
When you open a new Web page in Visual InterDev, it inserts this simple HTML code for you.

Testing a Web page with the Quick View

The great value of the Quick View tab in the Visual InterDev Editor is that you see what a visitor to your Web page sees. And, in most cases, you can interact with the components of the page, just as a visitor does when the page is loaded into a browser. This interaction enables you to get a sense of how the page looks, and also test its behavior.

To see exactly how the check box example looks and acts, click the Quick View tab, and you see the check boxes and the descriptions. Note that in this example, Design View and Quick View essentially have the same appearance. However, the boxes behave differently in the two views. In Quick View, when you click a check box component, the check box isn't selected. Quick View is very much as if a visitor were viewing this page in a browser. In other words, the components, like a check box, do their thing as they normally do in the real world. In Design View, a component such as a check box becomes selected and can be resized or dragged around to reposition it, or even deleted.

In Design View, you have two ways to *select* a component. As far as I know, Visual InterDev is unique among Windows applications in permitting this dual-selection technique. If you click one of the check boxes, Visual InterDev adds drag handles and a crosshatched frame. These additions enable you to drag the check box to reposition it on the page. (Some components, like a TextArea, can also be resized by dragging one of the drag handles. Check boxes can't be resized.).

The second way to select a component is to drag your mouse cursor over the component. This action causes a blue shadow to cover the component (shown on the top in Figure 5-2). When you select a component in this fashion, you can manipulate the component as if it were selected text in a word processor: press Ctrl+C to copy; Ctrl+V to paste; Ctrl+X to delete; or Ctrl+Z to restore a deleted component. The alternative Shift+Ins, Ctrl+Ins, and Delete keys also work.

Figure 5-2:
Design
View gives
you two
ways to
select a
component.

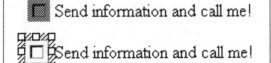

Instead of dragging your mouse across a component to select it, you can hold down the Shift key while using the arrow keys to expand the high-lighted selection block.

Setting up secondary windows

Just as you arrange things on your desktop in the real world, you also arrange the virtual tools in the virtual working environment in your computer. You want to display or hide whatever windows and toolbars that you find useful in Visual InterDev. My favorite working environment has the Toolbox on the left (with all its components ready to drag into a Web page or Windows application). I put the editor in the middle. On the right side, I have the Project Explorer on top of the Properties window. Then I add and subtract any windows I need, as necessary. (Refer to Figure 5-1.)

If you haven't worked with the Visual Studio IDE, you may want to try my setup first, and then personalize it later. To adjust the windows in Visual InterDev, follow these steps:

1. **Choose View⇨Toolbox to display the toolbox.**

2. **Drag the Toolbox to the left side of the window, and stretch or shrink it to resize it to fit on the left side, without covering the Editor window.**

   The three windows that I always leave visible (Toolbox, Project Explorer, and Properties) are also the three that have separate entries in the View menu and have their own shortcut keys.

3. **Choose View⇨Project Explorer and then choose View⇨Properties Window.**

   The Project Explorer window and the Properties window appear.

4. **Arrange these two new windows as shown in Figure 5-1 along the right side. Resize them as necessary.**

If you find the windows hard to control because they seem to be attaching themselves to the sides of the Visual InterDev main window, you've got docking turned on. Right-click the Toolbox, Project Explorer, or Properties window and deselect the Dockable option. Or, you can just press the Ctrl key while dragging a window to prevent it from docking. For a detailed discussion of docking, see Chapter 2.

Working with Toolbars and Buttons

A *toolbar* is a bar that houses a set of buttons that trigger features when clicked. The set of buttons is collected together on a particular toolbar because they offer related features; for example, all the debugging tools are on the Debug toolbar.

Setting up toolbars

Most people leave their toolbars at the top of the main window. However, if you wish, drag and dock your toolbars against any of the four sides of the main window. You can even be a little wild and drag them into the center of the main window and let them float.

You can also drag toolbars around to reposition them relative to each other. Some toolbars appear automatically when Visual InterDev thinks that you may want them. For example, you can test a Web page by pressing F5. This puts you in debug mode. (See Chapter 14 for a thorough exploration of the Visual Studio 6 excellent debugging tools.) And as soon as you press F5, Visual InterDev knows that you're going into debug mode, so it displays the Debug toolbar.

To display or hide toolbars, follow these steps:

1. **Choose View⇨Toolbars.**

    A menu appears with all the toolbars listed for you to choose from.

2. **Click a toolbar from the menu to display it.**

    If that toolbar is currently displayed, it becomes hidden.

You can also display the menu of toolbars by right-clicking any toolbar on your screen. The context menu of toolbars appears, and you can choose other toolbars to display, or select toolbars that you want to hide.

Customizing toolbars

Toolbars are yours to change if you want to. To customize a toolbar, follow these steps:

1. **Right-click any toolbar and choose Customize from the context menu that appears.**

    The Customize dialog box opens. This dialog box enables you to add or remove icons on your toolbars, make the icons larger on the toolbars, and create animation effects for drop-down menus.

All about toolbars

Toolbars are popular because they're quicker to use than navigating a menu. You just click a button on a toolbar and something happens. Toolbars can be freely moved around anywhere you want to position them in the Visual Studio IDE. Toolbars can be docked or floating. A docked toolbar is attached to the top, bottom, or one of the sides of the main window (It may also be attached to other toolbars.) A docked toolbar has a small set of parallel bumps on its far left (if the toolbar is attached to the top or bottom of the main window). The bumps are on the top of the toolbar, if the toolbar is attached to one of the sides of the main window. In any case, you can move a docked toolbar by holding down your mouse button with the pointer positioned on the bumps and then dragging the toolbar. If you drop the toolbar against the top, bottom, or one of the sides of the main window, the toolbar docks there. If you drop the toolbar. anywhere else, it becomes a floating toolbar. (It no longer has the bumps but now has a title bar, with its name displayed.) You drag a floating toolbar as you do any typical window, by dragging it by its title bar. You can have as many toolbars open as you want at a given time.

2. **Click the Commands tab and notice that you can select any menu in the left pane under Categories.**

3. **Click Project in the left pane.**

   The items in the Project menu are listed in the right pane.

4. **Try dragging** HTML page **from the right pane onto a toolbar.**

   HTML page (representing the add HTML page feature of the Project menu) becomes a new button on whatever toolbar you dropped it into.

5. **To move a button to a different location on its toolbar, drag the button and drop it where you want.**

   If you decide that you don't want to move the button after all, press Esc.

6. **If you want to remove a button from a toolbar, drag the button off the toolbar and then drop it anywhere in the Visual InterDev Editor** *except* **on a toolbar.**

   The button disappears. If you decide that you don't want to remove it after all, press Esc.

Creating custom window layouts

You may find that you use a particular group of windows when programming, but you want a different set when testing a Web page. Visual InterDev makes it easy to create personal layouts that you can quickly switch between. This way you don't have to display and hide windows one-by-one. Nor do you have to reposition or resize them. Just choose your custom programming layout, and you're ready to go.

To create a custom layout, follow these steps:

1. **Display, hide, and arrange the windows in the Visual InterDev Editor as you want them for your custom layout.**

   Remember that the current size and position of each window are saved.

2. **Choose View⇨Define Window Layout.**

   The Define Window Layout dialog box opens.

3. **Type in a name for your new layout in the View Name text box.**

4. **Click the Add button.**

   Your new layout is added to the list labeled Views in the Define Window Layout dialog box.

5. **Click the Close button.**

Whenever you want to switch to a window layout, choose View⇨Define Window Layout. Click the view that you want in the left pane of the Define Window Layout dialog box and then click the Apply button.

If you want to make life really easy for yourself, add a button for the Define Window Layout dialog box to your Standard toolbar (as described in the section "Customizing toolbars," earlier in this chapter). That way, switching between layouts is only a click away.

The various elements of the Define Window Layout dialog box perform the following functions:

- **View Name text box:** Gives your custom layout a memorable name.
- **Close button:** Shuts the dialog box.
- **Apply button:** Changes the current layout to the one you've selected in the Views list.
- **Add button:** Creates a new layout (based on the current window settings in Visual InterDev).
- **Delete button:** Removes the currently selected View.
- **Rename button:** Changes the name of the currently selected View.

Using the Toolbox

Visual InterDev's three views — Design, Source, and Quick View — are best illustrated by working with the Toolbox. That's because the fastest way for you to add major features to a Web page is to drag a component from the Toolbox to Design View or Source View.

The Toolbox in the Visual Studio IDE is where components are categorized and stored. A component is a prebuilt object that you can add to your Web page or Windows application. Typical components include text boxes, drop-down list boxes, check boxes, and so on.

In this section, you see how to use the Design View and the Toolbox to quickly add components to a Web page.

Adding components the easy way

To get a feel for using the Toolbox and working with the three views, try this next example. You provide a list of options for the user. Each option includes a check box component and some text describing it. Then you see how to interact with the check boxes by testing the Web page in Quick View. Check boxes are useful when you want to allow a visitor to indicate preferences. To add check boxes to a Web page, follow these steps:

1. **Choose File⇨New File in Visual InterDev.**

   The New File dialog box opens.

2. **Click Visual InterDev in the left pane of the New File dialog box.**

3. **Double-click the HTML Page icon in the right pane.**

   The dialog box closes, and you have a blank Web page in Visual InterDev. Also, you're in Visual InterDev's Design View.

4. **Click the HTML tab in the Visual InterDev Toolbox.**

   A list appears in the Toolbox, showing you the set of HTML components that you can drag into your new, blank Web page. For this example, assume that you want to create a set of four check boxes.

5. **Create your four check boxes in one of two ways: Double-click the check box icon in the Toolbox four times, or drag a check box onto your blank page four times.**

   At this point, you see a line of four check boxes, such as those shown in Figure 5-3.

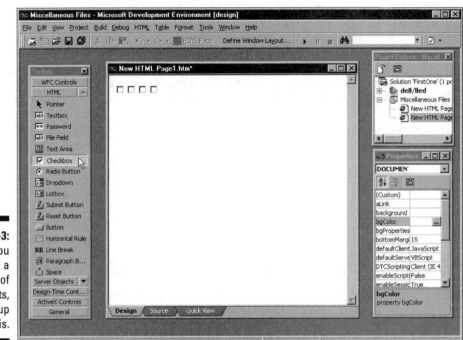

Figure 5-3:
When you
add a
group of
components,
they line up
like this.

6. **Click the Source View tab at the bottom of the Editor window.**

You see the HTML code that tells a browser to display four check boxes.

The HTML code to create four check boxes looks like this:

```
<INPUT id=check box1 name=check box1
type=check box><INPUT id=check box2 name=check box2
        type=check box><INPUT
id=check box3 name=check box3 type=check box><INPUT
        id=check box4 name=check box4
type=check box>
```

The best way to arrange your check boxes is to align them vertically rather than horizontally. When the check boxes are aligned vertically, you can type a description next to each one. However, by default, HTML components are added horizontally until they fill the width of the page.

You can handle the formatting in two ways. The first option is to fiddle with the HTML code to change the alignment of your check boxes. The HTML codes for a new paragraph are a <P> to start the paragraph and a </P> to indicate the end of that paragraph. You can insert <P> and </P> around each check box when you have the editor in Source View. Inserting those codes moves the boxes into a vertical column. Although this code fiddling gets the job done, it may be a bit intimidating to some people. The second (and easier) option is to change the alignment graphically in Design View. The following steps lead you through this method:

1. **Click the Design tab.**

   The editor switches to Design View.

2. **Position your insertion pointer (the blinking vertical line) between the first and second check boxes.**

   Use the left and right arrow keys.

3. **Press the Enter key.**

   You move three of the boxes down one line.

   Pressing the Enter key adds a paragraph ⟨P⟩ HTML element. (Browsers display a blank line between the components or text when they come across a ⟨P⟩ element.) If you want a tighter set of boxes (with no blank lines), press Shift+Enter. The ⟨BR⟩ element (Break) replaces the ⟨P⟩ ⟨/P⟩ elements in the HTML source code.

4. **Continue to move the insert cursor and then press Enter (or Shift+Enter), until each box is on its own line.**

If you want to continue on to give each of your check boxes a descriptive label, follow these steps:

1. **Now move the cursor to the right side of the top check box and type in a description.**

   Make the description of the check box's purpose clear for your Web page viewers. For example, type **Send all information immediately!**

2. **Press the down-arrow key to move to the right of the second check box and type a description for that check box.**

   If you used the description example in Step 1, your second description could be "Send information and call me!"

3. **Continue repeating Steps 1 and 2 until you've defined each check box with a description.**

At this point, click the Source View tab, and you see this HTML source code:

```
<P><INPUT id=check box1 name=check box1
          type=check box> Send all information
          immediately!</P>
<P><INPUT id=check box2 name=check box2 type=check box>
          Send information and call me!</P>
```

(continued)

(continued)

```
<P><INPUT
id=check box3 name=check box3 type=check box> Call
me and visit me, I'm lonely.</P>
<P><INPUT id=check box4 name=check box4
type=check box> Don't
darken my door.</P>
```

Modifying the Toolbox's features

Exactly which components appear on your Toolbox depends on which operating system you're using (Windows or NT) and which applications you've installed on your computer. Some applications add components to the collection available to your computer. For example, if you choose to add Visual J++ during the Visual Studio setup process, the WFC Controls tab appears on your Toolbox. Otherwise, that tab doesn't appear. (WFC means Windows Foundation Class, a set of components used by Visual J++.)

Even individual components can be added to or removed from the Toolbox. The HTML components tab is a standardized set, so you can't modify the contents of that tab. But you can change the components available on the other tabs.

To add or subtract components from the Toolbox, follow these steps:

1. **Click the ActiveX Controls tab in the Visual InterDev Toolbox.**

   ActiveX Control is one of Microsoft's names for a component, like a text box.

2. **Right-click the Calendar component in the Toolbox.**

   You can right-click any component; just don't right-click one of the tabs. You see the context menu.

3. **Click the Customize Toolbox option in the context menu.**

   The Customize Toolbox dialog box (shown in Figure 5-4) opens, listing all the components currently registered on your system.

   Add or remove Toolbox components by using this dialog box. The components listed here are installed on your system. You can find the checked components on the Toolbox.

4. **In the Customize Toolbox dialog box, click the ActiveX Controls tab.**

   Notice that some of the components listed in the ActiveX Controls tab end with the letters DTC. This stands for design-time control, and these controls also appear listed under the Design-Time Controls tab.

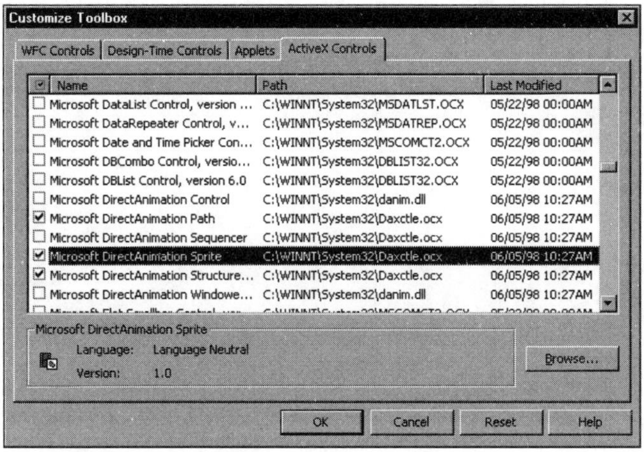

Figure 5-4:
The
Customize
Toolbox
dialog box.

5. **Locate a component that's checked, and uncheck it by clicking.**

   This action removes the component from the Toolbox.

6. **Also try clicking an unchecked component to add it to the Toolbox.**

7. **Click the OK button.**

   The dialog box closes, and you see the effect of your changes. You can see (or not see) the icons that you added or subtracted from the Toolbox.

Organizing Toolbox tabs

You can also modify the Toolbox's tabs. Right-click one of the tabs, and you can see a context menu. From this menu, you can move the tab up or down in the list of tabs and rename or delete it. If you click the Add option, a new, blank tab appears at the bottom of the Toolbox, ready for you to type in a new title. After that, you can use the Customize Toolbox dialog box (refer to Figure 5-4) to populate your new tab with components.

Understanding the Project Explorer

Of the four main windows that I usually leave displayed in Visual InterDev, the Project Explorer is the best one to show you the big picture. It's a graphic representation of the entire Web project. Project Explorer shows the folders and the files within those folders, similar to what you see in Windows Explorer. A simple Project Explorer is shown in Figure 5-5.

Note that at the top of the tree list displayed in Figure 5-5, you can see the Solution (and how many projects are currently active in this Solution). The term *Solution* means the entire set of projects and files in this distributed application. Below that is the name of the Web server.

The rest of the folders and files you'll see in the Project Explorer depend on what kind of Web site you're building and how you've organized it.

However, the Project Explorer isn't just for seeing a tree view of the current Web site. You have several ways you can use the Project Explorer, as you can see in this list:

- ✓ If more than one project is in the Visual InterDev Workspace, you can click one of the projects to make it the currently active one.

- ✓ Double-click a file (a Web page) to bring it into view in the Editor window.

- ✓ You can rename projects or pages by right-clicking the name and choosing Rename from the context menu that appears.

- ✓ Also the right-click context menu provides the usual Cut, Copy, and Delete options. You can also view any links to the current page; view the page in any browser; choose Open With to view the source code in a special editor; and interact in various ways with the Master copy of the site on the server.

- ✓ You can select which page or project is the *startup* (the page or project executed first when the site is loaded into a browser).

- ✓ You can choose Mark As Scriptlet to use the source code as an object in other pages. (See Chapter 10.)

- ✓ Choose Apply Theme and Layout to add a predefined look or navigation structure to the current page.

Not all options appear on the context menu for all types of Web pages. For example, an .Asp page (active server page) is designed to work on the server, not to work in the user's browser. Therefore, no Apply Theme option appears on its context menu. In other cases, you see options listed, but they're gray (disabled) and can't be activated. For example, the Apply Theme option is enabled only if you're currently working online (in communication with the server).

As you can see in Figure 5-5, you have five buttons across the top of the Project Explorer (when a file is selected in the Project Explorer). From left to right, the buttons are as follows:

- ✔ **Open:** Opens the Editor window for the currently highlighted file.

- ✔ **Refresh:** Updates the tree list if files have been added, deleted, or reorganized in the Project Explorer.

- ✔ **Synchronize:** Makes sure that files in the local version (on your workstation) and master version (on the server) are in sync. This means that you have a view of the current status of the Web application.

- ✔ **Copy:** Use this button after you're finished creating your Web site and are ready to deploy the site. You can copy the entire Web application to another server, ready to be viewed and used by people on an intranet within your company or by the entire world on the Internet.

- ✔ **Properties:** Displays a special tabbed dialog box (not the Properties window) describing various qualities of the selected file, project, or solution. This feature is becoming more and more popular in Windows applications, but it isn't yet available for all objects, nor is it standardized.

Adjusting Properties

Nearly all Microsoft RAD applications now feature a Properties window. This window shows a list of properties of the currently selected object — a Web page, a project in the Project Explorer, a component in the editor's Design View, and many other items.

Properties is the fancy term that computer programmers use for *qualities* or *characteristics*. It's been suggested that everyone already knows basic grammar from school, so why not just use those categories we all know when we're talking about computer language? That would make sense, but alas, it's not happening. If we were using grammar terms for computer language categories, a property would be an adjective.

Using the Properties window to change a color

The Properties window displays a list of an object's qualities. What object? Whatever object that's currently selected. (For an in-depth discussion of objects, see Chapter 10.) To see how this process works, follow these steps:

1. **Choose File⇨New File in Visual InterDev.**

2. **Click Visual InterDev in the left pane and then double-click HTML page in the right pane.**

   A new, empty page appears in Visual InterDev.

3. **Click the Design tab in the new page's Editor window.**

   The page is ready for text, graphics, and other kinds of editing.

4. **Click the HTML tab in the Toolbox.**

   The HTML components are displayed. If the Toolbox isn't visible, choose View⇨Toolbox.

5. **Drag the button component icon from the Toolbox and drop it onto your blank page.**

   A button component appears on your page. Notice that the button remains selected, and because it's the selected object, the Properties window displays the list of properties for that button.

6. **Click .backgroundColor in the Properties window.**

   You see a button with three dots on it appear next to the .backgroundColor property, as shown in Figure 5-6.

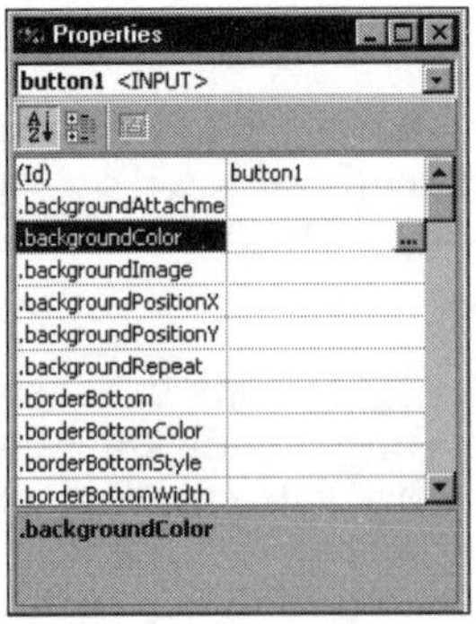

Figure 5-6: When you see a button with three dots next to a property, click it to display a dialog.

7. **Click the button with three dots (...).**

   You see the Color Picker dialog box.

8. **Click a color and then click the OK button to close the dialog box.**

   The color's name is entered into the Properties window, and the button is now colored with the tint you chose, as shown in Figure 5-7.

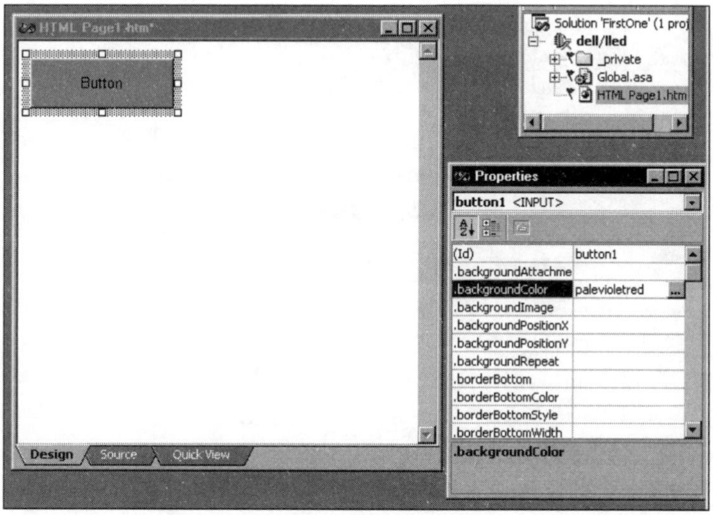

Figure 5-7:
Whatever
color
appears
in the
Properties
window
on the
right also
appears on
the button
in the
editor.

Changing a property

If you decide that you want to change the color, you can either click the button with three dots again and then pick a different color, or you can delete the current color and type in, for example, **blue**. As soon as you finish typing **blue**, press the Enter key and, whammo, the button is now blue.

Of course, you don't know what colors are available. What names, beyond the obvious names like yellow and blue, can you type in? Try light blue. It works. But to really make an informed choice, use the dialog box.

Many properties don't offer a dialog box, though some dialog boxes do have a drop-down list from which you can make choices. Click .fontSize in the Properties window with an object, such as a command button, selected in the editor. Notice the small, down-arrow icon. Click the icon. You see a list of possible fantasizes for the button. Click xx-small in the list and check out the effect on the button's caption.

Even though some properties offer a dialog box or a drop-down list, the majority of properties offer neither. If you don't know what to type in for a property, press F1 with the property or the object selected. Sometimes this action brings up a help screen describing the property or the object. If you see a help screen for the object, you probably can find the words Properties, Methods, and Events at the top of the help window. Click Properties, and you see a list like the one shown in Figure 5-8.

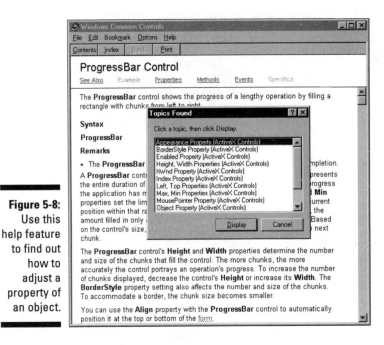

Figure 5-8:
Use this help feature to find out how to adjust a property of an object.

Some components are more equal than others

Not all objects have all properties. For example, some components enable you to change their size. Buttons do. And some components are a fixed size, like the HTML check box.

Also, you have two kinds of Properties:

✔ **Design-time properties:** These are any properties that you see listed in the Properties window. You can change them while designing your Windows application or Web page. (Many design-time properties can also be changed by programming, but not all.)

✔ **Run-time properties:** These properties can be changed *only* by programming. (They're not listed in the Properties window at all.) This programming (called *script*) sits in a Web page along with the HTML source code. After the page is loaded into a browser like Internet Explorer, the browser notices the script programming and interprets it. At this point, a run-time property can be changed by commands written in the script. If you want to get into script programming, look at Chapter 12.

The Properties window icons

You see three icons at the top of the Properties window. The Alphabetic icon, on the left, is the default and orders the properties alphabetically. The second icon is called Categorized, but I find the categories often rather vague or arbitrary. The third icon is called Properties Pages and brings up a tabbed dialog box for some objects. To activate the Properties Pages icon, click the name of an .Htm page or other file in your Project Explorer.

Don't mistake the Properties window for a Properties dialog box (or *Property Pages* as the dialog box is sometimes called). Although the Properties window and Properties dialog box often contain identical or at least similar lists of properties, they're not the same feature. To see the difference, click the name of your server (which appears in boldface, just below the project) in the Project Explorer. That action selects your server. Then click the button on the right side in the Properties window, labeled Property Pages. You then see a *tabbed* dialog box.

Suit Yourself: Customizing Visual InterDev's Editor

Visual InterDev is extraordinarily easy to customize. For example, you have shortcut keys for most things you may want to do in Visual InterDev. Ctrl+Shift+N brings up the New File dialog box, as one of many examples. And if you don't like a shortcut key, you can change it. Or you can create a shortcut key to most any menu item. In fact, you can even create several *sets* of keyboard maps for different uses.

You can also customize the style of interior windows, choosing between windows that attach to other windows, or a style where windows float free, even going outside the main Visual InterDev window. Beyond that, you can specify editor, debugging, security, and other options.

Customizing the keyboard

You often may find yourself needing to view your Web pages in your browser. For example, if you do a good amount of work involving components, some of them won't work correctly when you switch to Quick View in Visual InterDev's Editor window. You must frequently choose View⇨View In Browser. That can become tedious. You decide to create a shortcut key for the View In Browser feature. To create that shortcut key, follow these steps:

1. **Choose Tools⇨Options in Visual InterDev.**

   The Options dialog box opens, with a large list box of categories on the left.

2. **In the list box on the left, click to expand the Environment category and then highlight the Keyboard category.**

3. **In the Categories list box, choose View.**

4. **In the Commands list box, choose View In Browser.**

5. **Click in the Press New Shortcut Key text box.**

   The blinking insertion pointer appears in the text box, indicating that you can type something.

6. **Press the F8 key.**

   The dialog box doesn't report that F8 is assigned to any other job, so assigning it to the View In Browser feature is okay. If you press the wrong key, click in the Press New Shortcut Key box just to the right side of the key description. Then press the Backspace key to delete the key.

7. **Click the Assign button and then click the OK button.**

   The dialog box closes, and your shortcut key is assigned and ready to use.

Now press F8 to see what happens.

Other preferences, other options

You accomplish most customization in Visual InterDev by choosing Tools⇨Options. The Options dialog box contains many ways that you can personalize Visual InterDev to suit your preferences and your style of working. Often, the options are obvious. For example, in the list box on the left of the Options dialog box, choose the General option (under Environment), as shown in Figure 5-9.

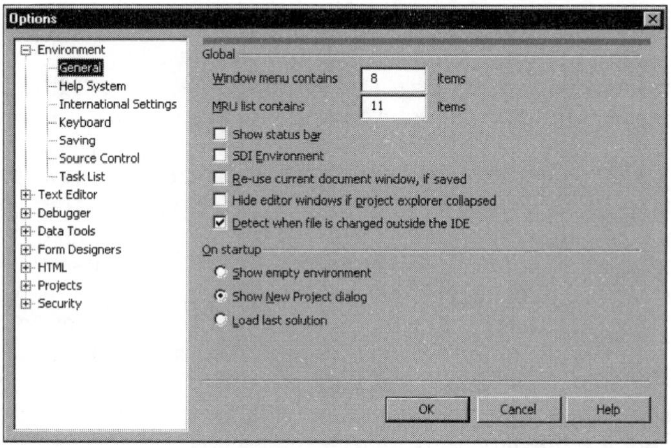

Figure 5-9:
The default
page in the
Visual
InterDev
Options
dialog box.

Understanding the meaning of the Show New Project Dialog option button under the On Startup section of the dialog box is easy. The other startup options are equally obvious: You can have Visual InterDev fire up in an empty state with no project loaded, or have it load the project you worked on the last time you ran Visual InterDev.

However, not all options are so obvious. Take a look at the options in Visual InterDev that meet two criteria: They're important and they're not obvious.

Environment options

Environment options are customizations that won't fit comfortably into any of the other options categories.

- ✔ **MRU:** On the General page under Environment, the term *MRU* means most-recently-used. This setting defines how many of the files and projects that you've recently worked on appear at the bottom of the File menu. It defaults to 4, but you can make the number as many as 24.

- ✔ **SDI:** Switches between a multiple document window and a single-document window. These features are covered in Chapter 2. By default, Visual InterDev is in MDI mode: The main parent window contains all child windows — like the toolbox and the Project Explorer. Move the main window, and all the other windows move with it (though this rule has exceptions). The SDI mode makes all child windows independent — every window resides on the desktop, not within the parent application.

Text Editor options

The Text Editor options includes fonts, tab settings, and such typical text-entry items as an optional horizontal scrollbar. Click Text Editor in the Visual InterDev Options dialog box and then click General.

✔ **Clickwait:** Operates when you click in a different window (to give it the focus — meaning it's the window where any typed characters are displayed). However, after you give it the focus, the blinking vertical line (insertion point) does not automatically go to this new window. *Normally* the blinking vertical line immediately goes to the window with the focus, assuming that window has a text box or other component into which you can type. For example, if you set Clickwait to 2000 milliseconds (2 seconds) and you press the mouse button before 2 seconds elapse, the insertion point won't move. I'm sure Clickwait has a use, but it eludes me. Any ideas?

✔ **Drag and Drop Editing:** This permits you to select some text in Source View in the editor and then drag and drop it to a new location within the source code.

Debugging options

Debugging options specify how Visual InterDev should behave when you're testing a Web page or a Web site.

The *Just-in-time debugging* feature, when activated, causes the debugger to start if an error occurs in a *running script* (a program written in JavaScript or VBScript). The debugger also starts if a remote procedure (one running on a different machine) executes.

Projects options

Projects options are those customizations that apply to a project as a whole. You see the Create Global.Asa For New Web Projects option on the Web Projects page of the Projects options. You may want to leave this option selected. It's turned on by default. This merely means that whenever you begin a new project in Visual InterDev, a file named Global.Asa is created for you and appears in the Project Explorer. This file is the rough equivalent of the Startup folder found in `Profiles\All Users\Start Menu\Programs\Startup` in Windows. (If you're old enough to remember DOS, think Autoexec.BAT.)

You can put programming in the Global.Asa file and run it when an application (or session) starts or ends, as you specify. To see just how to program initialization or shutdown behaviors, double-click the Global.Asa file in your Project Explorer. The instructions are in the file itself.

Security options

Security options don't include *your* permissions that enable you to create new Web sites or add new Web pages to an existing site. Those permissions are set by your network's administrator. Instead, Security options in Visual InterDev are limited to the Sign Cabinet option, a supposed protection for visitors to your Web site.

The *Sign Cabinet* option adds a digital signature to a .CAB file in your project. Such signatures are supposed to provide a safeguard against viruses. The idea is that you've added your company's name to your page, certifying that the page does no harm. The page can then be traced back to you, holding you accountable. The weakness of this system, it seems to me, is that bad people can get signatures, too.

Chapter 6

The FrontPage Editor: The Visual Studio 6 Content Designer

• •

In This Chapter

▶ Choosing between Visual InterDev and FrontPage

▶ Starting a new project in FrontPage

▶ Working with Webbots

▶ Letting the wizards do it

▶ Managing graphics in FrontPage

• •

*I*n my view, FrontPage is often superior to Visual InterDev. Some people may disagree, but Microsoft doesn't. The company includes FrontPage in Visual Studio for a reason. You have an even more convincing argument for the value of FrontPage: It's bundled with Visual InterDev when the latter is sold separately from Visual Studio. FrontPage is an essential tool for Web site design. Why? Because FrontPage includes wizards and other shortcuts that aren't available elsewhere. Visual InterDev is a great application, but for many jobs — working with Web page graphics, for example — many people consider FrontPage the superior tool.

If you specialize in site administration or programming, you may never have a reason to run FrontPage. If you do other work with distributed applications or Web sites, you're likely to come to value FrontPage as one of your best resources. And if you doubt me, see if you still disagree after looking through this chapter.

Visual InterDev versus FrontPage: The Choice Is Yours

Visual InterDev is a brilliant tool for both programmers and project administrators. But FrontPage is the tool of choice for many of the other people who frequently contribute to the creation of a Web site: artists, writers, designers, CEOs — anyone who wants to create or edit Web page *content*. FrontPage boasts loads of shortcuts, Wizards, and utilities that make Web programming painless. If you're not a programmer, you may find that FrontPage's tools make creating attractive, functional, Web pages easy. Often FrontPage can ask you a set of questions and then write programming to do the job that you need done.

Programmers prefer Visual InterDev. And Visual InterDev is a great tool for Web site administrators, too. Web site administrators are responsible for organizing a group of people who work together to design, build, and maintain a Web site. Keeping people from stepping on each other's toes when working on a Web site can be a major undertaking.

But for all Visual InterDev's power, sophistication, and complexity, at times FrontPage is indispensable.

Understanding the distinction between Visual InterDev and FrontPage and knowing when to use which tool are important.

Use Visual InterDev for

- ✔ Programming
- ✔ Debugging
- ✔ Prototyping and site management
- ✔ Coordinating group efforts

Use FrontPage for

- ✔ Page design
- ✔ Content work (adding or editing text and graphics)
- ✔ Working with Themes
- ✔ Inserting forms, frames, tables, and other elements

In the spirit of the preceding distinction, roll up your sleeves and get working in the FrontPage Editor. You can find many great features.

When you start FrontPage, you're not in the editor. Instead, you're in the FrontPage Explorer. The Explorer is like Visual InterDev, because it takes a site-wide view of things. You can make global changes in the Explorer. Often, though, you want to use Visual InterDev rather than the Explorer for global (site-wide) work.

Note: Nearly all the examples in this chapter require that you be in FrontPage Editor's Normal View. (Click the Normal tab at the bottom left of the Editor window.) If an example requires a different View, it's specifically mentioned.

Opening the FrontPage Editor

To get to the FrontPage Editor, follow these steps:

1. **Start FrontPage by clicking its icon on your desktop.**

   You see the Getting Started dialog box. Unless you choose the Always Open Last Web option in the lower left, you see this dialog box when you first run FrontPage.

2. **Select the Open An Existing FrontPage Web option button and then click the OK button.**

   If you have no existing FrontPage Web, select the Create A New FrontPage Web option button and then choose One Page Web when the Wizard asks.

   You see the Name and Password Required dialog box for security, shown in Figure 6-1, if you haven't yet logged in at the necessary permission level. Type in your password. If you don't know it, contact your administrator.

   The Explorer is now running, but you want to get to the FrontPage Editor.

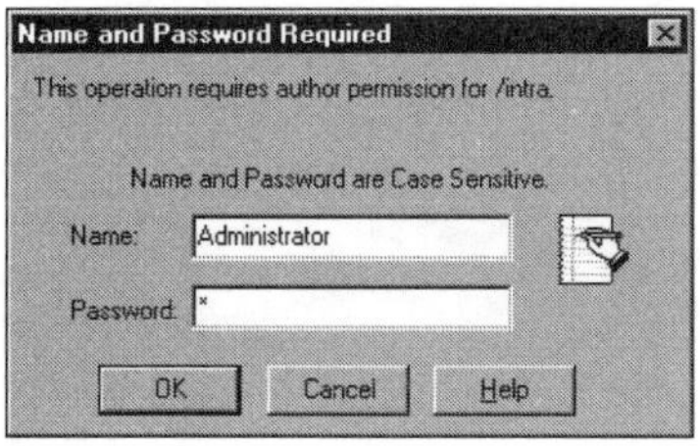

Figure 6-1:
Type in your password in the Name and Password Required dialog box.

3. **Choose Tools⇨Show FrontPage Editor.**

   The FrontPage Editor opens, and displays a blank page. If the page isn't blank, the Web you opened has a Theme. To remove the Theme from this page, choose Format⇨Theme. Click the This Page Does Not Use Themes option button. Click the OK button.

A *theme* in Visual Studio is a professionally designed *look* that can be added to a Web site — a Theme is a set of typefaces, backgrounds, colors, custom elements, such as shaded buttons, and other graphics. This look is created by artists working for Microsoft, and many of the 54 Themes included in Visual InterDev and FrontPage are excellent. When you choose a theme, you can apply it to all pages in a Web site, making the whole site look both cohesive and more attractive. Chapter 7 explores the subject of themes in depth.

You now see a blank page ready for editing, as shown in Figure 6-2.

If you've checked the Always Open Last Web check box in the lower left of the Getting Started dialog box, you won't see the Getting Started dialog box again. However, you can bring it back. Switch to the FrontPage Explorer and then choose Tools⇨Options. Click the General tab. Select Show Getting Started dialog box.

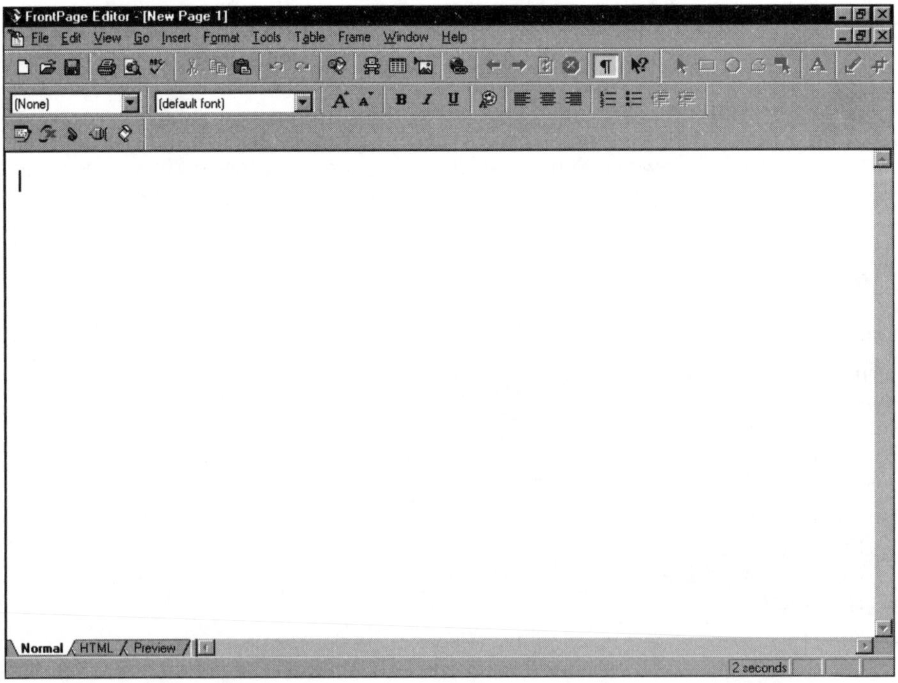

Figure 6-2:
The
FrontPage
Editor,
ready for
you to add
contents
and design.

Creating a new Web

You don't want to ignore one of FrontPage's most powerful features: the Web Wizard. This wizard can create a fairly complete Web for you. All you do is customize the text and modify the pages to reflect your particular needs. This approach (modifying an existing Web) is often a lot easier than starting from scratch. The Web Wizard is available when you start a new Web. Follow these steps:

1. **Go to FrontPage Explorer, or start it running.**

   If you've got an open Web currently active in FrontPage, choose File⇨Close FrontPage Web in the FrontPage Explorer.

   You see the Getting Started dialog box. If you don't see the Getting Started dialog box, choose File⇨Open FrontPage Web.

2. **In the Getting Started dialog box, click the Create A New FrontPage Web option button.**

3. **Click the OK button.**

   You see the New FrontPage Web dialog box, as shown in Figure 6-3. In this dialog box, you can run a new Web Wizard, import a Web, or create a single-page Web.

4. **Click the From Wizard Or Template option button.**

5. **Choose Customer Support Web in the list of available wizards and templates.**

6. **Click the OK button.**

   You see the animated message box indicating that a new Web is being built, as shown in Figure 6-4.

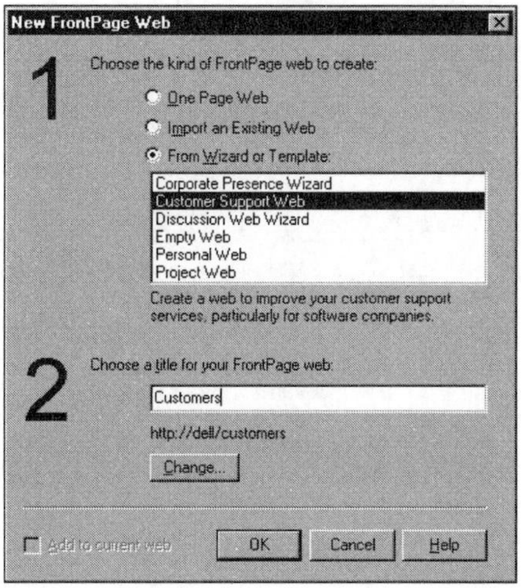

Figure 6-3: The New FrontPage Web dialog box.

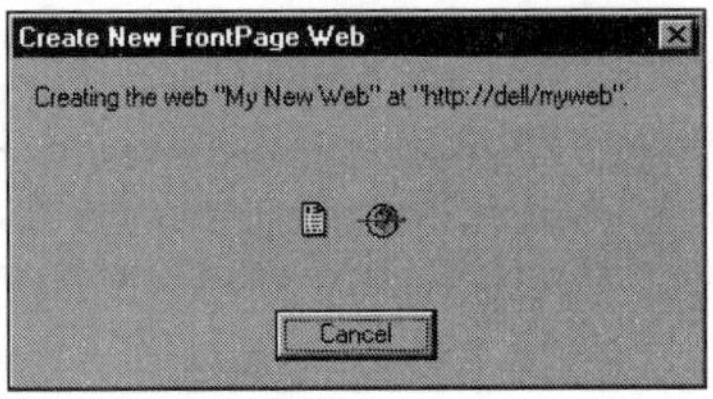

Figure 6-4:
Be patient
for a
minute as
FrontPage
builds a
fairly
complex
site for you.

Figure 6-4:
Be patient for a minute as FrontPage builds a fairly complex site for you.

After all is quiet again in FrontPage, you see the customer service Web that's been built for you, as shown in Figure 6-5. Now all you have to do is customize it. See the following section, "Customizing a template."

In under a minute (unless you're trying to use Visual Studio on a very slow computer), FrontPage has built a complete set of customer service pages. You have a home page and group of secondary pages, each devoted to an aspect of cheerful, perky customer assistance.

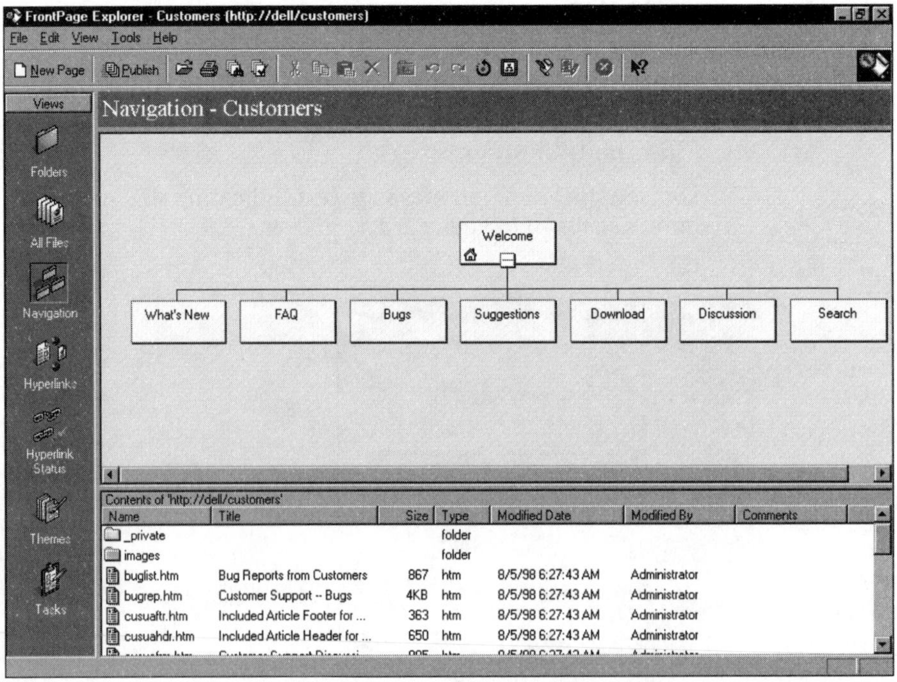

Figure 6-5:
See your full-featured customer-support Web site.

Customizing a template

The previous section, "Creating a new Web," shows you how to quickly create a Web by using the Web Wizard. This wizard adds a theme to the entire Web, and each page in the Web is also filled with text and perhaps graphics. Consider each page to be a *template* that you need to customize, to personalize the Web with your own information. In Navigation View of FrontPage Explorer, double-click the home page (usually named Welcome). FrontPage launches its editor and loads the page into Normal View. As you can see in Figure 6-6, the home page is divided into several zones, including a set of hyperlinks on the left that a visitor can click to navigate to the various pages in your site.

Assume that you decide to actually use this Web site to deal with customers. You have to edit the site so that it displays your company's name and other details. Among other things, you want to change the large Welcome banner at the top of the page shown in Figure 6-6 so that it says "Welcome to ZWorld." To customize this template, follow these steps:

Figure 6-6:
In the FrontPage Editor, look at a template and you usually find the page divided into several zones.

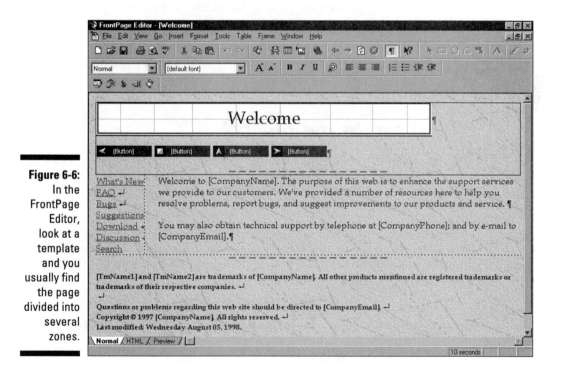

1. **Follow Steps 1 through 6 in the previous section "Creating a new Web." You see the Customer Support Web displayed in Figure 6-6.**

2. **Press Alt+Tab until you switch to FrontPage Explorer.**

   To change the banner at the top of this page, you must switch from the FrontPage Editor to FrontPage Explorer. The reason is that this banner is a *Webbot,* FrontPage's name for what is usually called a *component* or *control* in the other applications in Visual Studio. You can't directly edit a Webbot in the FrontPage Editor.

3. **Make sure that you're in Navigation View (click Navigation in the left pane of the FrontPage Explorer).**

4. **Right-click the icon labeled Welcome, and choose Rename from the context menu that appears.**

   The context menu disappears, and the word Welcome becomes editable. You can now change it. (You can edit the same way that you can rename a filename in Windows Explorer.)

5. **Type in** Welcome to ZWorld. **After you're finished, click outside the icon (on the blank background) to set the new name.**

6. **Double-click the Welcome To... icon to return to the FrontPage Editor.**

   Notice that, the change you made in the FrontPage Explorer is also changed in the Editor. It says ZWorld.

What's with the robots?

As you work in FrontPage, you're probably seeing robots. Whenever you move your mouse pointer over a Webbot, the pointer displays a little robot. That's not an attempt to drive you out of your mind. The robot tells you that you're looking at a Webbot.

The set of four navigation buttons, just below the Welcome banner, is also a Webbot. If you want to adjust this component, right-click it. A context menu appears. Choose FrontPage Component Properties from the context menu. You see the Properties dialog box.

Changing the Table of Contents Webbot

As you look at a template home page, you may be startled to find that the table of contents list on the left of the template (What's New, FAQ, Bugs, and so on) is also a Webbot. In fact, it's the *same* kind of Webbot as the four navigation buttons shown in Figure 6-6! The table of contents list is another way to display a Navigation Bar Webbot.

You may not have noticed that the table of contents is a Webbot because the mouse cursor doesn't turn into a robot until you *select* the table of contents by clicking it. The cursor *usually* turns into a robot, but doesn't in this case. Are you listening, Microsoft?

Try putting your mouse pointer over the various Webbots on the Welcome page displayed in the FrontPage Editor. To change a couple of these items so that they're appropriate to your business, follow these steps:

1. **Click the table of contents list to select it.**

2. **Right-click the table of contents list and choose FrontPage component properties from the context menu.**

   You see the Navigation Bar Properties dialog box. Sure enough, this table of contents list is a Navigation Bar disguised as a list of text items. Note the TIP at the bottom of the dialog box. To change the labels on the buttons, you have to switch to FrontPage Explorer.

3. **Press Alt+Tab to switch to the FrontPage Explorer.**

4. **Click the Navigation icon in the left pane of the FrontPage Explorer.**

   The Navigation View appears, displaying your Web site in a tree diagram.

5. **Right-click the page that says Bugs and choose Rename from the context menu.**

   Your cursor appears in an editing box in the Bugs box in the diagram, where you can rename Bugs.

6. **Change the name from Bugs to** Surprise Features.

7. **Click the background to set the change.**

   The new name becomes official.

8. **Switch back to the FrontPage Editor.**

   Notice in the FrontPage Editor that the change also has been made to this page. Bugs is no longer a hyperlink in the table of contents.

One more Webbot is on the Welcome page shown in Figure 6-6. Have you found it yet? It's not obvious. This Webbot is hidden as part of the copyright information. See if you can find it by watching your mouse cursor change. Then, right-click it and choose FrontPage Component Properties to see what options you can adjust.

Modifying regular text

Templates include placeholder text, such as `CompanyName` and `Company Email`. You replace that default text with text that describes your company or is otherwise appropriate for the page you're creating. Make sure that you substitute your information for all these placeholders, or your Web page may look like an unfinished form letter. ("We care about you, customer name here.") An easy way to update all the placeholder text is to use search and replace. Follow these steps:

1. **Choose Edit⇨Replace.**

   You want to change CompanyName to ZWorld. The Replace dialog box opens.

2. **Type** CompanyName **in the Find What text box and type** ZWorld **in the Replace With text box.**

3. **Click Replace All.**

4. **Click the OK button.**

   Notice that this replaces the CompanyName only in the upper zone of this page. Click the copyright information section of the Welcome page and repeat these steps to replace CompanyName with ZWorld in the lower section of this page.

Also, you can edit the CompanyEmail and TMName text. You can just click it to select it and then retype the correction, as you do in any word processor.

Previewing your Web site

FrontPage makes creating your Web site an easy process. And by the time you finish creating it, you're anxious to get a look at the completed Web site. You want to see what visitors see when they look at your Web page. Click the Preview button. Whoa! Most of the page looks okay, but the buttons at the top say [Button]. That can't be right.

In fact, Webbots can't really do their thing in Preview mode. You have to actually look at the page in your Internet browser to activate the Webbots. This is one of the few cases where the FrontPage Preview tab (or the Visual InterDev Quick View tab) simply can't do the job of presenting your page as What You See Is What You Get.

To view the page in the browser, choose File⇨Preview in Browser. You're shown a list of browsers on your system. Choose one and then click the Preview button. At this point, if you haven't saved your editing, you're asked if you want to save the changes. Say yes.

After the page is loaded into your browser, it looks something like Figure 6-7, depending on what editing you did to it.

Notice in Figure 6-7 that the navigation buttons are gone. That's because when the home page is first loaded, you don't need to have the Next, Previous, or Home buttons.

However, after a visitor penetrates your site, you have a use for the navigation buttons. Try clicking Suggestions or another of the hyperlinks in the table of contents. Then you see the Navigation Bar (the buttons) appear, as shown in Figure 6-8.

Try using the Navigation Bar buttons to move through the site. Notice that the copyright information appears on each page of your site. This feature is called *shared borders,* which acts similar to a running header in a word processor. You can define a format that appears across the entire Web site by using the shared borders feature. Read the "All about shared borders — and then some" sidebar if borders excite you.

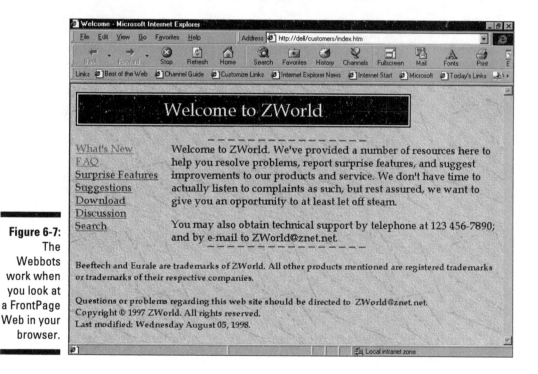

Figure 6-7:
The
Webbots
work when
you look at
a FrontPage
Web in your
browser.

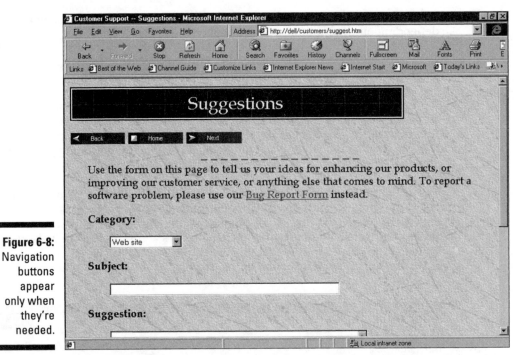

Figure 6-8:
Navigation
buttons
appear
only when
they're
needed.

If you're a propeller-head like me, by now you want to know what's going on down below, in the programming, to create all these borders, Navigation Bars, and all the rest of the tricks. Return to the Welcome To ZWorld home page in the FrontPage Editor. (The quickest way to get to a particular page in a Web is to switch to the FrontPage Explorer and then click the Navigation icon on the left pane. Double-click the icon for the page you're interested in.) Click the HTML tab at the bottom of the Editor. It's amazing how many effects are going on in this page, yet only this sparse HTML code exists.

One clue to the hidden functionality on this page is those two lines that begin with Meta:

```
<meta name="Microsoft Theme" content="expeditn 001,
        default"> <meta name="Microsoft Border"
        content="tlb, default">
```

These lines of HTML code alert a browser that a theme named expeditn 001 is being used. The theme supplies all the graphics such as the style of lines (brown dashes), the background that looks like stretched leather, the brown buttons, and all the rest of it. You could easily name this theme *Safari,* but another theme already has that name.

TECHNICAL STUFF

All about shared borders — and then some

Shared borders is a useful feature in FrontPage that enables you to create elements that appear on each page of your Web site. However, you can hide these elements on individual pages, if you wish.

In Normal View in FrontPage's Editor, right-click the current document and choose Shared Borders from the context menu. You see the Page Borders dialog box.

If you want to turn off (or adjust) the shared borders for the currently displayed individual page, use the Page Borders dialog box. This feature is useful for such items as date display, Navigation Bar, a set of hyperlinks, table of contents, running headlines, and information such as your telephone number or e-mail address.

If you disable the shared borders for a particular page, a visitor doesn't see that content in the browser, and vice versa. You can define shared borders for a particular page (if the entire Web doesn't have them). Then you can share that border with other individual pages in your Web site by using the Page Borders dialog box.

Note that if you want to add or modify shared borders for an entire Web site, switch to the FrontPage Explorer. Choose Tools⇨Shared Borders in *Explorer* (not the FrontPage Editor) to make a Web-wide adjustment.

Avoid using the shared borders feature in pages that have frames. (I deal with frames later in this chapter.)

All FrontPage templates applied during the startup process (except for the Discussion Wizard) automatically create shared borders for you.

One final point. You can use the FrontPage Explorer to build a Web page-by-page. (I recommend that you use Visual InterDev to prototype and create a Web, but you can rebel.) If you did use the FrontPage Explorer to build a Web, you may notice that Explorer adds a Navigation Bar to each page automatically. This Webbot is placed in a shared border as you create each page.

Themes are so powerful and important that Chapter 7 is mainly about them. The second line of code defines the style of shared border. Now you know how so little source code produces so many effects. A good bit of programming code and lots of .Gif graphics files are hidden away in a folder for this theme. If you're still curious about the innards of the theme, take a look in `\Program Files\Microsoft FrontPage\themes\expeditn`.

Let the Wizards Do It

In addition to the useful templates and themes, FrontPage also boasts many wizards and shortcuts that help you add content to individual pages. A wizard is a series of dialog boxes that ask you to fill in various information and ask you various questions. A wizard takes you step by step through the process of creating something, such as a table or form. The wizard uses your answers to its dialog boxes' questions to ensure that your wishes are carried out. For example, whenever you use a Setup program to install a new Microsoft application, you're using a wizard.

Talk to me: Adding a form

Unlike people watching TV, people surfing the Web are active. They expect to be able to interact with what they see. They can jump around like fleas by clicking buttons, by clicking their list of favorite sites, and by clicking other hyperlinks. They can order stuff from online bookstores or buy a VCR.

Perhaps more to the point, *you* can sell stuff. You want a way that people can buy whatever you're selling. What *are* you selling? Anyway, the quickest way to let visitors communicate back to you is to add a form.

Adding a form isn't simple if you have to type in all the HTML source code, but when you use the FrontPage Form Wizard, the process couldn't be easier. A *form* is an area in a Web page that contains input components such as option buttons and text boxes. You also have a button, usually captioned *submit,* that sends back to you whatever information the user has entered.

After the user clicks the submit button, a *form handler,* which is a program running on your Web server, gathers the information and saves it on the hard drive. Later you can harvest — I mean *process* — the orders for whatever you're selling. To create a simple form that sends you a user's name and address so that you can e-mail your company catalog to him or her, follow these steps:

1. **In the FrontPage Editor, choose File⇨New.**

   The New dialog box opens, listing many templates and a few wizards.

2. **Double-click Form Page Wizard.**

   The Form Page Wizard's first dialog box opens.

3. **Click the Next button.**

   The second wizard page appears, wherein you can type a Name and URL (address) for the page.

4. **Name the page** Catalog **and name the file** Catalog.Htm. **Click the Next button.**

   The next wizard page appears.

5. **Click the Add button.**

   A new dialog box opens, asking you to choose what kind of information you're after.

6. **Choose Contact Information from the Select The Type Of Input To Collect list box.**

7. **Click Next and then check the Name, Postal Address, and E-mail Address check boxes, as shown in Figure 6-9.**

   The Form Page Wizard writes the necessary programming to provide visitors' names, addresses, and e-mail addresses.

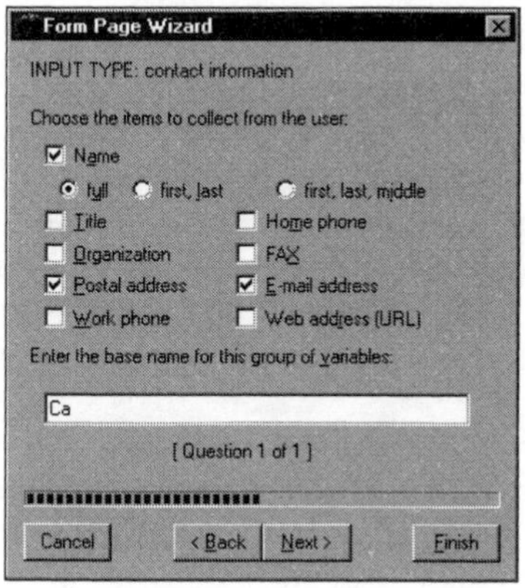

Figure 6-9:
In the Form Page Wizard dialog box, you can choose the type of contact information to collect.

Form Page Wizard

INPUT TYPE: contact information

Choose the items to collect from the user:

- ☑ Name
  - ● full ○ first, last ○ first, last, middle
- ☐ Title ☐ Home phone
- ☐ Organization ☐ FAX
- ☑ Postal address ☑ E-mail address
- ☐ Work phone ☐ Web address (URL)

Enter the base name for this group of variables:

`Ca`

[Question 1 of 1]

Cancel < Back Next > Finish

8. **Make the base name for these variables *Ca* and then click the Next button.**

9. **Click the Next button twice.**

   You see the Presentation Options dialog box.

10. **Choose Bulleted List, no table of contents, and request that tables be used. Click the Next button.**

11. **Choose to save the results to a text file and provide the name *Ca* so that the Wizard causes a submission to be saved in a file named Ca.Txt.**

12. **Click the Finish button.**

   The wizard closes up shop.

TIP

If you're still seeing the Expedition theme background and the shared borders from earlier examples in this chapter, you can remove them from this page easily. Choose Format➪Theme and select This Page Does Not Use Themes. Then click the HTML tab at the bottom of the Editor and remove these lines of code to eliminate the shared borders:

```
<meta name="Microsoft Border" content="tlb, default">
<meta name="Microsoft Theme" content="none">
```

To see how your new form looks to a visitor, click the Preview tab. And if you want a good scare, click the HTML tab and see all the HTML code you didn't have to understand and didn't have to type in. Chilling, isn't it?

Of course, you do have to replace the text `This is an explanation of the purpose of the form.` with your custom version. Wizards are smart, but they're not psychic. And maybe you want to goose up the page with some graphics. But the wizard did all the really hard, boring work.

Using the Forms toolbar

You can modify your form in several ways. In Normal View, you can adjust the text. If you want to make bigger changes, such as adding additional buttons or input components, choose View⇨Forms Toolbar. (You must be in Normal View for this process to work.) You see the toolbar shown in Figure 6-10.

One-line text box

Check box

Drop-down menu

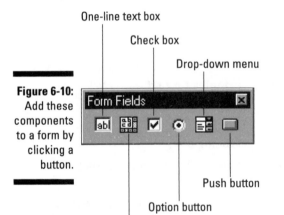

Figure 6-10: Add these components to a form by clicking a button.

Push button

Option button

Scrolling text box

Send it as e-mail: Adjusting form properties

The classic way to retrieve order forms and other kinds of information from people who visit your Web site is to store it in a text file on the server. However, now you have a better way. An easy way to gather messages from visitors to your site is to have form data sent to you as e-mail. This way, you don't have to keep checking the server's hard drive. The e-mail technique is quick and clean. If you've told the Form Page Wizard that you wanted incoming messages saved to a text file, you can change this easily enough. Follow these steps to change to e-mail submission:

1. **Click the Normal tab on the bottom of the FrontPage Editor.**

   Notice that a form is displayed with a dashed frame around it.

2. **Right-click the form to display the context menu.**

3. **Choose Form Properties from the context menu.**

   The Form Properties dialog box opens, asking you how you want a visitor's input sent back to you. (See Figure 6-11.)

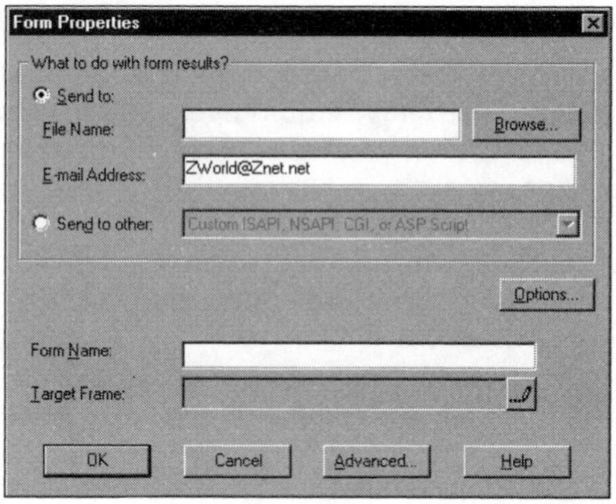

Figure 6-11:
User information sent to your e-mail account makes getting visitor information easier.

4. **Delete the file name in the What To Do With Form Results? section of the dialog box.**

5. **Type in your e-mail address in the E-mail Address text box.**

6. **Click the OK button to close the dialog box.**

Your server may not have been adjusted to permit the e-mail option. If so, a warning message appears, and you can inform your Web administrator or your Internet service provider.

After you've finished specifying your e-mail account, the wizard adds this Webbot to the HTML code to make your wish come true:

```
<!--webbot bot="SaveResults" startspan B-Label-
          Fields="TRUE"
  S-Email-Address="ZWorld@Znet.net" S-Email-
          Format="TEXT/PRE" --><!--webbot
  bot="SaveResults" endspan -->
```

But you need not worry about the code. As always, if possible just leave it to the wizards.

Line 'em up: Creating tables the easy way

They're blunt, boxy, and as design elements go, pretty boring. But tables have their place if you want to organize some information in a way that's simple to understand.

However, some designers suggest that it's a good idea, when possible, to avoid using classic, grid-like tables. They remind everyone of (shudder!) school textbooks. That's the last thing you want to do if you expect to encourage visitors to linger or revisit.

No wizard exists for creating tables, but you get some dialog windows to define a table rather than having to write the source code. That's just about as good as being guided by a wizard.

If you do decide to put a table into a Web page, follow these steps:

1. **Choose View in the FrontPage Editor.**

   The View menu drops down.

2. **Select these Toolbars in the View menu: Standard, Format, and Table.**

3. **Click the Normal tab at the bottom of the editor.**

4. **Click the blank page icon at the top left of the Standard Toolbar.**

   A new page appears.

5. **Choose Table⇨Insert Table.**

   Or, if you prefer to just drag a pencil icon to create the table, choose Draw Table.

   The Insert Table dialog box opens.

6. **In the Rows list box, choose 4, and in the Columns list box, choose 2. Leave the rest of the options set to the default.**

   Your new table should look like the one in Figure 6-12.

7. **Click the OK button to close the dialog box.**

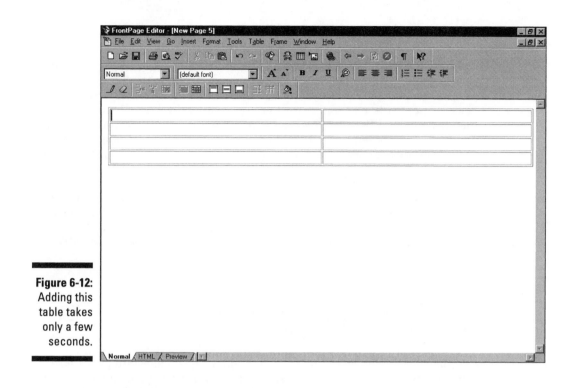

Figure 6-12:
Adding this
table takes
only a few
seconds.

Adding a color or texture to a table

If you've chosen to add a table to your Web page, you may as well add a
background color or texture under the table to make it look more interesting. Follow these steps:

1. **Right-click the table and choose Table Properties from the context
   menu.**

   You see the Table Properties dialog box, where you can adjust many
   properties of your tables.

2. **Click the Browse button to locate a .Jpg or .Gif graphic file on your
   hard drive, or download one from the Internet.**

3. **Click the OK button to close the dialog box.**

You can even provide texture or color as the background for *individual cells*
in a table. Just right-click the cell that you want to change and then choose
Cell Properties from the context menu.

Using the Draw Table features

If you prefer, you can actually design a table by using a pencil (to draw cells) and an eraser (to remove them). Click the pencil icon in the Table Toolbar (or choose Table➪Draw Table). Your cursor turns into a pencil, and you can draw vertical or horizontal lines, thereby creating rows or columns. Click the eraser icon in the same toolbar to remove unwanted cells. Note that you drag the pencil or eraser tool. To return to the normal arrow pointer for your mouse, click somewhere in the page outside the table. Or just click the pencil icon to toggle it off.

You can also widen or otherwise adjust the shape of cells by dragging the lines that define the table. To type text into the table, click the blank background in the editor. This action changes the pencil cursor to the I-beam cursor that indicates text-insertion mode. Now you can type. Press Tab or use the arrow keys to move among the cells.

Rezone your pages: Using the Frames Wizard

FrontPage's Frames Wizard makes subdividing your pages into panes easy. This process groups related content so that a visitor can quickly understand that items contained within a frame are, in some way, related to each other.

FrontPage behaves like any good RAD tool. (See Chapter 2 for details about RAD, Rapid Application Development, a set of techniques and features that make creating Windows applications and Web pages much more efficient.) As one of its RAD features, FrontPage enables you to manipulate WYSIWYG frames graphically. You can modify existing FrontPage templates, or if you prefer, you can create your own custom framing. In both cases, a wizard writes all the HTML source code programming for you.

You may want to display information to the visitor on a large right pane, and display various navigation links in a narrow left pane. To create a page with these two frames, follow these steps:

1. **Click the Normal View tab in the FrontPage Editor and then choose Frame➪New Frames Page.**

   The New dialog box opens, listing ten kinds of frames.

2. **Choose the Contents frame style, as shown in Figure 6-13.**

3. **Click the OK button.**

   The New dialog box closes, and you see the frame template that you selected in the FrontPage Editor.

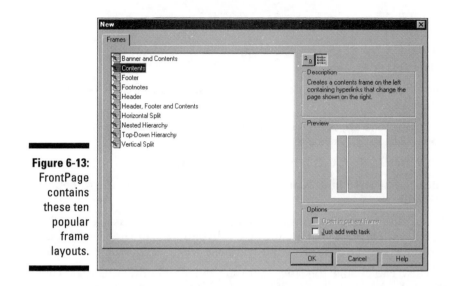

Figure 6-13:
FrontPage
contains
these ten
popular
frame
layouts.

Notice that at this point, two additional tabs have been added to the usual Normal, HTML, and Preview tabs on the bottom of the FrontPage Editor window. The No Frames tab shows you how the page looks in a browser that doesn't have the capabilities to display frames. Such browsers are, happily, extremely rare. You may say that they're more or less nonexistent these days.

4. Click the Set Initial Page button in the larger frame.

The Create Hyperlink dialog box opens, listing all the pages in your current Web, and also offering you the options of assigning a link to an Internet address, a location on your system's hard drive, an e-mail address, or a new page that you can then create.

5. Choose whatever page you want from the list of the available pages in the currently active Web.

If you're still working with the ZWorld example, you may want to choose the home page (the start page) named *Welcome*.

If you're working in the Normal View of the FrontPage Editor, you can edit frames just as you edit ordinary Web pages.

6. Click the OK button to close the dialog box and return to the FrontPage Editor.

7. Click the New button in the left pane (the left frame) in the FrontPage Editor.

You get a blank page. But if you have a theme in effect (like the Expedition theme used in the ZWorld example), the left pane conforms to the style that governs your entire site.

8. **Choose Insert⇨Active Elements.**

A pop-up menu appears, listing the available active elements.

9. **Select Hover Button.**

The Hover Button dialog box opens, enabling you to define its various Properties.

Hover Buttons are cool. When you move the mouse pointer over a Hover Button, it glows like it's being lit from within.

10. **In the Button Text text box, type** Order Goods.

11. **Click the Browse button and double-click the FAQ.Htm file or some other file.**

This action inserts whatever filename you double-click as the Link-To item in the Hover Button dialog box. A hyperlink is created that transfers the visitor to the selected target page when the button is clicked.

You also can change the Hover Button's color and other qualities while this dialog box is still open. If you're feeling wild, add sounds to the button by clicking Custom in the dialog box.

12. **Click the OK button to close the dialog box and add the button to your current page in the FrontPage Editor.**

If you want, repeat Steps 1 through 12 to add more Hover Buttons linked to other pages in your Web site.

The best way to add multiple buttons is to select (click) an existing button. Then copy (Ctrl+C) and paste (Ctrl+V), the existing button. Next, click the HTML tab and edit each `<param name="text" value="News">` line to change the `value=` to the names of the pages you want to link. Also type in the new URL (address) of each new button by editing this line: `<param name="url" value valuetype="ref">`. By using this copy/paste approach, you don't have to define the properties of each new button (its color and other elements, for example) by filling in a dialog box over and over again.

To see the results of your efforts in action, choose File⇨Preview in Browser.

A Picture Is Worth . . . A Lot

They say that a picture is worth a thousand words. Of course, that depends on who took the picture and who wrote the words. Though, you can't deny that adding color and graphics really improves your Web site.

As usual, there's a catch. Current Internet technology offers only a narrow bandwidth, which is like a tight pipe through which you must force all your site's graphics and content. When somebody has a Web page bloated with high-resolution pictures, it can take a long, long time to display that page on your screen.

If you're like most people, you become annoyed and click the Stop button in your browser. Or, even more likely, you jump to another Web site altogether.

When designing a Web site, one of your goals is to add enough graphics to attract visitors to your site without making your pages so graphics-intensive that your pages take too long to load.

One of the best FrontPage features is its tools for managing graphics (Visual InterDev is way, way behind in this area). FrontPage offers dozens of tools that simplify designing or adjusting the *look* of a Web site.

Using Auto Thumbnail

Here's one solution to the slow graphics download problem: Show users a small sample version of your picture. If they want to see the picture in more detail (the larger version), they can just click the graphic. The page loads quickly, and users can decide to view any graphics close up, if they're interested.

Have you ever seen a Web page that looks like a stamp album? It's a group of tiny graphics representations. A small version of a graphic is called a *thumbnail*. Thumbnails conserve space on a page, and also load a lot faster than the full-sized graphics that they represent. Each thumbnail is a hyperlink to a full-sized image.

Is adding thumbnail hyperlinks to your Web pages hard? In FrontPage? Are you kidding? Check out the other sections in this chapter — such as "Creating television transitions" and "Creating banner ads," — you see that FrontPage usually rushes to help you do sophisticated things quickly and painlessly.

Follow these steps to create a group of thumbnails:

1. **Choose Tools⇨Options.**

   The remarkably sparse FrontPage Options dialog box opens.

2. **Select the Auto Thumbnail tab.**

   The Auto Thumbnail page appears with options for sizing your thumbnails.

3. **Make any modifications that you want to the thumbnail's size and appearance in the dialog box.**

4. **Click the OK button to close the dialog box.**

If you set the width properties to 100 Pixels, the height is automatically resized to prevent the picture from being distorted. (All thumbs are then 100 pixels wide, but may vary in height.) Alternatively, you can specify the height in pixels and allow the width to vary as necessary. Or, as a final option, choose the Shortest Side, and FrontPage makes either the width or the height 100 pixels (or whatever you specify), but still preserves the aspect ratio to prevent distortion.

Now that you've specified the resizing method and the frame properties, it's time to try out the Auto Thumbnail feature.

5. **Choose Insert⇨Image to add images to the current page.**

Clip art cannot be thumbnailed.

Perhaps after adding your images to the page, you see that you have a collection of graphics of various sizes. Graphics are usually different sizes, as you can see in Figure 6-14.

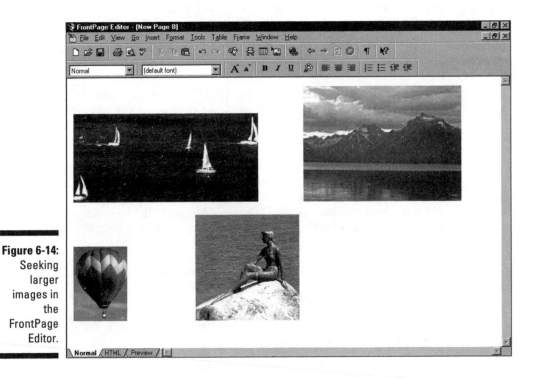

Figure 6-14:
Seeking larger images in the FrontPage Editor.

Larger images load fairly slowly. This is particularly true if the images are high-resolution files. Check the file size of the images that you put into your pages. Don't burden your site's visitors with what feels like an endless download.

6. **Click each image in turn to select it.**

7. **Choose Tools⇨Auto Thumbnail.**

The selected graphic is shrunk as appropriate, and a frame is added. You can see the result in Figure 6-15. This faster-loading group of thumbnails permits the user to get a quick view of your page, and also to expand any of the graphics to full size by clicking them if the user wants to see it displayed larger. Note the beveled edge feature that you can choose. Notice that the aspect ratio has been preserved so that the images aren't distorted.

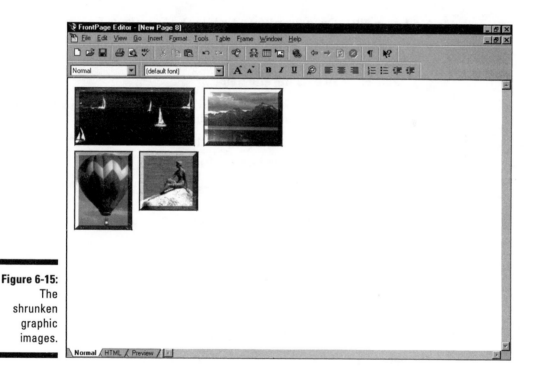

Figure 6-15:
The shrunken graphic images.

Creating television transitions

Moving from one Web page to another within a site is something like changing to a new scene in a TV show. Most often, TV uses a jump cut — simply replacing one view with the next. Now and then, though, more elaborate visual transitions are used. The most popular transition is the *dissolve* where the first scene seems to evaporate as the new scene emerges.

Another popular transition occurs most often when going to a commercial. This transition is called *fade to black*. The image becomes increasingly faint. But instead of seeing the next scene, like in a dissolve, you get a black screen briefly before the advertisement pops up.

Of course, you have hundreds of different kinds of transitions. You see some of the more drastic ones — revolving bars, checkerboards, and venetian blind effects — in news shows.

All these transitions have one thing in common: They notify you, the viewer, that you're seeing something new. Can you use TV-like transitions in your Web site? You bet.

Follow these steps to add a page transition (moving from one Web page to another) to the current page in FrontPage:

1. **Choose File➪Open FrontPage Web in the FrontPage Explorer.**

   The Getting Started dialog box opens, displaying a list of existing Web sites.

2. **Double-click an existing site name.**

   The Web site is loaded into the FrontPage Explorer. You can choose any site, as long as it contains at least two ordinary .Htm pages.

3. **Click the Navigation icon in the left pane of the FrontPage Explorer.**

   The Explorer displays the pages in the Web site.

4. **Double-click the page in Navigation View to which you want to add a transition.**

   The FrontPage Editor starts up, and the page you double-clicked is displayed.

5. **Click the Normal tab.**

   The current page is displayed in the Normal View, so that you can make your edits.

6. **Choose Format➪Page Transitions.**

   You see the Page Transitions dialog box, as shown in Figure 6-16.

7. **Choose one of the 26 effects by clicking it in the list.**

   Try Strips Right Down.

8. **Leave the Event set to Page Enter (so that the transition occurs each time this page is displayed by a browser).**

9. **In the Duration (Seconds) text box, enter a duration of 10 seconds. (Five to 15 seconds is a good choice.)**

10. **Click the OK button.**

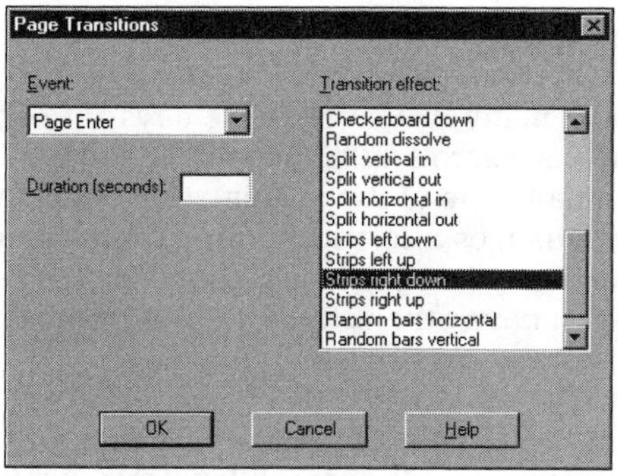

Figure 6-16:
Specify the
kind of
page
transition,
its duration,
and when it
should
occur.

Can't wait, can you? It's time to see the transition. Click the Preview tab at the bottom of the FrontPage Editor and then switch back and forth between this and another page. If the site uses navigation buttons, you can click the Next and Previous buttons to switch. To see the effect well, change the background by applying a different background color or texture to the two pages. (Choose Format⇨Theme, and then click the Use Selected Theme option button in the Choose Theme dialog box.) Figure 6-17 illustrates the Strips Right Down transition.

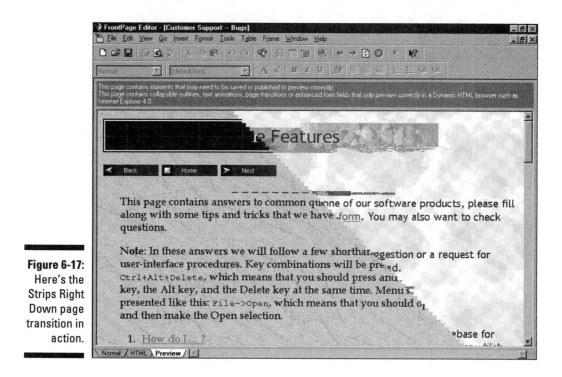

Figure 6-17:
Here's the
Strips Right
Down page
transition in
action.

Creating banner ads

A special effect that you see in many Web sites these days is the banner ad. You may think that name means a scrolling display like the news banner in Times Square. Wrong. It's actually one of those animation effects you see in many Web pages: One image changes into another and then changes back to the original. The effect looks best when you use dissolve as the transition effect between images, but you have other choices. (Note, some banner ads are not animated.)

FrontPage features a Webbot component that makes creating this kind of animation a snap. Also, the effect doesn't demand lengthy download times because you normally apply it to a graphic about the size of a postage stamp. You can also provide an Internet address (a URL) that makes your banner ad a hyperlink. If users click it, they're taken to another Web page.

To create a banner ad, follow these steps:

1. **Choose File⇨New in the FrontPage Editor.**

   The New dialog box opens with a list of page templates.

2. **Double-click Normal Page.**

   The dialog box closes, and a new Web page is displayed in the FrontPage Editor.

3. **Click the Normal tab at the bottom of the FrontPage Editor.**

4. **Choose Insert⇨Active Elements⇨Banner Ad Manager.**

   The Banner Ad Manager dialog box opens. In this dialog box, you specify which graphics you want to display, how quickly, and in what order.

5. **Click the Add button to select your series of images.**

   The Add Image for Banner Ad dialog box opens, displaying any images currently stored in the active Web site.

6. **Choose from the list of images displayed, or click the explorer icon on the right side of the Add Image for Banner Ad dialog box to locate image files stored elsewhere on your system.**

7. **Click the OK button to close the Add Image for Banner Ad dialog box.**

8. **Repeat Steps 5 through 7 until you've created the list of images that dissolve or otherwise transition into one another.**

   Normally, people use just two images for a banner ad.

9. **Choose among the three possible transition effects by using the drop-down list in the Transition section of the Banner Ad Manager dialog box.**

   The default dissolve is best. The venetian blind and exploding/imploding box effects are a bit rough and ugly.

10. **In the Transition section, adjust the transition time from the default 5 to 3 seconds.**

11. **Click the OK button to close the Banner Ad Manager dialog box.**

    To see this effect, you have to save the current page. (Choose File⇨Save.) Then you have to use Internet Explorer to see it in action. (Choose File⇨Preview in Browser.) A sample banner ad is shown in Figure 6-18. The image on the left is just beginning to fade out as the second image (with text in it), replaces it. When fully faded in, the second image looks like the graphic on the right. The overall effect is that the text repeatedly appears and disappears.

To edit a banner ad, right-click the banner ad in the FrontPage Normal View and then choose Java Applet Properties. The Banner Ad Manager dialog box opens.

Figure 6-18: The first and second images of a dissolve effect.

Chapter 7

Themes and Templates (Borrow Only from the Best)

*H*ave you ever tried to write a resume from scratch? The task is much easier if someone gives you a good, polished resume on which to build. This way, you already have all the formatting, organization, and other elements. All you have to do is customize the document to describe your work history. In other words, you can focus on the *content* and not worry about the style.

Visual Studio 6 includes 54 predesigned *themes*. To make your Web site look great, all you have to do is choose one of the themes. Then Visual Studio 6 automatically applies a consistent, professionally designed look to all the buttons, lines, typefaces, backgrounds, and other graphics in your Web site.

Microsoft's graphic designers are among the best in the business — so why not let them transform your Internet site from humdrum to handsome?

However, before you jump in and start selecting a theme, you may want to briefly look at how Microsoft uses the words *theme* and *template*. You may assume that *theme* is just another word for *template*. But, it isn't. Microsoft, which always has a special way with words, has decided to make a distinction. You know what a theme is. A theme is visual *style* that governs the look of things, such as buttons and backgrounds. But what's a template? It's a structure for the *content* of a Web site.

A template, by contrast, provides you with prewritten content: Sometimes it's text, perhaps pictures, and the basic organization of a page. For example, a table of contents page always follows some general rules. It lists the contents of the site and offers a way for the user to click hyperlinks or buttons to navigate to another location in the site. Starting with a template enables you to modify the page to suit yourself. But you're not in danger of forgetting an important component of such a page, or going radically off the rails when organizing the page.

To muddy the waters a little, FrontPage includes a Web Wizard that combines a theme with a set of predefined template pages. The result is a Personal Web or a Corporate Presence Web that you can then customize, adjusting both the visuals (the theme) and the content (the templates) to suit your needs. Chapter 6 explores the Web Wizard in detail.

(To muddy the waters even further, Visual Studio 6 also includes *layouts* and *style sheets*, two additional categories related to templates and themes, but don't give yourself a headache. You get to these concepts later in this chapter in the sections "Understanding Layouts and Navigation Bars" and "Working with Style Sheets.")

Using Visual Studio 6's Built-in Themes

Both FrontPage and Visual InterDev include 54 themes, and you can choose which ones to add during the Visual Studio 6 setup process. To add the full set of themes after installing Visual Studio 6, merely insert the Visual Studio 6 CD and re-run setup, this time choosing the themes.

The themes range from the sublime to the fairly ridiculous. You can find themes with such names as Bubbles, Cactus, Construction Zone, Tidepool, and Safari. Choose whatever look fits with the image you want your Web site to project. Bubbles is particularly appropriate if you sell 1950s retro lawn furniture. Other themes are less specific in their appeal.

Adding a theme to a Web site couldn't be easier. To select a theme, follow these steps:

1. **Have an idea of the feeling you want to convey to people who visit your site.**

2. **Load your project into the FrontPage Explorer.**

   If you're working in the FrontPage Editor, choose Tools⇨Show FrontPage Explorer. If the Web isn't currently loaded in Explorer, choose File⇨Open FrontPage Web in Explorer.

3. **In the Views pane, click Themes, as shown in Figure 7-1.**

   The Themes dialog box opens, displaying a list of all 54 built-in themes, and previewing the selected theme in a large, right pane.

4. **Click the Use Selected Theme option button.**

5. **Preview the themes by clicking their names in the list box.**

   Each theme that you click is displayed as a sample in the right pane.

6. **After you've found a theme you like, click the Apply button.**

   FrontPage takes a few seconds to apply that theme to the current Web.

Making minor design adjustments

Each theme can be quickly adjusted. You can tone down the colors; turn off animation and simplify the design; or remove the textured background. Perhaps you like everything about a theme except the background, for example. You can remove the background, or replace it with a different one. Or, maybe you're using a slow server or a slow Internet connection and you want to simplify the graphics so that your Web pages load faster when visitors browse your site. Whatever your reason, changing a theme is easy.

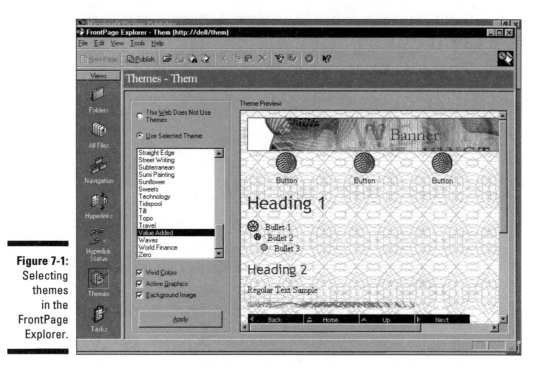

Figure 7-1:
Selecting themes in the FrontPage Explorer.

Follow these steps to modify the look of a theme:

1. **Decide if you want to emphasize the text in your Web by muting elements of the theme's graphics.**

2. **If you want less vivid colors, deselect the Vivid Colors check box (refer to Figure 7-1).**

3. **If you want no animation, and also want to simplify buttons and other designs, deselect the Active Graphics check box.**

   The difference between Active Graphics selected or deselected is shown in Figure 7-2. Adjusting the amount of detail is easy.

Figure 7-2:
Turn the Active Graphics option on (top) or turn it off (bottom).

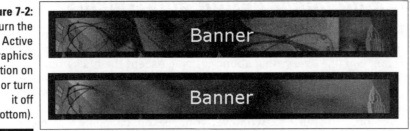

4. **If you want to remove background wallpaper from your pages, deselect the Background Image check box.**

   A color compatible with your theme remains in the background. Just the *texture* disappears.

If you want to look at additional themes, check out this page in the Microsoft Web site. The latest themes are posted here for you to download:

`www.microsoft.com/frontpage/resources/ttpack.htm`

Previewing pages with themes

After you've applied a new theme, follow these steps to see how your new theme looks in the various pages of your site:

1. **Click the FrontPage Explorer Navigation icon in the Explorer Views (left) pane.**

   A tree diagram appears, showing all the pages in the current Web and their relationships.

2. **Double-click one of the pages (an .Htm filename) listed under Name.**

   That page appears in the FrontPage Editor.

Follow Steps 1 and 2 to view any other pages in your Web. (You can also find a list of recently viewed pages if you drop down the FrontPage Editor File menu.)

Living dangerously: Applying themes to individual pages

The idea of a theme is to make your site look better. For example, a theme provides consistency of design across all the pages of your site. But perhaps you have a reason to violate that consistency. Maybe you've got a page where some really serious business is going on. The customer is about to order something, and you want no distractions — just a white background and black text. You think the customer may spend more money if the order form is stark.

Follow these steps to remove a theme from an individual page, while leaving it applied to the rest of your site:

1. **Figure out which pages in your Web (if any) should be simple and contain no theme at all.**

2. **In the FrontPage Editor, choose Format⇨Theme.**

   The Themes dialog box opens, displaying a list of all 54 built-in themes and previewing the selected theme in a large right pane.

3. **Click the option button labeled This Page Does Not Use Themes.**

   The Theme Preview pane goes blank.

4. **Click the OK button to close the Themes dialog box.**

You can also apply different themes to different pages in your site. Follow the preceding Steps 1 through 4, but in Step 3, click the option button labeled Use Selected Theme. Beware, though. Remember that by mixing more than one theme in your Web site, you're going further out on a limb than by just turning off the theme. Mix themes and you're in danger of losing one of the great benefits of themes: consistency of design.

Living even more dangerously: Messing with theme code

If you're really the adventurous type, you can modify individual elements within a page. Say you've decided, in your wisdom, that you want a particular button on a particular page to violate the general rule for buttons in the theme. You want it to be blue (when all the other buttons are green). Click the HTML tab in the FrontPage Editor. Locate the button's definition in the source code. (For details about working with HTML code, see Chapter 8.)

After you find the code that describes the button, edit the COLOR attribute from GREEN to BLUE. To make these kinds of changes, though, you need to understand HTML programming. If you're planning on going down to this level, you may want to pick up a copy of *HTML For Dummies,* 3rd Edition by Ed Tittel and Steve James (IDG Books Worldwide, Inc.).

Themes in Visual InterDev

FrontPage doesn't have the exclusive contract for themes in Visual Studio 6. Themes can also be added if you're working in Visual InterDev. To use a theme in Visual InterDev, follow these steps:

1. **Choose File⇨New Project in Visual InterDev.**

   The New Project dialog box opens with two panes.

2. **Click the OK button to close the dialog box.**

   New Web Project and Sample App Wizard icons appear in the right pane.

3. **Double-click New Web Project in the right pane.**

   The Web Project Wizard appears.

4. **Your active Web server is displayed.**

   Type in the correct Web server if it's not displayed. The wizard contacts your server, and the second page of the wizard is displayed.

5. **Type in a name for your new project and click Next.**

   The Apply a Layout page appears.

6. **Click Next.**

   The Apply a Theme page appears, as shown in Figure 7-3. Notice that the preview doesn't show the entire page, as does the FrontPage Theme preview.

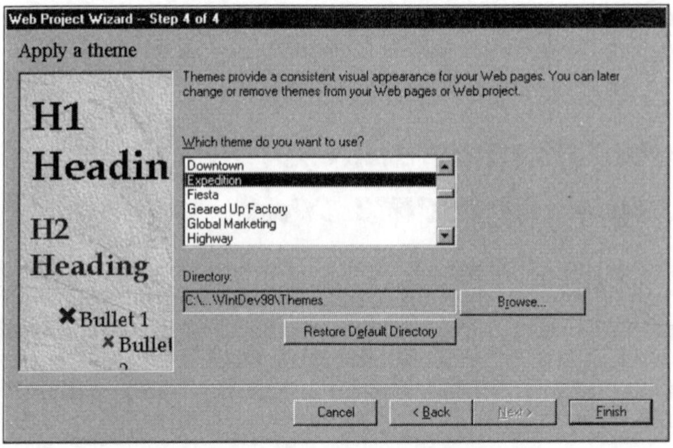

Figure 7-3:
The Visual
InterDev
version of
the Theme
dialog box.

7. **Click Finish to close the Wizard and see the new Web site, with your chosen theme in Visual InterDev.**

The Microsoft themes are generally effective, sometimes even gorgeous. But if you've got the artistic talent (or *think* you do), you may want to strike out and create your own theme. To see how to do this, you first want to look at the section later in this chapter titled "Working with Style Sheets." Then go to the end of the chapter and check out the section titled "Customizing Themes."

Templates: Saving Yourself a Lot of Time and Trouble

Similar to themes, templates are good ways to ensure consistency. But where a theme ensures a consistent look, a template ensures consistent (or at least organized and logical) content. A template in Visual Studio 6 is similar to a template in a word processor. For example, Word for Windows contains many templates: invoice, fax, memo, letter, and many others. Likewise, Visual Studio 6 includes a variety of common Web page templates: confirmation form, feedback page, FAQ, guest book, search page, and many more.

Choosing a built-in template

Although Visual InterDev has only four templates at the time of this writing, FrontPage has many. To use one of the templates in FrontPage, follow these steps:

1. **Run the FrontPage Editor.**

2. **Choose File⇨New.**

   The New dialog box opens, as shown in Figure 7-4. This dialog box includes many templates from which you can choose.

3. **Click a template to see a preview.**

   A thumbnail preview of the currently selected template appears in the Preview area of the New dialog box.

4. **Double-click the template you're interested in.**

   The New dialog box closes, and the template appears in the FrontPage Editor.

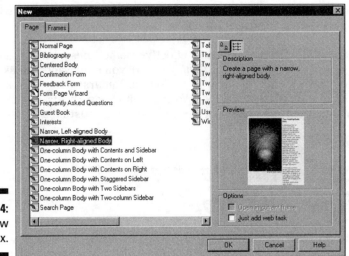

Figure 7-4:
The New
dialog box.

At this point, you can modify the template by replacing the headline, body text, and/or graphics that the template provides with your own, as shown in Figure 7-5.

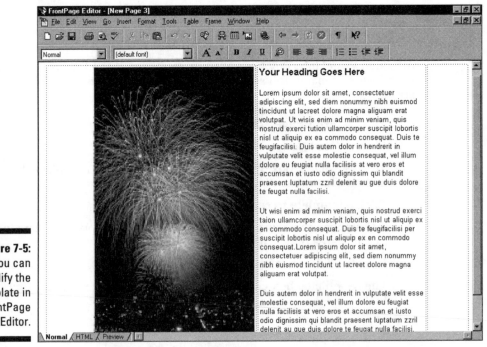

Figure 7-5:
You can
modify the
template in
FrontPage
Editor.

If you're curious about the underpinnings of this kind of page, the Narrow Right-Aligned Body template is built on a table that's divided into two large cells. Click the HTML tab in the FrontPage Editor and you see this table definition:

```
<table border="0" cellpadding="3" width="100%">
<td align="right" valign="top" width="50%">
<td valign="top" width="40%">
```

Modifying a template

You can use cut and paste techniques to modify an existing template. Load a template into FrontPage, as described in the section "Choosing a built-in template," earlier in this chapter. Then follow these steps to personalize the template:

1. **Click the Normal tab in the FrontPage Editor.**

   The page is ready to be edited.

2. **Select the template's headline by dragging your mouse over it (or pressing Shift+Arrow Keys).**

3. **Type in your new headline.**

   The existing, selected headline disappears and is replaced with whatever text you type in.

4. **Adjust the size of the new headline by selecting it and then clicking the Increase Text Size Icon (the large *A* on the FrontPage Format Toolbar).**

   If the Format Toolbar isn't visible, choose View⇨Format Toolbar.

   The headline grows larger each time you click the A icon.

You can also use the other facilities on the Format Toolbar to change the text color, style, and font, and otherwise manipulate the text, such as centering it.

Most of the familiar shortcut keys that work in word processors also work in the FrontPage Normal View. You can use Ctrl+C (copy), Ctrl+V (paste), Ctrl+X (cut), Ctrl+Z (undo), Ctrl+B (boldface), Ctrl+I (italics).

Creating your own templates

If you're working with other people to create or maintain a Web site, one very important consideration is that new pages you add to the site should resemble existing pages. In other words, you use themes and templates to enforce a consistent look and feel across the entire Web site. A visitor shouldn't find that some of your pages have body text in 18–point Arial and other pages feature body text in 10–point Times Roman typefaces.

If you establish templates for your Web, you can ask that everyone use those templates as the basis for creating new pages. You can see how to create your own themes at the end of this chapter in the section "Modifying an existing theme." To create your own template, follow these steps:

1. **Choose File⇨New from the FrontPage menu bar.**

   The New dialog box opens.

2. **Double-click the Normal Page option in the list on the left pane in the New dialog box.**

   The New dialog box closes, and a new, blank page appears in the FrontPage Editor.

3. **Click the Normal tab at the bottom of the FrontPage Editor.**

   The page is now ready for you to add content and structure.

4. **Add whatever Webbots, headlines, text, graphics, or other components that you want to the page.**

   After you're finished, you have your new template.

5. **Save the template by choosing File⇨Save As and then clicking the As Template button.**

   The Save As dialog box opens, as shown in Figure 7-6.

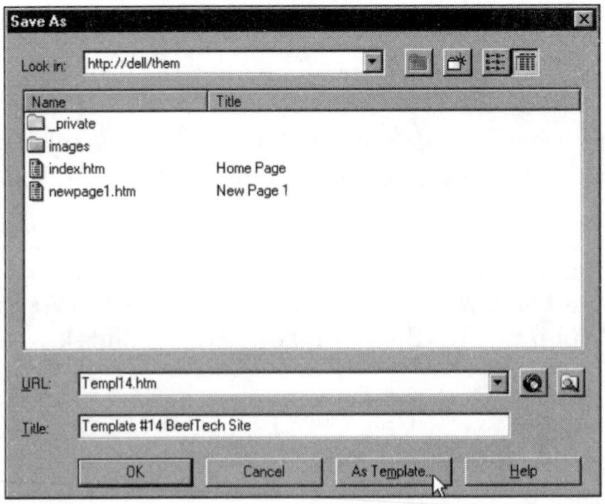

Figure 7-6: Click the As Template button to save a template.

6. **Add a description of the purpose of this template in the Save As dialog box.**

7. **Click the OK button.**

   If you have any graphics or background images in this template, the Save Embedded Files dialog box opens.

8. **Click the OK button in the Save Embedded Files dialog box to keep the necessary graphics together with your template.**

   The template is now saved.

Other users (or you later) may load and modify this page — using it as a basis for creating a new page that uses the same typestyles and that subdivides the page in the same fashion as your template (if you use frames, forms, tables, Navigation Bars, or other kinds of subdivisions).

Where is the new template when you want to use it again? It's been inserted right there in the list of predefined templates supplied with FrontPage. To see the template you just created, choose File⇨New and look at the list of templates in the New dialog box. You see that your template is now listed, as shown in Figure 7-7.

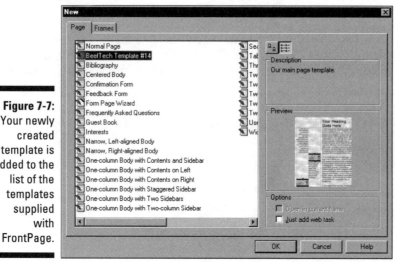

Figure 7-7:
Your newly created template is added to the list of the templates supplied with FrontPage.

Understanding Layouts and Navigation Bars

A *layout* is an arrangement of navigation bars. A layout creates a default placement of Navigation Bars in each page of your site. (A *Navigation Bar* is a set of hyperlinks that a visitor can click in order to jump to other locations in your Web site. A Navigation Bar can take several forms. For example, it can be a set of buttons with such labels as Next and Previous, or a Table of Contents list of pages in your site.) In Visual InterDev, you have three ways to apply a layout:

- ✓ **Choose File⇨New Project.** The New Project Wizard asks you whether you want to apply a layout during the series of four dialog boxes displayed as it creates the new project.

- ✓ **Apply (or modify) a layout in an existing project.** Right-click the name of the project (it's the name in boldface) in the Project Explorer and then choose Apply Theme and Layout from the context menu.

- ✓ **Apply (or modify) a layout for an individual page.** Right-click the name of the page in the Project Explorer and then choose Apply Theme and Layout from the context menu. You see the Apply Theme and Layout dialog box, shown in Figure 7-8.

The closest thing in FrontPage to the Visual InterDev layouts is the Navigation Bar Webbot described in Chapter 6. To add (or modify) a Navigation Bar in FrontPage, choose Insert⇨Navigation Bar. You see the Navigation Bar Properties dialog box.

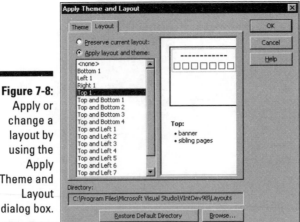

Figure 7-8:
Apply or change a layout by using the Apply Theme and Layout dialog box.

Working with Style Sheets

Style sheets are not a Microsoft invention, nor are they a feature found only in Visual Studio 6. A style sheet is a feature of HTML, the standard language of Internet communication. (**Hint:** Themes are a kind of style sheet.)

A *style sheet* enables you to redefine most of the elements (commands, or *tags*) in the HTML language. HTML consists of many elements that define the way text and graphics appear when loaded into a browser. The word *element* in HTML means a particular kind of text or graphic. You have a paragraph element, a blank line element, and so on. For example, the <H1> element means *level-1 headline,* and all text between <H1> and </H1> is the largest of the headlines in a Web page. (The ending</H1> element is a signal to stop using the H1 format and revert to body text, or if you see another element, use that element's definition.)

Reaping the benefits of style sheets

Why would you want to use a style sheet to redefine standard HTML elements? You get the following three primary benefits from using styles:

- **Make global format definitions:** A style sheet makes life easier for the Web designer and also for anyone who has to maintain a Web. Suppose that you want all your level-1 headlines to be green throughout your Web site. You can go through and change each <H1> in all your Web pages to <H1 color="green">, but that process is tedious and — be honest — not very efficient, either. Instead, you can redefine the meaning of <H1> in a style sheet and then import that style sheet into your FrontPage Web. That way, all your level-1 headlines turn green, without further effort on your part.

- **Edit formatting throughout a Web site:** If you make a global formatting definition and then later decide that all <H1> headlines should instead be blue, the only thing you have to do is make one little change to the style sheet: Change <H1 color="green"> to <H1 color="blue">.

- **Format in ways that HTML can't:** The final benefit of using styles is that you can specify formats that are simply not part of the HTML language, such as kerning (adjusting the spaces between individual letters) or leading (adjusting the space between lines of text). For an example of kerning, see the section "Redefining a single HTML element" later in this chapter.

When you include a style sheet in a Web page, a Web page may or may not be changed. Only those elements in the page that have a corresponding style redefinition in the style sheet change. Those elements are forced to conform to the format that the style sheet specifies.

Now it can be revealed. Themes are style sheets. A theme is simply a professionally designed series of Web page graphic elements. These elements are then specified in a style sheet, which is attached to each page in a Web. See the first few paragraphs in the introduction to this chapter for a description of themes.

Creating a cascading style sheet in FrontPage

A style sheet that can be applied to many Web pages at the same time (or an entire Web) is called a *cascading style sheet*. This type of style sheet touches multiple objects, like water cascading over a series of ledges.

To understand how to create a style sheet in FrontPage, no better way exists than to build one. So, follow these steps:

1. **Run Windows Notepad by clicking the Windows Start button and then choosing Programs⇨Accessories⇨Notepad.**

   Notepad appears. Notepad is a simple text document tool that's easy to use to create a style sheet.

2. **Type this:** H1 { color: green }

   This text redefines <H1> so that level-1 heads are always green.

   Note: You enclose the redefinition of the HTML element within braces {}. If you want to define several attributes of an HTML element at the same time, just separate them with semicolons, like this:

   ```
   H2 { font-size: large; color: red }
   ```

3. **In Notepad, choose File⇨Save As, and save the file as Mystyle.Css.**

   By saving the file with the .Css extension on its filename, you save it as a cascading style sheet.

4. **Choose File⇨Exit to close Notepad.**

That's it. You've now got a style sheet that makes all the level-1 headlines green in any page, Web, or project that you attach this style sheet to.

Of course, you can include many more HTML element redefinitions in a style sheet file. You can always rerun Notepad and edit the .Css file, adding to it or changing definitions.

Attaching a cascading style sheet to a page in FrontPage

If you want to enforce a set of styles to a Web page, you can add a style sheet to that page. The process of attaching a style sheet to a Web page is quite simple. To see how to do it, follow these steps:

1. **Run the FrontPage Editor.**

2. **Choose File⇨New.**

   The New dialog box opens.

3. **Double-click the Normal Page option in the list on the left pane in the New dialog box.**

   The New dialog box closes, and a new, blank page appears.

4. **Click the Normal tab at the bottom of the FrontPage Editor.**

   The page is now ready for you to add content and structure.

5. **Create a level-1 headline in the current page.**

   You can look at this heading to see the before-and-after effect of attaching the .Css file to this Web.

6. **Type** THIS IS A LEVEL ONE HEADLINE **into the Web page.**

7. **Drag your mouse across the headline to select it.**

   The words reverse to white on black after they're selected.

8. **In the Change Style drop-down list on the left side of the Format Toolbar, choose Heading 1, as shown in Figure 7-9.**

   If the Format Toolbar isn't visible, choose View⇨Format Toolbar.

9. **Click the HTML tab in the FrontPage Editor.**

10. **Near the top of your HTML code, anywhere between the** <HEAD> **and** </HEAD> **elements, type this:**

    ```
    <link REL="stylesheet" HREF="c:\mysheet.css"
          TYPE="text/css">
    ```

    Use whatever path (like D:\) and filename you gave to your style sheet, instead of c:\mysheet.css in the line that you type.

11. **Click the Preview tab in the FrontPage Editor to see your headline turn green.**

12. **Repeat Steps 9 and 10 to add the style sheet to any other pages in your Web.**

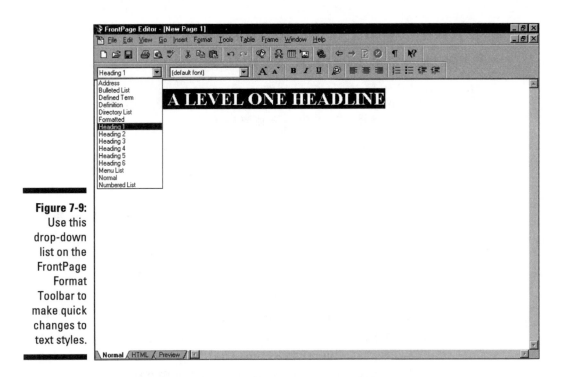

FrontPage Editor - [New Page 1]

File Edit View Go Insert Format Tools Table Frame Window Help

Heading 1   [default font]

Address
Bulleted List
Defined Term
Definition
Directory List
Formatted
Heading 1
Heading 2
Heading 3
Heading 4
Heading 5
Heading 6
Menu List
Normal
Numbered List

A LEVEL ONE HEADLINE

Normal / HTML / Preview /

Figure 7-9:
Use this
drop-down
list on the
FrontPage
Format
Toolbar to
make quick
changes to
text styles.

Adding an in-line style sheet

You can also insert (or *embed*) a style directly into the HTML code of a single page. The result is called an *in-line style*. It redefines the styles for that particular page. In fact, if the page also has a linked cascading style sheet attached to it, your in-line style overrules any styles defined in the .CSS.

To add an in-line style, follow these steps:

1. **In the FrontPage Editor, click the HTML tab.**

2. **Near the top of your HTML code, anywhere between the** <HEAD> **and** </HEAD> **elements, type this:**

```
<style>
  <!--
    H1 { font-size: small; color: red }
  -->
</style>
```

3. **Click the Preview tab in the FrontPage Editor to see any level-1 headline turn small and red.**

   Any redefinitions that you add between the ⟨!-- and --⟩ elements also take effect throughout the page.

Redefining a single HTML element

You can redefine HTML elements for multiple pages by linking the pages to a single .Css cascading style sheet file. Or, you can redefine a single page using an in-line style element placed between the ⟨HEAD⟩ and ⟨/HEAD⟩ elements (the header) of that page.

Anything between the ⟨HEAD⟩ and ⟨/HEAD⟩ commands in HTML source code is called the page's *header*. (Following the header is the *body* of the page, defined by the ⟨BODY⟩ and ⟨/BODY⟩ elements.) You put a link to a cascading style sheet or an in-line STYLE element in the header. Browsers read the header first. This way, the browser finds any redefinitions you've put into your style sheet before trying to interpret the actual body of the page where it must apply those redefinitions.

But can you just redefine *a single element* within a page, and yet not affect any other uses of that element in the page? You bet. You can stick a STYLE command right inside the element you want to redefine, like this:

```
<H1 STYLE="color: lightgreen"> THIS HEAD IS GREEN</H1>
```

This way you're only affecting that particular H1 headline. No other headlines on the page turn green.

Notice that three different punctuations are used (ugh!), depending on whether you're defining a style in a cascading style sheet (.Css) file, in a header (for the whole page), or in just a single element:

✔ **Defining a style for a .Css file:**

```
H1 { color: green }
```

✔ **Defining a style for a single page (by putting this in the header of the page):**

```
<style>
<!--
H1 {color: green}
-->
</style>
```

> ✔ **Defining a style for a single element:**
>
> ```
> <H1 STYLE="color: green">
> ```

Sometimes you use quotation marks; sometimes you don't. Sometimes you need braces; sometimes you don't. This d esign is impulsive and clumsy, but you have to live with dozens of these kinds of exceptions in computer languages. Luckily, the trend in many of today's applications and languages is toward wizards and Property dialog boxes. They can memorize all the exceptions and other kinks in the diction, syntax, and punctuation in computer languages. Let the wizards worry about it.

Here's a valuable technique you can use to *kern* the headlines on your pages. On a headline-by-headline basis, you can squeeze (kern) the letters of the headline together a little. This technique makes the headline easier to read and looks more professional. Newspapers and magazines frequently kern their heads. Studies have shown that most people read whole words, not individual letters. They scan *word shapes.* And if you move the letters a little closer together, it generally creates a more distinctive word shape. Hence: more readable headlines.

Kerning is one of those formatting tricks that you can't accomplish by using ordinary HTML commands, but that you can define with a style. You use *negative* letter spacing to pull the characters in your headline a little closer together, as in the following example:

```
<h1>THIS HEADLINE IS NOT KERNED</h1>
<h1 STYLE="letter-spacing:-1pt">THIS HEADLINE IS
        KERNED</h1>
```

Click the HTML tab on the bottom of the FrontPage Editor and then type the preceding HTML code into a page in FrontPage, somewhere between the `<BODY>` and `</BODY>` commands. Then click the Preview tab, and you can see the results, as shown in Figure 7-10.

Figure 7-10:
You have to use a `STYLE` command to kern your headline.

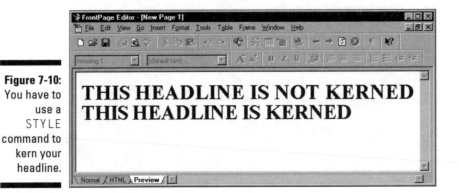

For a complete reference to style sheet commands and conventions, visit this site:

www.htmlhelp.com/reference/css

FrontPage's less-than-stellar stylesheet utility

FrontPage includes a Format Stylesheet dialog box that you can use, instead of typing in the HTML yourself. Click the Style button in the Format Stylesheet dialog box. A second Style dialog box opens, where you can redefine various elements of the current page. To bring up the Format Stylesheet dialog box, choose Format➪Stylesheet.

Unfortunately, the FrontPage Format Stylesheet utility is highly limited. It contains only a small set of elements and is rather clumsy. You don't, for example, get a preview of the styles as you redefine them. The Style Sheet Editor in Visual InterDev is by far superior. It's a utility that deserves the name *utility*.

Using Visual InterDev's superior Style Sheet Editor

The Visual InterDev Style Sheet Editor utility is superior to FrontPage's in several ways. Primarily, it's more logically arranged, includes all the HTML tags you're likely to want to redefine, and has an excellent preview window. Visual InterDev's Style Sheet Editor can be activated in two ways:

✔ Choose File➪Open File and then open a file that ends with .Css.

✔ Choose File➪New File, select Visual InterDev in the left pane of the New File dialog box, and then double-click the Style Sheet icon in the right pane of that dialog box.

To create a new style sheet using the Visual InterDev Style Sheet Editor, follow these steps:

1. **In Visual InterDev, choose File➪New File.**

   The New File dialog box opens.

2. **Click Visual InterDev in the left pane.**

   The right pane displays the three kinds of default files that you can create.

3. **Double-click the Style Sheet icon in the right pane of the New File dialog box.**

   You can see the Style Sheet dialog box, as shown in Figure 7-11.

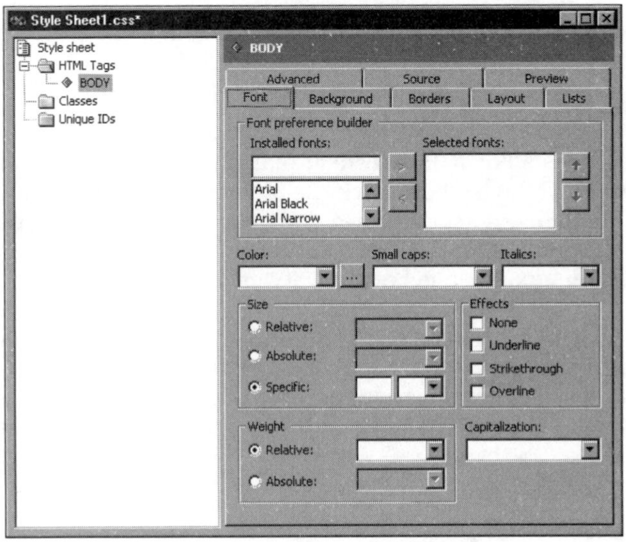

Figure 7-11:
Use this
dialog box
in Visual
InterDev to
redefine
HTML
elements
and create
a style
sheet.

4. **Redefine whatever HTML elements you want to change by using the various tabs, drop-down lists, and check boxes displayed in the dialog box shown in Figure 7-11.**

5. **After you're finished, click the x in the upper-right corner of the style sheet dialog box to close it.**

   A new dialog box opens (titled Microsoft Development Environment), asking whether you want to save your changes.

6. **Click the Yes button to save your changes.**

   The new .Css file appears in your Visual InterDev Project Explorer, under the folder named Miscellaneous Files.

Adding a Style Sheet to a Web page in Visual InterDev

Visual InterDev uses an unusual technique for adding a cascading style sheet (a .Css file) to a Web page. Follow these steps to link a Web page in the Visual InterDev Editor to a .Css file listed in the Visual InterDev Project Explorer:

1. **Click the Source tab at the bottom of the Visual InterDev Editor window that's displaying a Web page you want to link to a cascading style sheet.**

   The HTML source code for the Web page is displayed in the Editor window.

2. **Locate the HTML elements <HEAD> and </HEAD> near the top of the HTML source code.**

3. **Drag the style sheet's icon (in the Visual InterDev Project Explorer) into the HTML code in the Editor window, and drop the icon just to the left of the < symbol in the </HEAD> element in the source code.**

   This action puts the style into this page's header.

   The reason for being so specific about where to drop the style sheet icon within the HTML header is that if you drop it _between_ an existing pair of < and > symbols in the source code, the style sheet won't work. You made the style sheet link part of the definition of some other element in the header. It's also likely that you may damage the other element as well — so it won't work either.

4. **Click the Quick View tab at the bottom of the Visual InterDev Editor window for the Web page into which you just dropped the link.**

   You see the results of your new link to the style sheet in the Editor window.

Creating Style Classes

The style classes feature may seem like overkill to you; it does to me. But, you can probably imagine a Web site so complex that creating style classes would be valuable.

If a Web site has hundreds of pages and you want to simplify the process of modifying its appearance, you may consider creating some style classes. With a _style class,_ you can specify more than one redefinition of an HTML element. You give each redefinition a unique name; then you can have more than one style for an <H2> headline, for example. For instance, you can define three H2 headline style classes, such as H2.WARNING, H2.REMINDER, and H2.BRAGGING. Each of these versions of an H2 headline may use a different typeface or a different color. This style class technique is probably overkill, though, for small or medium-size Web sites.

The basic idea of styles is that you can redefine the standard HTML elements to suit your needs.

To understand what style classes do, try an example. Assume that the boss lays down the law. She says: All second-level headlines in our Web site must be colored red and be 18 pt. large.

That's easy enough. Also, instead of creating a separate .Css file, use the in-line style. With an in-line style, you just type the ⟨STYLE⟩ element in a page's header (between the ⟨HEAD⟩ and ⟨/HEAD⟩ elements near the top of a page's HTML source code).

To redefine the ⟨H2⟩ element the way the boss wants it, use FrontPage for this example and follow these steps:

1. **Start the FrontPage Editor.**

2. **Choose File⇨New.**

   The New dialog box opens.

3. **Double-click the Normal Page option in the list on the left pane.**

   The New dialog box closes, and a new, blank page appears in the FrontPage Editor.

4. **Click the HTML tab at the bottom of the FrontPage Editor.**

   The page is now ready for you to add content and structure.

5. **Locate the HTML element ⟨/HEAD⟩ near the top of the HTML source code.**

6. **Just to the left of the ⟨/HEAD⟩ element, type this:**

   ```
   <STYLE> H2 { font-size: 18pt; color: red }</STYLE>
   ```

7. **Click the Normal tab at the bottom of the Editor window and type the following text:**

   ```
   I'M A LEVEL-1 HEAD
   I'M A LEVEL-2 HEAD (WARNING)
   I'M A LEVEL-2 HEAD (REMINDER)
   I'M A LEVEL-2 HEAD (BRAGGING)
   ```

8. **Select the level-1 headline by dragging your mouse over it.**

   The headline reverses to white letters on a black background.

9. **In the Change Style drop-down list on the left side of the Format Toolbar, choose Heading 1.**

   If the Format Toolbar isn't visible, choose View⇨Format Toolbar.

   The headline is formatted as a standard level-1 head.

10. **Select all three level-2 headlines by dragging your mouse over them.**

11. **In the Change Style drop-down list on the left side of the Format Toolbar, choose Heading 2.**

    The headlines are *not* formatted as standard level-2 heads. Instead, they follow the rules of the STYLE element that you defined in Step 6.

The boss takes a look at the results and announces: "Too much red, not enough variety!" I never said the boss wasn't whimsical. Here's what she wants now: If a second-level headline is a warning, leave it red. If it's just a reminder, make it green. And if it's a bragging headline about how great our products are, make it blue.

But, boss! Our Web site has 236 pages. (Whine. Whine.) Do you want me to go through each page and change the colors of all the hundreds of headlines one by one, by hand!!??? (You know the answer.)

If you find yourself in a situation that dictates such changes, the solution is to use a style sheet to redefine <H2> into *three* different *classes* of the <H2> style. To do that, follow these steps to change the STYLE definition in Step 6 of the preceding example:

1. **Click the HTML tab at the bottom of the FrontPage Editor to return to Code View.**

2. **Locate the <STYLE> element in the header of this page.**

3. **Replace the existing style definition, which is**

   ```
   <STYLE> H2 { font-size: 11pt; color: red }</STYLE>
   ```

   with the following new definition:

   ```
   <STYLE>
   <!--
   H2.WARNING {font-size: 11pt; color: red}
   H2.REMINDER {font-size: 11pt; color: green}
   H2.BRAGGING {font-size: 11pt; color: blue}
   -->
   </STYLE>
   ```

   Now you can use H2 in your body text and add a CLASS command to it. CLASS defines which of the three new flavors of H2 you're referring to.

4. **Change the first <H2> element from <H2> to the class that you want to use, like this:**

   ```
   <H2 CLASS=WARNING>
   <H2 CLASS=REMINDER>
   <H2 CLASS=BRAGGING>
   ```

Now your HTML code for the entire page looks something like this:

```
<html>
<head>
<title>Styles</title>
<style>
<!--
H2.WARNING {font-size: 11pt; color: red}
H2.REMINDER {font-size: 11pt; color: green}
H2.BRAGGING {font-size: 11pt; color: blue}
-->
</style>
</head>

<body>
<h1>I'M A LEVEL-1 HEAD</h1>
<h2 CLASS="WARNING">I'M A LEVEL-2 HEAD (WARNING)</h2>
<h2 CLASS="REMINDER">I'M A LEVEL-2 HEAD
(REMINDER)</h2>
<h2 CLASS="BRAGGING">I'M A LEVEL-2 HEAD (BRAGGING)
</h2></body>
</html>
```

5. **Click the Normal or Preview tab to see the various colors of your
   <H2> heads.**

Your headings are now just what the boss wants.

Customizing Themes

As you know, Visual Studio 6 ships with 54 themes. Many of them are
excellent. But perhaps you decide to create your own theme by making
some serious (and great) modifications to one of the Microsoft 54. The
following sections show you how to customize themes.

Modifying an existing theme

The easiest way to modify a theme is to first copy an existing theme to a
new folder. You can find all the Visual InterDev Themes located in:

```
C:\Program Files\Microsoft Visual Studio\VIntDev98\Themes
```

(The location may not be C:\ or even Program Files if you modified the
default directory during Visual Studio 6 setup.)

Each predesigned theme is located in its own folder, and the folders are named after the theme. So, if you like the Nature theme, copy the following folder:

```
C:\Program Files\Microsoft Visual
          Studio\VIntDev98\Themes\Nature
```

And paste it to the following folder (for example):

```
C:\Temp\Nature
```

Now you can modify this theme without worrying that you'll mess up the original.

Import the copy of the theme into Visual InterDev. To see the steps necessary to add a theme when creating a Visual InterDev project, see the section "Themes in Visual InterDev," earlier in this chapter. Choose the theme using the Visual InterDev Apply Theme and Layout dialog box.

To add a theme to an existing Visual InterDev project, right-click the project's name (which is in boldface) in the Project Explorer. Then choose Apply Theme and Layout from the context menu. (You must be working online — connected to the server — or the Apply Theme and Layout option is gray, disabled, and doesn't work.) Choose the theme using the Visual InterDev Apply Theme and Layout dialog box.

Adding a theme to a Visual InterDev project

By default, the Visual InterDev Apply Theme and Layout dialog box displays the themes located in the default theme folder (`C:\Program Files\Microsoft Visual Studio\VIntDev98\Themes`). However, you want to import your *copy* of a theme. So, click the Browse button in that dialog box. Then you can locate the copy of the theme that you made earlier.

After you create a Visual InterDev project and specify a theme (or add a theme to an existing project), all the files necessary for the theme are copied to the project's directory. The files copied include:

- ✔ The .Css files that define the elements of the theme
- ✔ All the smaller graphics (usually .Gif files) used for buttons, bullets, lines, and other small elements
- ✔ The larger background (wallpaper) graphic (usually a .Jpg file)
- ✔ A couple of information (.Inf and a duplicate .Utf8) files that describe the version, file type, and title of the theme

You can see the files that have been copied into your project because they're listed in the Project Explorer within the folder named Themes, as shown in Figure 7-12.

One easy way to quickly survey all the .Gif files used in a theme is to use the Windows Explorer View as Web Page option. In Windows Explorer, choose View⇨as Web Page. Then you can see a sample view of any .Gif or .Jpg that you select in Explorer, as shown in Figure 7-13. (*Note:* If the View as Web Page option isn't available on your Explorer's View menu, you don't have the latest version of Windows. You won't be able to use this tip and will have to view the .Gif and .Jpg files using a graphics program instead.)

You have three main ways to modify a theme after it's in your project's folder:

- **Delete:** Suppose that you don't like the .Gif file that's used for an element. You can just delete it. Note, however, that if an element is referenced in a theme — such as the large bullet (Nabull1.Gif) in the Nature theme — but that graphic file is missing, the browser may display a broken image link symbol. So be sure to preview your Web pages if you modify a theme.

- **Replace:** Replacing is a different approach. Replace the .Gif or .Jpg file with one of your own. Use the same filename and your file is applied to the site rather than the original.

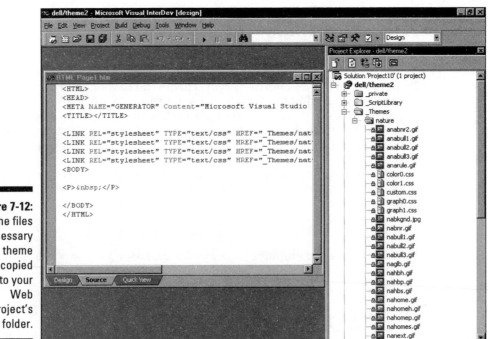

Figure 7-12:
All the files necessary for a theme are copied into your Web project's folder.

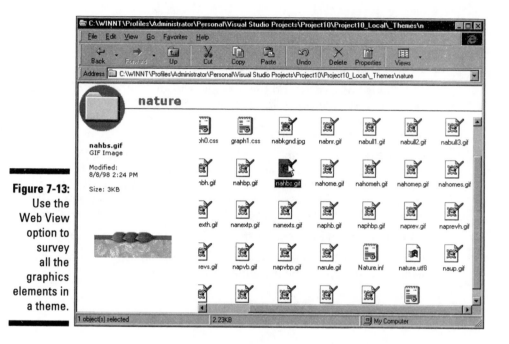

Figure 7-13:
Use the
Web View
option to
survey
all the
graphics
elements in
a theme.

> ✔ **Edit:** A third technique is to edit the .Css files, replacing the reference
> to an existing .Gif or .Jpg graphic with the name of some other .Gif or
> .Jpg file that you prefer. If you do this, make sure that you include your
> replacement graphic file in the folder so that the browser can find it
> when necessary.

Editing a theme's .Css file

You may like the Microsoft Sunflower theme just as it is. Or, you may really
dislike that large oval orange bullet (but like everything else). If you want to
make changes to a theme, you can go right into its cascading style sheet file
and make your adjustments. Then, after you're done, your changes are
displayed on each page in the Web where the theme is used.

To edit a theme's .Css file, follow these steps:

1. **Apply the Nature theme to a Visual InterDev project, as described in
   the section "Modifying an existing theme," earlier in this chapter.**

2. **Look in the Visual InterDev Project Explorer until you locate**
   `Theme.Css`. **It's located under the themes/Nature folders in the
   Project Explorer.**

3. **Right-click** Theme.Css **and choose Open With from the context menu.**

The Open With dialog box opens.

4. **Double-click Source Code (Text) Editor.**

The dialog box closes, and the .Css file is loaded into an editor where you can make changes to it, as shown in Figure 7-14. To change the background wallpaper, you can change Nabkgnd.Jpg to the name of a wallpaper file that you prefer.

Depending on how permissions are set up for the project, Visual InterDev may display a dialog box asking whether you want to view a read-only version of the .Css file (you can't change it), or if you want an editable version. Choose the editable version, or ask your network administrator to give you access if you can't open an editable version.

5. **Edit the name of an element that you want to change in the theme.**

In this example, change Nabkgnd.Jpg to Nabkgndx.Jpg, which is the name of your replacement wallpaper graphics file.

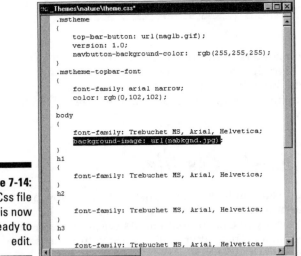

Figure 7-14:
The .Css file is now ready to edit.

6. **Be sure to save your new Nabkgndx.Jpg replacement file into the same Projectname_Local/Themes/nature folder where the** Nabkgnd.Jpg **file is located.**

7. **Click the x in the upper-right corner of the text editor to close it.**

A dialog box opens (titled Microsoft Development Environment), asking whether you sincerely want to "Save changes to the following files."

8. **Click the Yes button to save the changes you made to the Theme.Css file.**

   The dialog box closes.

Part III

Jazzing Up Your Web Site with Multimedia (Lights! Camera! Action!)

The 5th Wave   By Rich Tennant

"I did this report with the help of a satellite view atmospheric map from the National Weather Service, research text from the Jet Propulsion Laboratory, and a sound file from 'The Barfing Lungworms' new CD."

In this part . . .

For many people, Part III will be the fun part. Here you learn tricks of the trade — techniques to jazz up your Web site that are similar to techniques that TV and movie directors have used for years to add excitement and drama to their productions. Wipes. Fades. Split Horizontal In. (Curious about *that* trick, aren't you?) Dissolves. Vertical blinds. Text that flies around the screen and then stops and does the hula. All the step-by-step examples are here for you. Why not startle yourself?

Now, some "serious" programmers think that computers are grim, dry things that have everything to do with cold information and nothing to do with fun and entertainment. I have to disagree. The best information *is* entertaining. (It's called the joy of learning.) And people today expect animation, design, and color on a Web site. They won't stay around long if you present them with something that looks like a law textbook — all gray with no pictures.

Chapter 8

Animating Your Pages with Dynamic HTML

Dynamic HTML (DHTML) is a capability that first appeared in Microsoft Internet Explorer 4. That browser, and subsequent browsers, such as Netscape 4, can make Web pages perform startling effects right in the visitor's computer. In other words, the visitor's computer does the computing that can animate your pages and really bring them to life.

To understand why DHTML capabilities are startling, remember that ordinary HTML is not dynamic. It just sits there. HTML is a page description language: It specifies things such as the position and size — how big, what color, and where — at which the text should be displayed in the browser window.

However, if you want *dynamism* — if you want, for example, text to change color while the viewer watches — HTML can't help you. If you want text to grow larger if the viewer moves the mouse pointer over it, HTML can't do anything about that. But these and many other special effects are possible when you use Dynamic HTML.

This chapter and Chapter 9 are monkey-see, monkey-do chapters. You can find examples of some of the most exciting DHTML tricks in these two chapters. If you want to use a trick in your Web site, copy the source code from this book's CD and paste it into your own Web pages. If you really want to get deeply into DHTML, you may want to take a look at *Dynamic HTML For Dummies* by Michael Hyman (IDG Books Worldwide, Inc). However, these two chapters give you lots of goodies to work with.

Alas, you have two distinct flavors of DHTML at this time, the Microsoft Internet Explorer version and the Netscape Communicator version. This book sticks with the Internet Explorer version of DHTML because more people use Internet Explorer.

Exploring the Object Model

HTML contains 124 objects. These objects are the various HTML commands (called *elements* or *tags*) such as H1, the tag that specifies a large headline, and TABLE, which says a table should be displayed.

The term *DHTML object model* merely means the set of objects (headlines, paragraphs, buttons, whatever) that can be manipulated on a Web page. The object model is hierarchical, like an ordinary workplace. You know the hierarchy: the boss, vice presidents, the supervisors . . . and you.

In DHTML, the highest objects are the *window* and the *document*. The window is the currently running browser, such as Internet Explorer. The document is the currently loaded page in that window. Lower down in the hierarchy are other objects such as the *body* (as opposed to the *head*) of the Web page. The hierarchy of an object model is specified in programming by separating the higher-level objects from the lower-level objects by periods. For example, in your workplace, you may be given a raise using this line of "programming:"

```
Boss.vice president2.supervisor5.you.GetRaise()
```

Similarly, if you want to write programming that manipulates a range of text in a Web page:

```
document.body.createTextRange()
```

Or if you want to change the fontsize of a headline:

```
window.event.srcElement.style.fontSize = "35"
```

One thing to remember about hierarchies: The higher objects are said to "contain" the lower objects. In other words, the document object contains the body object. This containment is described by separating objects with a period in the programming. For instance, `document.body` tells you that the body is contained within the document.

If all this sounds a bit much, remember that this chapter and Chapter 9 include many monkey-see, monkey-do examples that you can copy and paste. You don't have to wrestle with the DHTML object model unless you really want to.

The exciting thing about DHTML is that it makes all these objects available to you, the programmer, so that you can make changes by repositioning them, changing their color or size, and otherwise manipulating them.

Not only is a Web page filled with objects, but each object can also be described in three ways:

✔ **Properties:** The qualities or characteristics of an object, such as *color* or *fontsize*.

✔ **Methods:** Things that an object knows how to do, such as the *close* method of the document object.

✔ **Events:** Things that can happen to an object, such as the `onclick` event that happens whenever a user clicks the object.

Taken together, the properties, methods, and events of a particular object are known as that object's *members*. If you list all the objects and all the members of all the objects, you're then looking at the *Document Object Model* (DOM). And, via the DOM, you can really go to town. You get dynamic control over all the items in your Web pages. (Note that the DOM is a subset of the objects in the DHTML object model. Why? Because the DHTML model also includes the window (browser) object. Don't worry about it.)

Using the OnMouseOver event

Users frequently interact with Web pages by moving the mouse pointer around. How would you like to be able to have your Web pages react to those movements? I'm not talking about clicking here. Just the fact that the user moves the mouse pointer over some text in your Web page can make that text (or other page elements) react.

To try this cool effect, follow these steps:

1. **Start FrontPage by clicking its icon on your desktop.**

   The FrontPage Explorer is displayed.

2. **Choose Tools⇨Show FrontPage Editor.**

   The FrontPage Editor is displayed.

3. **Choose File⇨New in the FrontPage Editor.**

   The New dialog box opens, showing a list of various page templates you can select.

4. **Double-click Normal Page.**

   The dialog box closes and a new, blank page appears.

5. **Click the HTML tab.**

   You see basic, blank-page HTML source code.

6. **Drag your mouse across all the HTML source code to select it.**

   The entire page of HTML code is highlighted.

7. **Press the Del key to delete all the source code.**

   The HTML View is now entirely white — no source code at all.

8. **Type in the following source code, or paste it from this book's CD.**

```
<html>
<head>
<script LANGUAGE="VBScript">

function Changeme(vcolor)
  window.event.srcElement.style.color = vcolor
  window.event.srcElement.style.fontSize = "35"
end function
</script>
</head>

<body>
<h3 ID="Thisone" onmouseover="Changeme('blue')"
       STYLE="color:black;font-size:18">
I dare you to move your mouse over me!
</h3>
<h2 ID="Thatone" onmouseover="Changeme('red')"
       STYLE="color:black;font-size:10">
Try me too.
</h2>

</body>
</html>
```

If you're interested in how all this works, you have several things to notice in the header of this HTML page. If you're not interested, skip this next section and go right to the hands-on examples in the section "Experimenting with Dynamic HTML," later in this chapter.

✔ In the header (between the `<head>` and `</head>` tags) is a `<script>` section. This is Web programming. See Chapter 12 for details about script.

✔ The script defines a *function,* which is a job that is carried out. The function is named `changeme`.

✔ The changeme function asks for information when it's triggered. The function wants to be told a color to change something to. This color is sent using the name vcolor.

✔ The phrase window.event.srcElement represents an object (whatever object calls the changeme function). In other words, the object that asks the changeme function to do it's job will be the one that the job is done to. You can refer to this requesting object as the *caller*. If an H1 headline calls on changeme, that H1 headline's color is changed. Changed to what color? Any color that the H1 headline requests, by assigning the color to the vcolor.

✔ Just for fun, the changeme function also changes the caller's fontsize to 35 points.

Here are several things to notice in the body of the HTML page created by the previous code:

✔ In the body (between the <body> and </body> tags), you have two elements, an H1 headline and an H2 headline.

✔ For purposes of identifying each element, each is given an ID. You can use these IDs to cause things to happen to the elements (to change their color, for example). However, often the easiest way to identify an object is to use the srcElement object. It's full name is: window.event. srcElement. It represents whatever element (the *source element*) in the Web page that triggers the function. For example, if the user moves the mouse pointer onto the element <h2 ID="Thatone", the changeme function is triggered. The changeme function knows which headline on the page triggered it because the srcElement object contains that information. This is how the changeme function knows which headline to adjust the fontsize and change the color of.

✔ The onmouseover command is the key to this whole example. Onmouseover is called an *event*. An event is something that happens to an object. In this case, the mouse pointer moves across the object (the H1 headline, or the H2 headline). As a result, the onmouseover event for that H1 object is *triggered*. When triggered, the ="do this" happens. For example, the onmouseover event for the H1 headline says: Changeme('blue'). The color blue is sent to the changeme function. The changeme function finds out what color was sent, then does its job of turning the text I dare you to move your mouse over me! from black 18–point. font to blue 35–point font.

You can use other events, such as onclick, which means "react if the user clicks you."

Testing the code example from the previous steps is simple. Click the Preview tab in the FrontPage Editor. You see two headlines, as shown in Figure 8-1.

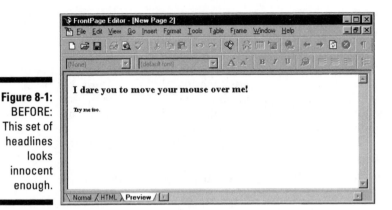

Figure 8-1:
BEFORE:
This set of
headlines
looks
innocent
enough.

Then move your mouse pointer over each headline, and watch how the headlines change, as shown in Figure 8-2.

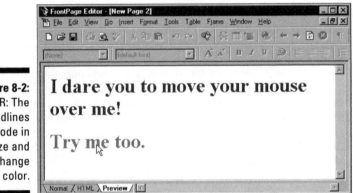

Figure 8-2:
AFTER: The
headlines
explode in
size and
change
color.

Experimenting with Dynamic HTML

DHTML is remarkably flexible. You can try substituting various colors, type sizes, and other effects (these characteristics are called *properties* of the object). You can also use various events to trigger the DHTML effect.

DHTML contains a total of 39 events, though not all objects have all 39. Here is a list of the events: Onabort, onafterupdate, onbeforeunload, onbeforeupdate, onblur, onbounce, onchange, onclick, ondataavailable, ondatasetchanged, ondatasetcomplete, ondblclick, ondragstart, onerror, onerrorupdate, onfilterchange, onfinish, onfocus, onhelp, onkeydown, onkeypress, onkeyup, onload, onmousedown, onmousemove, onmouseout, onmouseover, onmouseup, onreadystatechange, onreset, onresize, onrowenter, onrowexit, onscroll, onselect, onselectstart, onstart, onsubmit, onunload.

Probably the most common events are: onchange, onclick, ondblclick, onkeypress, and onmouseover.

To experiment with DHTML a little, try creating a headline that changes to italic whenever the mouse pointer is over it, but returns to normal when the mouse pointer is elsewhere in the page.

To create a trick italic headline that wavers between italic and normal, type this code into a blank page in the FrontPage Editor with the HTML tab selected:

```
<html>
<head>
<script LANGUAGE="VBScript">
function mousein()
   window.event.srcElement.style.fontstyle = "italic"
end function
function mouseout()
   window.event.srcElement.style.fontstyle = "normal"
end function
</script>
</head>

<body>
<h1
onmouseover="mousein()"
onmouseout="mouseout()">

I can change myself if you move your mouse over me.
</h1>
</body>
</html>
```

Try this example: Click the Preview tab in the FrontPage Editor and then move your mouse on, and then off, the headline.

The script in this example has two functions. One of them, named mousein, changes an object's font to italic. The other, mouseout, changes an object's font to normal (non-italic).

Down below in the <BODY> is the headline. It has two events: onmouseover and onmouseout. These events trigger the correct function to carry out the job that's required.

Try clicking the HTML tab and then changing the word mousein. Change it to whatever you want, perhaps heretheyare. But be sure to change it in both the H1 definition and in the script. Also, be sure that you include the empty parentheses. They're required, even if you're not passing any information to the function.

Now test the example again by clicking the Preview tab and moving your mouse on, and then off, the headline. It still works fine. What you've done is to change the name of the `mousein` function. It doesn't matter what name you give a function. People usually give it a name that means something, though, so you can tell at a glance what the function does.

Don't change the `onmouseover` or `onmouseout` terms. They're built into the script language, so you have to use them as they are. Think of it this way: You created the function, so you can name it whatever you want to, just as you can pick the name of your child. But you didn't create the `onmouseover` or `onmouseout` events, so you have to leave them alone. You can't change the name of the Mona Lisa, can you?

Simplifying events

As usual with computers, you have many ways to do things. When working with DHTML effects, you can often avoid using scripts and functions altogether. Just put the DHTML right inside the definition of an HTML element.

To make a paragraph turn italic when the mouse is over it, but return to normal when the mouse pointer moves off of it, follow these steps:

1. **Choose File⇨New in the FrontPage Editor.**

   The New dialog box opens, showing a list of various page templates that you can select.

2. **Double-click Normal Page.**

   The dialog box closes and a new, blank page appears.

3. **Click the HTML tab.**

   You see basic, blank-page HTML source code.

4. **Drag your mouse across all the HTML source code to select it.**

   The entire page of HTML code is highlighted.

5. **Press the Delete key to delete all the source code.**

   The HTML View is now entirely white. As a result, no source code exists.

6. **Type in the following source code, or paste it from this book's CD.**

```
<html>
<head>
</head>

<body>
<p onmouseover="this.style.font='italic'"
        onmouseout="this.style.color='purple'">
I'm a special paragraph. I go italic while your mouse
        pointer is on top of me, and then I change to
        purple when you leave me.
</p>
</body>
</html>
```

You have several things to notice in the preceding DHTML programming:

- **No script:** All the programming takes place inside the HTML paragraph element, between the `<P>` and `</P>` tags.
- **The `<P>` element:** This element can respond on its own to the `onmouseover` and `onmouseout` events (and any other events it is sensitive to, such as `onclick`).
- **The entire action:** The action is enclosed in quotation marks, so you have to use single quotation marks around the properties `'italic'` and `'purple'`.
- **The object:** The object whose properties are being adjusted is referred to as `this`.

Working with properties

Currently 362 properties are in DHTML's document object model. Of course, many objects have only a few properties, and no object has all the 362 properties.

Yet, properties have multiple values. At the least, each property has a minimum of two values: true or false. For example, the visible property can have a value of either true or false.

A *value* is something a property can be. For example, the font-style property can be italic or normal. When you describe the value of a property, you separate the property from the value with an equals sign, like this:

```
color="lightblue"
```

Some properties have many, many values. For example, properties that define color (backgroundcolor, bordercolor, color, linkcolor, and so on) have 140 colors that you can assign to them. Internet Explorer 4 can display any of these, if the user's video card can handle them. Some of the colors have great names. And some of the colors are so rare that you never even hear them mentioned unless you're around when an interior decorator goes into a spitting frenzy and loses it. Here's a small sample of the colors you can specify:

aliceblue, antiquewhite, bisque, blanchedalmond, cadetblue, cornflowerblue, darkorchid, indigo, lavenderblush, mediuaquamarine, mintcream, mistyrose, navajowhite, oldlace, papayawhip, saddlebrown, teal, thistle, and whitesmoke.

I suggest you experiment with papayawhip for your Web page background color, but the final decision is, as always, yours alone.

To see the complete list (so that you know about lightgoldenrodyellow is also available), choose Help⇨Search in any Visual Studio 6 application. The Help dialog box opens. Type **sienna** in the *Type In The Word You Want To Search For* text box. (Only the color table contains the word sienna in the entire billion-word MSDN help engine, as you probably guessed.) Click the List Topics button. The entry Color Table shows up in the list box. Double-click Color Table. All 140 colors are listed in the right pane of the Help dialog box, and a sample of each color is also displayed.

Try this experiment. See how the various colors look in your browser by following these steps:

1. **Click the HTML tab in the FrontPage Editor.**

2. **Drag your mouse across all the HTML source code to select it.**

   The entire page of HTML code is highlighted.

3. **Press the Del key to delete all the source code.**

   The HTML View is now entirely white. No source code is left.

4. **Type in the following source code, or paste it from this book's CD.**

```html
<html>
<head>
<title></title>
</head>
<body>
<p onmouseover="this.style.color='papayawhip'"
        onmouseout="this.style.color='darkorchid'">
People can distinguish between millions of shades and
        tones of color. Try moving your mouse over this
        paragraph. </p>
</body>
</html>
```

5. **Click the Preview tab in the FrontPage Editor.**

 The paragraph in the preceding source code is displayed.

6. **Try moving your mouse on and off the text, to watch it change color.**

7. **Substitute other colors for papayawhip and darkorchid to see how different colors look in the browser.**

Controlling the Position of Objects

You've probably noticed that when you type some text into the FrontPage Editor, you don't have much control over where that text appears on the page when it's finally displayed to the viewer. This result is true of the Visual InterDev Editor and every other editor. (It's actually a feature of the way HTML piles things together, smack up against each other, unless you tell it otherwise.)

Similarly, you insert an image or drag a component like a button onto a Web page in an editor. You then look at that page in the browser or editor's Preview (or Quick View) feature. The browser determines where that item is positioned on screen. (Images and components are piled up against each other by default, too.)

Sure, you can move images and components on top of or below each other vertically to some extent, but you've got very little control over where they appear horizontally. They act like magnets: They want to stick together if at all possible.

Using absolute positioning

With the `position` command, you can have complete control over position within a Web page. You have two kinds of positioning: absolute and relative. When you use *absolute positioning*, you specify the precise Top and Left location, in pixels. For example, if you specify `Top:200; Left:300`, you're telling the browser to start displaying this text 200 pixels down from the top of the document window, and 300 pixels over from the left of the window.

When you use *relative positioning*, you specify the location in terms of some other object. For example, `document.objectsname.left + 23` means "put this object 23 pixels further right than the thing called `objectsname`." It's understood by the browser that the Top stays the same as the other object.

The difference between absolute and relative positioning is the difference between telling someone to sit in the chair next to the window, or to sit to the left of Elizabeth, wherever Elizabeth ends up sitting. In other words, an absolute position is fixed within the container (the room or the browser window). A relative position is defined by another object that can move within the container. If Elizabeth moves, so do you, because your position is "attached" to hers. Your position is relative to Elizabeth's.

By default, a browser window includes a top and left margin. Therefore, if you want to position an object up against the top or left of the window, you have to eliminate the default margin by adding these commands to the `<body>` tag in the HTML source code:

Change the default body definition:

```
<body>
```

To this new definition that eliminates the margins:

```
<body tomargin="0" leftmargin="0">
```

The DIV element is used with the position command because DIV can enclose a whole group of objects (text, graphics, components such as buttons) and position that entire group with one position specification.

To see how absolute positioning works, follow these steps:

1. **Choose File⇨New in the FrontPage Editor.**

   The New dialog box opens, showing a list of various page templates you can select.

2. **Double-click Normal Page.**

   The dialog box closes and a new, blank page appears.

3. **Click the HTML tab and drag your mouse across all the HTML source code to select it. Then press the Delete key to delete all the source code.**

   The HTML View in the FrontPage Editor is now entirely white. No source code exists.

4. **Type in the following source code, or paste it from this book's CD:**

```
<html>
<head>
<title></title>
</head>

<body>
<div style="position:absolute; left:50; top:130">
<p>You can position text or other page elements
        anywhere you want.</p>
```

```
</div>
<div style="position:absolute; left:70; top:123">
<h1>Even on top of each other!</h1>
</div>
</body>
</html>
```

5. **Click the Preview tab and you can see the results shown in Figure 8-3.**

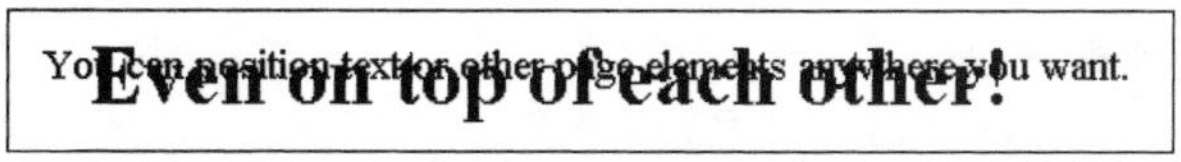

Figure 8-3:
Define
exactly
where you
want to
display any
element
with the
`position`
command.

You can position text or other page elements anywhere you want.
"Even on top of each other!"

Using relative positioning

If you want to use relative positioning to specify one object's (or group of objects') position in relation to another object's (or group's) position, all you have to do is give the `DIV` element a name. You can name things in source code by using the `ID` tag. Then, when defining the position of the second object, you say something like this: `itsname + 100`.

To see how to position a piece of text relative to a graphic, follow these steps:

1. **Choose File⇨New in the FrontPage Editor.**

   The New dialog box opens, showing a list of various page templates you can select.

2. **Double-click Normal Page.**

   The dialog box closes and a new, blank page appears.

3. **Click the HTML tab and drag your mouse across all the HTML source code to select it. Then press the Delete key to delete all the source code.**

   The HTML View in the FrontPage Editor is now entirely white. You see no source code at all.

ON THE CD

4. **Type in the following source code, or paste it from this book's CD:**

```html
<html>
<head>
<title></title>
</head>

<body>
<div style="position:absolute; left:30; top:30">
<p><big><big><big>Here is the text and it's
        absolute...</big></big></big>

<img src="file:///C:/Program Files/Microsoft
        FrontPage/temp/TN00054A.gif"
style="position: relative; left:-380">
</p>
</div>
</body>
</html>
```

5. **Change** `src="file:///C:/Program Files/Microsoft FrontPage/temp/TN00054A.gif"` **so that it points to a .Gif graphic file on your hard drive.**

6. **Click the Preview tab and you see the results shown in Figure 8-4.**

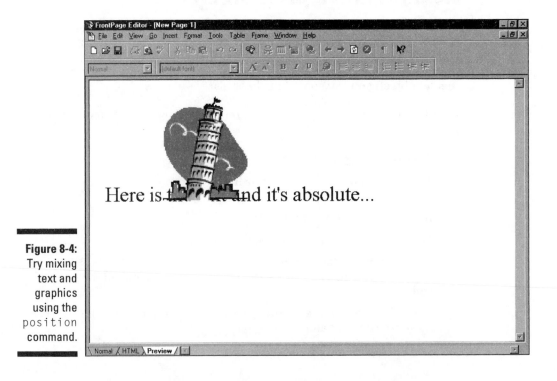

Figure 8-4:
Try mixing text and graphics using the position command.

The key point in this example is this programming: `style="position: relative; left:-380"`, which specifies that the graphic is placed 380 pixels to the left of the end of the text. This is a *relative* specification and it depends on the location of the text. The graphic is, in this way, bound to the text. If you animate this page by moving the text, the graphic moves with it to maintain its relative position. (Chapter 9 includes examples showing how to move objects around in a page, as the user watches and, no doubt, gasps.)

Notice in Figure 8-4 that the graphic covers the text. Ordinarily, you want the text superimposed on the graphic. Is there any way to fix this? DHTML to the rescue! A `z-index` command enables you to specify which items overlap other items, when they superimpose. To put the text on top of the graphic shown in Figure 8-4, change this line:

```
style="position: relative; left:-380"
```

to:

```
style="position: relative; left:-380; top:55; z-index:-1"
```

The `z-index:-1` command moves the graphic behind the text. If you also add the `top:55` command, the graphic is forced down the page, relative to the top of the text. The final result is shown in Figure 8-5.

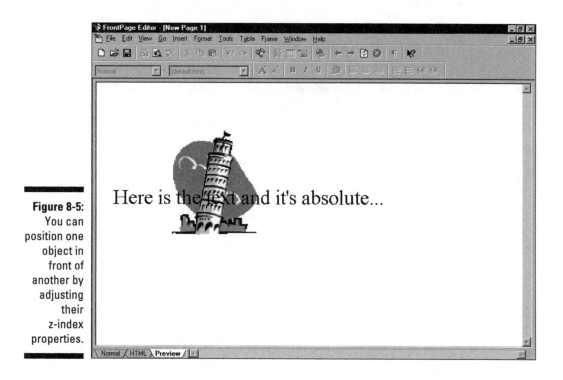

Figure 8-5:
You can position one object in front of another by adjusting their z-index properties.

Understanding TextRange

Doubtless you suspect that you can do hundreds of tricks with DHTML, and you're right. This chapter and Chapter 9 only touch on some of the more fascinating techniques.

You may also suspect that if you can manipulate all the HTML elements and their attributes, you can probably get at the text in the document, too. Right again. The intriguing TextRange object is your gateway to a document's words.

The TextRange object includes all the text in the body of the document (between the <BODY> and </BODY> tags). However, you can also use TextRange with a more limited item, such as a TextArea, Button, or Input.

Using the single-line version of TextRange

You can do some great things with the TextRange object. In this next example, you create a Web page that reacts to the user's mouseclick by replacing the text that's displayed with different text. To understand how the TextRange object works within a single line of programming, follow these steps:

1. **Choose File⇨New in the FrontPage Editor and then double-click Normal Page in the list of FrontPage page templates.**

   The New dialog box closes and a new, blank page appears.

2. **Click the HTML tab and drag your mouse across all the HTML source code to select it. Then press the Delete key to delete all the source code.**

   The HTML View in the FrontPage Editor is now entirely white. You see no source code at all.

3. **Type in the following source code, or paste it from this book's CD:**

```
<html>
<head>
<script language="vbscript">
function changeit()
document.body.createTextRange().pasteHTML("<h1>NEW
        HEADLINE</h1>")
end function

</script>
</head>
<body onclick="changeit()">
<p>This text will be replaced if you click it.</p>
</body>
</html>
```

4. **Click the Preview tab in the FrontPage Editor and then click the page to see the existing text replaced with the new headline.**

Notice that all the `TextRange` activity takes place in a single line (the line between the `Function` and `End Function` commands). You also have a multi-line format involving `TextRange`, where you assign the `TextRange` to a variable and then use that variable to manipulate the text.

After a `TextRange` object is brought into existence (with the `createTextRange ()` command), you can accomplish various tasks with it. A `TextRange` object has a set of methods — things it knows how to do. `PasteHTML` puts HTML source code into the `TextRange`, as illustrated in the code in the preceding steps. Other `TextRange` methods enable you to replace, highlight, change words to italic, and otherwise adjust text.

Note, too, the line that reacts when the user clicks anywhere in the entire document: `<body onclick="changeit()">`. This line specifies that if the user clicks the body of the document, the `changeit` function is executed in the script.

Working with TextRange in a variable

The most common way to use the `TextRange` object is to assign the `TextRange` to a variable and then use that variable to adjust the text. In VBScript, an object variable is assigned a value by using the set command. To understand how to work with an object variable, follow these steps:

1. **Choose File⇨New in the FrontPage Editor and then double-click Normal Page in the list of FrontPage page templates.**

   The New dialog box closes and a new, blank page appears in the FrontPage Editor.

2. **Click the HTML tab and drag your mouse across all the HTML source code to select it. Then press the Delete key to delete all the source code.**

   The HTML View in the FrontPage Editor is now entirely white. No source code exists.

3. **Type in the following source code, or paste it from this book's CD:**

```
<html>
<head>
<script LANGUAGE="VBScript">
function viewit()
dim tobj
set tobj = document.body.createTextRange()
msgbox (tobj.text)
```

(continued)

(continued)

```
end function
</script>
</head>

<body onload="viewit()">
<h1>Major Headline. MAJOR! MAJOR!</h1>
<p>A little explanation in the body of the
        document.</p>
</body>
</html>
```

4. Click the Preview tab to see the results, as shown in Figure 8-6.

The key lines in this example are:

```
dim tobj
set tobj = document.body.createTextRange()
```

The `dim` command creates a new variable with the name `tobj`. Then the `set` command assigns the `TextRange` (in the document's entire body) to that object variable. Later, you can display the object variable to the user by putting the variable into a message box, like this:

```
msgbox (tobj.text)
```

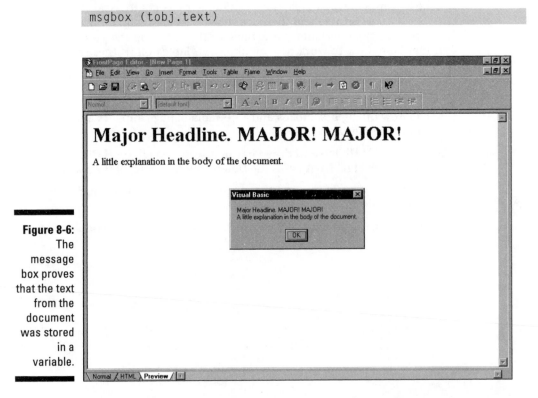

Figure 8-6:
The message box proves that the text from the document was stored in a variable.

You may also be interested in this line: `<body onload="viewit()">`. This line of code tells the browser to execute the `viewit` function as soon as this page loads into the browser. No user activity, such as clicking, is required to activate the script in this example.

Using the MoveToPoint method

The `TextRange` object knows how to move itself to a particular point on the screen, by using its `MoveToPoint` method. The point is defined by two parameters: x (the horizontal location in pixels) and y (the vertical location in pixels). You can provide those coordinates using a pair of properties: `window.event.x` and `window.event.y`. These `window.event` objects know the location where the user clicked the mouse.

The `TextRange` object also has an `expand` method, enabling you to extend it to embrace a character, word, sentence, and so on.

Copy this example from this book's CD into the FrontPage Editor and then click the Preview tab. Test the example by clicking a word in the message. The word you click is displayed in the `messagebox`.

```
<html>
<head><script LANGUAGE="VBScript">
function Showme()
dim tobj set tobj = document.body.createTextRange()
tobj.movetopoint window.event.x, window.event.y
tobj.expand ("word")
msgbox (tobj.text)
end function
</script>
</head>

<body onclick="showme()">
<p>Just click one of the words in this message.</p>
</body>
</html>
```

Note that after you've captured a word that the user clicked, you can then *use* that word in many ways in your programming. You can display some information about the word to the user, for example. Perhaps you list five items on sale at your auto supply store. If the user clicks one of those items, a fuller description of the item is then displayed in a `TextArea`, message box, or other display technique.

You have many other techniques to manipulate a word, sentence, or whatever else is currently in the TextRange object. For example, if you want to transform each clicked word into italics, instead of showing the word in a message box, change this:

```
msgbox (tobj.text)
```

to:

```
tobj.execCommand("ITALIC")
```

Then click the Preview tab. Now each word that you click is italicized.

Searching with TextRange

The TextRange object includes a findtext command that, as you may guess, can search through the entire TextRange object and locate the requested text.

This example behaves like a search utility in a word processor. All the text is searched for a particular word, then that word is highlighted. Try this example by copying this source code from the book's CD into the FrontPage Editor and then click the Preview tab and click anywhere in the document to trigger the search:

```
<html>
<head><script LANGUAGE="VBScript">
function Findit()
dim tobj
set tobj = document.body.createTextRange()


if tobj.findText("this") then
  tobj.select()
end if
end function
</script>

</head>
<body onclick="findit()">
<p>Just click somewhere in this document and I'll locate a
         word for you, then highlight it.</p>
</body>
</html>
```

Notice that after the `findtext` method has located the target text, the `TextRange` object contains only that target text. Therefore the `select` method highlights only the target, and nothing more.

If you can search, you can also replace, right? The remarkably versatile `TextRange` object can, of course, replace a piece of text after it's been tracked down and located.

To replace `this` with `not this` in the previous code example, change this:

```
tobj.select()
```

to:

```
tobj.text = "not this"
```

Now, when you test this in the FrontPage Preview window, click the document to activate the `Findit` function. The word `this` is replaced with `not this` right before your eyes.

Chapter 9

Dazzle 'Em with Special Effects

. . . .

In This Chapter

▶ Exploring DHTML timers

▶ Using a countdown timer

▶ Doing expert transitions with filters

▶ Creating fade and wipes

. . . .

*B*y one of its definitions, *animation* means that something comes alive. However, the more common definition of animation is that something which is normally still changes before your very eyes. Text could scoot onto the screen, or perhaps a graphic wiggles. Whatever it is, if it's animated it moves; it's active, not passive.

How do you get something to move in a browser? DHTML does the job. After all, the *D* in DHMTL does stand for *dynamic*.

Some DHTML effects use timers to repeatedly adjust the position, size, color, or other attribute of a graphic or piece of text. This way, text can gradually grow larger, or an image can gradually slide off the bottom of the browser screen. Many other effects are possible, too, after you get the idea of how to work with timers.

Other effects, called *transition filters*, contain their own built-in timing. You specify the duration of the effect and the transition filter handles the rest. One cool transition is called *BlendTrans* and you can use it to make objects fade from full strength to invisibility. For example, you can make text gradually appear, as if white smoke slowly evaporated and it became gracefully visible (see the section at the end of this chapter titled "Using Transition Filters for Fades and Wipes" for this particular effect).

Exploring DHTML Timers

The first thing that you should know about timers is that they behave in two different ways:

- ✔ **Like a kitchen timer:** You set the timer to a particular time, and it counts down to zero and rings its bell.
- ✔ **Like a metronome:** You set the timer to go off repeatedly at a regular interval that you specify.

How many timers can you "set"? As many as you want. They're free for the asking.

The first kind of timer — the kitchen-timer type — can be used to display a message or splash screen and then make it disappear after a certain amount of time elapses.

Many applications use this technique to display a *splash screen* before the program's normal user-interface appears. For example, the Visual FoxPro splash screen is shown in Figure 9-1.

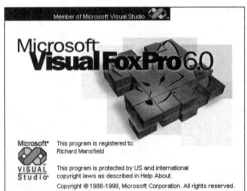

Figure 9-1:
The Visual
FoxPro
splash
screen.

Using a countdown timer

A countdown timer (they act like a kitchen timer) is created by using the setTimeout command, like this:

```
timerhandle = setTimeout("movep",3000)
```

You can use most any name instead of `timerhandle` here (except a word already used by VBScript, such as `End` or `Function`). However, `timerhandle` seems like a good name for it. The `timerhandle` is just a name that's given to the timer when it's created by the above line of script (when the page with this script loads into a browser). Then you can later destroy this timer by using its name, as in this line:

```
clearTimeout(timerhandle)
```

The `clearTimeout` command removes the timer from the computer's memory (destroys it, really). The `clearTimeout` command isn't strictly necessary. Generally, you can count on the computer to destroy timers that are no longer in use. However, explicitly killing off a timer when your program is finished using it is considered good programming.

The important point in the earlier code example is the word "`movep`", which is the name of the script you want executed when the timer finishes its countdown.

`Movep` or whatever function name you provide is carried out automatically after the interval is over. What interval? The 3000 in the above example specifies three seconds. Timer intervals are specified in milliseconds. They're very precise. So to specify one minute you'd write it like this:

```
timerhandle = setTimeout("movep",60000)
```

To create a paragraph that turns slate blue and grows to 22–point type size three seconds after the page is loaded into a browser, follow these steps:

1. **Start FrontPage by clicking its icon on your desktop.**

   The FrontPage Explorer is displayed.

2. **Choose Tools⇨Show FrontPage Editor.**

   The FrontPage Editor is displayed.

3. **Choose File⇨New.**

   The New dialog box opens, showing a list of various page templates you can select.

4. **Double-click Normal Page.**

   The dialog box closes and a new, blank page appears.

5. **Click the HTML tab.**

   You see basic, blank-page HTML source code.

6. **Drag your mouse across all the HTML source code to select it.**

   The entire page of HTML code is highlighted.

7. **Press the Delete key to delete all the source code.**

   The HTML View is now entirely white. You see no source code.

8. **Type in the following source code, or paste it from this book's CD:**

```
<html>
<head>
<script LANGUAGE="VBScript">

function startTimer()
        timerhandle = setTimeout("movep",3000)
end function
function stopTimer()
        clearTimeout(timerhandle)
end function
function movep()
 para.style.color = "slateblue"
 para.style.fontSize = "22"
end function
</script>
</head>

<body onload="startTimer()" onunload="stopTimer()">
<p ID="para">Some paragraphs can change, all on their
        own...</p>
</body>
</html>
```

9. **Click the Preview tab.**

   Wait three seconds to see the effect on the Web page.

Here's what happens, blow by blow, when you load the source code from Step 8 into a browser:

✔ When the page is loaded (onload), the startTimer function is executed.

✔ The startTimer function specifies that after 3000 milliseconds, the movep function is started: timerhandle = setTimeout("movep",3000)

✔ After the timer counts down three seconds, the movep function does two things to the style of the para object. It changes the color and adjusts the fontsize:

```
para.style.color = "slateblue"
para.style.fontSize = "22"
```

✔ Notice that you can name a paragraph (or a headline or other HTML element) by using the ID attribute, like this: `<p ID="para">`. Then in a function, you can adjust that element's name by specifying its name: `para` or whatever ID you gave the element.

✔ Finally, when the page is unloaded (`onunload="stopTimer()`), the `stopTimer` function uses the `clearTimeout` command to destroy the timer.

Getting visitors' feet wet with a splash screen

You may want to show visitors an attractive graphic screen for a few seconds before displaying your web site's home page. Consider displaying a 10-second splash screen to intrigue them. Then display your real home page automatically (the user doesn't have to click anything — a timer does the work).

A *splash screen* is usually an attractive graphic, it may be your company's logo, that's displayed while an application or web page is loading. Therefore, a splash screen can be particularly useful if your home page is heavy with graphics and loads slowly. Figure 9-1 shows the Visual FoxPro splash screen.

To show a splash screen, you display the graphic page until a timer counts down; then you hide that page and show your home page proper. To create a splash page for your web site, follow these steps:

1. **Choose File⇨New in the FrontPage Editor.**

   The New dialog box opens, showing a list of various page templates you can select.

2. **Double-click Normal Page.**

   The dialog box closes and a new, blank page appears in the FrontPage Editor.

3. **Click the HTML tab.**

   You see basic, blank-page HTML source code.

4. **Drag your mouse across all the HTML source code to select it.**

   The entire page of HTML code is highlighted.

5. **Press the Delete key to delete all the source code.**

   The HTML View is now entirely white. No more source code.

6. Type in the following source code, or paste it from this book's CD.

Be sure to replace the "file:///C:/cheese.htm" in the following source code with an .Htm file on your system. This file is the home page you want to automatically display after five seconds. Also, replace the <img src="file:///D:/bark.jpg"> in the following source code. That's the graphic you want to use in the splash screen.

```html
<html>
<head>
<script LANGUAGE="VBScript">

function startTimer()
        timerhandle = setTimeout("jump",5000)
end function
function jump()
document.location = "file:///C:/cheese.htm"
end function
function stopTimer()
        clearTimeout(timerhandle)
end function
</script>
</head>

<body onload="startTimer()" onunload="stopTimer()">
<img src="file:///D:/bark.jpg">
</body>
</html>
```

7. Click the Preview tab to test this code.

The browser first displays the splash screen (<img src="file:///D:/bark.jpg">) for five seconds, as shown in Figure 9-2. Then the browser automatically jumps to "file:///C:/cheese.htm" (which you replaced with your equivalent to specify the home page for your Web site).

The key line in the source code in this example is found in the function named jump: document.location = "file:///C:/cheese.htm". This line tells the browser to load the document named cheese.htm found at the URL location file:///C:/.

Jumping automatically to a new URL

Sometimes you switch to a different Internet service provider, or for some other reason your Web site relocates to a different URL address. Most people simply display a notice and a hyperlink to the new address:

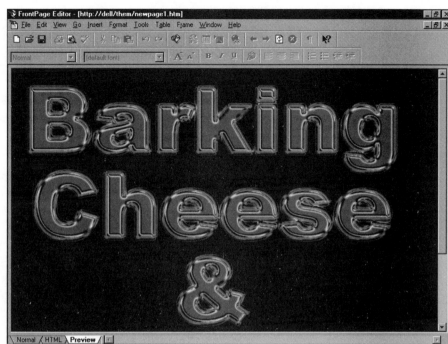

Figure 9-2:
A visitor
sees this
splash
screen
graphic
before the
actual
home page
appears.

```
We have moved to a different address: click here to go to
               our new home!
```

But an even better way to automatically jump them to the new address, after displaying the notice for a few seconds, is as follows:

```
We have moved to a different address. You'll be transferred
          there in a few seconds. Please add our new address
          to your Favorites!
```

You can inform the visitor of your new address using a timer, or you can use the following `meta` command in FrontPage to accomplish the same thing. Type the following source code into a blank FrontPage document, making sure that the HTML tab is selected in the FrontPage Editor:

```
<html>
<head>
<title>Jump to new address</title>
<meta name="GENERATOR" content="Microsoft FrontPage 3.0">
<meta http-equiv="refresh" content="6;
          url=http://www.mynewaddress.com">
```

(continued)

(continued)

```
</head>
<body>
<p>We have moved to a different address. You'll be
           transferred there in a few seconds.
Please add our new address to your Favorites! </p>
</body>
</html>
```

The significant line in the preceding example is `<meta http-equiv="refresh" content="6; url=http://www.mynewaddress.com">`. Replace the 6 with the number of seconds you want FrontPage to wait before the browser switches to the new address, and replace `http://www.mynewaddress.com` with the actual new URL address of your Web site.

Using a metronome timer

The metronome type of timer is created by using the `SetInterval` command, like this:

```
timerhandle = setInterval ("movep",60000)
```

Notice that the items in parentheses (the name of the function to execute, and the interval of time) are the same for the `setInterval` command that you're working with here, as they were for the `setTimeOut` command described in the section "Using a countdown timer," earlier in this chapter. The difference is that with `setInterval`, the function (`movep`, in this example) is executed repeatedly instead of executed only one time.

Try an example of the metronome timer. The following source code causes the color of a paragraph to switch rapidly between black and blue. To see how to create an effect like this, follow these steps:

1. **Choose File⇨New in the FrontPage Editor.**

   The New dialog box opens, showing a list of various page templates you can select.

2. **Double-click Normal Page.**

   The dialog box closes and a new, blank page appears.

3. **Click the HTML tab.**

   You see basic, blank-page HTML source code.

4. **Drag your mouse across all the HTML source code to select it.**

   The entire page of HTML code is highlighted.

5. Press the Delete key to delete all the source code.

The HTML View is now entirely white. You see no source code.

6. Type in the following source code, or paste it from this book's CD:

```
<html>
<head>
<script LANGUAGE="VBScript">

dim toggle
function startTimer()
        timerhandle = setinterval("movep",80)
end function
function stopTimer()
        clearTimeout(timerhandle)
end function
function movep()
toggle = not toggle

if toggle then
 para.style.color = "slateblue"
else
 para.style.color = "black"
end if
end function
</script>
</head>

<body onload="startTimer()" onunload="stopTimer()">
<p ID="para">This text vibrates a little bit!</p>
</body>
</html>
```

7. Click the Preview tab in the FrontPage editor.

The text vibrates and it looks a little strange as it flashes. Don't stare at it too long, or you may get disoriented and flip out.

The following list shows the major events that happen as you run the preceding code example:

1. When a Web page contains a section of *script*, any lines of programming that aren't enclosed in a `Function...End Function` (or `Sub...End function`) are executed immediately. In other words, in the preceding example, the line `dim toggle` is outside any `Function` or `Sub`. Therefore, the variable `toggle` is created when this page first loads into a browser. (The `dim` command creates a variable.)

The main value of using the `dim` command to create a variable outside of any `Function` or `Sub` is that the variable can then be used by *all* the `Functions` and `Subs` anywhere in the current Web page. (Variables created *within* a `Function` or `Sub` can be used only by other lines of source code within the same `Function` or `Sub`.)

In this example, you wanted to have a variable, `toggle`, that could hold information no matter what function was, or was not, currently executing. Because you create `toggle` outside the `Functions`, it can hold the information you give it as long as this page remains in the browser.

2. When the `startTimer` function is executed (with the `body onload` command), the browser is told to execute the `movep` function every 80 milliseconds. Note that this execution happens quite often because 1000 milliseconds is one second.

3. The meat of this program is in the `movep` function. The line `toggle = not toggle` is like flipping a light switch. If the variable `toggle` was true, it becomes false when you use the `not` command. Or, if it was false, it becomes true.

4. The variable `toggle` is tested. If it's true (`if toggle then`), the paragraph is displayed blue. If `toggle` is false (`else`), the paragraph turns black.

5. The `movep` function continues to toggle on and off, quite rapidly, until the `stopTimer` function is executed when the browser unloads this page, triggering the `onunload="stopTimer()"` command.

Changing text dynamically

If you want to make text grow, shrink, or otherwise animate, you can use the `setInterval` command to establish the frequency of the animation. Then adjust the style of the text.

In the following example, the paragraph named `heade` (in this line: `<p id="heade">growth.</p>`) grows from its normal size to about six times its normal size. Then it switches back and starts growing all over again.

To try this example, follow these steps:

1. **Click the HTML tab in the FrontPage Editor.**

   The source code page of the FrontPage Editor is displayed.

2. **Select any source code by dragging your mouse across it.**

   The source code is displayed in reverse — white text against a black background.

3. **Press the Delete key to delete all the source code.**

4. **Type in the following source code, or paste it from this book's CD:**

```
<html>
<head>
<script LANGUAGE="VBScript">

dim counter
function startTimer()
        timerhandle = setInterval("sizeit",60)
end function
function stopTimer()
        clearTimeout(timerhandle)
end function
function sizeit()
counter = counter + 1
if counter > 70 then counter = 10
heade.style.fontSize=counter
end function
</script>
</head>

<body onload="startTimer()" onunload="stopTimer()">
<p>Not growth.</p>
<p id="heade">growth.</p>
</body>
</html>
```

5. **Click the FrontPage Preview tab to see the growing text.**

Try adjusting the interval (60) to see the effect of slowing or speeding the animation. Also try adjusting the counter size from +1 to perhaps +5 to see the effect of increasing the jumps between font sizes.

The key source code in the preceding example is found in the `sizeit` function. A variable named `counter` is raised by 1 each time the `sizeit` function is executed. The VBScript uses the `if...then` command to reset the `fontsize` to 10 each time it reaches 70. Then the paragraph named `heade` is set to the `fontsize` currently in the variable `counter`.

Using the display and visibility properties

You want to be aware of two ways to hide text (or graphics). The `display` property causes surrounding objects to make space for a hidden object. The `visibility` property holds space open for the hidden object. In other words, when you use `visibility:hidden` in describing a paragraph's properties, the space taken up by that paragraph remains visible as white space, as you can see in Figure 9-3.

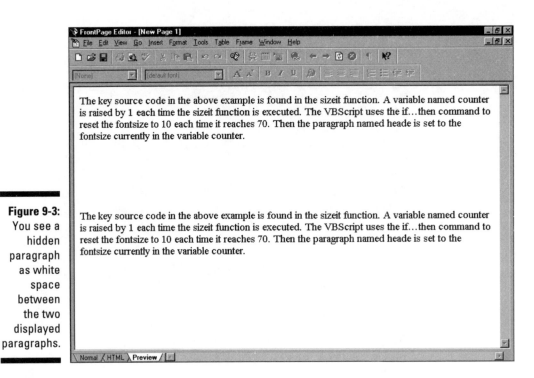

Figure 9-3:
You see a hidden paragraph as white space between the two displayed paragraphs.

The key source code in the above example is found in the sizeit function. A variable named counter is raised by 1 each time the sizeit function is executed. The VBScript uses the if...then command to reset the fontsize to 10 each time it reaches 70. Then the paragraph named heade is set to the fontsize currently in the variable counter.

The key source code in the above example is found in the sizeit function. A variable named counter is raised by 1 each time the sizeit function is executed. The VBScript uses the if...then command to reset the fontsize to 10 each time it reaches 70. Then the paragraph named heade is set to the fontsize currently in the variable counter.

To create the effect shown in Figure 9-3, type the following code into the FrontPage Editor:

```
<html>
<head>
<script LANGUAGE="VBScript">

function startTimer()
      timerhandle = settimeout("showit",2000)
end function
function stopTimer()
      clearTimeout(timerhandle)
end function
function showit()
par.style.visibility = ""
end function
</script>
</head>
```

```
<body onload="startTimer()" onunload="stopTimer()">
<p>The key source code in the above example is found in the
      sizeit function. A variable named counter is raised
      by 1 each time the sizeit function is executed. The
      VBScript uses the if&#133;then command to reset the
      fontsize to 10 each time it reaches 70. Then the
      paragraph named heade is set to the fontsize
      currently in the variable counter. </p>


<p id="par" style="visibility:hidden">The key source code
      in the above example is found in the sizeit
      function. A variable named counter is raised by 1
      each time the sizeit function is executed. The
      VBScript uses the if&#133;then command to reset the
      fontsize to 10 each time it reaches 70. Then the
      paragraph named heade is set to the fontsize
      currently in the variable counter. </p>


<p>The key source code in the above example is found in the
      sizeit function. A variable named counter is raised
      by 1 each time the sizeit function is executed. The
      VBScript uses the if&#133;then command to reset the
      fontsize to 10 each time it reaches 70. Then the
      paragraph named heade is set to the fontsize
      currently in the variable counter. </p>
</body>
</html>
```

Click the FrontPage Preview tab to see the results. In this example, the browser waits two seconds and then makes the middle paragraph visible between the two paragraphs that surround it. Note that when first loaded, the middle paragraph's style is set to invisible: `style="visibility:hidden"`. However, after two seconds, the function `showit` is executed, and the paragraph is made visible with this code: `par.style.visibility = ""`. (When you set a visibility or display property to `""`, the object becomes visible.)

Now try changing two lines of source code to test the display property and see how it differs from the `visibility` property.

Change the line in the function from this:

```
par.style.visibility = ""
```

to this:

```
par.style.display = ""
```

And down in the body of the page, change the middle paragraph's style definition from this:

```
<p id="par" style="visibility:hidden">
```

to this:

```
<p id="par" style="display:none">
```

Now click the Preview tab again and this time, no space appears between the first and third paragraphs when the page is first displayed. Then as soon as the middle paragraph's display property is set to "" (meaning: display this paragraph), the bottom paragraph moves down to make room for the now-visible middle paragraph.

Creating Expert Transitions with Filters

DHTML offers a set of built-in filters that you can apply to text and graphics. These filters are built into Internet Explorer 4 and the entire filter effect takes place in the visitor's browser (no computing is required by the server where the web site resides). You can apply the filters using script. This way, the filter effects can also change over time. The word *filter* is just a name Microsoft chose, in its search for a word that describes the idea of *transformation*. One kind of filter, for example, can change a headline's look by adding a shadow. Another filter (wave) smears the headline as if it were written in finger paint and a child pulled her fingers across it, distorting it by dragging parts of the characters out of alignment. Try some of the following experiments to get an idea of how the various filters affect the look of text or graphics.

The built-in filters are as follows:

- Blur
- Chroma
- Drop shadow
- Flip
- Glow
- Grayscale

- ✔ Invert
- ✔ Light
- ✔ Mask
- ✔ Opacity
- ✔ Shadow
- ✔ Wave
- ✔ X-Ray

The following sections show you how to apply some of the more interesting filters, and also how to make them change by using timers.

Fogging it up: Varying opacity over time

The Opacity filter determines how visible an object is. When the Opacity filter is set to 100, the object is fully visible — just as it looks when the filter is not applied. When set to 0, the object is invisible. In between 0 and 100 an object looks like it is seen through a white fog. The closer the filter is set to 100, the less fog.

If you change the opacity from 0 to 100, you are, in effect, creating a fade-in effect. The object gradually appears.

To add an Opacity filter to some text and a graphic and then decrease the opacity effect dynamically, follow these steps:

1. **Click the HTML tab in the FrontPage Editor.**

   The source code page of the FrontPage Editor is displayed.

2. **Select any source code by dragging your mouse across it.**

   The source code is displayed in reverse — white text against a black background.

3. **Press the Delete key to delete all the source code.**

4. **Type in the following source code, or paste it from this book's CD.**

   Replace the `<img src="D:\butterfl.jpg">` in the following source code with a .Gif or .Jpg graphic file stored on your system.

```
<html>
<head>
<script LANGUAGE="VBScript">
```

(continued)

(continued)

```
dim counter
function startTimer()
        timerhandle = setInterval("lightit",20)
end function
function stopTimer()
        clearTimeout(timerhandle)
end function
function lightit()
counter = counter + 2
if counter > 99 then counter = 1

n = "alpha(opacity=" & counter & ")"
divider.style.filter= n
end function
</script>
</head>

<body onload="startTimer()" onunload="stopTimer()">
<div id="divider" STYLE="position: absolute; filter:
        alpha(opacity=1)">
<h1 align="center">Opacity effects over time</h1>
<dd><img SRC="D:\butterfl.jpg"> </dd>
</div>
</body>
</html>
```

Both the text and the graphic in this example are located within a zone defined by the <DIV> and </DIV> tags. The DIV is given a name, given a divider, and also assigned a filter named alpha that governs the amount of visibility of an object. To start with, the opacity is set to a value of 1, which means that the text and graphic in this DIV are not visible when the page first loads into a browser.

Nevertheless, a timer is also started when the page loads (body onload). This timer executes a function named lightit every 20 milliseconds.

The lightit function increments a variable named counter each time the function executes. Then counter is tested and reset to 1 each time it reaches 100. The opacity variable can be set anywhere from 0 to 100. Then a variable named n is created that specifies the opacity based on whatever the counter currently is. Finally, the filter for the divider zone is assigned the opacity.

You may want to try increasing the 20 in the StartTimer function to slow down the effect.

Figure 9-4 illustrates how the opacity effect looks when set to 50, halfway between invisible and fully visible.

Figure 9-4:
The opacity
effect set
to 50.

Playing tricks with the blur filter

The blur filter makes text or any other object look smeared. The blur effect
can be adjusted to move in any direction, and to leave the original object
visible (as shown in Figure 9-5), or to merely show the blur itself.

Figure 9-5:
The blur
effect.

You can use the blur filter to manipulate a shadow, making an object of some
text look like it's in motion. To try the shadow move effect using the blur
filter, type this source code into the FrontPage Editor with the HTML tab
selected:

```
<html>
<head>
<script LANGUAGE="VBScript">
```

(continued)

(continued)

```
dim counter
function startTimer()
      timerhandle = setInterval("sizeit",20)
end function
function stopTimer()
      clearTimeout(timerhandle)
end function
function sizeit()
counter = counter + 1
if counter > 49 then counter = 1
n = "blur(add=1, direction=125, strength=" & counter & ")"
divider.style.filter= n
end function
</script>
</head>

<body onload="startTimer()" onunload="stopTimer()">

<div id="divider" STYLE="position: absolute; filter:
            blur(add=1, direction=125, strength=90">

<h1>This is a blur effect over time. </h1>
</div>
</body>
</html>
```

Adding drop shadows

One of the most valuable visual effects is the drop shadow. A page has a 3-D look because drop shadow creates realistic shadows underneath text or other objects, as you can see in Figure 9-6.

Figure 9-6:
You can add a realistic 3-D look to your pages with the drop shadow filter.

The drop shadow filter is a subtle, yet highly effective, tool. It adds dimension to your pages and looks quite realistic as you can see in Figure 9-6. To experiment with the drop shadow filter, type this source code into the FrontPage Editor with the HTML tab selected:

```
<html>
<head>

<script LANGUAGE="VBScript">
dim counter
function startTimer()
        timerhandle = setInterval("sizeit",120)
end function
function stopTimer()
        clearTimeout(timerhandle)
end function
function sizeit()
counter = counter + 1
if counter > 16 then counter = 1


n = "dropshadow(color=lightgrey, offx=8, offy=" & counter &
        ", positive=positive)"
divider.style.filter= n
end function
</script>
</head>

<body onload="startTimer()" onunload="stopTimer()">
<div id="divider" STYLE="position: absolute">
<h1 align="center"><font face="Engravers MT">Shadow effects
        over time</font></h1>
<p align="center"><font size="48" face="Engravers
        MT">Q</font></p>
</div>
</body>
</html>
```

Notice the key line in the preceding source code example:

```
n = "dropshadow(color=lightgrey, offx=8, offy=" & counter &
        ", positive=positive)"
```

You can use any color for the drop shadow filter, but lightgrey is the most realistic against a white background. The offx and offy specify how far from the object the shadow falls, with offx representing the horizontal measurement and offy the vertical. This measurement is in pixels. In the above example, the variable counter is used to stretch the y-axis over time to provide animation.

The fourth parameter can be 1 or 0. If positive, a shadow is created for any transparent pixel in the object; if negative (0), non-transparent pixels are used as the basis for the shadow.

Using the wave filter to create a hula effect

The wave filter offers you five parameters that you can adjust to get just the jiggly look you want. To try the wave filter, type the following source code into the FrontPage Editor with the HTML tab selected. As is the case with most filters, if you want to apply them repeatedly, you have to use a timer. This way, you can vary their parameters repeatedly. In this example, the fourth parameter of the wave filter (the parameter is called *strength*) is continually increased until it reaches a value of 8. At that point, the wave filter has twisted the letters fairly far out of shape (it looks a little as if someone has moved their hips way out during a dance). As soon as the strength parameter reaches 8, it is decreased back to zero. This decrease slowly restores the characters to their normal upright appearance.

The following code example applies and then removes the wave filter, over and over. It makes the letters look like they're doing the hula.

```
<html>
<head>
<script LANGUAGE="VBScript">

dim toggle
dim counter

function startTimer()
        timerhandle = setInterval("sizeit",90)
end function
function stopTimer()
        clearTimeout(timerhandle)
end function
function sizeit()
if counter > 8 then toggle = 1
```

```
if counter = 1 then toggle = 0
if toggle then
counter = counter - 1
else
counter = counter + 1
end if

n = "wave(add=0, freq=2, lightstrength=50, phase=0,
         strength=" & counter & ")"
divider.style.filter= n
end function
</script>
</head>

<body onload="startTimer()" onunload="stopTimer()">
<div id="divider" STYLE="position: absolute">
<h1 align="center"><font face="Bradley Hand ITC">SMEAR
         ANIMATION, or, the hula effect</font></h1>
</div>
</body>
</html>
```

The five parameters of the wave filter are set like this in the above example:

```
n = "wave(add=0, freq=2, lightstrength=50, phase=0,
         strength=" & counter & ")"
```

The add parameter defines whether or not to leave the original object visible in addition to the distorted version. Normally, you turn this off by setting add=0. The freq parameter specifies how many waves you have when the object is smeared. The lightstrength parameter is supposed to govern the lighting (0 to 100), but appears to have no effect when the value is changed. Phase describes where in the object the wave ripples appear. You can set the phase from 0 to 100. Finally, the strength parameter defines how far the smearing is dragged. This is the parameter that the above example varies over time.

Combining filters to create new effects

You can apply more than one filter to an object. Try the following example that applies the shadow and invert filters to a headline. Type this code into the FrontPage Editor with the HTML tab selected:

```
<html>
<head>
```

(continued)

(continued)

```
</head>

<body>
<div

STYLE="position:absolute;height:233;
filter: shadow(color=gray, direction=145) invert()">
<h1>Shadow and INVERT.</h1>
</div>
</body>
</html>
```

After you've typed in the above source code, click the FrontPage Preview tab and you can see the result shown in Figure 9-7. You can also try combining various filters to see what happens.

Figure 9-7:
The shadow
and invert
filters
are both
applied
to this
headline.

Shadow and INVERT.

The embossed effect illustrated in this example is created by combining the shadow filter with the invert filter. The invert filter transforms colors to their opposite (black, in this example becomes white).

Notice that to add more than one filter to an object, all you do is type in the new filter's name, separated from previous filter definitions by a space:

```
filter: shadow(color=gray, direction=145) invert()
```

Some filters combine differently, depending on which filter you specify first in the source code. The first filter specified is applied to the object first when the browser translates the source code. Then the next filter is applied to the result. Therefore, you can sometimes get different effects depending on which filter is put first in the code. For example, if you put the glow filter before the shadow filter in the code, the result looks quite different than if you reverse their order and put the shadow filter first.

Using Transition Filters for Fades and Wipes

The blendtrans filter is probably the most excellent filter of the entire bunch. Unlike some other animation effects, the blendtrans filter performs gently and gracefully. There's no jerky, awkward jumping during the animation. Instead, the object changes smoothly.

Blendtrans offers fades. A sister filter, revealtrans, is equally smooth and professional. Revealtrans offers wipes (such as box in, circle out, checkerboard, and so on). A *fade* looks as if an object gradually disappears, becoming more and more transparent until it's not there at all (the background gradually overtakes it and finally all you see is the background color, wallpaper, or whatever). A fade is similar to a dissolve, though a dissolve can include a more grainy, or pixilated disappearance. Fades can also work in reverse: The object gradually appears out of the background, becoming increasingly solid and blocking the background. A *wipe* is a more visually drastic transition. For example, the *circle out* wipe replaces an object with the background (or with another object) by gradually expanding a circle. At the start, the background can only be seen as a pinpoint circle in the center of the object. But that circle continues to expand until the object has been replaced by the background (or a second object).

The blendtrans filter gives you a result that's similar to the opacity effect (refer to Figure 9-4). Blendtrans, in fact, permits a faster, smoother fade in and fade out than you can get using the opacity property.

To try the blendtrans filter, type the following source code into the FrontPage Editor with the HTML tab selected:

```
<html>
<head>
<script language="VBScript">

function fadein()
        displaythis.filters(0).Apply()
        displaythis.style.visibility = "visible"
        displaythis.filters(0).Play()
end function
</script>

</head>
<body onload="fadein()">
```

(continued)

(continued)

```
<div id="displaythis"
style="width: 100%; visibility: hidden;
          filter:blendTrans(duration=4)">
<h1 align="center">Fade up into visibility.</h1>
</div>
</body>
</html>
```

Notice that the initial style of DIV is visibility:hidden. You don't see the headline when the browser first loads. But, immediately after this page loads (onload), the fadein function is executed. It uses the Apply method to officially add the blendtrans filter to the DIV named displaythis; then it sets the style to visible. Finally, the filter's behavior is actually initiated with the Play method. You can see that the blendtrans filter operates differently from the other filters. You complete several steps before the filter takes effect. Think of it like a tape player: First you push in the tape (Apply), and after setting visibility, you press the button that starts the action (Play).

Try adjusting the Duration parameter to speed up or slow down the fade.

Also, in the preceding code, try replacing this line:

```
style="width: 100%; visibility: hidden;
          filter:blendTrans(duration=4)"
```

with this new line:

```
style="width: 100%; visibility: hidden ;
          filter:revealTrans(duration=3,transition=3)"
```

You can use either the blendtrans or the revealTrans filter with any of the following HTML objects: BODY, BUTTON, DIV, IMG, INPUT, MARQUEE, SPAN, TABLE, TD, TEXTAREA, TFOOT, TH, THEAD, or TR.

The revealTrans filter enables you to specify the transition. The transition parameter defines what kind of *wipe* is used to reveal the object. The 24 transition values are listed in Table 9-1.

Table 9-1	The transitionwipe values
Transitionwipe	**Value**
Box in	0
Box out	1

Transitionwipe	Value
Circle in	2
Circle out	3
Wipe up	4
Wipe down	5
Wipe right	6
Wipe left	7
Vertical blinds	8
Horizontal blinds	9
Checkerboard across	10
Checkerboard down	11
Random dissolve	12
Split vertical in	13
Split vertical out	14
Split horizontal in	15
Split horizontal out	16
Strips left down	17
Strips left up	18
Strips right down	19
Strips right up	20
Random bars horizontal	21
Random bars vertical	22
Random	23

Part IV
The Basics of Internet Programming

The 5th Wave   By Rich Tennant

Re'al Pro'gram·mers

OH WOW!

MONDO-TECH

Real Programmers do their best work between 1 and 5 a.m.

In this part . . .

This part of the book zeros in on programming — in plain English. You see how similar the Internet programming languages JavaScript and VBScript are and how easily you can translate between them. You find out how to make things happen in a Web page, beyond what plain-vanilla HTML programming can do. You also see how to fix bugs when your programs don't work the way you hoped they would.

Chapter 10

Objects, Objects Everywhere

. . . .

In This Chapter

▶ Finding out what objects actually are

▶ Adding components in the Visual Studio 6 Applications

▶ Understanding the Object Browser

▶ Using the Visual Component Manager

. . . .

*I*f you use any Rapid Application Development (RAD) tools — such as the applications that make up Visual Studio 6 — you're using objects.

But if you think about it for a minute, you realize that the word *object* can mean pretty much anything. Regardless of how imprecise it is, *object* is the word that people in computing use to mean a group of *things*.

What things? The Visual Studio 6 applications — Visual Basic, Visual FoxPro, FrontPage, Visual InterDev, Visual C++, and Visual J++ — include a set of pre-built objects. To make matters confusing, the Help feature and the documentation that comes with Visual Studio 6 does not call them simply *objects* (most of the time). Instead, Visual Studio 6 calls them by various names such as components, Webbots (in FrontPage 97), Active Elements (in FrontPage 98), scriptlets, applets, design-time controls, ActiveX controls, or just plain controls. Microsoft, bless them, is not like France. In France, an official grammar committee ensures the purity of *La Belle Francaise.* No such purity disturbs the glorious diversity of computer diction.

To be fair, minor distinctions do exist between some of these entities. A design-time control, for example, inserts source code into an application while you're designing (programming) the application. By contrast, a component, properly named, does not insert any source code into your application. A component hides its source code. (You just drop the component into your source code like you drop a cherry on top of a sundae.)

However, these objects, by whatever name, offer you, the programmer, the same benefit: They contain prewritten functionality. In other words, somebody else spent time building them, and you can just drop them into your programming and use them. A check box is a typical object. A user can click it while your application runs, selecting or deselecting it. Your application can detect the status (checked or not checked) of the check box and take appropriate action. Perhaps the check box is labeled Boldface, and if the user clicks it, your application changes all the text in a text box to boldface.

But in spite of the many words used to describe essentially the same thing, you can find at least one happy result. Most of the Visual Studio 6 applications put the components/objects/applets/design-time controls/scriptlets/ Webbots on a Toolbox. So, if something is on a Toolbox, it's an object.

In computer programming, the idea of *object* is more extensive than the definition used in this chapter. An object can be something as elementary as an HTML headline, for example. (So, objects are not limited to the things that you see on a Visual Studio 6 application's Toolbox.) However, to make the definition of *object* somewhat manageable, it's useful to limit it, in this chapter anyway, to things that you find on a Visual Studio 6 application's Toolbox. If you think of it that way, you'll get the idea. And the idea of objects, like other notoriously abstract ideas (love, hope, beauty), is impossible to really define precisely, even for poets.

In most Visual Studio 6 applications, you can choose View⇨Toolbox, and you see objects on a Toolbox, ready for you to use them. (As always, you encounter exceptions to the rule that you find objects only on a Toolbox. For example, Visual FoxPro uses a Toolbox-like window that it calls Form Controls.)

These minor eccentricities aside, objects are a key feature of *Visual* applications (RAD applications). Objects/controls/components assist you in Rapid Application Development. Be glad that you have them, even if objects do have different names.

After all, if you're working on an application in Visual Basic and you need a set of option buttons, you don't want to have to actually write the low-level programming that makes option buttons work. All you want to do is double-click them in the Visual Basic Toolbox and watch the set of buttons appear — fully functional — in your application's user interface. No programming is involved.

You know, before 1991 when Visual Basic introduced pre-built components, programmers the world over were spending most of their time reinventing the wheel. These programmers put most of their efforts into concocting the various objects that make up a Graphical User Interface, as well as common utilities, such as spell checkers and search and replace features. Now, life is much easier. And because of objects, in combination with other shortcuts such as wizards, Rapid Application Development is now a reality.

Introducing Objects

The word *object* has always been a bit of a problem. Even in normal English, *object* is a pretty vague word. But in the past few years, this word has been even more misused by the computer community. The word isn't quite meaningless yet, but it's close.

In computing, an object is pre-built and mainly self-sufficient. An object usually has properties, methods, and events:

> ✔ **Properties** are qualities (or characteristics), like blue or two inches wide.
>
> ✔ **Methods** are abilities, like the ability to calculate state tax.
>
> ✔ **Events** are things that can happen to an object, like Click or Resize.

Collectively, an object's properties, methods, and events are called its *members*.

Recall that objects are called by various names in computing today: controls, components, design-time controls, Webbots, scriptlets, or applets. What all these objects have in common is that they're reusable, pre-built *somethings* with members. In the real world, an example of a component is a plastic drink holder: You just buy it in the auto store and hang it on your car window. You can stick a Coke in it. You get usefulness out of it, without having to build the thing yourself.

The most popular word for objects currently is *component*, so I use that term in this book. Examples of common components are a text box, label, option button, command (general purpose) button, check box, picturebox, scrollbar, and list box.

Adding a component

The best way to understand specifically what a component does is by using one. When you're creating an application in Visual Basic, you can easily add functionality to your project by dropping components from the Visual Basic Toolbox onto a Form. To see how to do this, follow these steps:

1. **Start Visual Basic by clicking its icon on your desktop.**

   You see the New Project dialog box with icons for a variety of kinds of projects you can create.

2. **Double-click the Standard EXE icon.**

   The New Project dialog box closes, and the standard Visual Basic workspace appears.

3. **Double-click a command button component in the Visual Basic Toolbox.**

   The command button appears on the currently selected form.

   If the Toolbox isn't visible, Choose View⇨Toolbox.

Now that you've added a command button component to your Visual Basic application, you can make it do something.

Programming a component in Visual Basic

Programming a component is generally quite easy. In Visual Basic, you simply double-click the component and then write some programming into the Code View window that appears.

To see how to put some programming into a command button, follow these steps:

1. **Put a command button on a Visual Basic form and then double-click the command button.**

   Follow the steps in the section "Adding a component," earlier in this chapter.

   The Code View opens. Code View in Visual Basic is the equivalent of Source View in Visual InterDev and HTML View in FrontPage. It's where you write programming that's carried out in response to events in the component, as shown in Figure 10-1.

2. **Type** Width = Width - 20 **into the Code View window.**

   Notice in Figure 10-1 that two drop-down lists are at the top of the Visual Basic code window. If you drop them down, the one on the left lists all the objects in the current form; the one on the right lists all the events for the current object. By default, the most commonly used event is displayed first. In the case of the command button, by far the most common event is Click.

3. **Now test the programming by pressing F5 to run the program you've just written.**

   Form1 appears on screen as if it's actually running in Windows as a normal program.

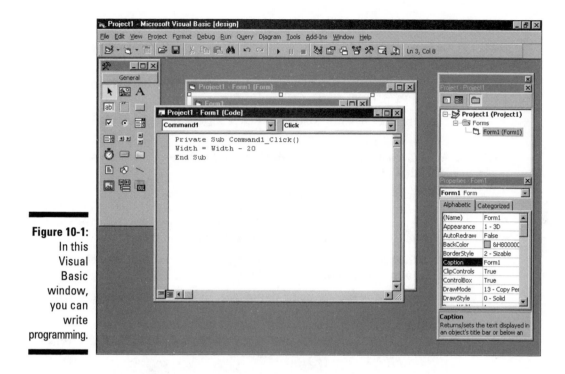

Figure 10-1:
In this
Visual
Basic
window,
you can
write
programming.

4. **Click the command button several times**.

Each time you click the command button, the form becomes 20 pixels narrower.

When you program a property like Width, Visual Basic assumes that you mean the form's width unless you specify otherwise. For example, if you want to make the command button grow narrower, you must specify the command button by using its name, like this: `command1.width = command1.width - 20`.

5. **Click the x in the upper-right corner of the form to stop execution and return to programming mode in Visual Basic.**

Adding a component in Visual FoxPro

To add a component to a Visual FoxPro form, you click to select the object and then you click on the form where you want the object placed. Follow these steps to add a set of check boxes to a Visual FoxPro form:

1. **Start Visual FoxPro by clicking its icon on your desktop.**

You see the standard Visual FoxPro Editor window with no project loaded unless you've selected the Open Last Project on Startup Option in the Tools⇨Options, View tab page.

2. **Load an existing project by selecting File➪Open.**

   A FoxPro project is opened, and the Project Manager window is displayed.

3. **Locate and then click to select a form in the tree list on the left side of the Project Manager window.**

   If the project has no existing form, click New in the Project Manager and then select New Form.

4. **With a form highlighted (selected) in the Project Manager window, click the Modify button.**

   The Visual FoxPro Form Designer window opens, displaying the form you selected. The Properties window and the unique Form Controls window also open, as shown in Figure 10-2. (The Form Controls window is called a Toolbox in all other Visual Studio 6 applications.)

5. **To add three check boxes to the displayed form, click the check box icon in the Form Controls window.**

   The check box icon remains depressed, indicating that it's selected.

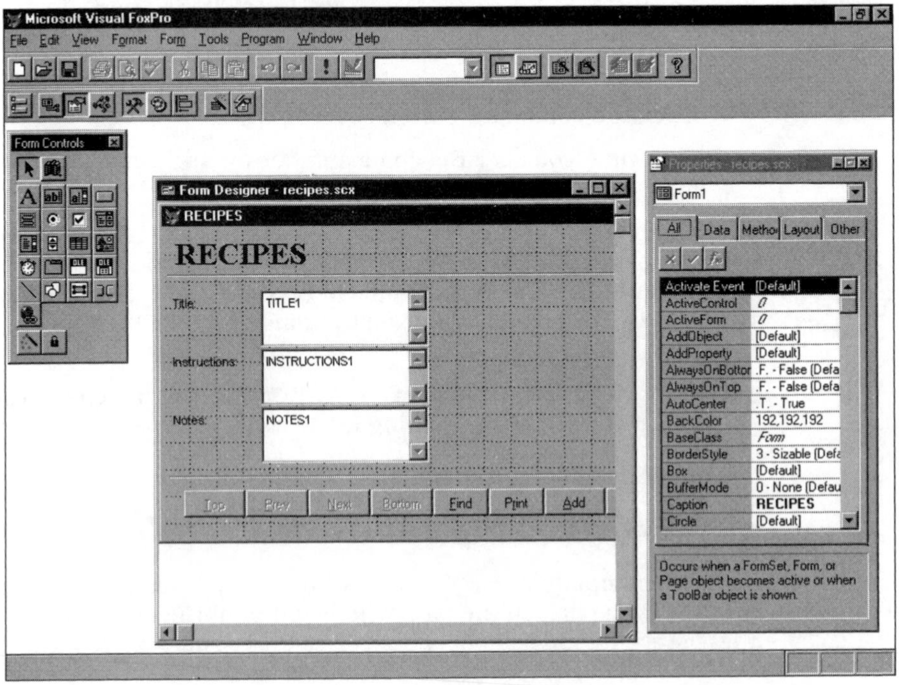

Figure 10-2:
The Visual
FoxPro
Form
Controls
and Form
Designer
windows.

6. **Click anywhere on the form in the Form Designer window where you want the first check box placed.**

   A check box appears in the form, right where you clicked the form. By default, it's named Check1.

7. **Repeat Steps 5 and 6 twice to place two additional check boxes on this form.**

   The resulting three check boxes in the Form Designer look like those shown in Figure 10-3. The most recently added check box still has the selection frame around it.

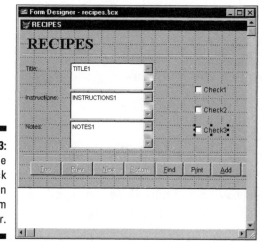

Figure 10-3:
Three
check
boxes in
the Form
Designer.

Adding components in Visual InterDev

Visual InterDev includes a set of HTML components, arranged as you may expect, on a Toolbox window. These components are standard, familiar HTML controls like submit buttons.

However, Visual InterDev also includes other sets of components on its Toolbox, such as ActiveX Controls and design-time controls. Follow these steps to add HTML components to a Visual InterDev page:

1. **Select File⇨New Project in Visual InterDev.**

   The New Project dialog box opens.

2. **Click the Recent tab.**

3. **Double-click the name of a project to open it.**

4. **Double-click an .Htm file in the Project Explorer.**

   A Web page opens in the Visual InterDev Editor window.

5. **Click the Design tab in the Visual InterDev Editor.**

   The page is ready to receive components.

6. **Click the HTML tab in the Toolbox.**

   Visual InterDev's set of HTML components is displayed. (If the Toolbox isn't visible, choose <u>V</u>iew➪Toolbo<u>x</u>.)

7. **Drag a Submit Button icon from the Toolbox onto the editor window.**

   A Submit button appears on the Web page in the editor window.

8. **Click the Source tab at the bottom of the editor window.**

   You see that dragging the Submit button onto this page caused Visual InterDev to insert the following HTML source code:

   ```
   <INPUT id=submit1 name=submit1 type=submit value=Submit>
   ```

9. **Click the Design tab at the bottom of the editor.**

   You return to design mode.

10. **Click the ActiveX Control tab in the Toolbox.**

    A new list of components appears.

11. **Drag a progress bar component onto the editor window.**

    A progress bar component appears on the editor.

12. **Click the HTML tab to see what the progress bar looks like in the source code.**

    You see a graphic representation of the progress bar, just as it looks when you add it in Design View.

13. **To see the actual source code that describes the progress bar, right-click the progress bar and choose Always View as Text from the context menu.**

    You see the OBJECT definition, like this:

    ```
    <OBJECT classid=clsid:0713E8D2-850A-101B-AFC0-
            4210102A8DA7
    height=23 id=ProgressBar1 style="HEIGHT: 23px; WIDTH:
            239px" width=239 VIEWASTEXT>
            <PARAM NAME="_ExtentX" VALUE="6324">
            <PARAM NAME="_ExtentY" VALUE="609">
            <PARAM NAME="_Version" VALUE="327682">
            <PARAM NAME="BorderStyle" VALUE="0">
    ```

```
<PARAM NAME="Appearance" VALUE="1">
<PARAM NAME="MousePointer" VALUE="0">
<PARAM NAME="Enabled" VALUE="1">
<PARAM NAME="OLEDropMode" VALUE="0">
<PARAM NAME="Min" VALUE="0">
<PARAM NAME="Max" VALUE="100"></OBJECT>
```

Most of this definition makes you glad that Visual InterDev handles the job of writing this source code for you. You can be especially grateful that you don't have to write the long `classid` code.

Adding components to Visual J++ projects

Visual J++ operates somewhat like its parent language C++. The toolbox in Visual J++ displays the WFC (Windows Foundation Class) set of components. To add a component to a Visual J++ project, follow these steps:

1. **Start Visual J++ by clicking its icon on your desktop.**

   The New Project dialog box opens.

2. **Click the Recent tab.**

3. **Double-click the name of a Visual J++ project to open it.**

4. **Click a form in the Project Explorer.**

   A form window opens, ready for you to add components to the form. You can double-click, or drag, a component onto a Visual J++ form, as shown in Figure 10-4.

5. **Drag a Picture Box component onto the form.**

   An empty picture box appears on the form.

6. **To add a picture to the empty box, click the Image property in the Properties window.**

   The image property is highlighted in the Properties window.

7. **Click the button with three dots (...) on the right side of the Image property in the Properties window. You can see the three-dot button right next to the word *(Bitmap)* in the lower-right corner of Figure 10-4.**

   The Open dialog box opens. It's a typical file Open dialog box.

8. **Double-click the graphic file that you want to insert into the picture box.**

   The graphic appears in the picture box.

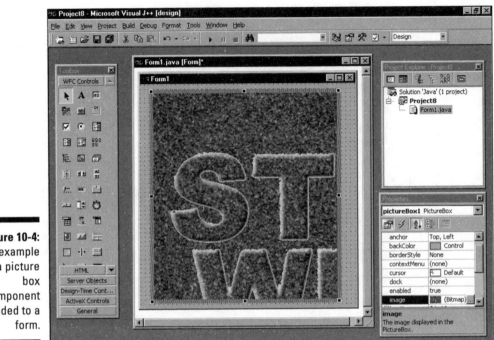

Figure 10-4:
An example
of a picture
box
component
added to a
form.

The Visual J++ Properties window has a unique feature. Take a look at the top of the Properties window, and you see a button with a lightning bolt on it. Click this button, and the Properties disappear and are replaced by all the events available to the currently selected object. Double-click the name of one of these events to bring up the code window. Also, if you're used to programming in Visual Basic, you may be surprised at the amount of over-head code required to load libraries and otherwise handle a simple event, such as a click. Take a look at the default code provided in the Visual J++ code window.

Employing FrontPage's Components

FrontPage has a unique way of dealing with components. Instead of a toolbox, FrontPage simply lists components on its editor's Insert menu. FrontPage 97 referred to components as Webbots, but recently Microsoft has been using the term *components*.

But it would be boring if consistency were to dominate creativity. Therefore, just to keep you on your toes, a component in FrontPage 98 is now called by two names: a FrontPage Component, or an *Active Element*. You find these categories both listed on FrontPage 98's Insert menu. What's the difference between a FrontPage Component and an Active Element? Don't ask me. I see no difference at all. Neither does anyone else. To prove my point, you can find the hit counter object available in *both* the FrontPage Component category and the Active Element categories in the FrontPage Insert menu.

The hit counter is a typical FrontPage whatchamacallit. A hit counter displays how many times a page has been loaded into a visitor's browser. To find out how to add a hit counter to a Web page, follow these steps:

1. **Start FrontPage by clicking its icon on your desktop.**

   The FrontPage Explorer appears.

2. **Choose Tools⇨Show FrontPage Editor.**

   The FrontPage Editor appears.

3. **Choose File⇨New.**

   The New dialog box opens, showing a list of various page templates you can select.

4. **Double-click Normal Page.**

   The dialog box closes, and a new, blank page appears.

5. **Click the Normal tab.**

   You see the basic, blank-page Design View.

6. **Choose Insert⇨FrontPage Component.**

   The Insert FrontPage Component dialog box opens.

7. **Double-click hit counter in the list of available components.**

   The Hit Counter Properties dialog box opens, as shown in Figure 10-5.

8. **Click the option button next to the style of hit counter you want to use.**

9. **Specify how many digits you want to display in the Fixed Number Of Digits text box and also specify whether you want the counter to reset to zero in the Reset Counter To check box.**

10. **Click the OK button.**

    The dialog box closes, and the words Hit Counter appear in the FrontPage Editor.

11. **Click the HTML tab on the bottom of the FrontPage Editor.**

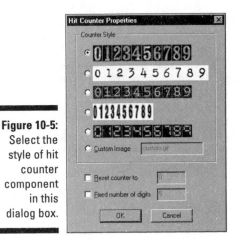

Figure 10-5:
Select the
style of hit
counter
component
in this
dialog box.

This source code for the new hit counter component is displayed:

```
<!--webbot bot="HitCounter" i-image="0" i-digits="0"
    b-reset="FALSE"
PREVIEW="&lt;strong&gt;[Hit Counter]&lt;/strong&gt;"
    u-custom i-resetvalue="0" -->
```

If you try to view the hit counter (or any other FrontPage component) in
the FrontPage Preview View (by clicking the Preview tab), nothing happens.
FrontPage components can be viewed only in a running browser. To see the
Webbot, choose File⇨Preview in Browser from the FrontPage Editor menu
bar. You see the hit counter in your browser, as shown in Figure 10-6. Try
pressing F5 several times to refresh (reload) the page in the browser. Sure
enough, the hit counter counts up by one, each time you reload the page.

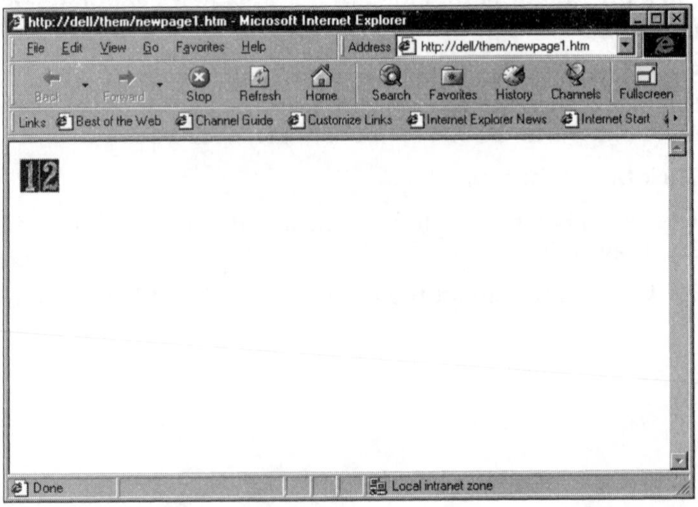

Figure 10-6:
You can see
a FrontPage
component
such as the
hit counter
in your
browser.

Managing Objects

Not all objects are installed with RAD applications. You can get objects from other sources as well. Objects can be purchased from third-party vendors, and you can even create your own. (Chapter 13 is all about building your own custom components.)

The default set of objects that come with an application appear on its Toolbox (or its menus). However, you must have a way to add (or remove) components from a project. Also, you must have a way to get information about the members of a component. Visual Studio 6 applications offer several tools to accomplish these jobs. The following sections give you the details on how to use some of these tools.

Working with the Object Browser

Most Visual Studio 6 applications include a utility called the Object Browser. You can find it available in Visual J++, Visual Basic, and even several Microsoft Office applications. The Object Browser is a kind of help system: It lists a component's members (properties, methods, and events) along with any constants that are used in connection with the component.

To see how to get help using the Object Browser in Visual Basic, follow these steps:

1. **Start Visual Basic by clicking its icon on your desktop.**

   You see the New Project dialog box with icons for a variety of projects you can create.

2. **Double-click the Standard EXE icon in the New Project dialog box.**

   The New Project dialog box closes, and the standard Visual Basic workspace appears.

3. **Choose** <u>V</u>iew⊏>**<u>O</u>bject Browser (or just Press F2).**

   The Object Browser appears, as shown in Figure 10-7. The Object Browser is a quick-reference help system, describing the members of components available for use in your projects.

4. **Click the drop-down list in the upper-left corner of the Object Browser.**

   A list of the various libraries of components appears.

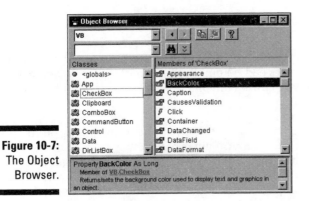

Figure 10-7:
The Object
Browser.

5. **Select *VB* from the drop-down list.**

All the default components available to Visual Basic are displayed in the Classes list box on the left of the Object Browser. All the members of the currently selected component are displayed in the right list box.

6. **After you've found the information you were looking for, close the Object Browser.**

Objects listed in the Object Browser (or available on the Toolbox) must first be registered with the Visual Studio 6 application. In Visual Basic's case, you can register third-party or other components by choosing Project⇨ References. You see a list of components that are installed in your system. To register them for Visual Basic, click the check box next to the component. After you click the OK button to close the References dialog box, any components you selected are registered.

Managing objects with the Visual Component Manager

All Visual Studio 6 applications (except FrontPage and Visual FoxPro) can use the Visual Component Manager tool. This utility's job is to help you locate, organize, and work with components. To see how to use the Visual Component Manager, follow these steps:

1. **With Visual InterDev running, choose View⇨Other Windows⇨ Visual Component Manager.**

The Visual Component Manager dialog box opens, displaying a single folder, the Local Database. This folder contains a group of additional folders you may want to look at.

2. **Click the drop-down list on the top left of the Visual Component Manager.**

   A tree displaying the contents of the Visual Component Manager appears, as shown in Figure 10-8. The Visual Component Manager enables you to add examples, add-ins, scriptlets, and other components to your project.

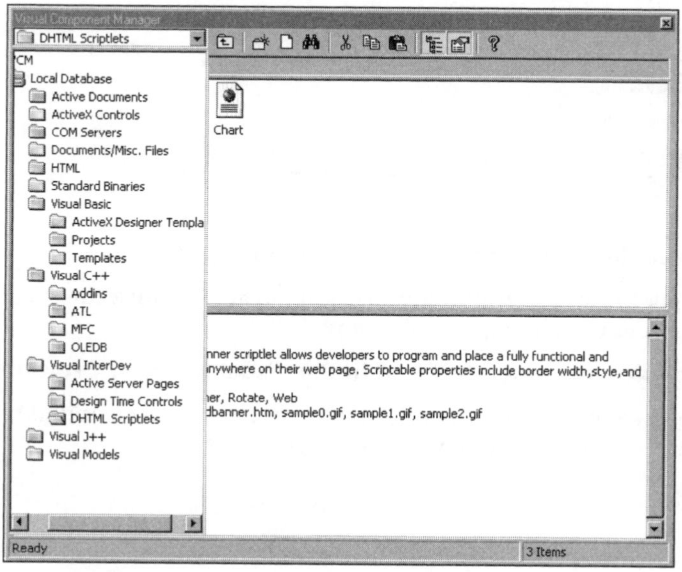

Figure 10-8: The Visual Component Manager.

3. **Click the folder named Visual InterDev in the tree view.**

   Several folders appear including Active Server Pages, design-time controls, and DHTML Scriptlets.

4. **Click the folder named DHTML Scriptlets.**

   Several additional folders appear, including AdBanner, Calendar, and Chart.

5. **Click the Calendar folder.**

   A thorough description of the Calendar component appears in the lower pane of the Visual Component Manager dialog box, as shown in Figure 10-9.

6. **Now right-click the Calendar icon.**

   A context menu appears, enabling you to save, relocate, copy, and otherwise manage this component.

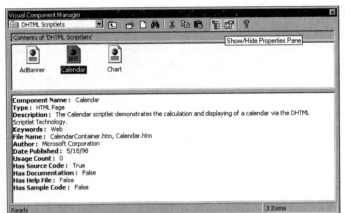

Figure 10-9:
The Visual
Component
Manager
dialog box.

7. **From the context menu, click Add to Project.**

8. **Click the x icon in the upper-right corner to close the Visual Component Manager dialog box.**

9. **Double-click Calendar.HTM in the Visual InterDev Project Manager.**

   You see the calendar scriptlet component has been added to your current project, along with its support files.

Chapter 11

The Rosetta Stone: JScript or VBScript

Computer languages aren't like normal human languages. Ordinary languages include many thousands of words; computer languages typically contain 50 to 100 primary words, and perhaps a couple hundred additional, less common words. Ordinary language is fairly loose and ambiguous; computer languages are highly precise: misplace a comma and the entire statement probably makes no sense at all to the computer. Finally, ordinary language is something you're taught before you know what's happening; you can choose which computer language you want to use.

You have two specialized computer languages, JScript and VBScript, that are designed for Web page programming (you mix them right in with the usual HTML Web programming).

You may ask: Why do you need scripting languages when you've got HTML? Well, HTML is not really a computer language. It describes the appearance of text and graphics — that is, where they are on the page, how big they are, and so on. But HTML can't compute. It can't even add 2+2.

So, to compute in Web pages, you have to supplement HTML with one of two popular scripting languages: VBScript or JavaScript (which is also known as JScript, Microsoft's version of JavaScript). This is how the process works: You can write whatever you want your script to do in either VBScript or JScript and insert the code into your HTML document between `<SCRIPT>` and `</SCRIPT>` tags. A browser knows that it's supposed to interpret as *script* (not HTML) the commands in the lines of source code between those tags. The `SCRIPT` tag also defines which scripting language is used:

```
<script LANGUAGE="VBScript">
```

Or, to use JScript:

```
<script LANGUAGE="JScript">
```

Scripting can be used in many ways. One popular use is to verify that the visitor has correctly entered some information. For example, when the visitor clicks a submit button to send her e-mail address to you, a piece of script can check the e-mail address and, if no @ is in the address, display a message to the visitor saying that she didn't type a correct e-mail address and asking her to please try again.

Note that this chapter demonstrates various scripting techniques, but it's not designed to cover all elements of script programming. In this chapter, I compare JScript to VBScript. They're similar in many ways. If you already know how to use one of them, it's nonetheless useful to be familiar with the other one. That way, you can understand and adapt example scripts no matter which script language the examples are written in. Translating between VBScript and JScript is surprisingly easy. For more information, check out *VBScript For Dummies* by John Walkenbach and *JScript For Dummies,* 2nd Edition by Emily A. Vander Veer (both by IDG Books Worldwide, Inc.).

Choosing Your Language

Your choice of language mainly depends on any programming you've done previously. If you've worked with Basic, you're likely to find VBScript easier to use. If you've used C or Java, JScript is probably your language of choice.

In any case, these two scripting languages are subsets of their parent languages, Visual Basic and Java. The scripting languages have been stripped of any commands that can manipulate peripherals. For example, no commands in VBScript or JScript access a hard drive.

The reason the scripting languages are stripped down is simple. People surfing the Internet don't want to load a page into their browser that destroys the contents of their hard drive. If a format command existed in VBScript or JScript, an evil person can type this into a Web page:

```
<html>
<head>
<script LANGUAGE="VBScript">
```

```
format c:

</script>
</head>
<body>
</body>
</html>
```

Anyone visiting a Web site with a home page that looked like this could be in serious trouble.

Comparing VBScript and JScript

You may find that understanding VBScript is fairly easy if you've worked with JScript, and vice versa. In the following sections, you can see comparisons of their major features side-by-side. Trying these examples in either FrontPage or Visual InterDev is easy, but for simplicity, you can use the FrontPage Editor.

JScript is case sensitive; VBScript isn't. Therefore, when using JScript, you must remember that if you use four different capitalizations of a word — such as vname, VName, Vname, and VNAME — you have created four *distinct* variable names. (In VBScript, they all refer to the same variable because VBScript ignores capitalization.) JScript is also case-sensitive with function names, variable parameters passed to functions, and so on.

The moral? To avoid causing bugs in their programs, many people *always use lowercase* letters when they write programs in JScript. You should, too. Perhaps you noticed that in the programming examples in this book, programming code is sometimes in all-lowercase, and other times in mixed upper- and lowercase. The reason is that, most scripting examples in this book are written in VBScript, where capitalization issues cause no problems.

Understanding procedures

A *procedure* is a group of source code lines that, together, do a particular job. You have two kinds of procedures in VBScript, a *sub* and a *function.* The difference between a sub (subroutine) and a function is that a function can return a value (a result), but a sub does not. JScript only uses functions. It has no provision for subs.

A procedure is often a few lines of programming code, but these lines accomplish a useful job. For example, if you want to create a procedure that adds 7 percent sales tax to the cost of any item, follow these steps:

1. **Start FrontPage Explorer.**

   Depending on how you have FrontPage set up, you may, or may not, see a Getting Started dialog box.

2. **Click Cancel if you're asked if you want to create a new FrontPage Web in the Getting Started dialog box.**

   The dialog box closes.

3. **Choose Tools⇨Show FrontPage Editor.**

   The FrontPage Editor appears, containing a blank, empty page.

4. **Click the HTML tab in the FrontPage Editor.**

   You see the window where you can type in source code that executes when the page is loaded into a browser (or when you click the Preview tab in the FrontPage Editor).

5. **Right-click the editor window and then choose Select All from the context menu.**

   The entire default source code template is selected.

6. **Press the Del key.**

   All source code in the editor is deleted.

7. **Type this source code into the editor:**

```
<html>
<head>

<script LANGUAGE="VBScript">

Function AddTax (costofitem)
AddTax = costofitem * 1.07
Msgbox AddTax
End Function

</script>

</head>

<body onclick="AddTax(23.34)">
</body>
</html>
```

Functions are usually typed into a Web page's header (meaning between the <HEAD> and </HEAD> tags).

8. Click the FrontPage Preview tab.

The Web page is displayed as it would be in a browser. You can test it in the Preview view.

9. Click your mouse anywhere in the page.

A message box appears displaying the result: 24.9738.

The procedure has done its job. It took the 23.34, added 7 percent to it, and then displayed the result in a message box.

The only difference in the way that JScript and VBScript handle procedures is that VBScript permits Sub procedures and JScript does not. Both languages use functions.

For example, you can get the result from the AddTax function, like this:

```
N = AddTax(33.10)
MsgBox N

Function AddTax (costofitem)
        AddTax = costofitem * 1.07
        Msgbox AddTax
End Function
```

The variable N in the preceding example receives the result when it calls the AddTax function. Then you can display N or otherwise manipulate the result.

Recall that a function returns a result to the line that calls it in the source code (invokes it by using the name of the function). A Sub does not return a result to the caller, but it can cause messages to be displayed and so on. For example, to accomplish the same result (showing a message box to the user) as the JScript function example above, you can write the code for a Sub like this:

```
<html>

<head>
<script LANGUAGE="VBScript">

AddTax(23.32)
```

(continued)

(continued)

```
Sub AddTax (costofitem)
        Tax = costofitem * 1.07
        Msgbox (Tax)
End Sub

</script>
</head>

<body>
</body>
</html>
```

The line `AddTax(23.32)` calls (or *triggers*) the Sub. You can, if you wish, omit the parentheses when calling a Sub, like this: `AddTax 23.32`.

Working with variables

In both JScript and VBScript, you can define variables in two locations:

✔ Inside a procedure. (This is called a *local variable.*)

✔ Outside a procedure. (This is called a *global variable.*)

If a variable is defined inside a procedure (a *local variable*), it works only within that particular procedure. As soon as the procedure concludes (with the End Function or End Sub command), the variable no longer exists and cannot be used elsewhere in the script. Here's an example of a local variable named `firstv`. It's local because it's defined inside this function:

```
function whichone () {

        var firstv = 5;
        a = alert ("In this function, the variable firstv
             is: " + firstv)
}
```

If a variable is defined globally — outside any subroutine or function — it can then be used by any script in the entire document. A global variable holds whatever contents you give it, no matter whether the browser is working with other script, working with HTML, or just sitting idle.

To define a global variable in JScript or VBScript, you can just assign some value to it, as you can see in this JScript example:

```
<html>
<head><script LANGUAGE="JScript">

firstv = 122

function whichone () {
        var firstv = 5;
        a = alert ("In this function, the variable firstv
            is: " + firstv)
}

</script>
</head>

<body onload="whichone()">
</body>
</html>
```

Compare the preceding source code to the following source code, which is a translation of the example into VBScript:

```
<html>

<head><script LANGUAGE="vbscript">

firstv = 122

function whichone ()
firstv = 5
msgbox ("In this function, the variable firstv is: " &
            firstv)
end function

</script>

<title></title>
</head>

<body onload="whichone()">
</body>
</html>
```

Compare the two scripting languages in these examples. You notice several things that distinguish them:

- ✔ **Braces:** VBScript doesn't use the { } braces for punctuation, but JScript uses them to show where a function's commands begin and end. VBScript shows that a function ends by using the End Function command. The End Function command does not exist in JScript. JScript uses the brace } to conclude a function.

- ✔ **Msgbox:** VBScript can use either the msgbox or the alert command to display a message to the user. JScript uses the alert command only.

- ✔ **Concatenation:** VBScript uses & and JScript uses + to add two pieces of text together (or *concatenate* them).

- ✔ **End of statement punctuation:** JScript uses a semicolon to show the end of a complete statement. A complete statement is something that fully describes an action (b = 5, for example, or a = alert ("those")). The semicolon is optional if a statement occupies a line all by itself, but you must use it to separate statements if the statements are on the same line, like this: b = 5; a = alert ("those"). In VBScript, if two statements are on the same line, they're separated by a colon, like this: b = 5: msgbox ("those"). VBScript never uses the colon when a statement is on a line of its own. The statement just ends with no punctuation.

- ✔ **Variable definition:** JScript requires that you use the Var command when defining a local variable (inside a Function). VBScript has a comparable command, Dim, to define variables. However, Dim is always optional.

Copy either of the preceding two code examples into the FrontPage Editor with the HTML tab selected. Then click the Preview tab. You see a message box displaying this: In this function, the variable firstv is: 5.

You've used the variable name firstv twice in the example, once locally and once globally. Note that the local version gets displayed. (You see a 5 not a 122 when the message is shown.) If you remove the line that defines the local variable, the global version will be displayed.

Arrays: cluster variables

You can group variables together into an *array*. Each variable in an array uses the same name but is distinguished by an index number. Arrays are useful precisely because all the variables in the array are *numbered*. As a result, you can easily work with variables as a set rather than individually, and you can also manipulate them *arithmetically.* For example, you can search through variables by counting from `arrayitem(1)` up to `arrayitem(12)` much more easily than if each variable had a unique name. Also, you can more easily change all the variables to the color blue, or delete them all, or do whatever else you want to them. You can make these changes by referring to the variables by their index number rather than working with each of them, one-by-one, using unique names for each variable. Put another way, arrays are particularly useful in loops. See the section later in this chapter titled "Going round and round with loops."

Here's how you define an array in JScript:

```
<SCRIPT LANGUAGE=JScript>

myarr = new Array(2);

myarr[0] = "This ";
myarr[1] = "That ";
myarr[2] = "The other ";

alert (myarr[0] + myarr[1] + myarr[2]);

</SCRIPT>
```

If you try running this script by clicking the Preview tab in the FrontPage Editor, you see a message box displaying: `This That The other`.

Here's the VBScript version of the same array:

```
<SCRIPT LANGUAGE= VBScript>

Dim myarr(2)

myarr(0) = "This "
myarr(1) = "That "
myarr(2) = "The other "

alert (myarr(0) & myarr(1) & myarr(2))

</SCRIPT>
```

Here are the points to notice when comparing these two versions:

✔ **The Array-defining command:** In VBScript, an array is created with the `Dim` command. (`Dim` is not optional with arrays, though it is optional when defining a variable.) In JScript, you define an array with the `new Array` command.

- **The "Zeroth Oddity":** Both script languages specify the number of items that the array holds (in this example, it's three): `Dim myarr(2)` and `myarr = new Array(2);`. Why do they say 2 when these commands create room for 3 items? Because arrays start counting with item 0: `myarr(0)` is the first item. This silly convention has caused countless errors in computer programming, but like the year 2000 problem, it's one of those oversights that happened years ago when computing was in its infancy, and we all just have to live with it now.

- **Brackets versus parentheses:** JScript encloses array index numbers in brackets; VBScript uses parentheses.

Using built-in events

Browsers have a set of *events* to which they can react. In other words, if a visitor clicks the page currently displayed in the browser, the onclick event triggers. Events are things that happen to an object. A text box, for example, has various events including KeyPress, OnClick, MouseMove, and others. You, the programmer, can write source code in an event, thereby defining how the text box reacts when clicked. Perhaps you write code in the text box's OnClick event that turns all the text in the box boldface if the user clicks the text box.

You also have other built-in events. You have sets of events for the document object (a Web page that's been loaded into a browser), and for the window object (the browser itself is called the "window object").

Most components and other objects in Windows programming include a set of events for which you can write programming. Also, many events are found in nearly all objects (OnClick, for example, is nearly always available). Others are highly specific to a particular object. (OnRowEnter, for example, is only available to objects that potentially contain a table.)

Here are a few of the events for the document object, just to give you an idea of what events are available to many other objects as well: onafterupdate, onbeforeupdate, onclick, ondblclick, ondragstart, onerrorupdate, onhelp, onkeydown, onkeypress, onkeyup, onmousedown, onmousemove, onmouseout, onmouseover, onmouseup, onreadystatechange, onrowenter, onrowexit, onselectstart.

Here is the set of events for the window object, for comparison: onbeforeunload, onblur, onerror, onfocus, onhelp, onload, onresize, onscroll, onunload. Use the onload event to make something happen as soon as a document loads into the browser.

You can write script to react to a click or any other event. To cause the background to change to a medium sea green color when the visitor clicks it, follow these steps:

1. **Start FrontPage Explorer.**

   Depending on how you have FrontPage set up, you may, or may not, see a Getting Started dialog box.

2. **Click Cancel if you're asked if you want to create a new FrontPage Web in the Getting Started dialog box.**

   The dialog box closes.

3. **Choose Tools⇨Show FrontPage Editor.**

   The FrontPage Editor appears, containing a blank, empty page.

4. **Click the HTML tab in the FrontPage Editor.**

   The source code editing window is displayed.

5. **Right-click the background of the editor window and then choose Select All from the context menu.**

   Any source code in the editor is selected.

6. **Press the Del key.**

   All the source code is deleted and the editor page is left empty.

7. **Type this into the FrontPage Editor, or paste it from this book's CD:**

```
<html>
<head>
<script LANGUAGE="vbscript">

sub document_onclick()
document.bgcolor="mediumseagreen"
end sub

</script>

</head>
<body>
</body>
</html>
```

8. **Click the FrontPage Editor Preview tab.**

   A blank document appears in the editor, with a white background.

9. Click anywhere in the document.

The background turns sea green.

Using VBScript to handle events is easy because all you have to do is write a Sub with the name of the object and the event, separated by an underline (_)symbol. For example, to have the background change to sea green automatically when the page first loads into the browser, change the name of the sub from `sub document_onclick` to this:

```
sub window_onload()
```

JScript, however, is another story. JScript isn't as straightforward when handling window or document events. The VBScript language recognizes events when you use them as the name of Subs in your script. JScript does not.

With JScript, you must create two separate Functions, one to trap the event and a second one that actually does the work of responding (because it contains the script that turns the background sea green or whatever other response you want).

For example, to trap the `onload` event using JScript, you must first describe it in the `<BODY>` tag, pointing to another function located within the `<SCRIPT>` section of the source code, like this:

```
<html>

<head>
<script LANGUAGE="JScript">

function win_onload() {

n = alert ("That triggered the event");
}

</script>
</head>

<body onload="win_onload()">
</body>
</html>
```

Going round and round with loops

In computers, as in life, repeating something over and over is often necessary. Computer languages use *loops* to do this. As you may expect, JScript and VBScript differ in the details of how they set up loops.

For and For...Next loops

The JScript version of the For loop follows the For command with three parameters enclosed in parentheses and separated by semicolons. Got it?

In this JScript example, the loop counts backward down from 4 to 0 (the > 0 means keep counting down as long as the counter variable i remains greater than zero).

Each of the four times the loop runs, it puts more characters into the variable named count. Each time through the loop, it adds a character representing the current index variable i. After the loop is finished (as soon as it's counted down to 0), a messagebox is displayed showing the result: 4 3 2 1.

```
<html>
<head><script LANGUAGE="JScript">

var count = ""

for (i=4; i > 0; i--){
count += i + " ";
}

alert(count)

</script>
</head>

<body>
</body>
</html>
```

You need to follow several steps to set up a For loop in JScript:

1. **If a variable is to be used in the body of the For loop, you must define it first.**

   Define the variable outside the loop, as count is in the preceding code example.

2. **Following the** `For` **command, you use parentheses to enclose three items:**

   - The initial value of the counting variable (`i=4`).

   - The condition that prevents the looping from stopping (`i > 0`, meaning that the looping continues to repeat as long as the counting variable `i` remains greater than zero).

   - How much to increase (or decrease) the counting variable each time through the loop. In this example, it is decreased by 1 each time (using the command).

3. **Following the parentheses, a set of braces describe the action to take each time through the loop:**

```
{
count += i + " ";
}
```

   In this example, you add the value of `i` to the text variable count, separating them each time by a blank space `" "`.

4. **Finally, after the counter variable goes down to zero, the program goes past the final brace } and displays the message box containing the result:**

```
4 3 2 1.
```

The VBScript version is somewhat shorter and more understandable. It's a bit more like plain English:

```
<script LANGUAGE="VBScript">

for i = 4 to 1 step -1

count = count & i & " "

next

msgbox (count)

</script>
```

VBScript describes the counter and end condition following the `For` command (and on the same line). In this example, the language says: count down from 4 to 1, counting down each time through the loop by 1 (`step -1`).

The action to take each time through the loop is contained between the line where the `For` command appears and a line with the command `Next` on it.

Do loops

Probably the most powerful and flexible looping command is the Do structure.

Do loops are flexible. Nearly all loops have a test condition that specifies when the loop should stop its repeated looping and allow the program to go on to the source code following the loop structure. A typical test condition, for example, is $x < 0$. This means keep re-running the loop until the variable x is less than zero. Another typical test condition is Name = "Nancy" or $x = 12$. In any case, a Do structure enables you to put the test condition at the start or the end of the loop structure. That's one of the Do structure's flexibilities.

JScript tests the loop (to see whether it should continue) at the end of the structure, like this:

```
<SCRIPT LANGUAGE="JScript">

c = 1

do {
        alert(c)
        c ++
}while (c < 4)

</SCRIPT>
```

This language translates as follows: A variable named c is given the value of 1. Keep doing this do...while looping as long as the variable c remains less than 4. Increase the value of c by 1 each time through this loop.

The VBScript version of this do...loop looks pretty much the same:

```
<SCRIPT LANGUAGE="VBScript">

c = 1

do
        alert(c)
        c = c + 1

loop while c < 4
```

```
</SCRIPT>
```

The primary differences between the VBScript and the JScript versions of this example are that the VBScript version uses less punctuation and increments the counter with c = c + 1 but JScript increments with a special increment command ++.

You can use a slightly different alternative syntax in VBScript as well, substituting the until command for the while command, like this:

```
c = 1

do
        alert(c)
        c = c + 1

loop until c = 4
```

The distinction between the until and while versions is a matter of semantics. It's like the difference between "sit near the fire until you're warm" versus "sit near the fire while you're still cold." Use whichever version sounds most natural to you.

While loops

The final kind of loop structure begins with a while command. The while structure continues to loop as long as (while) some condition remains true. Here's a VBScript example of a while loop (note the strange word wend that ends the while loop):

```
<script LANGUAGE="VBScript">

c = 1

while c < 4
        c = c + 1
        alert(c)
wend

</script>
```

Here's the translation into JScript:

```
<script LANGUAGE="JScript">
```

```
c = 1

while (c < 4){
        c ++
        alert(c)
}

</script>
```

The primary differences between the VBScript and JScript versions of the `while` loop are punctuation. JScript uses braces to enclose the action, and VBScript defines the end of the action with the command `wend`.

Take action: Using operators

Operators is the formal word for commands that take action on variables or compare them. For example, the + in 1 + 1 is an operator. The following list explains the important operators in VBScript and JScript:

- **Arithmetic:** The arithmetic operators +, -, *, and / for addition, subtraction, multiplication, and division are identical in both languages.

- **Comparisons:** Asking a question, such as "Is *a* greater than *b?*," is often necessary. Both languages use > for greater than and < for less than. VBScript uses = to ask whether two variables are equal, but JScript uses the = = symbol, like this: If n = = m. To express inequality, VBScript uses <> and JScript uses !=, as in If n != m.

- **Increment:** It's common in computer programming to need to raise a number by 1 (for example you often raise a variable by 1 each time through a loop). This is a kind of *incrementing.* JScript and VBScript use different approaches to incrementing by 1. JScript increments a variable by 1 using the ++ symbol, like this: i++. But VBScript increments a variable by 1 using this format: i = i + 1.

- **Decrement:** JScript and VBScript also use different approaches for the opposite of incrementing, which is decrementing by 1. To decrement by 1, JScript uses i−. VBScript decrements using i = i - 1.

The big If

Both VBScript and JScript, like all human languages, have ways of asking *if.* Asking an *if* question is how decisions are made. As always, JScript uses more punctuation, but both JScript and VBScript work with if in a similar way. Here's a JScript example that displays a message if a variable equals "Joan":

```
<SCRIPT LANGUAGE="JScript">

a = "jo"

if (a == "joan")
        alert ("It's joan!");
else
        alert ("It's not joan.");

</SCRIPT>
```

The VBScript version includes less punctuation, but two additional commands then and end if:

```
<script LANGUAGE="vbscript">

a = "jo"

if a = "joan" then
        alert ("It's joan!")
else
        alert ("It's not joan.")
end if

</script>
```

Because the VBScript version signals the conclusion of the If structure with the end if command, it doesn't need extra punctuation. However, JScript doesn't require braces unless you use several lines between the if and else commands and the end of the structure. In that case, you do need to use braces around the actions taken, like this:

```
a = "john"

if (a == "jon") {
alert ("It's jon.");
alert ("It's truly jon.");
}
```

A structure similar to the If structure also makes decisions. In VBScript, this structure is called Select...Case. In JScript, it is called Switch. Think of this structure as a version of If, with multiple Ifs all contained in a single structure. (You can, in fact, use multiple If structures to accomplish the same thing that Select...Case and Switch accomplish.)

The JScript version of this structure requires that you use a `break` command in each of the `If` tests, like this:

```
<script LANGUAGE="JScript">
z = 1
switch (z) {
      case 1:
         alert("z equals one.");
         break;
      case 2:
         alert("z equals two.");
         break;
      default:
         alert("z isn't one or two.")
}
</script>
```

Here's the VBScript version of the preceding code structure:

```
<SCRIPT LANGUAGE="VBScript">

z = 1
select case (z)

      case(1)
         alert("z equals one.")
      case(2)
         alert("z equals two.")
      case else
         alert("z isn't one or two.")

end select

</SCRIPT>
```

Chapter 12

Writing Your First Script in Visual Studio 6

....

....

*W*hen you create Web pages, you use HTML, or HyperText Markup Language. But HTML has limitations, and it's often useful to supplement HTML with a *script* language. For details about HTML's limitations and the uses of script programming, see the introduction to Chapter 11.

This chapter explores various ways to create scripts. You find out how scripting can improve the performance of your Web site (making it respond faster for the visitor, and taking a burden off your server). You write some useful, real-world scripts, and even find a way to directly modify existing HTML tags and text *after* visitors load a Web page into their computers.

Why Write Scripts?

Why put script source code in a Web page? Scripting wasn't always a feature in Web pages. For many years, the only source code in a Web page was HTML. Any necessary computing was done on the Internet server, not in a visitor's browser. (An *Internet server* is a computer that contains a Web site on its hard drive and makes the site available to visitors who surf the Internet.) The only thing sent to a visitor was a complete, unchangeable page of HTML.

In many situations, though, you want a Web page to react to the needs of a visitor to your Web site, right there in the visitor's computer. For example, one common task is to accept input from a visitor. Perhaps a visitor is asking for a catalog from your company and therefore types in his or her name and address. Before scripting was available, the visitor would fill out a form and then click a Submit button. This action would send the address information back to the server. Then the server contained programming that would check the address information to see, for example, whether the zip code was included. If not, a message was sent back to the visitor requesting that the zip code be typed in. And the whole process would start over again.

But this process is clumsy: Back-and-forth transmission over the Internet is slow and unnecessary. It should be possible to check the visitor's input *within the visitor's own computer,* before anything is sent back to the server. This kind of computing in a visitor's machine is a feature that's been added to today's browsers. These browsers can interpret programming that is placed into HTML, but set off by <SCRIPT> and </SCRIPT> tags, which alert the browser that either JScript or VBScript is being used.

This server-side programming is called CGI (for Common Gateway Interface), a protocol allowing data to be received, and then returned (or stored), using an agreed-upon format. Even today, CGI programming remains the most common way that a Web site's server interacts with users. However, *client-side* scripting is becoming increasingly popular. When programming is run on the client's (visitor's) machine instead of the Web server, a load is taken off the server. And this load can be considerable, if the site has many visitors. Serious delays can occur because each time a CGI program runs (and a separate, new CGI program runs for each individual data submission from each visitor), a new *process* is started on the server. In other words, each data submission starts a new, individual program running on the server! You can imagine how quickly this bogs down the server if a lot of people are interacting with the site. The solution is to use components and scripting that execute on the client-side, so the visitor's computer carries the burden of processing the user's form submission or other submission. (A visitor's data can even be sent to your server in a way that *entirely* frees the server from any realtime processing: just have a form sent to the server via e-mail. To see how to use this technique, see Chapter 6.)

A Web site is a *distributed application.* This term means that a Web site isn't like a traditional word processor that resides entirely in the user's local computer. A Web page is loaded into a user's browser, but it also resides in the server (where other people can visit the site). Even more, a Web site may be located on a particular hard drive in an Internet service provider's building in San Diego, but the site can contact a database located at your company's main building in Toronto. In other words, applications can now be spread around (distributed) instead of having all their components located on a single hard drive.

Scripting is one feature that makes distributed applications possible; you can split your programming between scripts that execute within a visitor's machine, and scripts or other programming that execute on the server.

A script language is a subset of a larger, more powerful language. JScript (also known as JavaScript) is a subset of the Java language. VBScript is a subset of the Visual Basic language. For information on the limitations of script languages, see Chapter 11.

Writing Your First Original Script

Visual InterDev is the application of choice when writing scripts in Visual Studio 6. You can write script, of course, anywhere. You can use FrontPage's excellent editor or even just write it in Notepad. But Visual InterDev contains a whole set of useful tools that assist programmers in creating and testing their scripts.

In Chapter 11, you find an overview of the two main scripting languages, JScript and VBScript, to help you choose which one may be right for you. After you've decided which scripting language you prefer, you can tell Visual Studio 6 to always default to that language. When first installed, the scripting language in Visual InterDev is set to JavaScript (JScript). If you plan to write your scripts in VBScript, you want to adjust this default. To make VBScript the default, right-click your project's name in the Project Explorer. Choose Properties from the context menu and click the Editor Defaults tab in the Properties dialog box. Change the Default Script Language from JavaScript to VBScript. (This chapter deals with client scripting, but you'll likely want to make both client and server scripting VBScript, if it's your language of choice.) Click the OK button to close the dialog box.

Assume that you want visitors to your Web site to send you their e-mail addresses so that you can e-mail them a list of your products. When they click a Submit button, you want to activate a script that checks to be sure that they have typed in their e-mail addresses. To create a script that checks a text box, follow these steps:

1. **Start Visual InterDev by clicking its icon on your desktop.**

   The New Project dialog box may open (depending on how you've set your preferences). If it does appear, click the Existing or Recent tab (it doesn't matter which one) and double-click a project's name. The New Project dialog box closes, and the project you chose is loaded into Visual InterDev.

2. **Choose File➪New File in the Visual InterDev Editor.**

   The New File dialog box opens.

3. **Click Visual InterDev in the left pane of the New File dialog box.**

   The three templates for Visual InterDev pages appear in the right pane: HTML Page, ASP Page, and Style Sheet.

4. **Double-click the HTML Page icon in the right pane of the New File dialog box.**

   A new, empty Web page appears in the Visual InterDev Editor. The Design View tab is selected.

5. **Click the HTML tab in the Visual InterDev Toolbox.**

   The HTML components appear on the Toolbox.

   If the Toolbox isn't visible, choose View➪Toolbox.

6. **Drag a Text Box icon from the Toolbox onto the empty page in the Editor window.**

   A text box is placed in the Web page you're designing.

7. **Drag a Submit Button icon from the Toolbox onto the Editor window.**

   A Submit button appears next to the text box in the editor.

8. **Click the Source tab in the editor.**

   The source code for the components appears in the Source Code window. The source code should look like this:

```
<HTML>
<HEAD>
<META NAME="GENERATOR" Content="Microsoft Visual
        Studio 6.0">
<TITLE></TITLE>
</HEAD>
<BODY>

<P>
<INPUT id=text1 name=text1>
<INPUT id=submit1 name=submit1 type=submit
        value=Submit>
</P>
</BODY>
</HTML>
```

9. **Add an `onclick` event trap to the Submit button. Type in the change yourself so that the source code changes from:**

```
<P><INPUT id=submit1 name=submit1 type=submit
        value=Submit></P>
```

to this:

```
<INPUT id=submit1 name=submit1 type=submit
        value=Submit onclick="checkit()">
```

You typed `onclick="checkit()"`. This event trap tells the browser
that when anyone clicks this Submit button (a click is an event), a
script Function named `checkit` should be executed. An *event trap* is
just a shortcut way of describing what happens when an event is
triggered. The event trap contains programming that describes how the
browser should react if the event occurs. In the preceding source code,
you're saying: React to a click by running the *checkit ()* function. (You
haven't yet written the *checkit* function, so it doesn't appear in the
preceding source code.)

If you're writing this script in VBScript, you can avoid having to add an
event trap to the Submit button. VBScript allows you to create a
function with the name of the object (submit1) separated by an underline (_) from the event you're handling (`onclick`). So, in VBScript, you
can omit the `onclick="checkit()"` and just name your function like
this: `Function Submit1_OnClick`. If you name the function like that,
it will be executed when someone clicks the button named Submit1.
However, to make things easy for those who prefer the JScript language,
I use the event trap technique and put `onclick="checkit()"` into the
definitions of objects like buttons in the examples in this book.

10. **Click in the source code just above the** `</HEAD>` **tag.**

    This places your blinking insertion cursor right at the bottom of the
    header in this page. This is where you want to write your script.
    (Scripts are usually placed in a Web page's header, between the `<HEAD>`
    and `</HEAD>` tags.)

    Now you can type in the `<SCRIPT>` tag, type in all the lines of your
    script, and then type in and end the script with the `</SCRIPT>` tag.
    However, Visual InterDev has a shortcut for you (demonstrated in the
    following step).

11. **Create a script block by choosing HTML⇨Script Block⇨Client.**

    A *script block* is a template into which you type a script. It's a shortcut
    because you don't have to type in the SCRIPT tags or the language
    definition, as shown in this next source code that was generated for
    you by Visual InterDev's Script Block menu option:

    Visual InterDev inserts the following script template:

```
<SCRIPT LANGUAGE=javascript>
<!--

-->
</SCRIPT>
```

12. Fill in the script block by typing in this VBScript source code:

```
<SCRIPT LANGUAGE=vbscript>
<!--

Function Checkit()
If text1.value = "" then
n = Msgbox ("Please type your email address into the
          text box.")
End if
End Function

-->
</SCRIPT>
```

13. Test this script by clicking the Quick View tab in the Visual InterDev Editor.

The Web page appears as it would to a visitor to your Web site.

14. Click the Submit button without typing anything into the text box.

If a visitor clicks this Submit button without having entered an e-mail address into the text box, an error message is displayed, as shown in Figure 12-1.

15. Type something into the text box and then click the Submit button.

No error message box opens.

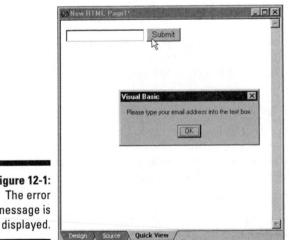

Figure 12-1:
The error message is displayed.

You may be wondering about the meaning of those <!-- and --> symbols that Visual InterDev inserts into the source code when you request a script block. These symbols mark the beginning and end of a comment in HTML. A *comment* is a note by a programmer to herself or himself. A comment is not treated as HTML and, therefore, isn't displayed by the browser. Old browsers did not recognize the <SCRIPT> tags, so they displayed the script source code to a visitor. If the comment tags are put into the script, a browser does not display the script. This problem, though, is largely no longer an issue. Almost everyone uses the latest versions of Internet Explorer or the Netscape browser, where accidentally displaying script source code is not a problem. But just in case your visitors are using older browsers, you may want to keep the comment tags in. They do no harm, and your script will still run as you intend.

Directly Modifying the Document Object

You may be surprised to find out that you can use scripting to create actual HTML source code on the fly. You can cause things to happen to modify the HTML source code in your Web pages after that code gets into the visitor's computer.

Normally, a Web page works this way:

1. **You type HTML source code into a Web page.**
2. **When you're finished with it, you store that Web page on a server.**
3. **A visitor to your Web site downloads the Web page when visiting your site.**
4. **The HTML in the page is scanned by the visitor's browser.**
5. **The page is then displayed to the visitor, based on whatever HTML source code you originally wrote.**

That's what happens normally.

Dynamic HTML (which is covered in Chapter 8) and scripting make it possible for you to animate a Web page and do other clever things, right there on a visitor's computer. For example, you can cause the visitor's browser to create brand-new HTML code, or modify existing HTML code — on the *client-side* (in the visitor's machine, rather than sending new or modified HTML from your Web site's server, a technique that is both clumsy and slow).

Calculating based on when the user visits your site

To see how to create and display new HTML in a visitor's browser, consider the date problem. You don't know, when writing your Web page's source code, when a particular visitor will visit your Web site. The scripting languages contain various commands that deal with date and time.

Suppose that you're writing a Web site for the traffic police. People are told to visit the site the day they get a traffic ticket, and they can find out how long they have to pay the ticket. The problem is that they get 70 days from the day they load your Web page. You have to add 70 days to the current day, whatever the current day is when they load your page into their browser.

To create some HTML source code by using script, follow these steps:

1. **Start Visual InterDev by clicking its icon on your desktop.**

   The New Project dialog box may open (depending on how you've set your preferences). If it does open, click the Existing or Recent tab (it doesn't matter which one) and double-click a project's name. The New Project dialog box closes, and the project you chose is loaded into Visual InterDev.

2. **Choose File⇨New File in the Visual InterDev Editor.**

   The New File dialog box opens.

3. **Click Visual InterDev in the left pane of the New File dialog box.**

   The three templates for Visual InterDev pages appear in the right pane: HTML Page, ASP Page, and Style Sheet.

4. **Double-click the HTML Page icon in the right pane of the File dialog box.**

   A new, empty Web page appears in the Visual InterDev Editor. The Design View tab is selected.

5. **Click the Source tab.**

   The Source Code window is displayed.

6. **Delete all the default source code in the Source Code window.**

7. **Type the following source code:**

```
<HTML>
<HEAD>
<SCRIPT LANGUAGE="VBScript">
```

```
d = DateValue(now) + 70

document.Write "<H1>YOUR COURT DATE</H1>"
document.write "<strong>"
document.Write "<P>You must turn yourself in to
        traffic court on or before " & d
document.write "</strong>"
document.write "<BR><BR>"

</SCRIPT>
</HEAD>

<BODY>

Failure to respond will result in subpoenas,
        citations, writs, summonses and anything else
        we can think of.
</BODY>
</HTML>
```

8. **Click the Quick View tab, and you see the results, shown in Figure 12-2.**

Notice that the document.Write command is very flexible. This command can insert three completely different kinds of content into a Web page:

- Ordinary text
- HTML tags such as <H1> (headline) and <strong> (boldface) and HTML formatting commands like
 (move down one line)
- Variables, like the variable d in the example in the preceding Step 7

As you can imagine, you can probably find many, many uses for this technique of scripting HTML. Based on how a visitor fills in a form, or which check boxes the visitor checks, your script can modify information displayed, and how it is displayed, in the browser right then and there. When you use this technique, HTML becomes freely adjustable and under your remote control. You can write script defining what changes should take place in the HTML, based on what happens on the visitor's end.

Anticipating needed changes to the source code

You can even anticipate changes. For instance, your company may have a different area code for its phone number after a certain date. Rather than worry about changing the phone number displayed in your Web page, just write code like this:

```
<SCRIPT LANGUAGE="VBScript">
thisday = datevalue(now) changephoneday =
          datevalue("12,12,98")
oldcode = " (445)"
newcode = " (266)"

document.write "Our phone number is:"
if thisday > changephoneday then
        document.write newcode
else
        document.write oldcode
end if
document.Write " 777-7777<BR>"
</SCRIPT>
```

This example illustrates how you can take action based on the date that each visitor loads your Web page (`datevalue(now)`) and then compare that `datevalue` to a specific date (`datevalue("12,12,98")`). If the current day comes after the specified date (`>`), use the greater-than comparison operator (`>`) and then you display the new area code. If not (the `else` command means, "if not"), display the old code.

Changing Existing HTML with the Innertext and Outerhtml Commands

Can you edit existing HTML source code from a script? Yes. Not only can you use the `Document.write` command to create new HTML source code, but you can actually change *existing* HTML source code, too. To change existing *text*, you use the `innertext` command; to change HTML elements (tags) or attributes, you use the `outerhtml` command.

With the `innertext` and `outerhtml` commands, you can dynamically (in the visitor's browser) rewrite your HTML source code! And you're not even there when the visitor visits the Web site. It's all automatic because you write script programming that responds to a visitor clicking on a graphic or typing in some text. In the following examples, you find out how to work with this sometimes useful technique.

Replacing HTML text

What if you want to change a paragraph or headline if the visitor clicks it? To do that, put an `onclick` event into the target paragraph or head (or whatever HTML element you want to adjust). Give the element a name. Then use the `innertext` command to replace the existing HTML text with your new text. Follow these steps to see how this is done:

1. **Start Visual InterDev by clicking its icon on your desktop.**

   The New Project dialog box may open (depending on how you've set your preferences). If it does open, click the Existing or Recent tab (it doesn't matter which one) and double-click a project's name. The New Project dialog box closes, and the project you chose is loaded into Visual InterDev.

2. **Click the Source tab in the Visual InterDev Editor.**

   You see the Source Code Editor window.

3. **Delete any source code.**

   The Source Code Editor window is empty.

4. **Type the following source code into the Source Code Editor window:**

```
<html>
<head>
<script language="vbScript">

function changehead()
thehead.innertext = "New, for you, new text"
end function

</script>
</head>

<body>
<h3 id="thehead" onclick="changehead()">
When in the course of events...blah, blah...</h3>
</body>
</html>
```

5. **Click the Quick View tab at the bottom of the Visual InterDev Editor.**

   You see the text `When in the course of events...blah, blah...` displayed in the Quick View window.

6. **Click that text.**

   The text is replaced with `New, for you, new text`.

Replacing HTML elements

The `innertext` command replaces existing text in a Web page. But you can also replace HTML *elements,* the formatting tags like `<STRONG>` or `<H1>`, as well as replace HTML attributes, such as `LEFTMARGIN` in the `HTML <BODY LEFTMARGIN = 0>`). (*Attributes* are qualities or properties of HTML elements.)

To change HTML elements or attributes, you use the `outerhtml` command.

In the following example, the script changes the `<H3>` headline in the HTML source code named *thehead* (`id="thehead"`). It is changed from a level three headline `<H3>` to ordinary body text in a paragraph. This change is accomplished by using the `outerhtml` command to replace the `<H3>` headline tags with paragraph tags `<P>`.

This change happens when a visitor clicks the text `onclick="changehead()"`.

```
<html>
<head>
<script language="vbScript">

function changehead()
thehead.outerhtml = "<p>When in the course of
          events...blah, blah...</p>"
end function
</script>
</head>

<body>
<h3 id="thehead" onclick="changehead()">
When in the course of events...blah, blah...</h3>
</body>
</html>
```

If you want to leave the existing HTML source code alone and just insert a new piece of HTML, you can use the InsertAdjacentHTML command. You write the command like this:

```
object.InsertAdjacentHTML location, text
```

The location parameter can be any of the following four options (see the example at the end of this chapter to find out how to use these parameters in actual source code):

- ✔ BeforeBegin: Insert just before the specified HTML element. In the previous source code listing, you would insert the new source code just before the <h3>.

- ✔ AfterBegin: Insert just after the specified HTML element. In the previous source code listing, you would insert the new source code just following the <h3>.

- ✔ BeforeEnd: Insert just before the end tag in the specified HTML element. In the previous source code listing, you would insert the new source code just before the </h3>.

- ✔ AfterEnd: Insert just after the end tag in the specified HTML element. In the previous source code listing, you would insert the new source code just following the </h3>.

Here's an example of how to use the InsertAdjacentHTML command. Here you add a new <H1> headline to the page, placing it just before an existing <H3> headline by using the BeforeBegin parameter:

```
<html>
<head>
<script language="vbScript">

function changehead()
thehead.insertAdjacentHTML "BeforeBegin", "<H1>Famous
          Quotes</H1>"
end function
</script>
</head>

<body>
<h3 id="thehead" onclick="changehead()">
When in the course of events...blah, blah...</h3>
</body>
</html>
```

Chapter 13

Creating Components

● ●

In This Chapter

▶ Understanding what components are and what they do

▶ Building a new component based on an existing one

▶ Testing your new component

▶ Using the ActiveX Control Interface Wizard

▶ Registering your new component

▶ Creating component icons

● ●

*I*f you've tried using any of the Visual Studio 6 applications, you've used components. Being able to drag a check box, text box, or button from a Toolbox onto one of your projects is quite a convenience. A *component* is a pre-built object, such as a text box, that you don't have to create from scratch every time you write a new program that needs a text box. Instead, you use the pre-built object. For details about how various components are used in Visual Studio 6 programs, see Chapter 10.

You can also design and build your *own* custom components, and then add them to the Toolboxes in the Visual Studio 6 applications. Creating your own component offers you great flexibility, enabling you to define precisely how your component looks and acts. Yet, as with all components, you can reuse your custom component as often as you want, just by dragging it from a Toolbox into one of your Web pages or Windows applications.

In this chapter, you discover how to create useful components. You may be surprised at how easy building a component can be. You can use Visual Basic, Visual C++, or Visual J++ to create components. Because many people find it the easiest language to use, this chapter demonstrates how to build components with Visual Basic. Visual Basic is by far the most popular programming language in use today.

The Purposes and Structure of Components

Visual Basic includes various tools that simplify the job of creating or modifying custom components. Here is a list of some of the most useful things Visual Basic can help you with as you set out to create or customize your own components:

- ✔ Create components that include whatever methods, properties, or events that you want them to have. (A wizard helps with this.)

- ✔ Design the user-interface as you wish.

- ✔ Build a new component based on an existing component or even a group of components (for example, you can modify the existing text box to make it only accept passwords of a certain length, or make a specialized label that centers whatever text the component's user wants to display in it).

- ✔ Add property pages to your components (a wizard can help you do this).

- ✔ Create a control that displays the contents of databases (is *data-aware*). See Chapter 16 for a discussion of data-aware components.

- ✔ Make your component automatically downloadable into visitors' browsers over the Web (another wizard helps with this).

- ✔ Enable users (developers) of your component to resize it by dragging.

- ✔ Create components that have no user-interface, but provide services that developers or programmers need (such as a set of procedures collected into a single component that handles financial calculations).

- ✔ Build components that can be visible, invisible, or have transparent backgrounds (so whatever container they're put onto shows through).

But before you build a component, you should be aware that each component has three primary features, called its *members*. If you create a component using Visual Basic's many helpful tools, your primary job is specifying the component's members. Visual Basic does much of the remaining work for you. Your job is to figure out how you want the new component to act, look, and react. Roughly speaking, a component's three members define it three ways: its actions (called *methods*), its appearance (called *properties*), and its reactions (called *events*).

The three members of a component are:

- **Methods:** Methods are a component's built-in capabilities. For example, a list box component has a `clear` method that removes all items in its list. A list box also has an `AddItem` method you can use to add new items to the items already in the list. In other words, a method is to a component what spinning is to a dancer — a trick they know how to do.

- **Properties:** A Property specifies a characteristic of a component, such as its color, size, or caption. Typical properties include height, backcolor, and alignment. Properties are to a component what hair color or shoe size are to people — aspects of their appearance mostly.

- **Events:** Events are sensitivities, things components react to. Think of an event as a feature where a programmer can define how a component reacts if clicked, double-clicked, or if other things happen to the component. Events are to a component what a teacher's fire drill instructions are to a student: a description of how they should act when a specific eventuality takes place.

Building a Component from an Existing Component

The easiest way to create a new component is to modify an existing one. Its features can become part of your new component, or you can change its features to suit your needs. But at least you're starting out with a framework rather than starting from nothing.

Suppose that you work for an emergency organization and you constantly deal with emergencies (and nothing else). All messages that are sent in your organization should be composed in uppercase letters because the messages are EMERGENCY REPORTS. But employees keep forgetting to use uppercase letters. So you want to create a text box that employees can use that permits only uppercase letters, no matter what is typed into it.

To create this custom text box component, follow these steps:

1. **Start Visual Basic by clicking its icon on your desktop.**

   The New Project dialog box opens. If it doesn't appear, choose File⇨New Project.

2. **Double-click the ActiveX Control icon in the New Project dialog box.**

   A new project displaying UserControl1 appears, empty and ready for you to define its properties or add existing components for the new component that you're building, as shown in Figure 13-1.

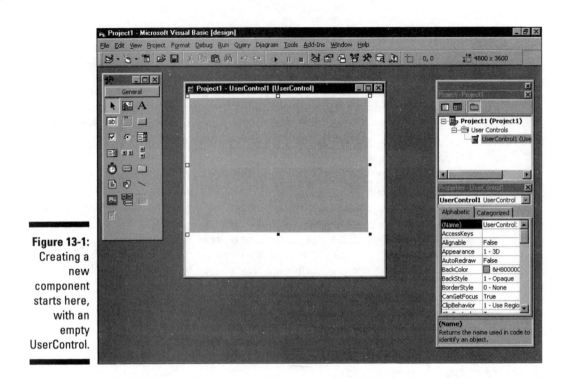

Figure 13-1:
Creating a
new
component
starts here,
with an
empty
UserControl.

3. **Double-click the Text Box icon in the Toolbox.**

   A text box opens on the UserControl. If the Toolbox isn't visible, choose
   View⇔Toolbox. By default, two properties are set in a text box in ways
   that you don't want. The next step shows you how to change the
   properties to make them more useful.

4. **Double-click the Multiline property in the Properties window.**

   The Multiline property changes from the default False to True. This
   way, a user can type in more than one line in the text box.

   If the Properties window isn't visible, press F4.

5. **Click the Text property in the Properties window. Click the drop-down
   list arrow and delete** Text1 **(the default contents of a text box control).**

   Now, when users first see your text box, it's empty. Note that different
   properties behave differently when you click them in the Properties
   window. Some, like the Text property, display a down-arrow icon,
   showing that if you click that icon, a list drops in which you can type,
   edit, or select the property. Other properties display an icon with three
   dots (...), and if you click on that icon, a Property Pages dialog box
   opens. Still other properties do nothing when you click them in the
   Properties window. (However, try double-clicking. You often find that
   double-clicking cycles the options for a property — sequentially

displaying all possible settings for that property, such as displaying True, then False, then starting over with True, as you continue double-clicking.)

6. **Drag the text box into the upper-left corner of the UserControl.**

7. **Resize the UserControl so that it's about the same size as the text box. All you see, after you resize, is the text box surrounded by a thin bit of the UserControl showing around the edges, as shown in Figure 13-2.**

   After your new text box control is placed into a Web page or an ordinary Windows application, it won't have an extra border.

8. **Double-click the text box.**

   The Code window appears (where you can write programming).

9. **Type the following source code into the Change event of the text box:**

```
Private Sub Text1_Change()
    Text1.Text = UCase(Text1.Text)
    Text1.SelStart = Len(Text1)
End Sub
```

This source code causes anything typed into this text box to become uppercase. The Change event is triggered each time a change occurs (when a new character typed, for example) in the text box. Each time the event is triggered, any source code in the event is carried out.

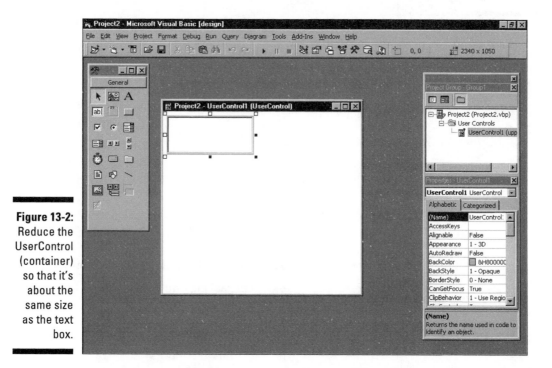

Figure 13-2:
Reduce the UserControl (container) so that it's about the same size as the text box.

First the UCase command changes the existing text in the text box to uppercase. However, this causes the insertion cursor in the text box to be reset to the start of the text. When people are typing, the insertion cursor needs to be at the end of the text. The second line tells the SelStart command to place the cursor at the end of the text. (Len means length-of.)

10. **Click the x button in the upper-right corner of the Code window.**

    The Code window closes.

11. **Click the x button in the upper-right corner of the design window.**

    The design window closes and the new component appears on the Toolbox, as shown in Figure 13-3.

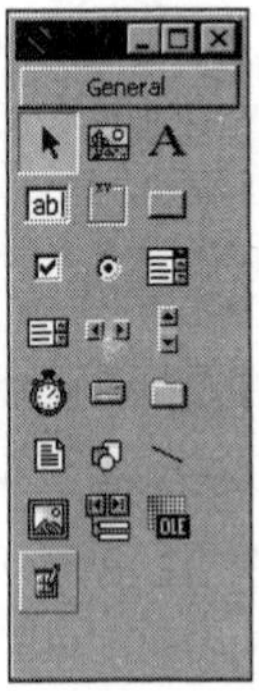

Figure 13-3:
Your new
component
has been
added to
the Toolbox.

12. **Choose File⇨Add Project to add a new project.**

    The Add Project dialog box opens. The reason you're adding a second project is that you can't save a UserControl as a project and then load it in later as a project; you can only save it as a .Ctl file (Ctl stands for *Control*).

13. **Double-click the Standard EXE icon.**

    An ordinary Windows-type program project is added to your Project Explorer. If the Project Explorer isn't visible, choose View⇨ Project Explorer.

    You've now created a Project Group (made up of your UserControl named "Project1," and a standard Windows application named "Project2."

14. **Save the Project Group by choosing File⇨Save Project Group.**

    The Save File As dialog box opens, asking you to save the .Ctl file.

15. **Click the Save button.**

    Visual Basic saves the UserControl.

    The default filename for Project1 is displayed: `Project1.Vbp`.

16. **Agree to use Project1.Vbp as the filename for the UserControl project group (this is Project1) and then click the Save button.**

    Project1 is saved.

    If you have the Enterprise version of Visual Studio 6 and have installed Visual SourceSafe (VSS), at this point you see a dialog box asking if you want to add your project. However, this book is about the Professional version of Visual Studio 6, which does not include VSS, so in the examples, VSS is not mentioned. If you're using the Enterprise version, you see VSS pop its head up now and then, asking for clarification or permission. For example, it makes an appearance following Step 18 below.

    You're shown a default filename for `Form1.frm`. This is the form in the Standard.Exe project.

17. **Click the Save button.**

    The form is saved, and you see the default name for Project 2: `Project2.Vbp`.

18. **Click the Save button.**

    Project 2 is saved.

    Finally, a name for the Project Group (a file that lists all the above files) appears, `Group1.Vbg`.

19. **Type over `Group1.Vbg`, changing the name of this group to BigText.Vbg.**

20. **Click the Save button.**

    The dialog box closes and the project group file is saved to the hard drive.

Testing a new component

You can't debug a component the way you normally debug a regular Windows application. Components aren't self-sufficient like ordinary Windows applications. They're designed to be just a part of other programs. A component is *contained* by a Windows application or an HTML page for a Web site. In other words, you put your BigText box into a container application or Web page. The box can't just appear all by itself, nor can it be tested all by itself.

Fortunately, you have a very simple way to test a component. You don't even leave Visual Basic. You just create a project group, as you did in the section "Building a Component from an Existing Component," earlier in this chapter.

In other words, you test a new component by adding a Standard.Exe to the UserControl project. (A Standard. EXE program is a normal Windows application, such as Notepad or Microsoft Word or some application you wrote that runs in Windows.) However, when testing a UserControl, you don't need to create a real Windows application. You just use that Standard.Exe program as a testing ground, a container to see how your UserControl behaves when contained by another application. You drop your new component into the Standard.Exe and then put the component through its paces to make sure that everything works as you want it to.

To test a new component, follow these steps:

1. **Start Visual Basic by clicking its icon on your desktop.**

   If the New Project dialog box opens, click the Cancel button to close it.

2. **Choose File⇨Open Project.**

   The Open Project dialog box opens, displaying a list of existing and recent projects.

3. **Double-click the BigText.Vbg project group to open it.**

   If you don't see the BigText project group, I suggest that you create it by following the steps in the "Building a Component from an Existing Component" section earlier in this chapter.

   The Open Project dialog box closes and your BigText project group is loaded into Visual Basic. The BigText project group consists of your modified Text box component (in Project1) and a Standard.Exe Windows-type program (Project2).

4. **Click the Forms icon under Project2 in the Project Explorer window.**

   A new icon Form1 appears beneath the Forms folder in the Project Explorer.

   If Project Explorer isn't visible, choose View⇨Project Explorer.

5. **Double-click Form1 in the Project Explorer.**

   The design window appears, displaying Form1 (of the Standard.Exe program).

6. **Double-click the UserControl icon in the tool box.**

   Your UserControl appears on Form1.

If the UserControl is grayed (disabled and doesn't respond to double-clicking), you have Project1's UserControl design window displayed. Close that window by clicking the x button in the upper-right corner. The UserControl's design window must be closed before you can test it in a Standard.Exe.

7. **To test the UserControl, press F5.**

The Project Properties debugging dialog box opens, as shown in Figure 13-4.

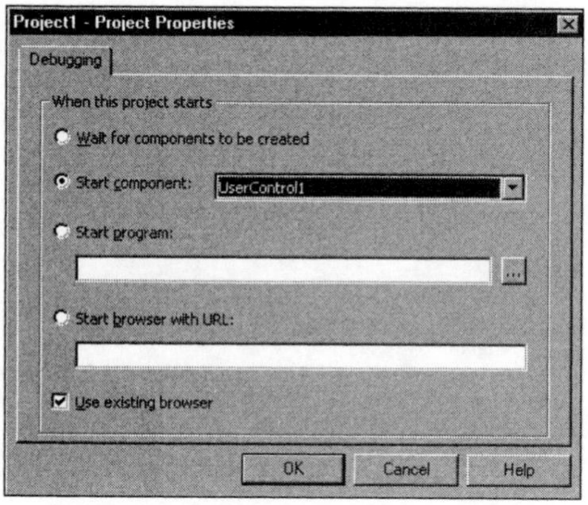

Figure 13-4:
This dialog
box allows
you to
customize
how Visual
Basic
behaves
when you
start a
project (to
test the
project).

Project1 - Project Properties	[x]

Debugging

When this project starts

○ Wait for components to be created

● Start component: `UserControl1` ▼

○ Start program:

○ Start browser with URL:

☑ Use existing browser

[OK] [Cancel] [Help]

8. **Make no changes to the Project Properties debugging dialog box, just click its OK button.**

The dialog box closes and the UserControl appears, fully functional, as shown in Figure 13-5.

9. **Try typing into the text box component.**

Notice that anything you type is shifted to uppercase letters.

Modifying a component

If you refer to Figure 13-5, you can see an example of a component that requires some modifications because it has some appearance problems. The BigText Text Box UserControl component has a gray frame around it. (This is actually the backcolor of the UserControl on which the text box resides.)

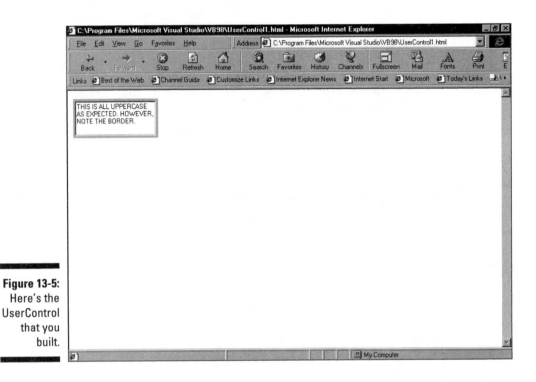

Figure 13-5:
Here's the
UserControl
that you
built.

In many cases, after you test a UserControl, you find that you need to make some changes. That's the purpose of testing, after all.

If you've found a problem, like the gray border shown in Figure 13-5, you probably want to fix it. To fix a problem, all you do is return Visual Basic to design mode. (After you press F5, you put Visual Basic into Run mode, so you can do your testing.) To return Visual Basic to design mode and then fix the gray border problem, follow these steps:

1. **Follow Steps 1 through 6 in the preceding section "Testing a new component."**

    The BigText UserControl Project group is loaded into Visual Basic.

    If the Standard Toolbar isn't visible, choose View⇨Toolbars⇨Standard.

2. **Double-click UserControl1 in the Project Explorer.**

    The Design window containing your component appears. You can still see the gray frame around the text box.

3. **To get rid of the gray frame and make the UserControl container exactly fit the text box, double-click the text box.**

    The Code window opens for the text box and UserControl.

4. **Click the drop-down list in the upper left of the Code window.**

   You see (General), Text1, and UserControl in the list.

5. **Click UserControl in the drop-down list.**

   All the events for the UserControl now appear in the drop-down list in the upper right of the Code window.

6. **Click the drop-down list in the upper right of the Code window.**

   You see a list of all the events available for use with a UserControl.

7. **In the drop-down list of events, click Resize.**

   The Resize Event appears in the main Code window.

8. **Type the following source code into the Resize event in the Code window:**

```
Private Sub UserControl_Resize()
Text1.Top = Top
Text1.Height = Height
Text1.Width = Width
End Sub
```

The preceding lines of source code in the Resize event set the text box's height and width to exactly match the position, height, and width of the UserControl itself. Setting the height and width this way has two effects:

- The gray border around the text box is no longer visible.

- If a developer wants to change the size of the text box (by dragging its sides or corners), they can now do that. Until you added the source code in Step 8, a developer could resize the container UserControl, but the text box inside the UserControl remained fixed. This code is very useful and you may want to put it into the Resize event of your UserControls. No matter what kind of UserControl you're building, if it has a visible user interface, you want to permit developers to resize it. If, for example, you're creating a new kind of command button, just replace the previous source code with this:

```
Command1.Top
Command1.Height = Height
Command1.Width = Width
```

9. **In the Properties Window, change the text box's Left property to 0.**

   Now the left side of the text box always lines up with the left side of the UserControl — thus, no extra frame around the text box when it's used by a developer.

10. Close the Code window and the design window of UserControl1.

The UserControl again appears enabled on the Toolbox.

11. Double-click Form1 in the Project Explorer.

Form1 in the Standard.Exe program now appears, but if your component is no longer on Form1, double-click UserControl1 in the Toolbox. Your text box component reappears on the Standard.Exe Form.

12. Try dragging the sides of the text box to make it larger.

You're now able to resize the component at will. Any developer you give the component to will also be able to resize the text box.

13. Press F5 to run the application.

A problem still exists. Debugging always takes some time!

Notice that after you finish the preceding steps, you still see a thin frame around the UserControl. You may like this effect; the frame does show a user where to type if you place the text box against a white background. But if you want to remove the frame, you can do that. You can create a completely neutral component, a text box with no border whatsoever. This neutral text box completely blends into any container application that you place it in. Assuming that you completed the preceding steps, continue with the following steps to create the neutral component:

1. Choose Run⇨End.

This puts you back into design mode, where you can adjust the component's properties again.

2. Double-click UserControl1 in the Project Explorer.

The Design window containing your component appears.

3. Click the text box to select it.

The Properties window displays the properties of the text box.

4. Double-click the BorderStyle property in the Properties window.

The BorderStyle for the text box switches from Fixed Single to None.

Now, no lines are visible when you press F5 to test the component again.

Using the ActiveX Control Interface Wizard to create members

When you create a component, you're in charge. You decide what color the component is, what jobs it can do, and everything else about it.

Sometimes you create components just for your own use. But you may also want to give your components to others (such as developers) for use.

Remember that components have properties such as Left and Top that define the component's position, or BorderStyle that defines whether or not a frame appears around the component. Properties are qualities. Some properties you want to adjust as the creator of the component, but not make available to developers.

Deciding which properties you make available to users of your component is up to you as the creator. You can expose or hide a component's properties (or methods or events) using the ActiveX Control Interface Wizard built into Visual Basic 6. Follow these steps to specify which properties developers are able to manipulate:

1. **Start Visual Basic by clicking its icon on your desktop.**

   If the New Project dialog box opens, click the Cancel button to close it.

2. **Choose File⇨Open Project.**

   The Open Project dialog box opens, displaying a list of existing and recent projects.

3. **Double-click the BigText.Vbg project group to open it.**

   If you don't see the BigText project group, I suggest that you create it by following the steps in the "Building a Component from an Existing Component" section earlier in this chapter.

   The Open Project dialog box closes and your BigText project group is loaded into Visual Basic. This project group consists of your modified text box component (in Project1) and a Standard.Exe Windows-type program (Project2).

4. **Choose Add-Ins⇨ActiveX Control Interface Wizard.**

   The ActiveX Control Interface Wizard - Introduction screen appears. This introductory screen tells you that the wizard can help you define properties, methods, or events for your new component.

   If you don't see ActiveX Control Interface Wizard listed on the Add-Ins menu, choose Add-Ins⇨Add-In Manager. Then double-click VB 6 ActiveX Ctrl Interface Wizard to highlight it in the list of Available Add-Ins displayed by the Add-In Manager. Click the OK button to close the Add-In Manager. Then choose Add-Ins⇨ActiveX Control Interface Wizard.

5. **Click the Next button.**

   The Select Interface Members page of the wizard appears, as shown in Figure 13-6. On this page, Visual Basic selects a typical set of properties, methods, and events, and lists them in the Selected Names list box. However, you can choose additional members from the much larger list in the Available Names list box.

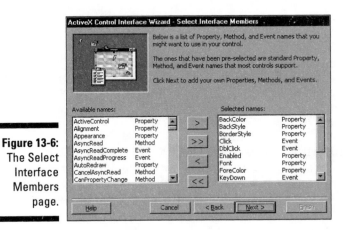

Figure 13-6:
The Select
Interface
Members
page.

6. **Examine the names in the Selected Names list box.**

You see six properties, eight events, and one method, which are the members that the wizard thinks you probably want to include with your component. These members are needed most often. The list of members chosen by the wizard looks like a reasonable set of members for the BigText component.

7. **Decide whether you want to add any of the members from the Available Names list box.**

If you're planning to enable users to attach this component to databases, for example, add the data methods and properties.

8. **Double-click the MultiLine property in the Available Names list box.**

The MultiLine property moves from the Available Names list to the Selected Names list on the right. Now developers can make the text box either the single or multiple line type.

9. **Double-click the SelLength, SelStart, and SelText properties in the Available Names list box.**

The SelLength, SelStart, and SelText properties move from the Available Names list to the Selected Names list on the right. Now, developers can manipulate the insertion cursor and select areas of text.

10. **Click the Next button.**

The Create Custom Interface Members page appears in the wizard.

You can create and define your own new properties, events, and methods by clicking the New button.

11. Click the Next button.

The Set Mapping Wizard page is displayed (as shown in Figure 13-7). Here is where you can *map* (borrow) the behaviors built into any component(s) that you placed into the UserControl. Suppose that you placed *two* items onto the UserControl — for example, a text box and a label. You can use the Set Mapping Wizard page to specify whether you want your new component to use the Font property (as it behaves in the traditional text box), or the traditional label. In this example, you can map all the members directly from the text box.

Figure 13-7:
You decide which component's functionality you want to borrow in this page of the wizard.

12. Hold the shift key and click the first and last items in the Public Name list box.

All the members in this list are selected.

13. Choose Text1 in the Control drop-down list.

The mapping you've specified is finalized after you click the Next button.

Notice that a Member drop-down list is also on the Set Mapping of the wizard. In the Member drop-down list, you can map a public name (from the Public Name list box) to any of the members in the text box component. For instance, you can cause the MouseDown Event to map — and, therefore, behave — like the MouseUp Event in the original text box. Making opposite actions behave the same by mapping them would be madness, but you can do it if you wish.

14. Click the Next button.

The mapping is completed and you see the Set Attributes page of the wizard. In the Set Attributes page, you can define different variable types and assign default values for any members that you included in your component but didn't map to existing members. You can define whether the unmapped members can be changed while Visual Basic is in design mode or run mode, or provide a description of what the member is or does. For this example, leave all the original text box definitions as they are for the traditional text box.

15. **Click the Next button.**

    The wizard shows you a View Summary Report check box asking whether you want to see the Summary Report. Leave this box checked. The Summary Report gives you a list of suggested additional things you may need to do before your component is finished. The wizard does most of the programming to create your new component, but it's not able to do everything.

16. **Click the Finish button.**

    You see a list of ways to test your new component and how to modify it to deal with such members as MouseMove that require special handling.

17. **Click the Close button.**

    The Summary Report closes and you're returned to the standard Visual Basic design mode.

18. **Click the UserControl in the Standard.Exe Form to select it.**

    The UserControl's properties appear in the Properties window.

19. **Examine the Properties window to see that the list of properties represents those properties you decided to give to this UserControl.**

20. **Double-click the UserControl in the Standard.Exe Form to get to its Code window.**

21. **Look through the list of events for this UserControl in the drop-down list in the upper right of the Code window. (Notice that they conform to the events you specified in the wizard.)**

If you ever want to adjust the members in your custom component in the future, just follow the preceding steps again. You can always run the ActiveX Control Interface Wizard any time you want to add or adjust the members of your component.

Using the Property Page Wizard

Visual Basic has more wizards than a Dungeons and Dragons convention. The Property Page Wizard helps you add Property Pages to a custom component that you designed. A Property Page is the tabbed dialog box you see when you right-click an object and then choose Properties from the context menu that appears. You can add Property Pages to your custom components, as a convenience for developers who want to adjust the properties of your component while they're in design mode in applications such as Visual Basic. Figure 13-8 shows you the Property Pages added to a custom component if you follow these next steps.

To add Property Pages to a custom component, follow these steps:

1. **Start Visual Basic by clicking its icon on your desktop.**

   If the New Project dialog box opens, click the Cancel button to close it.

2. **Choose File⇨Open Project.**

   The Open Project dialog box opens, displaying a list of existing and recent projects.

3. **Double-click the BigText.Vbg project group to open it.**

   If you don't see the BigText project group, I suggest that you create it by following the steps in the "Building a Component from an Existing Component" section earlier in this chapter.

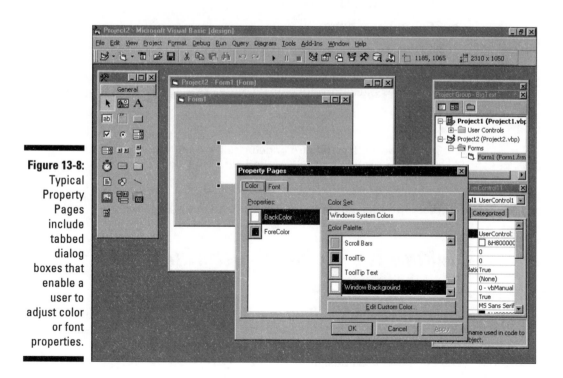

Figure 13-8:
Typical
Property
Pages
include
tabbed
dialog
boxes that
enable a
user to
adjust color
or font
properties.

The Open Project dialog box closes and your BigText project group is loaded into Visual Basic. This project group consists of your modified text box component (in Project1) and a Standard.Exe Windows-type program (Project2).

4. **Choose Add-Ins⇨Property Page Wizard.**

The Property Page Wizard's introductory screen appears.

If you don't see Property Page Wizard listed on the Add-Ins menu, choose Add-Ins⇨Add-In Manager. Then double-click VB 6 Property Page Wizard to highlight it in the list of Add-Ins displayed by the Add-In Manager. Click the OK button to close the Add-In Manager. Then choose Add-Ins⇨Property Page Wizard.

5. **Click the Next button to move past the introductory screen.**

You see a list of all property page-style dialog boxes available for the properties in the component you're working on. In this example, the BigText component can use a property page enabling users to define color or font. (These are the standard property page dialog boxes. Note that you can click the Add button in this wizard page to define unique property pages of your own.)

6. **Click the Next button.**

You see the Add Properties page, displaying a list of all available (appropriate) properties. However, because you're using two standard property pages in this example, you can't modify them. The Add Properties page is useful only if you're creating a custom property page.

7. **Click the Next button and then click Finish.**

The Property Page Wizard concludes its work and you now have a Font and Color property page included with your component.

8. **Click the OK button to close the dialog box.**

9. **Click the Close button to close the Summary Report.**

Making it official: registering a new component

After you've created a great new component, you want to save it in a way that enables you to add it to Toolboxes in applications such as Visual Basic or Visual InterDev. That way, you can drag it onto standard Windows applications or Web pages that you work on in the future.

You can make a new component officially available for use in your Windows applications and Web pages by:

- **Compiling the component:** The component must be compiled. Compiling occurs when you save the component from within Visual Basic as an .Ocx file. Doing that makes the component an official object. (You can also save a component as a .Ctl file from within Visual Basic, but that's just source code. You can work on a .Ctl file in Visual Basic to modify the component, but you can add the component to Toolboxes as a finished product only in its compiled .Ocx format.)

- **Registering the component:** The component must be registered on your system. As soon as Visual Basic finishes storing a compiled .Ocx version of your component, it's automatically registered on your system. The component can then be added to most applications' toolboxes for actual use in real world work.

Compiling and registering a component

To compile and register a new component, follow these steps:

1. **Start Visual Basic by clicking its icon on your desktop.**

   If the New Project dialog box opens, click the Cancel button to close it.

2. **Choose File➪Open Project.**

   The Open Project dialog box opens, displaying a list of existing and recent projects.

3. **Double-click the BigText.Vbg project group to open it.**

   If you don't see the BigText project group, I suggest that you create it by following the steps in the "Building a Component from an Existing Component" section earlier in this chapter.

   The Open Project dialog box closes and your BigText project group is loaded into Visual Basic. This project group consists of your modified text box component (in Project1) and a Standard.Exe Windows-type program (Project2).

4. **Double-click UserControl1 in the Project Explorer window.**

   The UserControl's design window becomes the active window.

5. **Choose File➪Make Project1.Ocx.**

   The Make Project dialog box opens, enabling you to specify where you want the .Ocx file stored.

6. **Click the OK button to store the .Ocx in the default directory.**

   You have a short pause as your component is compiled and saved to disk. The Make Project dialog box closes.

7. **Close Visual Basic.**

Verifying the registration of a component

Now see whether your new component, imaginatively named Project1, is available. See whether it's registered on your system. After you register a component, you can add it to the Toolbox in any of the various Visual Studio 6 applications. To see whether you can add a component that you've registered (as I explain in the previous section "Compiling and registering a component"), follow these steps:

1. **Restart Visual Basic.**

   The New Project dialog box opens. If it doesn't appear, choose File⇨New Project.

2. **Double-click the Standard EXE icon in the New Project dialog box.**

   A typical Windows application template appears.

3. **Right-click the Toolbox and then choose Components from the context menu that appears.**

   If the Toolbox isn't visible, choose View⇨Toolbox.

   The Components dialog box opens, as shown in Figure 13-9. Your newly created component, named Project1, is ready to be added to any application's Toolbox and put to good use.

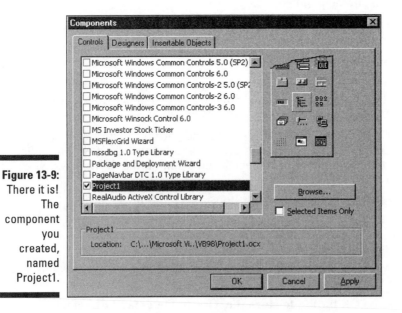

Figure 13-9: There it is! The component you created, named Project1.

4. **Click the check box next to Project1 in the Components dialog box.**

5. **Click the OK button.**

   The Components dialog box closes and your Text Box UserControl icon appears on the Toolbox, ready to be double-clicked and added to any Visual Basic Form.

6. **Double-click the UserControl icon in the Toolbox.**

   Your Text Box UserControl appears on the Visual Basic Form, ready to go to work. It's now just another component, an object for your use, just like all the standard objects (command buttons, labels, and so on) that come with Windows applications and make life easier for programmers, designers, and developers.

The preceding steps make a component available on your system. However, if you want to give your component to others not on your network, the component has to be registered on their system before they can use it. You can provide them with a version of the .Ocx that automatically registers itself on their system (and also stores any necessary support files on their hard drive). A Setup program takes care of this job very efficiently. To create a Setup program so that you can distribute your component, choose Add-Ins⇨Package and Deployment Wizard. If you don't see this on the Add-Ins menu, choose Add-Ins⇨Add-In Manager, and double-click the wizard after the Manager dialog box opens.

Chapter 14

Debugging in Visual Studio 6

- -

In This Chapter

▶ Finding and fixing simple bugs

▶ Using the Auto Syntax Check utility

▶ Testing a Web page

▶ Understanding breakpoints

▶ Locating bugs by single-stepping

- -

*W*hen you do any programming, you get bugs. It's inevitable. *Bugs* are errors in a program, places where you've mistyped a word, put a comma in the wrong place, made an error in logic, or otherwise confused things. When you write a program, you're trying to get the computer to do something. But if it can't understand your program, it behaves unpredictably or it simply does the wrong thing.

You often read in the press that someone got a $1,000,000,000 electricity bill, or experienced some other laughable mistake in their bill, as a result of a computer error. Actually, this kind of error isn't a *computer* error; it's a human error. Either someone typed in the wrong amount of money, or someone designed software that had a bug in it. The computer was just following orders, and the orders themselves were faulty.

Tracking down problems in computer programs is called *debugging,* and it works pretty much the same whether you're looking for an error in a Windows application component created in C++ or an error in an Internet Web page script written in Visual InterDev. The tools and techniques you use to debug are similar in nearly all applications.

Visual Studio 6 has two primary types of applications:

▶ **The languages (Visual Basic, Visual J++, and Visual C++):** These languages are traditionally used to create standard Windows applications (.Exe files that run within Windows). More recently, the languages have expanded to be capable of creating components (.Ocx and .Dll files) that run within standard .Exe or HTML applications. (The C language can always create components.) Now the languages are expanding further to include features for Internet or intranet page design, such as Visual Basic's DHTML Application and IIS Application features.

✔ **The Web development environments (FrontPage and Visual InterDev):** These IDE's (integrated design environments) are specifically designed for HTML and script programming. Visual InterDev, however, is the superior environment for programming. It has many features that benefit programmers, including powerful debugging facilities. (Visual FoxPro is the odd man out — it's a database creation and management application, so debugging is handled rather differently than it is in all the other Visual Studio 6 applications. Nevertheless, bugs are bugs, so there's a family resemblance you'll notice when you debug in any Visual Studio 6 application, including Visual FoxPro.)

In this chapter, I demonstrate debugging in two environments — Visual Basic and Visual InterDev — with notes on how you can use the same features in Visual C++ and Visual J++. This way, you can find out how to fix traditional applications designed to run in Windows. But you can also find out how to debug a Web page script designed to run in a browser.

As you see in this chapter, standard application languages, such as Visual Basic, and newer Web tools, such as Visual InterDev, offer powerful debugging tools including breakpoints and stepping. The set of debugging tools is pretty much the same in all the Microsoft Rapid Application Development (Visual) applications.

You must add components like Java Applets and ActiveX Controls to a container application before you can test and debug those components. Therefore, you must use special techniques when debugging components. I describe these special techniques in detail in Chapter 13.

Typos and Punctuation: Solving Minor Problems

Correcting some kinds of computer programming errors is fairly simple. Typos, for example, aren't much of a challenge. Most Visual Studio 6 applications have built-in typo-detectors and syntax checkers. They alert you to most spelling, syntax, and punctuation errors. To see how to deal with typos and other minor errors, follow these steps:

1. **Start Visual Basic by clicking its icon on the desktop.**

   The New Project dialog box opens. If it doesn't appear, choose File➪New Project.

2. **Double-click the Standard EXE icon in the New Project dialog box.**

   The dialog box closes and you can now write a traditional, ordinary Windows program (ending in .Exe).

3. **Double-click Form1 in the Project1 - Form1 (Form) Design window.**

   The Code window opens, where you can type in some programming. By default, the event for the Form is Form_Load (), meaning that whatever you type between Private Sub Form_Load() and End Sub is carried out when this form first loads into the computer (in other words, when this program starts running).

4. **Type this into the** Form_Load **event:**

```
Private Sub Form_Load()
open "afile"
End Sub
```

5. **Press the down arrow key (or Enter key) after you type** open "afile" **to get to the next line in your programming.**

   Two things happen: The line open "afile" turns red, and the *o* in *open* remains lowercase.

   Open is a command in Visual Basic that opens a disk file. If your line of programming were written correctly, Visual Basic would capitalize Open. When you write a line of Visual Basic programming and the commands, such as Print or Open are not automatically capitalized when you move down to another line, Visual Basic is telling you that it doesn't recognize what you've typed and can't interpret it.

   Also, when Visual Basic can't interpret a line of programming, it turns that line red.

6. **Change the line by deleting** open "afile", **typing the following text instead, and then pressing Enter:**

```
Private Sub Form_Load()
open "afile" as #1
End Sub
```

   As soon as you press Enter or the down arrow key, Visual Basic changes the line to this:

```
Open "afile" For Random As #1
```

   This tells you that Visual Basic understood your intentions (and also helped out by adding the For Random commands). Notice, too, that Visual Basic capitalized Open, For, Random, and As — the four commands in this line. Also, the coloring is no longer red. Instead, the commands are colored blue and the other words are black. All these cues mean that you've succeeded in typing in a correct line of programming.

Using auto syntax check in Visual Basic

You may have used that instant-spellcheck feature found in some word processors. Any time you type a word that's not in the word processor's dictionary, it immediately turns the word red, or underlines it in red, or provides some other cue. I find this feature really annoying. I'd much rather do a spellcheck of the entire document after I've finished writing it. But that's just me; some people love instant spellcheck.

Likewise, some programmers like to see an error message any time they mistype a line of programming code. Visual Basic has a feature called Auto Syntax Check that you can turn on if you want to be notified at once of any typos or punctuation errors while you're programming. To see how it works, follow these steps:

1. **Start Visual Basic by clicking its icon on your desktop.**

   The New Project dialog box opens. If it doesn't open, choose File➪ New Project.

2. **Double-click the Standard EXE icon in the New Project dialog box.**

   The dialog box closes and you can now write a traditional Windows program.

3. **Choose Tools➪Options.**

   The Options dialog box opens.

4. **Click to place a checkmark in the Auto Syntax Check check box under Code Settings.**

   The Auto Syntax Check feature is now active.

5. **Click the OK button.**

   The Options dialog box closes.

6. **Double-click Form1 in the Project1 - Form1 (Form) Design window.**

   The Code window opens, where you can type in some programming. By default, you see the Form_Load event.

7. **Type this into the Form_Load event:**

   ```
   Private Sub Form_Load()
   open "afile"
   ```

8. **Press the down arrow key (or Enter key) after you type open "afile" to get to the next line in your programming.**

   An error message pops up, telling you that you must use the As command when using the Open command, as shown in Figure 14-1.

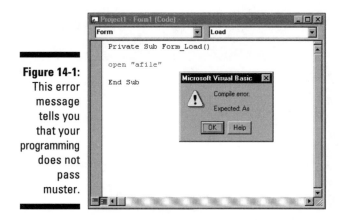

Figure 14-1:
This error
message
tells you
that your
programming
does not
pass
muster.

9. **Click the Help button in the error message box.**

   A help screen appears, describing several kinds of errors that can cause the expected type of problem. Alas, none of these descriptions apply to your particular problem with the Open command.

10. **Click the OK button on the error message dialog box.**

    The error message dialog box closes.

11. **Click the Open command in the source code.**

    The blinking insertion cursor appears in the Open command, where you clicked it. This enables you to identify the Open command as the target of a help query. You can get specific information about any Visual Basic command by using this technique.

12. **Press F1.**

    The Help window opens again (as shown in Figure 14-2), this time telling you all you need to know about the syntax of the Open command. You can press F1 when your insertion cursor (blinking vertical line) is located on any command in the Visual Basic source code. A Help window appears, showing you the correct syntax for use with that command and also providing you with examples of source code using the command.

Catching typos in Visual InterDev

The debugging features that trap syntax errors (typos and punctuation) in Visual InterDev are similar to the equivalent features in traditional programming languages like Visual C++ and Visual Basic. To see how to ferret out syntax errors in Visual InterDev, follow these steps:

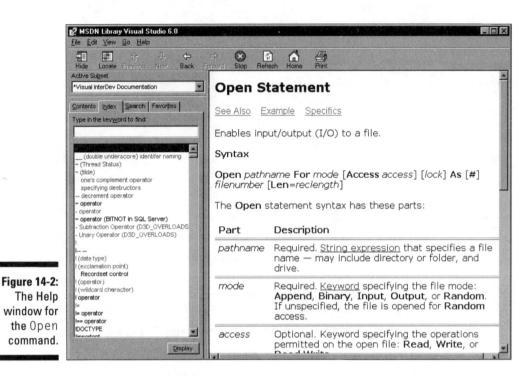

Figure 14-2:
The Help
window for
the Open
command.

1. **Start Visual InterDev by clicking its icon on your desktop.**

   The New Project dialog box opens. If it doesn't open, choose File⇨New.

2. **Click the New tab in the New Project dialog box.**

3. **Click Visual InterDev Projects in the left pane of the dialog box.**

   Two icons appear in the right pane of the dialog box: New Web Project and Sample App Wizard.

4. **Double-click the New Web Project icon in the right pane.**

   The Web Project Wizard starts running and displays its first page.

5. **Click the Next button.**

   The Web server is contacted and the second dialog box in this wizard appears. By default, the Create A New Web Application option button is selected. Leave it selected.

6. **Type in the name BigBugs in the Name text box in the New Project dialog box.**

7. **Click the Next button twice and then click the Finish button.**

   This way, you bypass the wizard pages that ask whether you want to use a theme or template. You don't.

8. **Click the Finish button.**

   A Name and Password dialog box may open. (Whether or not it does depends on your Web server.) If the dialog box opens, type in your password and, if the password is correct, your new site is built.

9. **Click the project's name in the Project Explorer.**

   The project name is BigBugs and it appears in boldface.

10. **Choose Project⇨Add Item.**

    The Add Item dialog box opens.

11. **Double-click the HTML Page icon in the Add Item dialog box.**

    A new page is added to your project, with the default name Page1.Htm.

12. **Click the Source tab in the Page1 Editor window.**

    The Source Code window opens, where you can type in HTML or script programming.

13. **Type this into the Source window:**

```
<HTML>
<HEAD>

<SCRIPT LANGUAGE=vbscript>
a = 2 +
</SCRIPT>
</HEAD>
<BODY>


</BODY>
</HTML>
```

14. **Press F5 to run (test) the programming on this page.**

    When you press F5, you test the page, as if you loaded the page into a browser.

    An error message pops up, as shown in Figure 14-3. This error message tells you that you can't debug in Visual InterDev until you define the starting page in the project (meaning the first page that's loaded into a visitor's browser).

15. **Click the OK button.**

    The error message box closes.

16. **Right-click HTML Page1.htm in the Project Explorer, and click Set As Start Page in the context menu that appears.**

    If the Project Explorer isn't visible, choose View⇨Project Explorer.

    The context menu closes and Page1 is now the starting page in this project.

17. **Press F5 to start running the page.**

    Whoa! Yet another complaint message from Visual InterDev. This time, a message box pops up telling you that ASP (Active Server Page) debugging isn't enabled. Who cares? The message asks, do you want to enable ASP debugging on this project. No, you don't have any ASP pages, nor do you plan to. So you answer No.

18. **Click the No button.**

    The error message box closes. Your browser loads Page1 and attempts to carry out your script. (Raw script like your a = 2 + is carried out as soon as a page is loaded. Script enclosed in a procedure, such as Function Runit(), won't execute until the Runit procedure is triggered.)

    Your script won't work. You've left out the final value, such as the *5* in a = 2 + 5.

    Internet Explorer displays the page, but a syntax error message is also displayed, as shown in Figure 14-4. This error message tells you that a syntax error has occurred in line six in your source code. More specifically, the error (probably) can be pinpointed to character 8.

19. **Click the Yes button.**

    You return to Visual InterDev, with the blinking insertion cursor located where the debugging system thinks the bug is to be found, as shown in Figure 14-5.

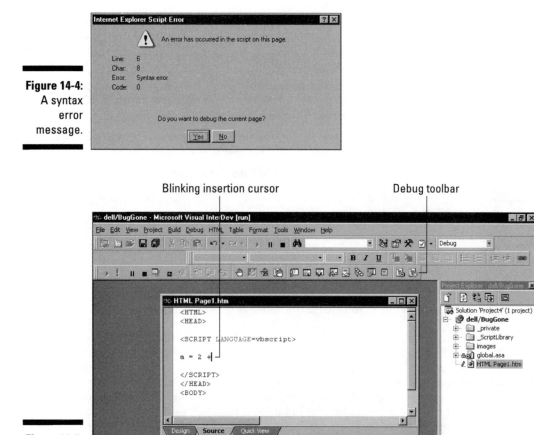

Figure 14-4:
A syntax
error
message.

Figure 14-5:
The
insertion
cursor
shows you
where the
problem is.

Also notice that some debugging windows have popped up in Visual InterDev, as shown in Figure 14-5. Both the Autos and Watch features, as well as the Debug toolbar, are added automatically to Visual InterDev when you're in debugging mode.

20. **To stop the debugging process and stop the page from executing, click the blue square icon (End) in the Standard Toolbar. (Or choose Debug⇨End, or press Shift+F5.)**

    The debugging windows and Debug toolbar disappear and you're back in normal Visual InterDev editing mode.

21. **Fix the problem by typing this into the script:**

```
<SCRIPT LANGUAGE=vbscript>
a = 2 + 4
document.write (a)
</SCRIPT>
```

22. **Press F5.**

    The page loads into the browser. The number 6 is displayed. All works as it should. No errors. No debugging necessary.

In many cases, you can debug a page in Visual InterDev without going through the process of pressing F5 and, thereby, loading the page into a browser. All you need to do is click the Quick View tab in the Visual InterDev editing window. If the error is in your source code, the same error message displayed in Figure 14-4 appears. However, some kinds of Web pages require that they be actually loaded in Internet Explorer or Netscape's browser before all their contents can be tested. So you may want to get into the habit of pressing F5 rather than trying to debug your Web pages by clicking the Quick View tab. That way, you can be sure that everything has been tested fully.

Calling All Breakpoints

Probably the single most useful debugging tool of all is the *breakpoint*. When you place a breakpoint on a line of source code, the program (or script) stops execution when it reaches the breakpoint. The program goes into pause mode. This process is similar to pressing the pause button on a VCR. You can later restart running the code again from the location where the break occurred. However, while in break mode, you can examine the contents of the program's variables to see whether things are as they should be.

Imagine, for example, that your program is telling you that you'll be 500 years old in three weeks. That's a wacky error. With this kind of bug, you can set breakpoints at several locations in your program and then examine the contents of the variable that holds your age to see where it suddenly balloons up to a huge number. After you find out where the age variable is becoming impossibly large, you've found the source code where the error is. You can then correct the bad code that's producing the wrong answer.

As you can see in the section "Setting a breakpoint in Visual InterDev" later in this chapter, you can even define conditional breakpoints that automatically break only when a condition becomes true. That makes this age example even simpler to solve. You just set breakpoints that say: `break if agevariable > 100`.

Breakpoints can help you locate the really tough bugs. The hardest bugs to find are logic bugs. Your program runs. It doesn't stop and displays an error message telling you that it doesn't understand the word `primt`. When you misspell a word, the program displays an error message and you then easily change `primt` to `print`.

Syntax errors — misspellings, bad punctuation, and typos — are easy to deal with. The tough bugs are those that result from errors in logic. The problem with these kinds of errors is that they're very sneaky because the program runs okay, the source code is understandable, and all the lines of code make sense and can be carried out.

But, somehow, the interaction between lines of code is producing the wrong results — side-effects, unintended consequences, call it what you will. Something is going wrong with your program, even though all the individual lines of code work okay by themselves.

One of the best tools to use when faced with a hard-to-find bug is the breakpoint. A breakpoint can cause the program to halt execution when it gets to the line where the breakpoint is located. You can set as many breakpoints as you want. When the program halts, you can then look to see what each variable holds, to see if somehow a variable holds the wrong amount.

Setting breakpoints in Visual Basic

To track down a logic bug by setting breakpoints in a Visual Basic program, follow these steps:

1. **Start Visual Basic by clicking its icon on your desktop.**

   The New Project dialog box opens. If it doesn't open, choose File⇨ New Project.

2. **Double-click the Standard EXE icon.**

   The dialog box closes and a traditional, ordinary Windows program (ending in .Exe) can now be written.

3. **Double-click the Text Box icon three times in the Visual Basic Toolbox.**

   Three text boxes are placed on Form1, the Default window. If the Toolbox isn't visible, choose View⇨Toolbox.

4. **Drag the text boxes so that they're lined up in a row, as shown in Figure 14-6.**

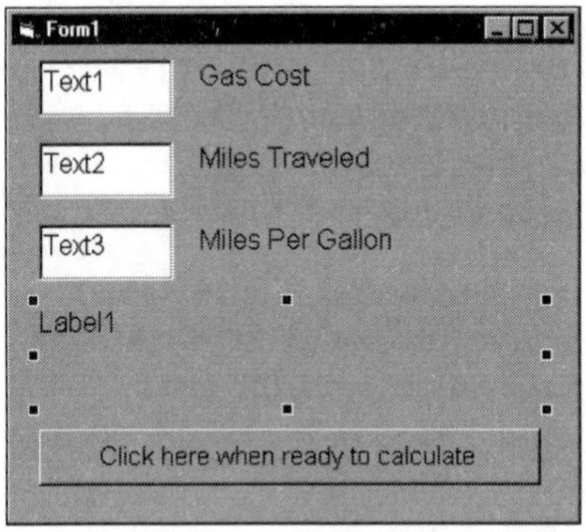

Figure 14-6:
Lined-up
text boxes
in the Form1
Default
window.

5. **Double-click the Label icon in the Toolbox four times.**

   Four labels appear on the Form.

6. **Drag three of the labels until they're lined up on the right side of each text box, with the fourth one (the one named *Label1*) at the bottom, as shown in Figure 14-6.**

7. **Double-click the Command Button icon in the Toolbox.**

   A command button appears on the Form.

8. **Drag the command button so that it's on the very bottom of the Form, as shown in Figure 14-6.**

9. **Click the topmost label. Then, in the Properties window, change its caption property to** Gas Cost.

   If the Properties window isn't visible, press F4.

10. **Click the second label and change its caption to** Miles Traveled.

11. **Click the third label and change its caption to** Miles Per Gallon.

12. **Click the command button and change its caption to** Click Here When Ready to Calculate.

13. **Double-click the command button.**

    The command button's Code window appears, ready for you to type some programming into its Click event (between Command1_Click() and End Sub). The Click event tells the program how to respond if a user clicks the command button.

14. **In the Code window, type the following programming into the Click event. This programming calculates how much money someone will spend on gas on a vacation trip:**

```
Private Sub Command1_Click()
gascost = Val(Text1.Text)
miles = Val(Text2.Text)
mpg = Val(Text3.Text)
totalcost = gascost / miles * mpg
Label1.Caption = "Total: $" & totalcost
End Sub
```

15. **Press F5.**

    The program starts running so that you can test it.

16. **Fill in the three text boxes with gas cost (per gallon), the number of miles you traveled, and the miles per gallon. (Delete the default text** Text1, Text2, Text3 **in each text box.)**

17. **Click the command button to trigger the calculation.**

    Your form appears, as shown in Figure 14-7. But you see a wrong result. (The E–02 means "move the decimal point two places to the left, so the actual result is $0.099 or about 10 cents.) The total gas expense result is clearly way too low. Time to debug this program!

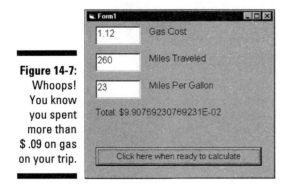

Figure 14-7: Whoops! You know you spent more than $ .09 on gas on your trip.

The program that you just created doesn't violate any Visual Basic syntax rules. All the lines of code make sense to Visual Basic and can be interpreted and carried out. There is only one violation: logic. You know the answer is wrong. Something is happening in this code to produce a bad result.

Now, this is a short program and you can probably look through the lines of code to find the error just by reading the source code. But in larger programs, tracking down the location of a logic bug can be a real head-banger. One of the best tools you can use to find a problem is to set breakpoints. To see how to use breakpoints to locate a logic error, follow these steps:

1. **Press Shift+F5.**

   The program stops running and you're back in editing mode.

2. **Click the line of source code that starts with** `Totalcost=`.

   That line now has the blinking insertion cursor.

3. **Press F9.**

   A breakpoint is set on this line. The line turns colors to white text on a red background. A breakpoint causes the program to halt execution when it gets to the line where the breakpoint is located.

4. **Press F5.**

   The program runs.

5. **Fill in the three text boxes with gas cost (per gallon), the number of miles you traveled, and the miles per gallon.**

6. **Click the command button to trigger the calculation.**

   The program automatically goes into break mode when it reaches the line where you set the breakpoint. The line is highlighted in yellow.

7. **Move your mouse pointer across the line and pause it on top of each variable name:** `gascost`, `miles`, **and** `mpg`.

   As you pause on each variable, a small window appears and you can see the contents of the variable, as shown in Figure 14-8.

As you can see by checking these variables, all is well. They each contain what you typed into their respective text boxes. Yet, the final result is incorrect.

You know that the variable `Totalcost` contains an incorrect value as soon as this line is executed. Therefore, because everything is correct up to this line and becomes incorrect as soon as the line is executed, the problem is on this line. Something is wrong with the way you're calculating.

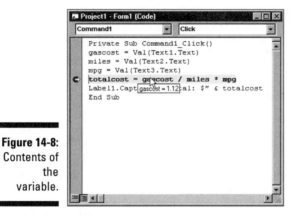

Figure 14-8:
Contents of
the
variable.

Take a hard look at the logic in the math here:

```
totalcost = gascost / miles * mpg
```

You're saying that to get the totalcost, you divide the cost of a gallon of gas by the miles traveled. Then you multiply the result by the miles per gallon. That method is not correct.

To get the right answer, you should divide the gas cost by the miles per gallon. That way, you know how much each mile costs. Then you multiply the cost of each mile by the total number of miles traveled. So, to fix this bug, change the line to the following and rerun the program:

```
totalcost = gascost / mpg * miles
```

Setting a breakpoint in Visual InterDev

One of Microsoft's goals with the six applications that make up Visual Studio 6 was to make the applications look and act as much alike as possible. Setting a breakpoint in a Visual InterDev script is quite similar to the way it works in Visual Basic and Microsoft's other Visual languages. To see how to set a breakpoint in Visual InterDev, follow these steps:

1. **Start Visual InterDev by clicking its icon on your desktop.**

   The New Project dialog box is displayed. If it isn't, choose File⇨
   New Project.

2. **Click the Recent tab.**

   A list of Web projects you've recently created is displayed.

3. **Double-click any project.**

   You merely want to get a blank, new .Htm page to work with. After you click the project, it's loaded into Visual InterDev.

4. **Choose File⇨New file.**

   The New File dialog box opens.

5. **Click Visual InterDev in the left pane.**

   Three icons appear in the right pane: HTML Page, ASP Page, and Style Sheet.

6. **Double-click the HTML Page icon in the right pane of the New File dialog box.**

   The dialog box closes and a new, empty Web page appears in the Editor window.

7. **Click the Source tab in the Editor window of your new Web page.**

   The HTML source code is revealed.

8. **Type this short script into the Source View of the Editor window:**

```
<html>
<head>

<script language="vbScript">
dim a
dim b
dim c

a = 12
b = 15
c = a + d
document.write (d)
msgbox ("The result of a + b is: ") & d

</script>
</head>

<body>
</body>
</html>
```

9. **Right-click the name of your page in the Project Explorer, and click Set As Start Page in the context menu that appears.**

   If the Project Explorer isn't visible, choose View⇨Project Explorer.

Page1 is now the starting page in this project. If this option isn't available on the context menu, copy and paste this source code to the page in this project that is the start page.

10. **Right-click the** c = a + d **line in the source code, and choose Insert Breakpoint from the context menu that appears.**

    (You can also set a breakpoint by clicking in the gray margin just to the left of a line in the Code window.)

    A red dot appears to the left of the line of source code in the Source View.

11. **Right-click the** c = a + d **line in the source code again, and choose Breakpoint Properties from the context menu that appears.**

    The Script Breakpoint Properties dialog box opens, as shown in Figure 14-9.

Figure 14-9:
Visual InterDev includes a special dialog box with advanced breakpoint options.

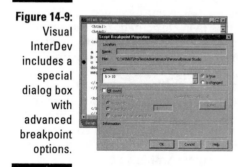

As you can see in Figure 14-9, Visual InterDev enables you to set many conditions determining when this breakpoint is activated. Specifying conditional breakpoints makes them effective, intelligent tools (though setting just plain breakpoints with no condition attached can be a useful debugging technique, too). Using the Script Breakpoint Properties dialog box, as shown in Figure 14-9, you can perform the following tasks:

• **Type in the Name of a function or sub to locate it in an application.** This Name feature is enabled only if you activate the Script Breakpoint Properties dialog box via the Debug menu: Choose Debug⇨Breakpoints and then click the Add button on the Breakpoints dialog box.

    If you type a name into the Name text box shown in Figure 14-9, Visual InterDev searches your entire current application to see if it can find any functions or subs with that name. Visual InterDev then inserts a breakpoint in the first line of source code within that function or sub. If Visual InterDev finds more than one function or sub with the name you typed, a Choose Breakpoints dialog box opens.

- **Describe a condition that triggers the breakpoint.** In the Condition text box you can tell Visual InterDev to continue to run the script *until* the condition is true. In other words, you can type into the Condition text box, for example, a $>$ 3 and Visual InterDev runs this script, only breaking (stopping) the execution of the script when (or if) the variable holds a value greater than 3. Likewise, you can click the Is Changed option button to the right of the Condition text box, as shown in Figure 14-9. If you use that option, the breakpoint halts the program only if the condition changes. For example, you can specify: Trigger a break if a $=$ 3 changes (the break occurs if the variable a ever holds something other than the number 3).

- **Specify that the program should halt based on the number of times the breakpoint is executed.** Sometimes you want to find out how often a line of source code is being executed. You can specify, for example, that the break should be triggered when the line has been executed eight times. (You can also specify that the break should trigger on any multiple of a number. For instance, you can specify a multiple of 4. In that case, if the line is executed any time such as 4, 8, 12, 16, and so on, the break occurs. Or you can specify that the break should trigger when the number of hits becomes equal to or greater than a particular number.) This hit count breaking can be useful in loops, for example. You may want to know if a line is executing more than 80 times within a Do...While loop, because it should never execute that many times.

Other Visual Studio 6 applications don't have the Script Breakpoint Properties dialog box. Instead of customizing breakpoints, other Visual Studio 6 applications use a technique called *watches* (a watch is the same thing as a conditional breakpoint). In Visual J++ or Visual Basic, choose Debug⇨Add Watch and a dialog box similar to the Visual InterDev Script Breakpoint Properties dialog box is displayed.

12. Click the OK button to close the dialog box.

You just examined its options, you didn't specify any conditions. Therefore, this breakpoint is plain and ordinary, and it *always* breaks when this line of source code is executed.

13. Press F5 to execute this script.

Your browser, perhaps Internet Explorer, starts running and loads this page. Then, because you have a breakpoint, you're immediately switched back into Visual InterDev and put into pause mode, with the breakpoint line highlighted in yellow and the blinking insertion cursor positioned within the line, as shown in Figure 14-10.

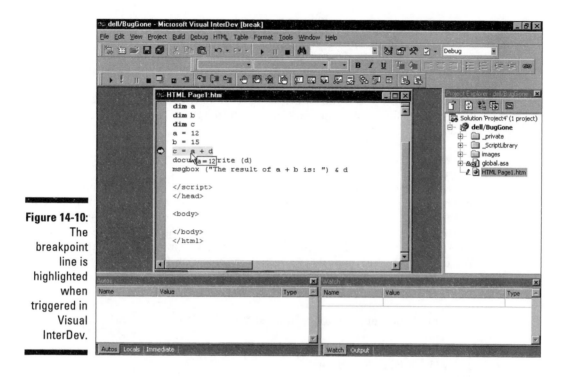

Figure 14-10:
The breakpoint line is highlighted when triggered in Visual InterDev.

Notice, in Figure 14-10, that examining the contents of any variable is quite easy. Just pause your mouse pointer over the variable name, and the contents of the variable are displayed in a small box.

Smart Stepping: When You've Narrowed It Down

Breakpoints are great when you don't know where a logic bug may be in your program. (See the section "Calling All Breakpoints," earlier in this chapter, for more information.) But after you've narrowed down the location of a bug to, perhaps, a particular script, another powerful debugging tool comes into play: stepping.

Stepping means that you can execute a program very, very slowly — one step (one line of source code) at a time. Press F11 and a line of source code is executed. Press F11 again and the next line of code is executed. And each time you press F11, the source code is executed one line at a time. (F11 works in Visual C++, Visual J++, and Visual InterDev. F8 is used in Visual Basic.)

Stepping works as if you'd placed a breakpoint on every line of source code in the script (or program).

When you single-step through a program in Visual Basic or a script in Visual InterDev, the line of source code where you're currently paused is highlighted in yellow and a yellow arrow appears in the left margin of the Code window. A yellow arrow appears in the left margin of the Code window in Visual J++, but the line itself is not highlighted.

You can start stepping from the beginning of the program or script by just pressing F11 (or F8 in Visual Basic). Or you can set a breakpoint and then, when execution halts on the breakpoint, begin single-stepping. While stepping, you can examine all the variables, just as you do when stopped by a breakpoint. (When in pause mode, you can examine variables by either pausing your cursor on the variable's name in the highlighted line of source code, or typing ?a and then pressing the Enter key in the Immediate window. You can display the Immediate window in pause mode — if it's not automatically displayed — by choosing View⇨Immediate Window in Visual Basic or View⇨Debug Windows⇨Immediate in Visual InterDev.)

Three kinds of stepping occur in most Visual Studio 6 applications:

✔ **Step Into:** This is the familiar single-stepping described above. Press F11 (or F8 in Visual Basic).

✔ **Step Over:** If you know that a particular Function or Sub (a *procedure*) that's called (triggered) in your source code is good and you don't want to single-step through it, choose Step Over and that Function or Sub is executed as a whole unit (it won't be single-stepped). Press F10 to Step Over (Shift+F8 in Visual Basic).

For example, if you know that the ShowIt function is good in the following source code, use Step Over when you get to that line by single-stepping. When you use Step Over, the ShowIt function is executed but not single-stepped:

```
Function Fina()
a = b
c = ShowIt(b)
c = n
End Function
```

✔ **Step Out:** This type of stepping is particularly useful when you're single-stepping and you come upon a loop, like a For...Next loop that repeats something 1000 times. You don't want to single-step through that. You have two options. You can click your mouse on the source code line below the For...Next loop, making that line the active line and press F11 (or F8 in Visual Basic) to resume single-stepping. Alternatively, if you're sure that the entire current procedure (the function or sub you're currently stepping through) is bug free, you can choose Step Out and the rest of that procedure is executed all at once. Then execution is halted on the line following the call to that procedure. Step Out is triggered by pressing Shift+F11 in most Visual Studio 6 applications, but Ctrl+Shift+F8 in Visual Basic.

If you're quick with your fingers, you can press Ctrl+Break to stop a Visual Basic, Visual J++, or Visual C++ program at any time. Breaking into a program stops it in its tracks — right at the spot where your program was executing when the break occurred. The applications behave the same way as they do when a breakpoint puts execution into pause mode.

Part V
The Database Connection

In this part . . .

Today's Web sites and Windows applications sites often display catalogs, order forms, delivery status, or other such information. This information is usually stored in databases. Attaching a database to an application or Web page used to be really hard to do. (You had to spend a lot of money to hire a hotshot programmer to hook up your database.)

Those days are over. Visual Studio has facilities that make attaching a database to an application or Web page a snap. (Technically, this is called *database connectivity*.) With Visual Studio, database connectivity is just a matter of dragging and dropping.

Chapter 15

Understanding the Visual Studio 6 Database Features

● ●

In This Chapter

▶ Working with FoxPro databases

▶ Creating new databases

▶ Translating other databases to FoxPro

▶ Using the Database Designer

▶ Using The Database Wizard

● ●

*I*t used to be difficult to connect a database to an application, not to mention connecting one to a Web site. (Web sites are notoriously complicated and are often worked on by several people and located on several hard drives — all of which can make merging databases into a Web site confusing.)

But times change. Visual Studio 6 now offers some efficient tools that enable you to connect applications created in Visual Basic, Visual C++, or Visual J++ to many different types of databases. Likewise, Visual InterDev also includes effective database connectivity components, enabling you to hook your Web site to your database with relative ease. Finally Visual FoxPro — a general-purpose database development environment — is included in Visual Studio 6 so that you can build, manipulate, and otherwise manage databases by using an application dedicated to databases.

In this chapter, I introduce you to Visual FoxPro. (Chapter 16 focuses on database connectivity features in Visual Basic and Visual InterDev, showing you how to connect databases to Windows applications as well as to Internet sites.) Of course, you can't completely explore a mammoth and powerful development environment like Visual FoxPro in a single chapter, but you *can* get a feel for how it works and try some of its interesting and important features by trying some of the step-by-step examples in this chapter. Then, when you're on your own, you're familiar with FoxPro and its features and can go more deeply into it as your needs require.

Introducing Visual FoxPro

Before you can connect a database to an application or a Web site, you must first build and manage the database. That's where Visual FoxPro shines. FoxPro used to be the poor stepsister of Microsoft's Access database application, but to many people's surprise, Microsoft has beefed up FoxPro to the point where it can generate some pretty powerful database applications.

Visual FoxPro also boasts many of the efficiencies — wizards, toolbars, templates, visual components, a Project Manager, drag-and-drop objects — that have made Visual Basic the world's most popular general-application computer language.

Opening an existing FoxPro database

Nothing is easier than opening an existing FoxPro database. And, after you have the database opened in Visual FoxPro, you can do many things with it. To see how to open an existing FoxPro-style database, locate one of the sample databases that are installed during the Visual FoxPro setup. To open a FoxPro database, follow these steps:

1. **Locate a sample FoxPro database by clicking the Windows Start button and then choosing Find⇨Files or Folders.**

   The Find: All Files dialog box opens.

2. **Type *.DBC in the Named text box. (Dbc stands for *database*.)**

3. **Click the down-arrow button on the Look In text box.**

   A drop-down list appears, showing the various hard drives or other storage devices on your system.

4. **Choose Local Hard Drives from the drop-down list.**

   The drop-down list closes, and all the local hard drives on your system will now be searched for .Dbc (FoxPro) database files.

5. **Click the Find Now button.**

   The Find utility searches your hard drives for all FoxPro-style databases. It displays a list of them to you after it finishes searching.

6. **In the Find utility's list of .Dbc-style databases, double-click a .Dbc database.**

   For example, you can double-click Recipes.Dbc (or any other .Dbc database that you choose). After you click it, the FoxPro database opens in Visual FoxPro, as shown in Figure 15-1.

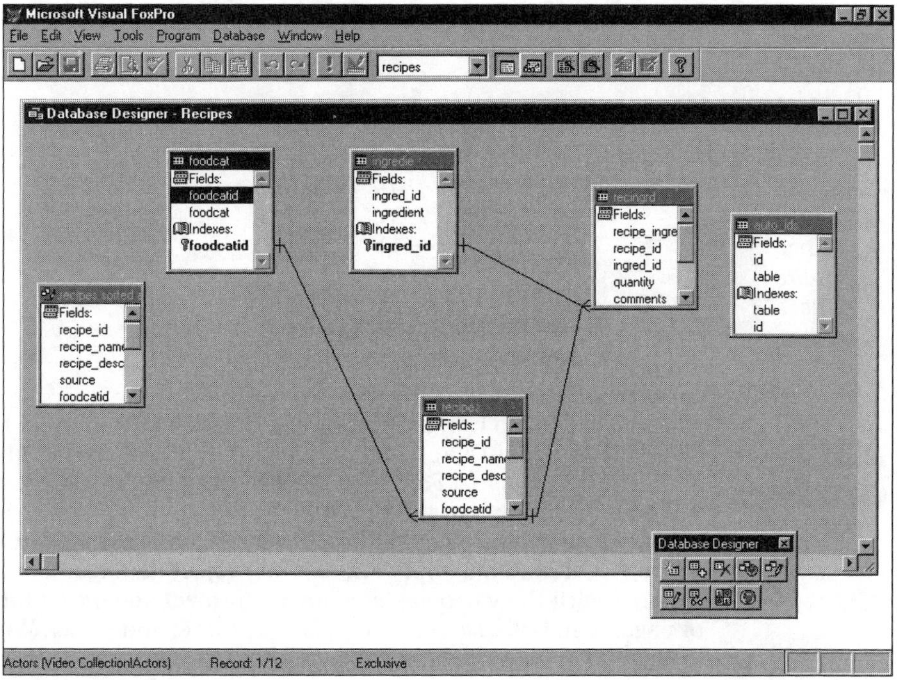

Figure 15-1:
A newly
loaded
FoxPro
database
graphically
illustrates
the
connections
between
the various
tables and
fields.

Examining data in an opened database

Visual FoxPro makes it easy to look at or edit the data and structure of an existing FoxPro database. All you do is double-click, and everything is revealed, ready for you to view or manage the database. To see how to work with the data or modify the organization (tables, fields, indexes, data types, and so on) of an existing database, follow these steps:

1. **Start Visual FoxPro by clicking its icon on your desktop.**

   If the Welcome to Visual FoxPro screen appears, click the Close This Window button to close it.

2. **Choose File⇨Open.**

   The standard Windows Open dialog box opens.

3. **Double-click any .Pjx file on your hard drive.**

   The .Pjx file extension signifies a FoxPro Project. You can find several sample .Pjx files in subfolders located in the C:\Program Files\Microsoft Visual Studio\VFP98\Tools folder. (Your VFP98 folder may be located in a different path, depending on where you installed it during the Visual Studio 6 setup process.)

   Visual FoxPro's Project Manager appears, with the database project that you selected loaded and displayed, as shown in Figure 15-2.

Figure 15-2:
The Project
Manager
helps you
view and
manage the
files in a
Visual
FoxPro
project.

The Visual FoxPro Project Manager is similar to the Project Explorer in other Visual Studio 6 applications. Notice that the Project Manager lists all the files in a Visual FoxPro project in the same tree structure used by Windows Explorer and the Project Explorer in other Visual Studio 6 applications such as Visual InterDev and Visual Basic. However, unlike other Visual Studio 6 applications, the Project Manager is a tabbed window, with the various elements of a project separated into a series of pages: All, Data, Documents, Classes, Code, and Other. With this arrangement, you can quickly view each category of file in your project, or click the All tab to see every file. The Visual FoxPro Project Manager displays all the files in the currently loaded project, including data, structure, and document files.

4. **Click the Data tab.**

   The database files are listed in the Project Manager.

5. **Display some of the tables in the data by clicking the + symbols in the tree diagram in the Project Manager.**

6. **Click a table.**

   The name of the table is highlighted in the Project Manager, and the table is selected.

7. **Click the Browse button.**

   A new window opens, displaying the data in the selected table.

8. **Click any cell in the Data window.**

   The cell is highlighted with a dark frame, and the blinking insertion cursor appears in the cell, as shown in Figure 15-3.

9. **Type in new data or edit the existing data in the selected cell.**

10. **Close the Data window.**

    The data is saved and the Project Manager is the only window open in Visual FoxPro.

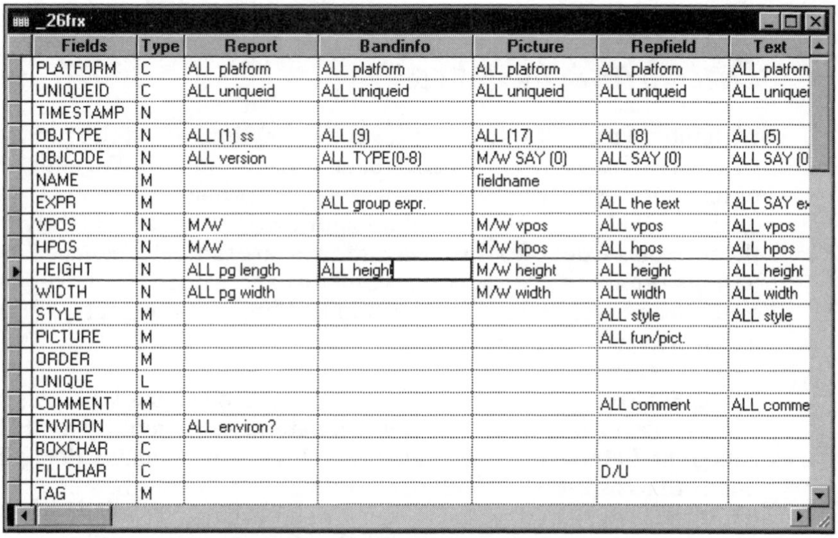

Fields	Type	Report	Bandinfo	Picture	Repfield	Text
PLATFORM	C	ALL platform	ALL platform	ALL platform	ALL platform	ALL platforn
UNIQUEID	C	ALL uniqueid	ALL uniqueid	ALL uniqueid	ALL uniqueid	ALL uniquei
TIMESTAMP	N					
OBJTYPE	N	ALL (1) ss	ALL (9)	ALL (17)	ALL (8)	ALL (5)
OBJCODE	N	ALL version	ALL TYPE(0-8)	M/W SAY (0)	ALL SAY (0)	ALL SAY (0
NAME	M			fieldname		
EXPR	M		ALL group expr.		ALL the text	ALL SAY ex
VPOS	N	M/W		M/W vpos	ALL vpos	ALL vpos
HPOS	N	M/W		M/W hpos	ALL hpos	ALL hpos
HEIGHT	N	ALL pg length	ALL height	M/W height	ALL height	ALL height
WIDTH	N	ALL pg width		M/W width	ALL width	ALL width
STYLE	M				ALL style	ALL style
PICTURE	M				ALL fun/pict.	
ORDER	M					
UNIQUE	L					
COMMENT	M				ALL comment	ALL comme
ENVIRON	L	ALL environ?				
BOXCHAR	C					
FILLCHAR	C				D/U	
TAG	M					

Figure 15-3: You can easily modify or view the data in any database by clicking the Browse button in the Project Manager.

11. **Click the Modify button in the Project Manager.**

    A Table Designer window opens, where you can modify the table. You can also use the Table Designer to modify fields and indexes and to specify default values and validation rules.

12. **Click the arrow icon next to Character under the Type label, as shown in Figure 15-4.**

    The drop-down list of field data types appears, as shown in Figure 15-4.

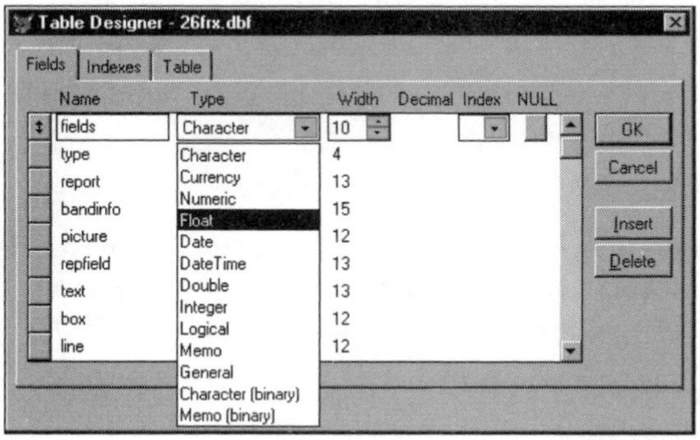

Figure 15-4: Selecting a field data type from the drop-down list.

13. **Click any of the field data types listed in the drop-down list.**

    The data type for the currently selected field is changed to your choice. The drop-down list closes.

Creating a new database with the Database Wizard

With most Visual Studio 6 applications, you don't need to start from scratch when creating a new project. Visual InterDev and FrontPage include dozens of templates, site wizards, and themes that provide you with professionally designed Web sites. You can build your own Web site by merely customizing those expert examples. Likewise, the Visual Studio 6 languages include various prewritten application templates and wizards to make your life easier when creating a Windows application, a component, or other kinds of applications.

Visual FoxPro is no different. It contains 22 predesigned databases that you can use as starting points to develop databases of your own. This feature is called the Database Wizard, and it employs professionally designed templates to assist you in building tables suitable to your needs. After the new database is designed, you can add it to an existing Visual FoxPro project. Or you can modify it. You can use the Database Designer utility to adjust and fine-tune the relationships, fields, data types, default data, indexes, and relationships — the whole structure — of your new database.

When you build a new database, you get a following choice of templates on which to base your database, including the following templates: Asset Tracking (tables that enable you to keep track of expenses and assets), Ledger (tables that assist in managing financial transactions), and Resource Scheduling (which covers customers, resources, and schedules for managers who want to really pay attention to details).

To create a new database in Visual FoxPro, follow these steps:

1. **Start Visual FoxPro by clicking its icon on your desktop.**

   If the Welcome To Visual FoxPro screen appears, click the Close This Window button to close it.

2. **Choose File⇨New.**

   The New dialog box opens, as shown in Figure 15-5. In the New dialog box, you can choose various elements for your project, and you can invoke a wizard to help you by clicking the Wizard button.

3. **Click the Database option button.**

4. **Click the Wizard button.**

   The Database Wizard appears.

Figure 15-5:
The New
dialog box.

5. **Click Recipes (or a different database template of your choice) in the Select Database list. (Oddly, double-clicking doesn't move you to the next page in the wizard.)**

The Select button enables you to choose an existing FoxPro or Access database to work with as your template in the Wizard. FoxPro databases end with a .Vbf filename extension; Access databases end with .Mdb. If you click the Select button, the traditional Windows Open dialog box opens, and you can browse your hard drive for an .Mdb or .Vbf database. If you do select one, it will appear in the Visual FoxPro Database Wizard's Select Database list, and then you can click the Next button. The chosen database will be used as the template for the rest of the wizard's activities. (Note that the actual data in the database is not loaded into your new database; only the structure of that database, such as its tables, is copied to your new database.)

6. **Click the Next button.**

The Select Tables and Views page of the Database Wizard appears, as shown in Figure 15-6.

7. **Click any of the check boxes in the Select Datasources list to deselect any tables or views that you don't want to include in your database.**

8. **Click the Next button.**

The Index Definition page of the Database Wizard appears.

9. **Decide which field you want to use as the primary index of the database. You can also add additional indexes if you wish.**

10. **Click the Next button.**

The relationship definition page of the Database Wizard appears. You see all relationships that currently exist in the database template. You can use this page of the Database Wizard to create new relationships or edit existing ones.

Figure 15-6:
On this
page in the
Database
Wizard, you
can choose
to include,
or exclude,
any of the
predefined
tables or
views in a
database
template.

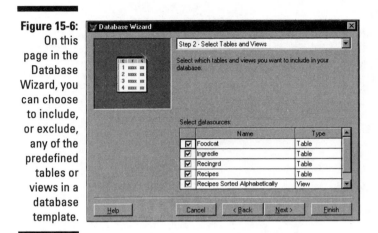

11. **Click the Next button.**

    You see the final page of the Database Wizard. You can choose to modify the database immediately after it's created. (The Database Designer utility is automatically displayed.) You can also choose to load sample data into the database.

12. **Click the Finish button.**

    A Save As dialog box opens.

13. **Type in the name you want to give your new database.**

    You can also optionally browse your hard drive and save the database in a folder other than the default VFP98 folder.

    The new database is saved to the hard drive. If you opted to modify the database in Step 10, the Database Designer is loaded.

Translating an existing Access database into a FoxPro database

Say that you have a database that you designed in Microsoft Access. Now you decide that you want to use that design to create a FoxPro database. Visual FoxPro makes it easy to open an existing database that was created in an alien database format (like Access) and to then build a FoxPro-style database based on that alien structure.

The process is quite similar to using the Database Wizard to build a new database by using one of the Visual FoxPro built-in templates, as described in the section "Creating a new database with the Database Wizard," earlier in this chapter.

To see how to create a new FoxPro database modeled after an existing Access database, follow these steps:

1. **Start Visual FoxPro by clicking its icon on your desktop.**

   If the Welcome To Visual FoxPro screen appears, click the Close This Window button to close it.

2. **Choose Tools⇨Wizards⇨Database.**

   The first Database Wizard page appears.

3. **Click the Select button.**

   The Open dialog box opens.

4. **Click the drop-down list named Files Of Type.**

   You see three options in the drop-down list: All Files, Database, and Microsoft Access Database.

5. **Click Microsoft Access Database in the drop-down list.**

   The drop-down list closes.

6. **Use the Open dialog box to browse your hard drive until you locate the path** C:\Program Files\Microsoft Visual Studio\VB98.

   This VB98 folder contains a sample Access-style database that you can open. You can also browse around and locate any other .Mdb file that you want to use instead.

7. **Double-click VB98.**

   The VB98 folder opens.

8. **Double-click Biblio.Mdb.**

   The sample database Biblio.Mdb is added to the Select database list in the Database Wizard dialog box.

9. **Click the Next button.**

   Visual FoxPro pauses for a relatively long time while it processes this database.

   If you see any error messages like "uniqueness is violated," don't panic; just click the OK button to close these messages.

   Finally, the second page of the Database Wizard appears.

10. **Click all the check boxes to select all the tables displayed in the list under Select Datasources on the second page of the Database Wizard.**

11. **Click the Next button three times and then click the Finish button.**

    You accept all the wizard's defaults in the wizard's last three dialog boxes.

    The Save As dialog box opens.

12. **Click the Save button in the Save As dialog box.**

    The new database is saved using the default name biblio.dbc.

    The wizard closes, and you're back in Visual FoxPro.

Following the steps described in this section creates a copy of the tables, indexes, fields, and other structural elements of an existing database. However, the actual *data* in the existing database will not be dumped into your new database. Just the *structure* of the alien database — its tables and fields and relationships — will be copied. If you do want to fill your new database with data from the alien database, that's easy to do. Just change Step 11 to: Click the Next button three times and then click the Populate Tables with Sample Data check box. Then click the Finish button. Some data, though, may not be copied into the new database. To populate your new database step-by-step, table-by-table, with data from an existing database, choose File⇨Import. Then click the Import Wizard button on the Import dialog box.

Using the Database Designer Utility

As you no doubt realize, if you've fooled around with Visual Studio 6 for a while, Microsoft has made every effort with Visual Studio 6 to make life easier for everyone who might use any of the Visual Studio 6 applications. One way that life can be made easier is to combine various views of a project or database into a single utility. For example, if you have a utility that enables people to redesign the organization (tables, indexes, data types, and so on) of a database, should they be able to change the actual data in the database, too? Why not? Less sophisticated applications provide two utilities: one that edited a database's structure and a separate utility that edited a database's data. But Microsoft realizes that people want to be able to work on *anything* they can see. There's no reason not to combine database editing with data editing, and that's exactly what you get with the Visual FoxPro Database Designer.

The Database Designer shows you all the views, relationships, and tables in any database. And, of course, you're free to edit any of these elements, as well as the data contained within them. To see how the Database Designer works, follow these steps.

1. **Locate a sample FoxPro database by clicking the Windows Start button and then choosing Find⇨Files or Folders.**

   The Find: All Files dialog box opens.

2. **Type *.DBC in the Named text box. (.Dbc stands for *database*.)**

3. **Click the down-arrow button on the Look In text box.**

   A drop-down list appears, showing the various hard drives or other storage devices on your system.

4. **Choose Local Hard Drives from the drop-down list.**

   The drop-down list closes, and Visual FoxPro searches all the local hard drives on your system for .Dbc (FoxPro) database files.

5. **Click the Find Now button.**

   The Find utility searches your hard drives for all FoxPro-style data-bases. It displays a list of them to you after it finishes searching.

6. **In the Find utility's list of .Dbc-style databases, double-click a .Dbc database.**

   For example, you can double-click Books.Dbc (or any other .Dbc database that you choose). After you choose a database, the FoxPro database opens in Visual FoxPro. Figure 15-7 shows that each window in the Database Designer is a table. And each table's fields and indexes are listed. The lines between the windows indicate relationships between fields.

7. **Drag the windows around until you can see the information that you want to see about this database's structure.**

   If you want Visual FoxPro to arrange the windows in the Database Designer, choose Database⇨Arrange.

8. **To edit the data in this database, double-click any field in any of the table windows displayed in the Database Designer.**

   An editor window opens up (such as the Authors window shown in Figure 15-8), displaying the data in the field that you double-clicked. You can click any cell in the window, and the blink insertion cursor appears in that cell. You can then delete, retype, or otherwise edit any data in the field.

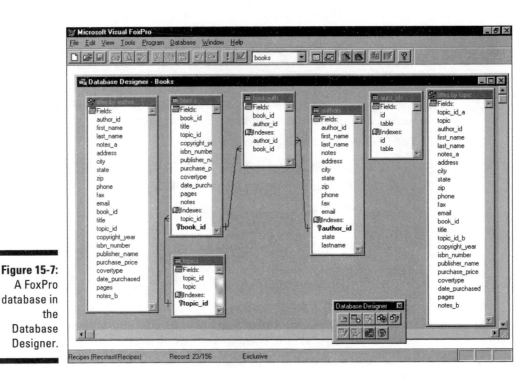

Figure 15-7:
A FoxPro
database in
the
Database
Designer.

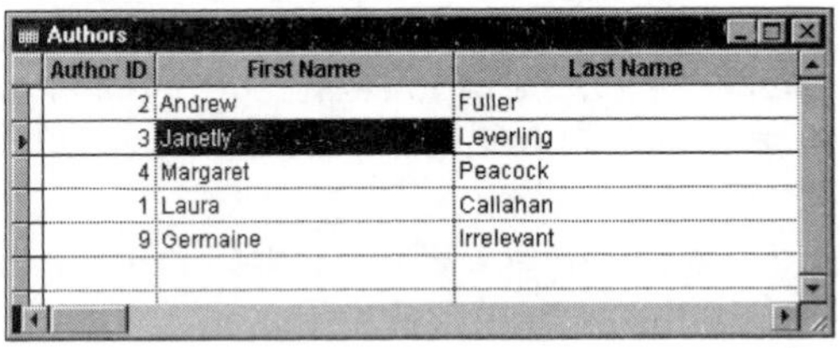

Figure 15-8:
Edit data in
any field in
a database
by using
this kind of
editor
window.

9. **Close the Editor window.**

10. **Right-click any of the opened windows (the tables) in this database and choose Modify from the context menu that appears.**

    A Table Designer window opens, so you can adjust the elements of the table if you want — its indexes, the properties of the fields, the name of the table, validation rules, and everything else.

Wizards, Wizards, and More Wizards

Visual FoxPro has more wizards than any other Visual Studio 6 application. Indeed it has more wizards than Camelot. A step-by-step wizard is available to guide you through pretty much anything you may want to do with a database.

To see the wizards that are available in Visual FoxPro, choose Tools⇔Wizards⇔All and the Wizard Selection dialog box opens, as shown in Figure 15-9. The Wizard Selection dialog box shows you a description of the purpose of each Visual FoxPro Wizard and also enables you to invoke a wizard by simply double-clicking it.

Figure 15-9:
The Wizard
Selection
dialog box.

Using the Web Publishing Wizard

If you want to quickly create a Web page that's connected to a database, Visual FoxPro has a wizard to help you do just that. The Web Publishing Wizard does all the dirty work (writing the HTML source code that fills the Web page with data from your database).

What's more, you get to choose from several different kinds of data displays. You also can add some pretty cool wallpaper designs behind your database display. Internet database connectivity (connecting a database to an Internet site) was never this easy, or the results this attractive.

To see how to use the Visual FoxPro Web Publishing Wizard to add a database to a Web site, follow these steps:

1. **Start Visual FoxPro by clicking its icon on your desktop.**

2. **Choose Tools⇔Wizards⇔Web Publishing.**

   The first box of the Web Publishing Wizard appears, as shown in Figure 15-10. In this box, you can choose the database, table, view, and fields that you want to show on your Web site.

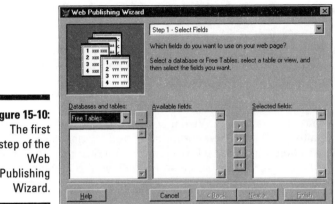

Figure 15-10:
The first
step of the
Web
Publishing
Wizard.

3. **Click the button with three dots on it (. . .), which is located next to the Databases And Tables list box.**

   This three-dot button enables you to load a database from your hard drive. After you click the button, the Open dialog box opens.

4. **Click the drop-down list named Files Of Type in the Open dialog box.**

   The drop-down list has three options: All Files, Table/DBF, and Database.

5. **Choose Database from the drop-down list.**

   The drop-down list closes.

6. **Use the Open dialog box to browse your hard drive until you locate a database file (a filename that ends with .Dbc) that contains data in it.**

   You can find several sample databases in subfolders under the C:\Program Files\Microsoft Visual Studio\VFP98\Wizards\Template\NameOfSample\Data folder. You can also use the Windows Find utility to locate .Dbc databases (Start⇨Find⇨Files or Folders).

7. **After you locate a .Dbc database name in the Open dialog box, double-click the .Dbc filename.**

   The Open dialog box closes, and the tables and fields available in this database are displayed in the various list boxes on the first page of the Web Publishing Wizard.

8. **Click a table or view in the Databases And Tables list.**

   The Available Fields list fills with all the fields that are in the table or view you selected.

9. **Double-click any fields in the Available Fields list that you want to display to visitors to your Web site.**

   Any fields that you double-click are moved to the Selected Fields list.

10. **Click the Next button.**

    The Sort Records page of the Web Publishing Wizard appears, where you can define which field will be used to alphabetize the records when they're displayed.

11. **Click the field in the Available Fields list that you want to sort by.**

    The field's name is selected.

12. **Click the Add button.**

    Your chosen field moves to the Selected Fields list.

13. **Click the Next button.**

    The page where you can choose the data layout and background graphic appears.

14. **Click Tabular List and click the check box next to whatever background graphic you want.**

15. **Click the Next button.**

    The final page of the Web Publishing Wizard appears, enabling you to select how you want the Wizard to generate your Web page.

16. **Click the Save Web Page And Open It In A Browser option button.**

17. **Click the Finish button.**

    The traditional Windows Save As dialog box opens.

18. **Type in a name for your new Web page.**

19. **Click the Save button.**

    The Save As dialog box closes, your Web page is saved to an .Htm file on your hard drive, and the Web page appears in your browser, as shown in Figure 15-11.

If your database contains too much data to display on a single page, Next and Previous buttons will be added to the Web page to allow visitors easy navigation through your database.

If you're curious about the source code that loads and displays data from a database, right-click Internet Explorer with your database .Htm file loaded. Then choose View Source from the context menu that appears. The HTML source code written by the Visual FoxPro Wizard is displayed in Notepad.

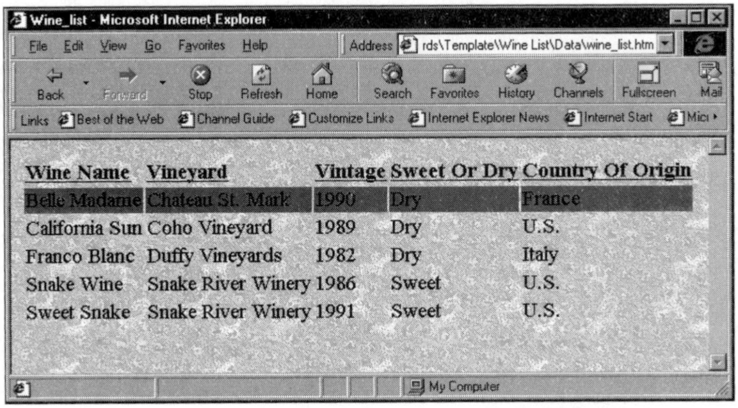

Figure 15-11:
Visual
FoxPro has
created a
Web page
that
displays the
data from
your
database.

Wine_list - Microsoft Internet Explorer

File   Edit   View   Go   Favorites   Help   Address rds\Template\Wine List\Data\wine_list.htm

Back   Forward   Stop   Refresh   Home   Search   Favorites   History   Channels   Fullscreen   Mail

Links   Best of the Web   Channel Guide   Customize Links   Internet Explorer News   Internet Start   Mic

Wine Name	Vineyard	Vintage	Sweet Or Dry	Country Of Origin
Belle Madame	Chateau St. Mark	1990	Dry	France
California Sun	Coho Vineyard	1989	Dry	U.S.
Franco Blanc	Duffy Vineyards	1982	Dry	Italy
Snake Wine	Snake River Winery	1986	Sweet	U.S.
Sweet Snake	Snake River Winery	1991	Sweet	U.S.

My Computer

Chapter 16

Managing Database Connections

. . . .

. . . .

*A*t first sight, database management may seem unrelated to Web site programming. But don't be fooled. The great majority of ordinary Windows business applications now require a database connection. If you're a programmer or a developer, you already know this. And, increasingly, Web site programming also requires a database connection or two. Or three.

Microsoft included a variety of database connection tools in Visual Studio 6. And Microsoft rarely does things without a good reason. In Visual Studio 6, you can find data-aware (also called data-bound) components such as text box controls that you can add to an application or Web page that automatically display data from a database.

Data-aware controls are said to be data-bound controls, meaning that they're bound to a particular database because they've been attached to a data control in Visual Basic, a recordset design-time control in Visual InterDev, or any other database connection component.

Also, wizards like Visual FoxPro's Web Designer Wizard save you lots of trouble. They generate the HTML source code necessary to display a database's contents on a Web page. (See the end of Chapter 15.)

In addition to the excellent Microsoft database application Visual FoxPro, Visual Studio 6 also includes other applications, such as Visual Basic and Visual InterDev, that are peppered with database management features, special data-related toolbars, design-time controls, Visual Database Tools (VDTs), and specialized data components.

The reason for all these database-related features is that connecting a Web site to a database is often useful. Such a connection can provide visitors with the following:

- ✔ Up-to-date information about your company and its products
- ✔ Reference look-up features, such as a database containing definitions of computer terms or frequently asked questions
- ✔ The ability to check order status, shipment method, or other information that is commonly stored in databases
- ✔ In special cases, the ability to modify the contents of a database

This chapter explores *data-aware components,* Microsoft's name for labels, grids, scrollbars, and other components that can be used to manipulate or display databases. Visual Basic was the first language to include data-aware components, and the approach it takes to connecting a component to a database set the standard (and was copied by Visual InterDev). Therefore, looking at how data-aware components are used in Visual Basic is worth your time. The second part of this chapter looks at how Visual InterDev deals with data-aware components.

Creating a Data-Aware Form in Visual Basic

Visual Basic uses the *form* in a way similar to the Design View in Visual InterDev or the Normal View in the FrontPage Editor. The form is a WYSIWYG (what you see is what you get) editor where you can prototype the user interface (or the visible surfaces) of your application. After a Visual Basic application is finished and the user interacts with it, the application's windows are what used to be its forms during the design and programming of that application.

Adding a database connection to a Visual Basic form is quite straightforward. To see how to add a database connection, follow these steps:

1. **Start Visual Basic by clicking its icon on the desktop.**

   The New Project dialog box opens. (If it doesn't open, choose File⇨ New Project.)

2. **Double-click the Standard EXE icon.**

   The dialog box closes and Visual Basic opens its template for a standard, ordinary Windows application.

3. **Double-click the data control on the Toolbox.**

   A data control appears on the form, as shown in Figure 16-1.

   If the Toolbox isn't visible, choose View➪Toolbox.

4. **Move the data control down on the form to near the bottom.**

   This way, the data control is out of the way so that you can add a text box.

5. **Double-click the text box control on the Toolbox (the icon near the top with abl in it).**

   A text box opens on the form.

6. **Drag and stretch the text box so that it looks like the box in Figure 16-2.**

   The form is now organized to display data. The text box at the top of the form displays data, and the data control at the bottom of the form enables a user to move through the records in the database.

Data control icon

The data control appears on the form.

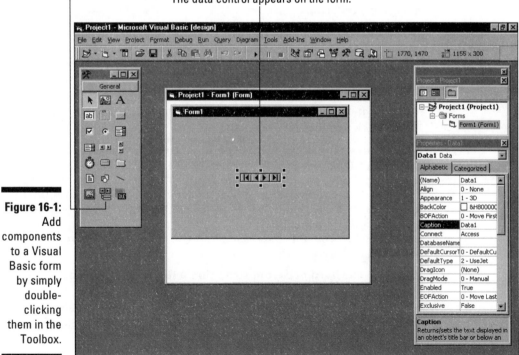

Figure 16-1:
Add components to a Visual Basic form by simply double-clicking them in the Toolbox.

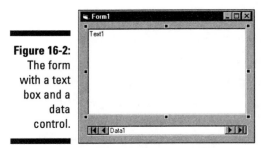

Figure 16-2:
The form
with a text
box and a
data
control.

7. **Click the text box on the form.**

   The text box is selected (and stretch tabs appear around it). The text box properties are displayed in the Properties window. If the Properties window isn't visible, press F4.

8. **Double-click the Multiline property in the Properties window.**

   The Multiline property of the text box changes from the default False to True. This change means that the text box can now display more than a single line of text.

9. **Now attach the text box to the data control by double-clicking the text box's Datasource property.**

   The Datasource property changes to Data1, the name of the data control.

10. **Click the data control.**

    The data control's properties appear in the Properties window.

11. **Double-click the data control's DatabaseName property in the Properties window.**

    The DatabaseName dialog box opens, where you can select a database to attach to the data control. By default, Microsoft Access-style databases (files with an .MDB extension) are listed. However, if you want to attach a different type of database, you can click the Cancel button to close the DatabaseName dialog box. Click the Connect property and then click the icon next to the Connect property. This action drops down a list of available database types (dBASE, Excel, FoxPro, Lotus, Paradox, and Text).

12. **Browse your hard drive until you find a database you want to use. Then double-click its filename.**

    You can find two sample Access (.MDB) databases in the C:\Program Files\Microsoft Visual Studio\VB98 folder. These are the standard Microsoft sample databases: Biblio (books) and Northwind (Nwind).

    The DatabaseName dialog box closes and your data control is now attached to the database you selected.

13. **Click the RecordSource property in the Properties window.**

14. Click the drop-down arrow icon next to the RecordSource property.

A drop-down list appears, displaying all the tables available in the database you're attached to. You can select which table's records you want to show in the text box, as shown in Figure 16-3.

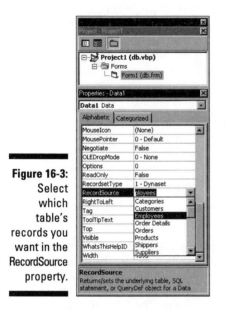

15. Click one of the recordsets in the dropdown list in the RecordSource property.

The recordset you chose now becomes the set of records that are displayed in the text box attached to this data control. (You can put as many different data controls as you want onto a Visual Basic form. You may also attach as many other controls as you want to this data control.)

16. Click the text box.

The text box gets the focus and its properties appear in the Properties window.

17. Click the DataField property in the Properties window.

A drop-down list icon appears (with a black triangle graphic) in the DataField property.

18. Click the drop-down list icon in the DataField property.

A drop-down list appears, displaying all the fields in the recordset (the table you selected in Step 15).

19. **Click the field that you want to display in the text box.**

    The DataField drop-down list closes and the field you chose is displayed as the chosen DataField.

20. **Press F5 to run your application.**

    You see a field in the first record displayed in the text box, as shown in Figure 16-4. You can move through the recordset by clicking the buttons in the data control on the bottom.

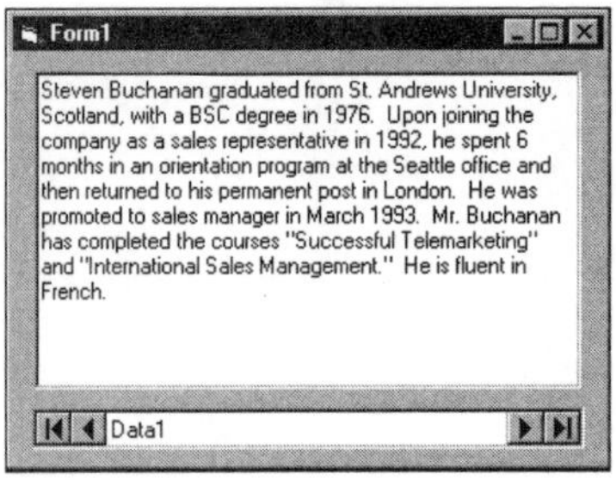

Figure16-4:
A user sees records displayed in this data-bound text box.

> **Form1**
>
> Steven Buchanan graduated from St. Andrews University, Scotland, with a BSC degree in 1976. Upon joining the company as a sales representative in 1992, he spent 6 months in an orientation program at the Seattle office and then returned to his permanent post in London. He was promoted to sales manager in March 1993. Mr. Buchanan has completed the courses "Successful Telemarketing" and "International Sales Management." He is fluent in French.
>
> |◄ ◄ Data1   ► ►|

A *recordset* is a copy of a table (or it can be a set of records returned after a query). A recordset is like an array, and usually it contains all the records in a particular table. If you have a data control on a form and that data control's DatabaseName and RecordSource properties are set to point to a particular database and table, a recordset copy of that table is automatically generated when the form is loaded (executed).

The recordset object is the essence of the data control. The data control uses its recordset as a window into the database that's attached to the data control. You have three kinds of recordsets: Table, Dynaset, and SnapShot. You can choose among them by adjusting the data control's RecordsetType property, but the default style is the Dynaset and it's also the most commonly used.

Each style of recordset specializes in a different kind of data manipulation. A Table-type recordset can read or write to a particular, single table within a database. A Dynaset-type recordset is more flexible. It can read or write to all (or just parts) of various tables, even from various databases; a Dynaset is sometimes the product of a query across several tables, providing, for example, all records prior to October 1993. A Snapshot-type recordset is like a Dynaset-type, but is read-only; no data can be edited, added, or deleted in the actual databases from which the snapshot was taken.

Each record in a database normally has several fields. For example, an employee's personnel record may contain Name, Address, Phone, SS#, Possibilities, Personality Drawbacks, Salary, and so on. Each of these elements within a record is called a *field*.

When you design a form that displays records, you often want to include several (or all) of the fields in each record. One way to do this is to put a data control on a form and add several text boxes (one for each field). You can also use several labels or other data-aware controls to display the fields.

To display several fields at once — by attaching several data-aware controls to a single data control on a form — follow these steps:

1. **Follow steps 1 through 19 in the previous numbered list in this section.**

   You have a Visual Basic form with a text box and a data control on it. These two components' properties are set so that they point to a table in a database on your hard drive.

2. **Drag the text box so that it's about the height of one line of text, and move it so that it's just above the data control.**

   You've now made room for several more text boxes above the original one on this form. Each text box displays a different field.

3. **Click the text box.**

   The text box is selected (small drag handles appear around it).

4. **Press Ctrl+C.**

   The text box is copied to the clipboard.

5. **Press Ctrl+V.**

   A message box opens, telling you that a text box named Text1 already exists. The message box asks whether you want to create a control array.

6. **Click the No button.**

   The message box closes and a new text box opens on your form named Text2, but otherwise has all the same properties as Text1 (Multiline, attached to Data1 as its data source).

7. **Repeat Steps 5 and 6 until you have a total of seven text boxes on your form.**

8. **Drag the text boxes so that they line up.**

9. **Click each text box in turn, and click the drop-down list in the DataField property in the Properties window.**

   A list of the available fields appears.

10. **Choose a different field for each text box's DataField property.**

    Now each text box displays a different field when the application runs.

11. **Press F5.**

    The application runs, displaying a different field in each text box, as shown in Figure 16-5.

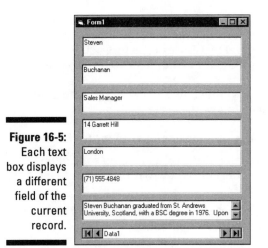

Figure 16-5:
Each text
box displays
a different
field of the
current
record.

Note that the bottom text box shown in Figure 16-5 contains a field (called Notes) that can include more data than can be displayed all at once; therefore, a scrollbar was added to enable the user to scroll through the field. To add a scrollbar, just locate the text box's ScrollBars property in the Properties window and then change it from the default None to Vertical.

Accessing a Database by Programming

You don't have to use data-aware components to attach an application to a database. All Visual Studio 6 languages include programming commands that enable you to connect an application to a database by writing source code. Although this approach takes more time, you do get greater, or *finer,* control over the behavior of an application when you hand-program it.

A database has two fundamental qualities: the structure of the database and the data contained in that structure. One advantage of programming is that you can find out the structure of a database, as well as its data, as the following example shows.

To see how to programmatically access a database, follow these steps:

1. **Start Visual Basic by clicking its icon on the desktop.**

   The New Project dialog box opens. (If it doesn't appear, choose File⇨New Project.)

2. **Double-click the Standard EXE icon in the New Project dialog box.**

   The dialog box closes and Visual Basic opens its template for a standard, ordinary Windows application.

3. **Double-click the text box control on the Toolbox (the icon near the top with abl in it).**

   A text box opens on the form.

4. **Choose Project⇨References.**

   The References dialog box opens, where you can choose the support files (.Dlls and other kinds of libraries) that you want to make available to your application.

5. **Click to put a checkmark in the box next to Microsoft DAO 3.51 Object Library in the Available References list box, as shown in Figure 16-6.**

   The Data Access Object (DAO) tools, such as database and recordset objects, now become available for use in your programming in this application.

Figure 16-6:
After you've
added the
DAO library
to your
project, you
can
connect to
databases
with
programming.

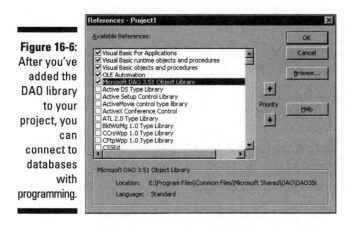

6. **Click the text box.**

   The text box is selected and its properties appear in the Properties window.

7. **Double-click the text box's MultiLine property in the Properties window.**

   The text box's MultiLine property changes to True and it can now display more than a single line.

8. **Double-click the form.**

   The Code window opens up, with the Form_Load() event displayed. The Form_Load event is automatically executed after the form is activated when the program runs.

9. **Type the following programming code into the** Form_Load **event:**

```
Private Sub Form_Load()
Show
cr = Chr(13) & Chr(10)
Dim MyDatabase As Database
Set MyDatabase = OpenDatabase("C:\Program
        Files\Microsoft Visual
        Studio\VB98\Biblio.mdb")
Dim MyTable As Recordset
Set MyTable = MyDatabase.OpenRecordset("Authors",
        dbOpenTable)
Dim n As Field
Set n = MyTable.Fields(1)
Text1 = "Contents of this field:" & n
Text1 = Text1 & cr & "Field Name: " & n.Name
Text1 = Text1 & cr & "AllowZeroLength: " &
        n.AllowZeroLength
Text1 = Text1 & cr & "Attributes: " & n.Attributes
Text1 = Text1 & cr & "CollatingOrder: " &
        n.CollatingOrder
Text1 = Text1 & cr & "DefaultValue: " &
        n.DefaultValue
Text1 = Text1 & cr & "OrdinalPosition: " &
        n.OrdinalPosition
Text1 = Text1 & cr & "Required: " & n.Required
Text1 = Text1 & cr & "Size: " & n.Size
Text1 = Text1 & cr & "SourceField: " & n.SourceField
Text1 = Text1 & cr & "SourceTable: " & n.SourceTable
Text1 = Text1 & cr & "Type: " & n.Type
Text1 = Text1 & cr & "ValidateOnSet: " &
        n.ValidateOnSet
Text1 = Text1 & cr & "ValidationRule: " &
        n.ValidationRule
Text1 = Text1 & cr & "ValidationText: " &
        n.ValidationText
End Sub
```

Replace (`"C:\Program Files\Microsoft Visual Studio\VB98\Biblio.MDB"`) with a path to an .Mdb database file on your hard drive. However, you're likely to find the biblio.Mdb database located in the same path as illustrated in this code example.

10. **Press F5.**

The program executes and you see the contents (and also the structure) of the second field, as shown in Figure 16-7.

Figure 16-7:
You can
display the
contents
and also the
structure of
a database.

```
Form1                                    _ □ ×
Contents of this field:Jacobs, Russell
Field Name: Author
AllowZeroLength: False
Attributes: 34
CollatingOrder: 1033
DefaultValue:
OrdinalPosition: 1
Required: False
Size: 50
SourceField: Author
SourceTable: Authors
Type: 10
ValidateOnSet: False
ValidationRule:
ValidationText:
```

Here's an explanation of how the programming code (shown earlier in Step 9) works. Fields(0) displays the first field of a record in the Authors table in the biblio.Mdb database. Fields(1) displays the second field, because the Fields collection begins counting with 0.

The contents of this field are displayed first, and that's accomplished by merely printing the variable n. (The line Set n = MyTable.Fields(1) in the source code assigns the first field to the variable n.) After displaying the contents of this field, all the properties (the structure) of the field are displayed by accessing properties of n such as its Name, SourceField, and Size. When you add text to a text box, if you want it to move down a line, you have to insert nonprinting carriage return/line feed characters. That's accomplished in the example above by defining a variable cr like this: cr = Chr(13) & Chr(10).

A database and a table within it are programmatically opened with this code:

```
Dim MyDatabase As Database
Set MyDatabase = OpenDatabase("C:\Program Files\Microsoft
        Visual Studio\VB98\Biblio.mdb")
Dim MyTable As Recordset
Set MyTable = MyDatabase.OpenRecordset("Authors",
        dbOpenTable)
```

You create database and recordset objects with the DIM command. Then you use the OpenDatabase command to assign a particular database on the hard drive to the database object variable. Likewise, you assign a particular table in that database to a recordset object variable using the OpenRecordset command.

There must also be a way to write programming that moves from record to record within a database. A data *control* contains four buttons, enabling a user to move to the first, previous, next, and last records in a recordset. Equivalent commands enable you to move among the records in a table by programming: `MoveFirst`, `MovePrevious`, `MoveNext`, and `MoveLast`.

To see how to write programming that enables movement among records, follow these steps:

1. **Follow Steps 1 through 10 in the previous numbered list in this section.**

   You have an application that displays information about a field in a text box.

2. **Double-click the form.**

   The Code window is displayed.

3. **Move the following two lines from the `Form_Load` event to a blank area above all events (at the very top of the Code window). Also change the `Dim` command in each of these lines to `Public`:**

```
Public MyDatabase As Database
Public MyTable As Recordset
```

   You've typed these variables into the General Declarations section of your form, as shown in Figure 16-8. When a variable is defined in General Declarations, all the events in the form can then access it (read it, use it, or change it). This kind of access is called *Form-wide scope.*

The General Declarations section

```
Project1 - Form1 (Code)                                     _ □ ×
(General)                    ▼   (Declarations)              ▼
      Public MyDatabase As Database
      Public MyTable As Recordset

      Private Sub Form_Click()
      Dim n As Field
      MyTable.MoveNext
      Set n = MyTable.Fields(1)
      Text1 = n
      Set n = Nothing
      End Sub

      Private Sub Form_Load()
      Show
      cr = Chr(13) & Chr(10)
      Set MyDatabase = OpenDatabase("E:\Program Files\Microsoft Visu
      Set MyTable = MyDatabase.OpenRecordset("Authors", dbOpenTable)
      Set n = MyTable.Fields(1)
      Text1 = "Contents of this field:" & n
      Text1 = Text1 & cr & "Field Name: " & n.Name
      Text1 = Text1 & cr & "AllowZeroLength: " & n.AllowZeroLength
      Text1 = Text1 & cr & "Attributes: " & n.Attributes
      Text1 = Text1 & cr & "CollatingOrder: " & n.CollatingOrder
      Text1 = Text1 & cr & "DefaultValue: " & n.DefaultValue
      Text1 = Text1 & cr & "OrdinalPosition: " & n.OrdinalPosition
      Text1 = Text1 & cr & "Required: " & n.Required
```

Figure 16-8: You can put variable definitions in the General Declarations section to give them form-wide scope.

4. **Type the following programming code into the** Form_Click **event, as shown in Figure 16-8.**

```
Private Sub Form_Click()
Dim n As Field
MyTable.MoveNext
Set n = MyTable.Fields(1)
Text1 = n
Set n = Nothing
End Sub
```

5. **Press F5.**

   Your program runs.

6. **Click the Form.**

   Each time you click the form, a new record is displayed.

Using Design-Time Controls

The job of connecting a database to a Web page is quite similar to connecting a database to a Windows application. You can add components that automate the process, or you can write the programming that does the job.

Visual InterDev includes a type of component called a *design-time control* (DTC). It's not your traditional component. True, you drop a DTC into your Web page as if it were an ordinary control (like a text box). And a DTC's appearance is solid like a typical control. But a DTC is really just a bunch of script source code that gets inserted into your Web page. You can see this by right-clicking a DTC and choosing Show Runtime Text from the context menu that appears. (ActiveX Controls or Java Applets never reveal their source code, so they're typical, classic, reusable components or objects.)

Creating an ODBC data source

Before you can attach a Visual InterDev Web page to a database, you must first make an ODBC (Open Database Connectivity) source that points to your database. To make this work, you must have chosen to install the appropriate ODBC driver during Visual InterDev setup. If you don't find the kind of database driver for your database type when you follow the steps below, rerun Visual Studio 6 setup and specify that the ODBC driver you need be installed. Visual Studio 6 ships with drivers for text files, Access, dBase, Excel, FoxPro, Oracle, Paradox and SQL Server. However, you may not have chosen one or any of them during your original Visual Studio 6 setup.

Open DataBase Connectivity is a set of tools (drivers) created by Microsoft that stands between a database and an application, assisting the application in communicating with the database. You have many incompatible database formats. ODBC uses database drivers, "filters" that translate an application's queries into a request that a particular database can understand. That way, an application can ask its query in a single format that can be understood by various different database formats (thanks to the various drivers). Applications that include programming commands able to ask ODBC queries, and databases that are able to respond to ODBC queries are said to be *ODBC-compliant.*

To point an ODBC driver to the Biblio.Mdb (Access-style) database found as a sample in the Microsoft Visual Studio\VB98 folder, follow these steps:

1. **Click the Windows Start button.**

2. **Choose Settings⇨Control Panel.**

   The Control Panel window appears.

3. **Double-click the ODBC icon, as shown in Figure 16-9 (in Windows 98, ODBC is referenced as ODBC Data Sources (32Bit)).**

   The ODBC Data Source Administrator dialog box opens with the User DSN tab on top, as shown in Figure 16-10.

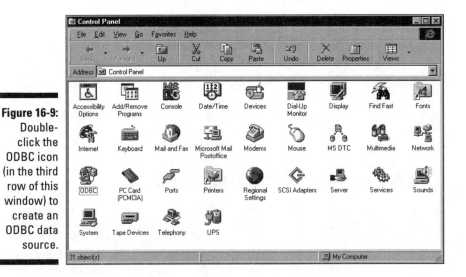

Figure 16-9: Double-click the ODBC icon (in the third row of this window) to create an ODBC data source.

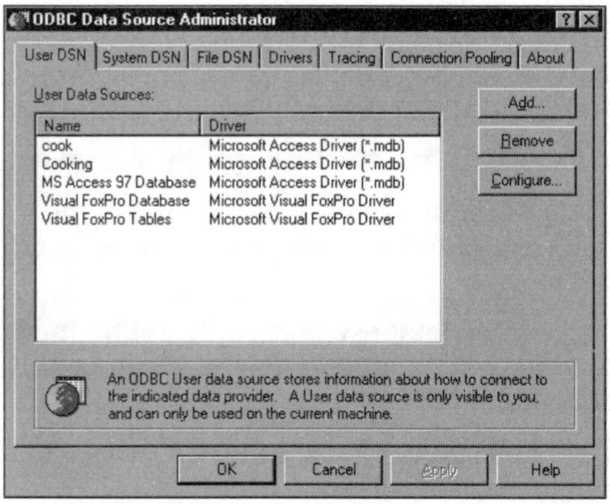

Figure 16-10:
The ODBC
Data Source
Administrator
dialog box.

4. **Click the A̲dd button in the User DSN page of the ODBC Data Source Administrator dialog box.**

   The Create New Data Source dialog box opens, as shown in Figure 16-11. In this dialog box, you choose the style of the database that you want to attach.

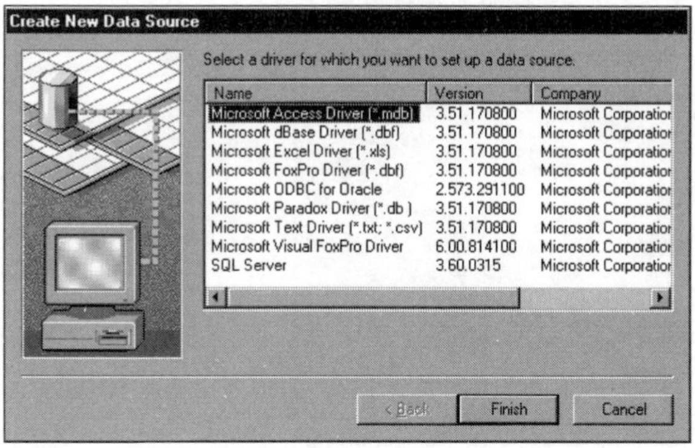

Figure 16-11:
The Create
New Data
Source
dialog box.

5. **In the list box of the Create New Data Source dialog box, double-click Microsoft Access Driver.**

   The ODBC Microsoft Access 97 Setup dialog box opens. In this dialog box, you give your data source a name and description.

6. **Fill in the Data Source N̲ame text box and the D̲escription text box (if you want your data source to have a name and description). You can use any name and description that makes sense to you, beginning the name with the prefix com as in comBiblio is customary.**

7. Click the Select button.

The Select Database dialog box opens. Here, you can browse your hard drive to find the .Mdb database that you want to connect to.

8. Browse your hard drive to find the Biblio.Mdb sample database.

The Biblio.Mdb sample database is usually located in the C:\Program Files\Microsoft Visual Studio\VB98 folder. You can use a different database if you prefer.

9. When the filename of the database that you want to open appears in the Database Name list box, double-click the filename (Biblio.Mdb or your chosen database).

The Select Database dialog box closes. Now you're back in the ODBC Microsoft Access 97 Setup dialog box.

10. Click the OK button.

The ODBC Microsoft Access 97 Setup dialog box closes. Now you're back in the ODBC Data Source Administrator dialog box. Notice that your new data source is now among the names in the User Data Sources list box, as shown in Figure 16-12.

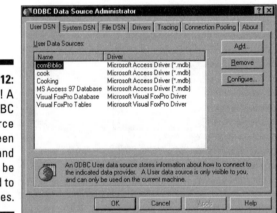

Figure 16-12: Success! A new ODBC data source has been created and can now be attached to Web pages.

11. Click the OK button.

The ODBC Data Source Administrator dialog box closes.

Making database connections in a Web page

After you've created a data source that points to a database you want to attach to your Web pages, you can then attach that database to your Web pages. (If you have not created a data source, follow the steps earlier in this chapter in the section "Creating an ODBC data source.")

Database connections can be pretty simple when you use components (design-time controls) in Visual InterDev. The first job when adding a database to a Web page is to create a data connection in a Web project. To see how that's done, follow these steps:

1. **Start Visual InterDev by clicking its icon on your desktop.**

   The New Project dialog box opens. (If it doesn't appear, choose File⇨New Project.)

2. **Click the New tab in the New Project dialog box.**

   The New page of the dialog box opens.

3. **Click Visual InterDev Projects in the left pane.**

4. **Type in whatever name you want to give your project in the Name text box.**

   Perhaps Biblio is a good choice for this project.

5. **Unless you have a compelling reason to change it, leave the folder names and path alone in the Location text box of the New Project dialog box.**

6. **Double-click the New Web Project icon in the right pane of the New Project dialog box.**

   The Web Project Wizard starts running, displaying its first page, which asks you what server you want to use. You find a list of any servers you've previously created projects on. You can either change the server, or leave the default as is.

7. **Leave the Master Mode option button selected on the New Web Project Wizard's first page.**

   Master mode automatically updates the project on the Web server whenever you save any files. *Local mode* means that you're working with a set of copies (of the official project stored on the server) in your workstation. Saving files when in Local mode saves them only to your workstation. You must explicitly update the official server project files when you're ready to do that; it doesn't happen automatically.

8. **Click the Next button.**

   The Web server is contacted and the second page in this wizard appears. By default, the Create A New Web Application option button is selected. Leave it selected.

9. **Click the Next button.**

   The third wizard page appears. Leave the default <none> option selected in the list box so that the Preview window displays `No theme/layout applied`.

10. **Click the Next button to get to the final dialog box in this Web Project Wizard.**

    You're asked if you want to add a Theme.

11. **Leave the default No Theme/Layout Applied option button selected and click the Finish button.**

    Visual InterDev builds your new Web project. (This process can take a few minutes as all the scripts in the script library are added.)

12. **Choose File➪New File.**

    The New File dialog box opens.

13. **Click Visual InterDev in the left pane of the dialog box.**

    HTML Page, ASP Page, and Style Sheet icons appear in the right pane of the dialog box.

14. **Double-click the HTML Page icon in the right pane of the dialog box.**

    A new HTML page is added to your project and the dialog box closes.

15. **Right-click the name of your project in the Project Explorer (the name is in boldface), and click Add Data Connection in the context menu that appears.**

    The Select Data Source dialog box opens (which may take several seconds). In this dialog box, you can choose which data source to connect to.

16. **Click the Machine Data Source tab.**

    The Machine Data Source page of the dialog box opens, showing you a list of user data sources.

17. **Double-click the name of the data source that you want to use.**

    If you've created a data source following the steps in the "Creating an ODBC data source" section and you want to use that data source, double-click comBiblio in the list box. (Otherwise, use whatever data source you want to use.)

The Select Data Source dialog box closes. This connection is named Connection1 by default, and a Connection1 Properties dialog box opens. In this dialog box, you can provide a different name for the data connection. (You can also change the source of the connection, but you don't want to do that in this example.)

18. **Leave the Connection Name as the default, Connection1.**

Note that you now have two features connecting you to a database. One, the ODBC data source is a feature of Windows; the other, called a *connection,* is a feature of Visual InterDev (that connects a Visual InterDev project to the ODBC data source). In other words, you've created the *Visual InterDev connection* (which you left at the default name *Connection1*) and the *Windows ODBC data source* that is used by that connection. The data source is the actual database you're accessing: comBiblio, or whatever database you selected in Step 17.

19. **Click the OK button.**

The Connection Properties dialog box closes, the data connection is added to your Global.Asa file (see it in the Project Explorer), and the Properties window changes to a Data View window, as shown in Figure 16-13. If the Properties window isn't visible, press F4.

You can use the Data View to see the structure — the tables, fields, and views — of the connected database.

Figure 16-13:
The Data
View
window.

Using design-time controls to display a database

After you've made a data connection to a project in Visual InterDev, you can then add DTCs (design-time controls) to Web pages. Put one or more DTCs anywhere in your Web site that you want to display the database to visitors.

Several data-bound DTCs are available in Visual InterDev: check box, formmanager, grid, label, list box, optiongroup, recordsetnavbar, and text box. Any of these components can be attached to a *Recordset DTC*. The Recordset is a special DTC. It is the component that all other data-bound components (DTCs) are attached to. This works the same way as in Visual Basic when you attach data-bound components to the Visual Basic data control. Both Visual InterDev's Recordset component and Visual Basic's data control provide a gateway into a database when other components are attached to the Recordset or data control.

After a Recordset DTC is attached to a data connection in a Web page, you can then add several data-bound components to that one Recordset if you wish. (Three text boxes could be attached to a single Recordset, for example.)

Conversely, you can put more than one Recordset on a page. That way, you can attach each Recordset to a different table in the database. As you can see, you can mix and match to display the database to a visitor in pretty much any way you want to display it.

To see just how easily you can use DTCs to connect a Web project to a database, follow these steps:

1. **Follow Steps 1 through 19 in the "Making database connections in a Web page" section to create a Web project that you can connect to a database.**

   Your Visual InterDev Web project is now ready for you to add DTCs to display a database in its Web page or pages.

2. **Click the Design View tab at the bottom of an empty, blank new HTML page.**

   The Design View is displayed in the editor.

3. **Click the Design-Time Controls tab in the Visual InterDev Toolbox.**

   All the DTCs are displayed. If the Toolbox isn't visible, choose View⇨Toolbox.

4. **Double-click the Recordset DTC in the Toolbox.**

   The Recordset1 control appears on your HTML page, as shown in Figure 16-14.

5. **If you wish, choose a different table in the Object Name drop-down box by clicking a different choice.**

6. **Right-click the Recordset control (on the HTML page) and choose Properties in the context menu that appears.**

   The Recordset Properties dialog box opens. In this dialog box, you determine which scripting language to use for this recordset.

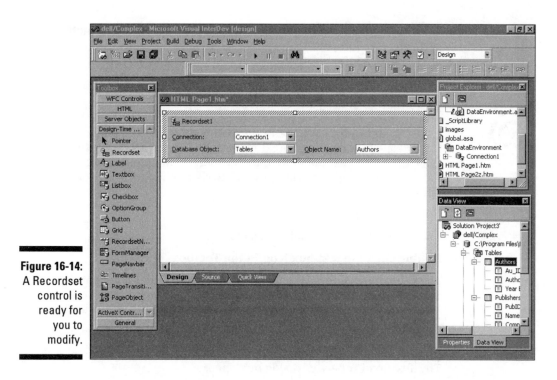

7. **Click the Implementation tab and choose Inherit From Page in the Scripting Platform drop-down list box.**

   This selection causes the Recordset to use the scripting that's in use on the host HTML page. (And any DTC components you add to the Recordset, such as a text box, also follow the same rule.) The page's DTCScriptingPlatform property can be Server ASP or Client DHTML. But, if you choose Client DHTML, your page runs on only Internet Explorer 4.0 and higher.

8. **Click the Close button.**

   The Recordset Properties dialog box closes.

9. **Click the Source tab at the bottom of your HTML page's Editor window.**

   You see the source code for the page.

10. **Right-click the page (not a component), and click Properties in the context menu that appears.**

    The page's Properties dialog box, where you choose the page's scripting platform, appears.

11. **Click the Server (ASP) option button in the DTC scripting platform section.**

    Now your page can run on browsers other than Internet Explorer 4.0 (such as earlier Internet Explorer versions and Netscape).

    If you want to specify the default scripting platform for your entire project, not just individual pages or DTCs, right-click the project name (which is in boldface) in the Project Explorer. A context menu pops out. Click Properties on the context menu. The Properties dialog box opens. Click the Editor Defaults tab in the Properties dialog box. Click one of the DTC Scripting Platform option buttons to choose Server or Client (IE 4 DHTML).

12. **Click the OK button.**

    The Page's Properties dialog box closes.

13. **Double-click the text box icon in the Toolbox.**

    A text box opens on the page. If you get an error message that the text box can't be placed in the current location, click elsewhere on your HTML page; then try double-clicking the icon in the Toolbox again.

14. **Right-click the text box and then choose Properties in the context menu that appears.**

    The Textbox Properties dialog box opens.

15. **Click the Recordset drop-down list.**

    You see a list of all Recordset components on the current page.

16. **Click Recordset1 in the drop-down list.**

    The drop-down list closes and Recordset1 is now attached to the text box component.

17. **Click the Field drop-down list.**

    All fields in the current table or view are listed in the drop-down list. Each Recordset points to a particular table (or view or query). The Field drop-down list displays all the fields in that table (or other kind of recordset).

18. **Click a field's name in the drop-down list.**

    The drop-down list closes and a field is now attached to the text box component.

19. **Click the OK button.**

    The Textbox Properties dialog box closes.

20. Press F5.

Your page is loaded in Internet Explorer or some other browser and displays the field in the table in the database you chose when setting up the properties of the Recordset and data-bound text box on this page.

21. Close Internet Explorer or your other browser.

This action stops the Web page from running and returns you to Design View in Visual InterDev.

To fill out this database page, you may want to add additional text boxes or other data-bound DTCs and set them to display the various fields in the table or view you're attached to. Likewise, you can add the RecordsetNavbar to your page, giving visitors four buttons to click to move through the records in your recordset: First, Previous, Next, and Last.

Often you can click the Quick View tab in the Visual InterDev Editor window, and thereby test your Web page by seeing what a visitor would see if that page were loaded into a browser. However, you can't see DTCs do their thing by clicking the Quick View tab. Quick View displays only HTML, some DHTML, or client-side scripting. Quick View can't handle any server-side scripting (programming distinguished by the % symbol or the RUNAT= Server command). Server-side scripting is intended to run on the server, not in a visitor's (a client's) browser. Any server-side script is just ignored in Quick View. DTCs run on the server-side because the databases that they access are on the server-side. Therefore, when you want to see or test a page with DTCs, you must press F5. This launches your browser and automatically loads the Web page into it for you to test and observe. Pressing F5 causes the page to display just as it does to a visitor — with server- and client-side scripting working as they do in the real world.

Viewing a design-time control's source code

A DTC adds HTML source code that attaches and displays a database's contents on a Web page. To see or modify the source code generated by a DTC, just click the Source tab at the bottom of the Editor window. Then right-click the design-time control, and choose Show Run-time Text from the context menu that appears. If you want to actually edit the source code for a design-time control, choose Convert to Run-time Text in the context menu.

Part VI
Managing Your Web Projects with Visual Studio 6

The 5th Wave   By Rich Tennant

New Age Web Designers

"QUIET EVERYONE—LET THE CRYSTAL DO ITS WORK."

In this part . . .

This part is where you find out how to take care of a Web site that you've already built. You see how to reorganize and update a site. (Maintenance sounds tedious, and, truth be told, it often is. The fun is usually in creating something, not in updating it. This part attempts to make maintenance fun, though, so don't run away screaming just yet.)

In this part, you also find out how to deploy the site when it's perfect and you're ready to send it out onto World Wide Web for all to see and enjoy.

Chapter 17

Using the FrontPage Explorer

In This Chapter

▶ Moving projects between Visual InterDev and FrontPage

▶ Working with hyperlinks

▶ Managing projects: creating new pages and folders

*F*rontPage is a great tool when you want to work with graphics, text, and other elements of a Web page. In fact, in many ways, FrontPage is easier to work with than Visual InterDev (which offers many of the same features as FrontPage). FrontPage includes many tools to help you easily insert forms, tables, and other Web page contents.

Yet, for all the strengths in FrontPage, Visual InterDev is really the best tool to write or edit programming. And it's also the best tool to manage a large, complicated Web site — and keep all the people who work on such a site from accidentally overwriting each others' files, duplicating efforts, and otherwise behaving in clumsy, uncoordinated ways.

However, FrontPage is usually where you want to be when working on individual pages in a Web site. And FrontPage includes special facilities enabling you to pull back from individual pages in a Web site and get an overall view of the site, or manipulate the links that connect the various pages in a site.

FrontPage is divided into two fundamental utilities: the FrontPage Editor and the FrontPage Explorer. The Editor is where you work on a single page at a time — designing how it looks and adjusting its contents (see Chapter 6). The Explorer is a tool for managing a FrontPage Web project — adding themes, manipulating the various pages, and creating hyperlinks within the project.

In this chapter, you see how to use some of the best features of the FrontPage Explorer. The Explorer pulls you back from the FrontPage Editor single page view. Instead, in the Explorer, you work with a FrontPage Web site as a whole.

Moving Projects between Visual InterDev and FrontPage

Before you can work with a Web site in the FrontPage Explorer, you must get access to the Web site. In many situations, a Web site is first prototyped in Visual InterDev. Later, the Web site is copied to FrontPage so that designers, artists, and writers can take advantage of FrontPage's excellent content-editing features. After these people have contributed their skills to the Web site, the site can be copied back to Visual InterDev for deployment and maintenance.

Loading a single Web page into FrontPage or Visual InterDev

If you need to work on a single Web page from a Visual InterDev project (an .Htm file), you can just load that file directly into FrontPage, if you know the location on the hard drive. In the FrontPage Editor, choose File⇨Open. Then click the Select A File On Your Computer icon on the lower right of the Open dialog box. Locate the .Htm file that you want to work on and double-click its filename. There it is, loaded into FrontPage. (This assumes that you have permission. If you ever have problems loading an .Htm file, you don't have sufficient permission. Speak to the network or Web site administrator, or try the various suggestions in Chapter 4.)

To merge an .Htm file into an existing FrontPage Web (a Web site you're building by using FrontPage), choose File⇨Import in the FrontPage Explorer.

Similarly, to load a single FrontPage Web page into Visual InterDev, choose File⇨Open File in the Visual InterDev menu bar. Then find the file you're interested in by navigating the hard drive.

Copying an application from Visual InterDev to FrontPage

FrontPage refers to an entire Web site that's under development as a *FrontPage* Web. Visual InterDev refers to an entire Web site under development as a *solution* or *application*. Whatever they're called, Web sites are a collection of files that make up a single site. These files, tied together by scripting and hyperlinks, are a coherent, individual site.

Sometimes you want to move an entire Visual InterDev Web site (application) to FrontPage. The Visual InterDev application then becomes a FrontPage Web, and you can work on the entire site by using FrontPage. Likewise, you sometimes want to go in the other direction and move a FrontPage Web to make it a Visual InterDev application.

To copy a Web site from Visual InterDev to FrontPage, follow these steps:

1. **Start the FrontPage Explorer by clicking its icon on the desktop.**

   The Getting Started dialog box is displayed with a list of existing FrontPage Webs (if any). If the dialog box isn't displayed, choose File➪Open FrontPage Web.

2. **If you don't see the name of the application that you want to open in FrontPage in the list displayed, click the More Webs button.**

   The Open FrontPage Web dialog box opens.

3. **Click the List Webs button.**

   The FrontPage Webs Found At Location list box fills with all the projects created in Visual InterDev that are available on your server or hard drive.

4. **Drop down the list labeled Select A Web Server Or Disk Location (if you want to switch to a different server or look on a hard drive for a Visual InterDev project).**

   You can see any additional Web servers. If you want to locate Visual InterDev projects on your hard drive that aren't listed in the list box (shown in Step 3), you can type in the file path (disk location) of the Visual InterDev application you want to import.

   The best way to locate a Visual InterDev application is to click the Windows Start button and then select Find➪Files or Folders. Search for the Visual InterDev application name. When located, type it into the Open FrontPage Web dialog box. Then click the OK button twice to close the dialog boxes and return to the FrontPage Explorer.

5. **Double-click (in the list box described in Step 3) the name of the Visual InterDev project that you want to work on.**

   The Visual InterDev application appears in the FrontPage Explorer, and the dialog boxes close.

Note that depending on how security is set up on your network, you may see a security dialog box asking for your name and password. (Your FrontPage security name and password may, or may not, be different than your network log-on name and password.) If you can't get past this dialog box, contact your network administrator or try the various suggestions listed in Chapter 4.

Copying a FrontPage Web to Visual InterDev

Moving a FrontPage Web over to Visual InterDev isn't much trouble. Maybe you've been designing some pages in FrontPage and you decide that it's time for programmers to add their scripting to your pages. (Programmers usually prefer to work in Visual InterDev.) So, to move your FrontPage Web to Visual InterDev and then save it as a Visual InterDev project, follow these steps:

1. **Start Visual InterDev by clicking its icon on your desktop.**

   The New Project dialog box opens. If it doesn't, choose File⇔ New Project from the Visual InterDev menu bar.

2. **Click the Visual InterDev Projects folder in the left pane.**

   The New Web Project and Sample App Wizard icons appear in the right pane of the dialog box.

3. **Double-click the New Web Project icon in the right pane.**

   The Visual InterDev Web Project Wizard appears.

4. **In the What Server Do You Want To Use? drop-down list, select the server where the FrontPage Web that you're interested in is located.**

5. **Click the Next button.**

   The second page of the Web Project Wizard appears, as shown in Figure 17-1.

6. **Click the Connect To An Existing Web Application On (*your server*) option button.**

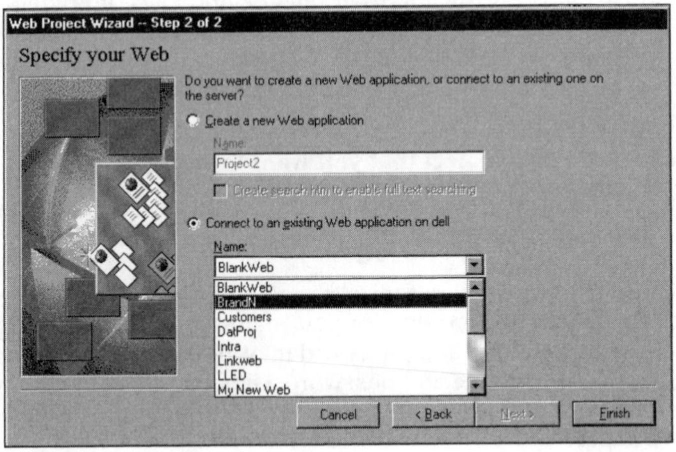

Figure 17-1:
The Visual InterDev Web Project Wizard.

7. **Click the FrontPage Web's name from the drop-down list, as shown in Figure 17-1.**

   The FrontPage Web's name is highlighted.

8. **Click the Finish button.**

   You may see a security dialog box asking for your name and password. If you can't satisfy this dialog box by typing in what you *think* are your proper name and password, contact your network administrator or try the various suggestions listed in Chapter 4.

   The wizard begins building the project in Visual InterDev. (If the Project Explorer window is visible, you see it fill with the new application.)

   You're likely to see a warning message informing you that the Visual InterDev Script library is not installed in this new Visual InterDev Web you're creating. You're asked if you want to install the Script Library. This library adds all the design-time controls to a project. These controls are used to help you attach a database to your Web site.

9. **If you're planning to use design-time controls (see Chapter 16 for a full description of these components), click the Yes button. If you aren't planning to connect a database to your Web site, you likely don't need the design-time controls, so you can click the No button.**

   The Web Project Wizard warning dialog box closes. The FrontPage Web is now loaded into Visual InterDev and ready to be worked with.

The Hype about Hyperlinks

The FrontPage Editor is Visual Studio 6's best tool for manipulating the content in individual Web pages. But the FrontPage Explorer utility can be used to view and manage the relationships, the *links,* between those pages. Although Visual InterDev is the best tool to use for managing large or complicated Web sites, the FrontPage Explorer does a fine job with smaller sites.

Creating a simple site in FrontPage Explorer

FrontPage includes wizards that help you to build particular kinds of sites. The Corporate Presence Wizard builds a typical company Web site, designed to show off the company's products and lure customers to buy, buy, buy. Another wizard creates a customer service site to take care of problems resulting from the aforementioned buying frenzy. The Customer Service Wizard creates several pages devoted to the assistance of confused or irate consumers, including pages titled Suggestions, FAQ, and Discussion. However, no page titled Fury exists.

To create a customer service site, follow these steps:

1. **Start the FrontPage Explorer by clicking its icon on your desktop.**

   The Getting Started dialog box opens. If it doesn't open, choose File⇨Open FrontPage Web.

2. **Click the Create A New FrontPage Web option button.**

3. **Click the OK button.**

   The New FrontPage Web dialog box opens.

4. **Click the From Wizard Or Template option button.**

5. **Click Customer Support Web from the list box.**

   Customer Support Web is highlighted.

6. **Type in the name you want to give this Web in the text box labeled Choose A Title For Your FrontPage Web.**

7. **Click the OK button.**

   The Create New FrontPage Web message box appears and then goes away. You may see a password dialog box at this point, which you must fill in and then click its OK button. If you have problems with the password dialog, contact your network administrator or try the various suggestions listed in Chapter 4.

   The FrontPage Explorer Navigation View now displays your new Web site, with a set of seven child windows underneath a Home Page, as shown in Figure 17-2.

 If you try to create a new FrontPage Web and you get the error message that the maximum number of Webs already exists, you must delete an existing Web before you can create a new one. FrontPage permits a total of only ten Webs. After that, it requires that you get rid of one before you can build a new Web. The only solution is to return to FrontPage Explorer and choose File⇨Open FrontPage Web to load a Web that you no longer want. Then, with the Web you're willing to discard currently loaded into the FrontPage Explorer, choose File⇨Delete FrontPage Web.

Manipulating page relationships in FrontPage Explorer's Navigation View

FrontPage Explorer features four views that you can switch between to examine and manage the pages in a Web site. You choose a view by clicking on an icon in the left frame titled Views of the FrontPage Explorer.

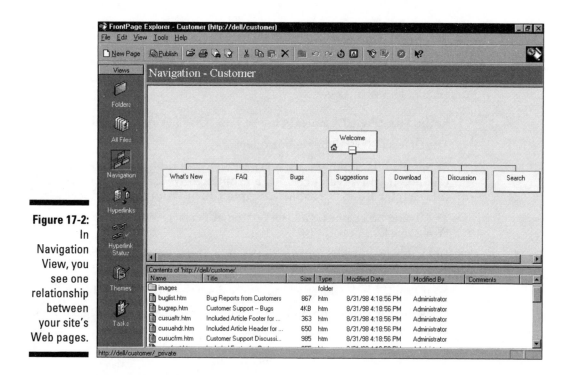

Figure 17-2:
In
Navigation
View, you
see one
relationship
between
your site's
Web pages.

Sometimes looking at a Web site a different way helps you to see relationships that went unnoticed, or problems that you didn't see before. The public pages that a visitor sees in a Web site are linked together with hyperlinks. Those links create hierarchies (parent pages with one or more child pages), sibling relationships (child pages with links to each other), and other structures.

One of the important jobs when building a Web site is to ensure that the site's links are logical. That is: A visitor should intuitively see how to navigate your site. The FrontPage Explorer Navigation View and Hyperlinks View are helpful when you want to consider (or modify) how a visitor traverses your Web site. For example, does a visitor have to click three hyperlinks before getting to a page that displays a table of contents for your site? The table of contents should be on the home page, not buried deep in the site.

The third and fourth views are useful when you're working with the files in a site. The Folders View is essentially the same view you get in Windows Explorer: folders and subfolders in the left pane, subfolders and files in the right pane. The All Files View displays every file in the site.

Seeing a rotated view

Two icons are on the toolbar along the top of the FrontPage Explorer that you can use to adjust the Navigation View. To see the effect of clicking the Rotate icon, follow these steps:

1. **In the FrontPage Explorer, choose File⇨Open FrontPage Web.**

   The Getting Started dialog box opens.

2. **In the list box, double-click a FrontPage Web that you previously created. If you haven't created a FrontPage Web, see the section in this chapter titled "Creating a simple site in FrontPage Explorer."**

   The dialog box closes, and the Customer Service Web is loaded into FrontPage Explorer.

3. **Click the Navigation button on the side of the FrontPage Explorer window.**

   Your FrontPage Explorer window now displays the Web graphically.

4. **Click the Rotate button on the top toolbar, as illustrated in Figure 17-3.**

   The Navigation View displays the parent/child relationship horizontally.

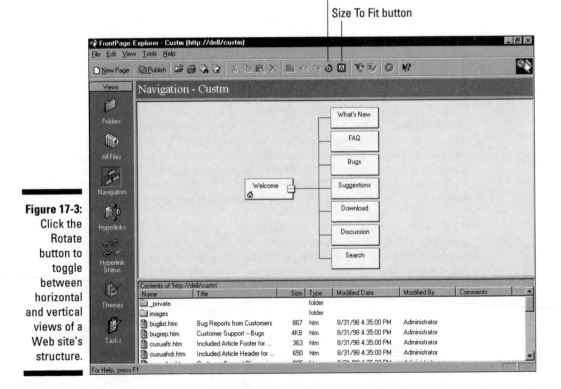

Figure 17-3: Click the Rotate button to toggle between horizontal and vertical views of a Web site's structure.

Your Web site may get too complicated and large to see in one screen without scrolling the Explorer Navigation or Hyperlinks Views. If that happens, click the Size To Fit button, as shown in Figure 17-3.

Adjusting page relationships

You can move the pages displayed in FrontPage Explorer's Navigation View. When you move the pages, you're actually changing their hyperlinks because FrontPage maintains hyperlinks for you automatically. To try editing the structure of your Web site, you can manipulate a Web that you've already created, such as the Customer Service Web. You can make its Bugs page a child page of the Suggestions page. To break a link and then create a new link, follow these steps:

1. **In the FrontPage Explorer, choose File⇨Open FrontPage Web.**

   The Getting Started dialog box opens.

2. **In the list box, double-click the Customer Service Web. If it's not listed, follow the steps in the "Creating a simple site in FrontPage Explorer" section, earlier in this chapter.**

   The dialog box closes, and the Customer Service Web is loaded into FrontPage Explorer.

3. **Click the Navigation button in the row of icons on the left side of the FrontPage Explorer window.**

   Your FrontPage Explorer window should now display the Customer Service Web in Navigation View, with the Welcome page as the parent page and seven child pages underneath it. Refer to Figure 17-2.

4. **Drag the icon labeled Bugs and drop it under the icon labeled Suggestions.**

   A new parent/child relationship is now created, as shown in Figure 17-4.

5. **To see exactly what happens when you rearrange the Bugs page to make it a child page of the Suggestions page, double-click the Suggestions page in the FrontPage Explorer.**

   The FrontPage Editor opens, with the Suggestions page loaded. Notice that a hyperlink has been added to the Suggestions page. This link is to the Bugs page, as shown in Figure 17-5.

Using the FrontPage Explorer Hyperlinks View

The Hyperlinks View is a more detailed illustration of the underlying structure of your Web site: All the hyperlinks in the site can be displayed.

Figure 17-4:
In
Navigation
View, you
can freely
rearrange
the Web
pages in
your
FrontPage
Web.

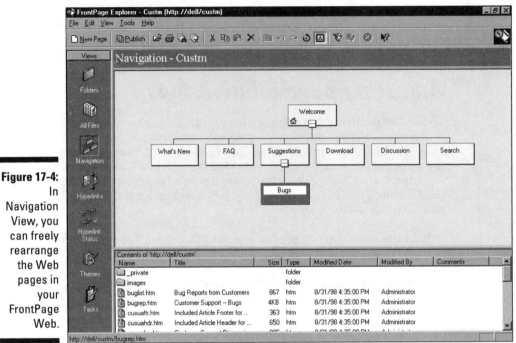

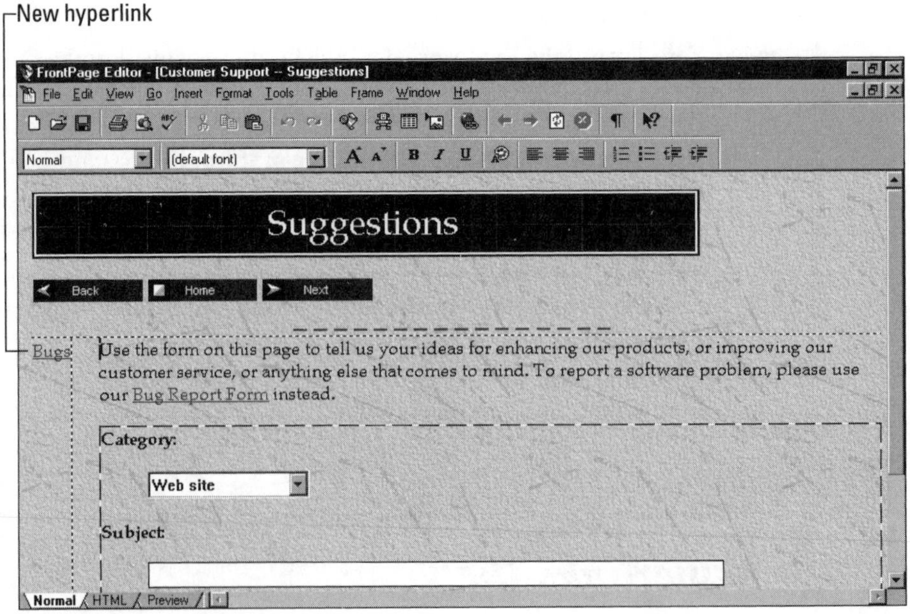

New hyperlink

Figure 17-5:
FrontPage
automatically
maintains
the correct
hyperlinks
when you
rearrange
your Web
site's
pages.

The Hyperlinks View shown in Figure 17-6 shows you which pages in your Customer Service Web have links to the home page (named Welcome). These links into the Home page are shown to the left of the Welcome page in the diagram. To the right of the Welcome page are the links in the Welcome page to other pages.

On the left, you see a pane listing the same pages, but they're displayed in a format similar to the familiar Windows Explorer tree diagrams. Notice the small + symbols next to each of the filenames in this list, as well as the + symbols in the diagram itself. This symbol tells you that if you click the icon or filename, an additional page or pages are displayed.

1. **In the FrontPage Explorer, choose File⇨Open FrontPage Web.**

   The Getting Started dialog box opens.

2. **In the list box, double-click the Customer Service Web. If it's not listed, follow the steps in the "Creating a simple site in FrontPage Explorer" section, earlier in this chapter.**

   The dialog box closes, and the Customer Service Web is loaded into FrontPage Explorer.

3. **Click the Navigation button in the row of icons on the left side of the FrontPage Explorer window.**

   Your FrontPage Explorer window should now display the Customer Service Web in Navigation View, with the Welcome page as the parent page and seven child pages underneath it. Refer to Figure 17-2.

4. **Click the Hyperlinks icon in the left pane of the Explorer window.**

   A different, more complex diagram is displayed, as shown in Figure 17-6. All the hyperlinks can be displayed in Hyperlinks View, so that you can track down circular links (pages that have links to each other, which is fine) or orphan links (pages that have links to deleted pages, which is not fine). You also get an overall view of the complexity (or simplicity) of how a visitor may travel through your Web site.

Try clicking the + symbol next to the filename Suggestions in the left pane. You see a list of links displayed underneath the filename. You also see the Suggestions page become the central icon in the diagram, as shown in Figure 17-7. When you click an icon in the diagram pane, or a + symbol in the filename pane, the page you click becomes the central page.

Notice the three buttons on the toolbar shown in Figure 17-7. They're all toggle buttons, which means that when clicked, they turn on a feature. But when clicked again, they turn off the same feature. These three buttons toggle the following features:

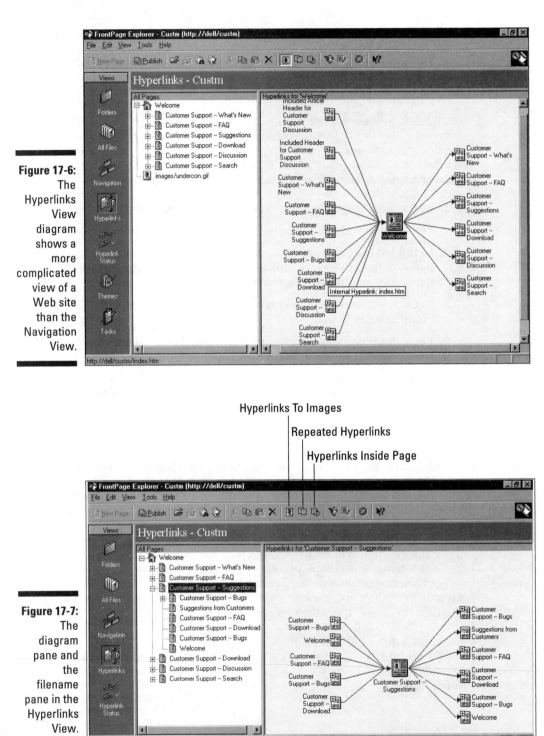

Figure 17-6:
The
Hyperlinks
View
diagram
shows a
more
complicated
view of a
Web site
than the
Navigation
View.

Figure 17-7:
The
diagram
pane and
the
filename
pane in the
Hyperlinks
View.

✔ **Hyperlinks To Images:** Displays any graphics files (.Gif or .Jpg) that have links to them. By default, graphics files aren't included in the Web diagram because they aren't that significant in the overall scheme of a Web site.

✔ **Repeated Hyperlinks:** Displays multiple links from a single page to another page. Sometimes a page has more than one hyperlink to a second page. But to keep things as simple as possible in the diagram, multiple links between two pages are normally displayed as only a single link.

✔ **Hyperlinks Inside Page:** Displays any links to other areas within the same page. Why would a page have links to itself? Some Web pages are quite long (perhaps five screens or more). As an alternative to the PgDn key or scrolling, some Web designers create a little table of contents for a large page, and when clicked, the page automatically scrolls itself to the target location within the page. Internal targets are called *bookmarks.* You often see this technique used with reference material like glossaries, product lists, and so on.

As you can see in Figure 17-7, when the Suggestions page becomes the central page in the diagram, four pages have links into Suggestions, and Suggestions has links to five pages. (The page named Bugs is displayed twice because it is a child page of Suggestions.)

If you click the + symbol and it changes to a – (minus) symbol, that means no lower levels are any further down. Clicking a – symbol hides secondary (lower) levels, and the – symbol change to a plus.

Using the FrontPage Explorer's Folders View

Some people find the FrontPage Folders View easier to use than the Navigation or Hyperlinks Views. Perhaps that's because the Folders View is the most familiar view to most people — it's exactly the same organization used by Windows Explorer to enable you to manage the files and folders on your hard drive. Click the Folders icon in the Views pane on the left side of the FrontPage Explorer.

With Folders View, you get the following details about each file in your Web site:

✔ Name

✔ Title

✔ Size

✔ Type

- ✔ Modified Date
- ✔ Modified By
- ✔ Comments

As in the Windows Explorer, Folders View lists top-level folders in the left pane, and files and lower-level folders in the right pane. If you double-click any .Htm file, it's loaded into the FrontPage Editor.

If you right-click any file, its context menu pops out, and you can perform the same actions on it that you can perform if you right-click a file in the ordinary Windows Explorer. The following options appear in the context menu:

- ✔ Open
- ✔ Open With
- ✔ Cut
- ✔ Copy
- ✔ Rename
- ✔ Delete
- ✔ Add Task
- ✔ Properties

If you move, rename, or otherwise modify a Web page in the Folders View, FrontPage handles all the link details for you. All pages that are linked to the modified page are automatically updated to keep the links accurate.

FrontPage always creates relative URLs (addresses) when defining new links within a Web. This means that the links are assumed to be located in the same server. Generally speaking, FrontPage handles the URLs for you. You can ignore the issue, unless you want to deliberately create a link to a specific address outside your FrontPage Web.

Testing and verifying hyperlinks

If you delete a Web page in a FrontPage Web, it's possible that another Web page will still point to it. In other words, you may have a hyperlink that's no longer valid. To see how this works, follow these steps:

1. **In the FrontPage Explorer, choose File➪Open FrontPage Web.**

   The Getting Started dialog box opens.

2. **In the list box, double-click the Customer Service Web. If it's not listed, follow the steps in the "Creating a simple site in FrontPage Explorer" section, earlier in this chapter.**

The dialog box closes, and the Customer Service Web is loaded into FrontPage Explorer.

3. **Click the Folders icon in the row of icons on the left side of the FrontPage Explorer window.**

Your FrontPage Explorer window displays the Web site the same way that Windows Explorer displays folders and files.

4. **Right-click the CUSUAFTR.HTM filename in the right pane of the Folders View.**

The context menu pops out.

If you don't see the list of files in the right pane that includes CUSUAFTR.HTM, double-click the top folder in the left pane that ends with the name CUSTM. This action cause all the files in the Web to be listed in the right pane.

5. **Click Delete in the context menu.**

The Confirm Delete dialog box opens, asking if you really, really mean to delete.

6. **Click the Yes button.**

The Confirm Delete dialog box closes and so does the CUSUAFTR.HTM file.

7. **Choose Tools⇨Verify Hyperlinks.**

The Verify Hyperlinks dialog box opens.

8. **Click Start in the Verify Hyperlinks dialog box.**

FrontPage checks all hyperlinks to make sure that they're still valid. Because you deleted CUSUAFTR.HTM in Step 5, the Verify Hyperlinks utility reports that a hyperlink in the CUSUPOST.HTM page that points to CUSUAFTR.HTM is broken. As indeed it is.

Whenever you delete any Web pages, use the Verify Hyperlinks utility to see whether any links were attached to it. Also, before using the Verify Hyperlinks feature, be sure to save a page you've been working on in the FrontPage Explorer — to make sure that page is included in the checking.

When you check for broken hyperlinks, only broken internal hyperlinks and any external (not in your Web) hyperlinks are displayed in the Hyperlinks Status page. If you want to see a list of every internal hyperlink, including those not broken, choose View⇨Show All Hyperlinks. This menu option is only available after you've followed the preceding Steps 7 and 8, and, as a result, the Hyperlink Status page is currently displayed in the FrontPage Explorer.

Repairing a broken hyperlink

Sometimes after you've used the Tools⇨Verify Hyperlinks utility, you find that, in fact, broken (no longer valid) hyperlinks are in some of your Web's pages. If you do find broken hyperlinks, you want to repair them, of course. Letting visitors click a link that points to outer space rather than to an actual, existing location would be rude. To repair a broken hyperlink, follow these steps:

1. **Choose Tools⇨Verify Hyperlinks.**

   The Verify Hyperlinks dialog box opens.

2. **Click Start in the Verify Hyperlinks dialog box.**

   FrontPage checks all hyperlinks to make sure that they're still valid.

   FrontPage displays the results in the Hyperlink Status page.

3. **If you see a broken hyperlink listed in the Hyperlink Status page, right-click it.**

   A context menu appears, giving you a choice of editing the hyperlink or editing the page on which it resides.

4. **Click Edit Hyperlink.**

   The Edit Hyperlink dialog box opens, as shown in Figure 17-8.

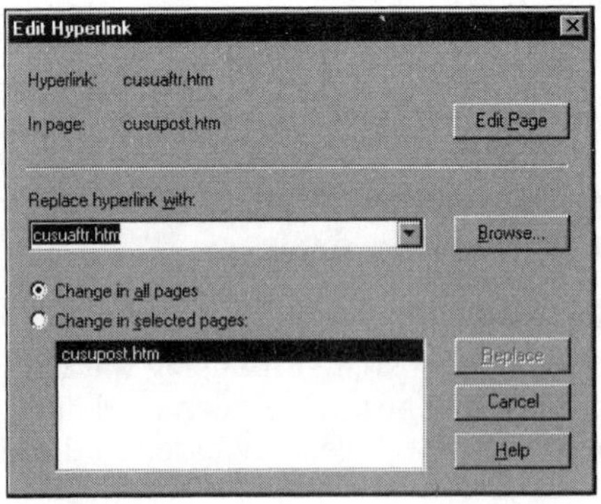

Figure 17-8:
Use this
dialog box
to fix
hyperlinks
that are no
longer
correct.

5. **In the Replace Hyperlink With text box, type a new, correct address (URL) for the hyperlink. (To delete the hyperlink, you have to use the FrontPage Editor, as explained in the following section, "Deleting a bad hyperlink.")**

6. **If you're repairing an external hyperlink (one on the Internet, but not in your Web site), click the Browse button.**

   Your Web browser opens, and you can search the Internet to locate the correct target of this external link.

7. **After you've located the correct Internet Web page that you want to be the target of this hyperlink, press Alt+Tab.**

   FrontPage Explorer reappears, and the correct address (URL) for this target Internet page is inserted into the Replace Hyperlink With text box.

8. **If you want to replace all the bad links in all the pages of your FrontPage Web, click the Change In All Pages option button.**

9. **If you want to repair the bad links in only certain pages in your FrontPage Web, click the Change In Selected Pages option button.**

10. **Click the Replace button.**

    The Edit Hyperlink dialog box closes.

Deleting a bad hyperlink

You may not want to replace a bad hyperlink with a different target. (Bad hyperlinks are called "broken" because they point to a Web page no longer in existence.) You may just want to delete the entire hyperlink. To delete a hyperlink, follow these steps:

1. **Follow Steps 1 through 4 in the preceding section, "Repairing a broken hyperlink."**

   The Edit Hyperlink dialog box opens.

2. **Click the Edit Page button.**

   FrontPage Editor starts running, and the page you want to edit is loaded into it.

3. **Click the HTML tab at the bottom of the FrontPage Editor.**

   The source code for this page appears.

4. **Locate the URL reference (the hyperlink) that you want to delete. In this example source code, you want to delete the link to CUSUAFTR.HTM.**

   The link to CUSUAFTR.HTM is located within a Webbot in the HTML source code:

```
<form method="POST" action="--WEBBOT-SELF--">
  <!--Webbot bot="Discussion" startspan S-Dir-
      Name="_cusudi" S-Article-Format="HTML/BR"
  U-Header-URL="cusuahdr.htm" U-Footer-
      URL="cusuaftr.htm" B-Make-TOC="TRUE"
  S-TOC-Fields="Subject,From,Date" B-Label-
      Fields="TRUE" B-Reverse-Chronology="FALSE"
  U-Confirmation-URL="cusucfrm.htm" S-Builtin-
      Fields="Date Time REMOTE_NAME"
  U-Style-Url="cusupost.htm" -->
```

Hyperlinks created for you automatically by FrontPage are enclosed within a Webbot (a component). They look like the preceding source code. For more details about Webbots, see Chapter 6 and Chapter 10.

However, most hyperlinks are ordinary HTML source code. Ordinary hyperlinks are found within a pair of ⟨A⟩ ⟨/A⟩ tags. Here is an example of a typical HTML hyperlink:

```
<a>href="http://dell/arc/bugrep.htm">
Click here to get to the Bugrep page</a>
```

5. **Delete the reference to** U-Footer-URL="cusuaftr.htm" **in the HTML source code.**

6. **Choose** File⇨Close.

   The FrontPage Editor dialog box opens, asking if you want to save the changes to this page.

7. **Click the Yes button.**

   The hyperlink is removed.

Recalculating hyperlinks

The FrontPage Explorer includes a feature that can recalculate all hyperlinks. This feature differs from the Verify Hyperlinks utility in three ways:

- ✔ It automatically repairs any broken links.
- ✔ It doesn't check external links.
- ✔ It's slower than the Verify Hyperlinks utility. (Running the Recalculate Hyperlinks feature on a big Web can take several minutes to finish.)

To recalculate hyperlinks, choose Tools⇨Recalculate Hyperlinks in the FrontPage Explorer menu bar.

Project Management: Creating New Pages and Folders in FrontPage Explorer

You can add new pages to a Web site in FrontPage Explorer by clicking the New Page icon on the far left of the FrontPage Explorer toolbar, just below the Explorer's menu bar. (You must be in Folders, All Files, or Navigation View by clicking one of those icons in the Views pane on the far left of the Explorer window.)

Or you can choose File⇨New⇨Page while in Folders, All Files, or Navigation View.

To create a new folder, follow these steps:

1. **Click the Folders icon on the Views pane on the far left of the Explorer window.**

   FrontPage Explorer switches to Folders View (which is virtually identical to the way the standard Windows Explorer displays files and folders).

2. **Click the folder in your Web where you want to add the new folder.**

   The folder you clicked is selected and becomes the parent folder of the new folder that you're adding.

   If you want to just add a folder at the same level as all the files in the right pane of the FrontPage Explorer pane, click anywhere on the background of the right pane. This action cancels any selections of any files or folders. Then, when you follow Step 3 to add a new folder, it appears in the right pane (and also the left pane).

3. **Choose File⇨New⇨Folder (or right-click in the right pane of the Folders View and then choose New Folder in the context menu that pops out).**

   FrontPage Explorer creates a new folder named New Folder, and that name is selected so that you can immediately begin typing in a new name for this folder. When you start typing, the name New Folder is automatically deleted and replaced by whatever name you type.

4. **After renaming your new folder, click anywhere on the background of the FrontPage Explorer to "set" the new folder's name.**

   FrontPage Explorer adds this new folder to your FrontPage Web.

Chapter 18

Deployment and Upkeep (A Web Site Is Never Finished)

. . . .

In This Chapter

▶ Web site deployment made easy

▶ Employing Visual InterDev's Link View feature

▶ Taking a look at the Microsoft Web site

▶ Repairing a broken link

▶ Using the automatic link repair tool

. . . .

*A*fter you create a really excellent Web site by using the various tools in Visual Studio 6, you can congratulate yourself on your awesome accomplishment. Relax and give yourself a pat on the back.

But your work isn't over yet. Next, you must deploy it. That means you must send your baby into the wide world, the World Wide Web. Luckily, deployment is fairly painless in Visual Studio.

Then, even after your site is out there on a server and attracting thousands of visitors a day (you hope), you're still not finished. You're never finished. You must perform routine maintenance to keep your site current, give people a reason to revisit it, improve its organization, or upgrade the graphics. You'll discover many reasons to revise your site. Luckily, maintenance is fairly painless in Visual Studio 6 because it has a strong collection of tools.

In this chapter, you see how to use Visual InterDev's deployment and Link View tools. You start with deployment first, because maintenance is something you do after a Web site is up and bringing in visitors. For maintenance, Visual InterDev's Link View feature helps you by showing you all the relationships between the pages in your site and by alerting you about any broken (no longer valid) links.

Deploying Your Site Easily

Put simply, you deploy a Web site by copying it. You copy it from your system to a server that's on the Internet. This Internet server can be part of your company's system, or on the other side of the earth at an ISP (Internet Service Provider) — it doesn't matter where the server is. (If your site is merely for in-house use, you copy the site to your intranet server.)

To deploy a Web application in Visual InterDev, follow these steps:

1. **Start Visual InterDev by clicking its icon on your desktop.**

   The New Project dialog box opens. If it doesn't open, choose File➪ New Project.

2. **Click the Existing or Recent tab.**

   You see a list of projects you've worked on in Visual InterDev.

3. **Double-click the name of the project you want to deploy.**

   The project is loaded into Visual InterDev.

4. **Click the name of the project (which appears in bold type) in the Project Explorer to select it.**

   The project's name becomes reversed (white text against black) in the Project Explorer after you click it.

5. **Choose Project➪Web Project➪Copy Web Application.**

   The Copy Project dialog box opens, as shown in Figure 18-1.

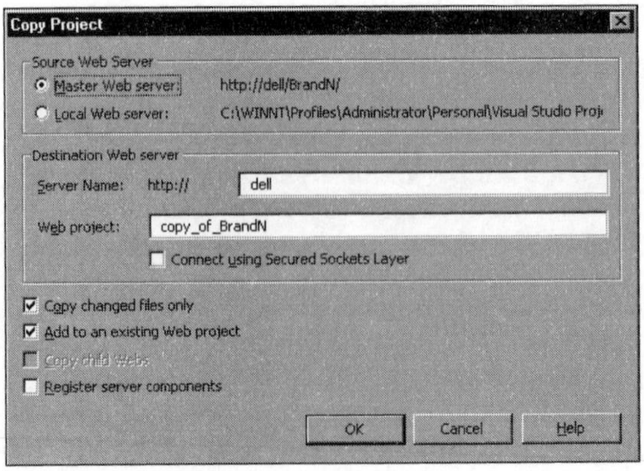

Figure 18-1:
Use this dialog box to send your Visual InterDev project to an Internet server.

6. Click the OK button.

The Copy Project dialog box closes and the entire project is copied to whatever target server is specified in the Destination Web server text box as shown in Figure 18-1. (By default, the Web is merely copied to the same server, but under a new project name beginning with copy of, as you can see in Figure 18-1.) In effect, this creates a backup copy of the project. To see how to adjust the other options in the Copy Project dialog box, take a look at the following sections in this chapter titled "Choosing the master Web server," "Choosing the local Web server," "Choosing the destination Web server," and "Selecting copy options."

You can use the Copy Project dialog box to make a backup of your Web project (or group of projects) on your local server. Just save the projects by using a different name. And note, too, that you can have more than a single project in the same Visual Studio 6 application. Choose File⇨Add Project from the Visual Studio 6 menu to add projects to the currently loaded solution. A *solution* is another term for Visual InterDev *application*. To see how this works, look at the Project Explorer in Visual InterDev (choose View⇨Project Explorer if it's not visible). Then note the top line in the Project Explorer. It says something like this: Solution 'Brand' (1 project). This description means that the entire application (solution) is named Brand and contains, at present, one project in this solution. Notice also that the first project you create gives its name to the solution. (Both the solution and the project, in this example, are named Brand.)

You, or others on your Web site development team, probably need to make changes to a Web site after it's been copied to a new server (or copied using a different name to the same server). To edit a deployed or copied Web site (a Visual InterDev application), first create a Web project in Visual InterDev. Then, after you've created that project, you connect it to an existing (the deployed) Web site.

You've got several choices to make when deploying (copying) a project or a whole solution (containing several projects). The Copy Project dialog box gives you several options for deploying your Web site. The following sections explain those options.

Choosing the master Web server

In the Copy Project dialog box, the Master Web Server option button specifies the server machine where the Web application is located, and where all people working on the Web application can access it. (This server may also optionally make the Web application available to the Internet or an intranet.)

People helping develop the application can "check out" copies of the application's files from the master Web server. Click the Master Web Server option button in the Copy Project dialog box if you want to copy files from there rather than from the local Web server.

Choosing the local Web server

Unfortunately, the Local Web Server option button has a really misleading name. The word *server* is being used strangely here. A local Web "server" is really just a *workstation,* not what we usually call a server. (Server usually indicates that more than one person is connected to the machine at once.) A local Web server actually refers to Microsoft's IIS (Internet Information Server), which is installed on workstations as well as server machines. (IIS is really a different use entirely of the word *server;* that's why it's so confusing.)

Anyway, you and other developers working on a Web site can test Web pages you're working on right in your local workstation because you've got IIS installed on your workstation. Click the Local Web Server option button in the Copy Project dialog box if you want to copy files from there rather than from the master Web server. If you want to copy files from the local Web server, no files are sent from the Master Web server at all — only those on your workstation are sent. Note that any editing that others have done to the files on the master Web server since you last released your local files to the master Web server aren't copied to the destination Web server. (You may want to choose the Local Web Server option as a way of backing up your work, but only your work.) For details about synchronization, see Chapter 5.

Visual InterDev always maintains two copies of an application that you're working on: the master and local versions. If others are also working on the same Web application, they have local versions, too. This causes a version problem. From time to time, you want to compare master and local versions. Update the master version by sending your edited local files to overwrite older master files. Or *synchronize* the local files with master files. Synchronization replaces all your local files with the latest versions, but you get read-only copies — files that you can look at, but can't change. You can accomplish these tasks by clicking a project's name in the Project Explorer (to select it) and then choosing Project⇨Web Files or Project⇨Web Project. You can also choose to work by selecting a project and then choosing Project⇨Web Project⇨Working Mode⇨Master (or Local). If you choose to work in Master Mode, you don't need to worry about comparing, updating, or synchronizing, because you're *in* the master files.

Choosing the destination Web server

In the Destination Web server area of the Copy Project dialog box, you can type in the URL for the target Web server (the location to which you want to copy your Web site). Or, if you're copying to the same server, or you've done this copying before, you may find the target server's URL listed in the Server name text box in the Copy Project dialog box.

In the Web project text box in the Copy Project dialog box you type in the name you want to give this project when it reaches the target Web server. (Give it a different name if you're merely making a backup copy onto your existing server.)

For information on the Secure Sockets Layer option — an encryption scheme to ensure privacy when you're sending a copy of your site to the target server — see Chapter 20.

Selecting copy options

You can click the Copy Changed Files Only check box to save some time if you've already deployed the entire Web previously. If you've already made a copy of this Web application on the target server, you don't need to resend *everything*. Just copy any files that have been edited since the last time the Web application was copied. This way you can quickly update the site on the Internet server as a way of maintaining the site and keeping it current. This option is checked by default.

Click the Add To An Existing Web Project check box if you want the project you're copying (specified at the top of the Copy Project dialog box under Source Web Server) to be saved to the destination server as a subfolder of an already existing Web project (the project specified under Destination Web Server in the Copy Project dialog box). The files you're copying are then *merged* into the target Web project. In other words, the files you're copying become part of the target Web project. This option is checked by default.

The Copy Child Webs check box is enabled only if the project you're copying is a main (root) Web application (and has secondary — child — Webs underneath it). You can choose to send the entire structure, child Webs and all, or just the main application without its child Webs. If you have no child Webs, this option is disabled (grayed and can't be clicked; refer to Figure 18-1).

Registration issues

Clicking the Register Server Components check box is necessary only if your Web site must have dependencies (special components) to function properly. If you choose this option, those special components are copied to the target server and also registered there so that they work. If you have added components that you want sent but have problems getting them registered on the target (destination) Web server, contact that server's administrator. You may not have permission to register components on the target server — and you need to arrange to get that permission. (For more details about components, see Chapter 10.)

Some readers may notice a Deploy option on the Project menu. You can use this feature to deploy a project to a Web server. However, it requires Visual Source Safe, a utility that isn't included in the Visual Studio 6 Professional Edition. Therefore, this book does not cover the Deploy tool, though it is quite similar to the Copy Project technique described in the section "Deploying Your Site Easily," earlier in this chapter. If you have the Deploy feature (because you purchased the Enterprise Edition of Visual Studio 6), check the help files for instructions on how to use it.

A Site with a View (Link View, That Is)

If you've deployed your site to an Internet server, you can take that well-deserved vacation. But don't kid yourself. A Web site requires ongoing maintenance.

After you've copied the Web site from your system to the Internet server, you can safely assume that the Internet server version remains secure and won't undergo any changes.

However, you'll probably use Visual InterDev or FrontPage to make changes to your local version of the Web site. Then you'll periodically update the Internet server's copy of the site. (To see an easy way to update the Internet server copy, look at "Selecting copy options," earlier in this chapter.)

Maintaining your Web site as it grows

As your business grows, your Web site likely grows, too. Your site increases in pages as well as in complexity.

And as a site becomes more complex, so does the job of maintaining it. Regular maintenance ensures that a visitor still finds it easy to understand and easy to navigate by using sensible, well-thought-out hyperlinks.

Here are some of the tasks you face when maintaining a Web site:

✔ Adding new pages.

✔ Replacing pages that have become outdated.

✔ Deleting links to pages that no longer exist. (These can be links within your Web site, or external links to now defunct locations elsewhere on the Internet.)

✔ Inserting whole new sections (multiple related pages).

Fortunately, Visual InterDev includes a variety of tools to help you keep your site both fresh and logical.

Playing with links

To see how to create links in a project, you can create a few pages in a brand-new site and then link the pages together in various ways. To try these linking activities, follow these steps:

1. **Start Visual InterDev by clicking its icon on the desktop.**

   The New Project dialog box opens. If it doesn't open, choose File⇨New.

2. **Click the New tab in the New Project dialog box.**

3. **Click Visual InterDev Projects in the left pane of the dialog box.**

   Two icons appear in the right pane of the dialog box: New Web Project and Sample App Wizard.

4. **Double-click the New Web Project icon in the right pane.**

   The Web Project Wizard starts running and displays its first page (of four).

5. **Click the Next button.**

   The Web server is contacted, and the second dialog box in this wizard appears. By default, the option button Create A New Web Application is selected. Leave it selected.

6. **Type in the name Complex in the Name text box in the New Project dialog box.**

7. **Click the Next button twice and then click the Finish button.**

   This way, you bypass the wizard pages that ask if you want to use a theme or template, because you don't. (See Chapter 7 for a complete explanation of themes and templates.)

A Name and Password dialog box opens. If you have problems (for example, Visual Studio 6 won't accept your password), you've got a permissions problem: You can't create the new Web project until you have permission to do so. Either contact your network administrator or look at Chapter 20.

Assuming your password passed muster, your new site is built.

8. **Click the project's name in the Project Explorer.**

In this case, the project's name is Complex and is in boldface.

9. **Choose Project⇨Add Item.**

The Add Item dialog box opens.

10. **Double-click the HTML Page icon.**

A new page is added to your project, with the default name HTML Page1.htm.

11. **Repeat Steps 8, 9, and 10.**

You now have two HTML pages in your project, named HTML Page1.htm and HTML Page2.htm.

12. **Click HTML Page1's Source tab.**

Page1 is selected, and the HTML source code is displayed.

13. **Choose View⇨Toolbars⇨HTML.**

The HTML Toolbar appears, with a link button on its far right.

14. **Click in HTML Page1's source code just before the `<BODY>` tag.**

The blinking insertion cursor appears where you clicked.

15. **Click the Link button on the HTML toolbar.**

The Hyperlink dialog box opens.

16. **You want to create a link to HTML Page2.Htm, so click the Browse button in the Hyperlink dialog box.**

The Create URL dialog box opens, as shown in Figure 18-2.

17. **Double-click the HTML Page2.Htm icon, shown in Figure 18-2.**

The Hyperlink dialog box reappears, with the following URL:

```
http://dell/Complex/HTML Page2.htm
```

18. **Click the OK button.**

The Hyperlink dialog box closes, and the following HTML source code is inserted into Page1's source code:

```
<A HREF="http://dell/Complex/HTMLPage2.htm">http://
          dell/Complex/HTMLPage2.htm</A>
```

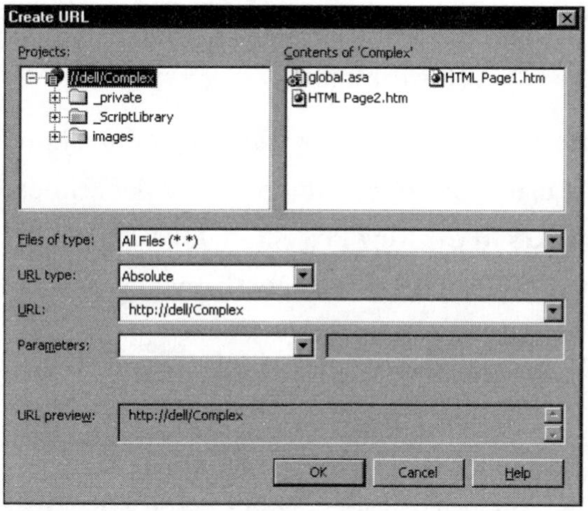

Figure 18-2:
Double-click on any page in the right pane of the Create URL dialog box to create a hyperlink to that page.

A hyperlink's source code contains two parts. The first part, located between <A and the closing > symbol, is the actual URL, the target page that a visitor sees after clicking the hyperlink:

```
<A HREF="http://dell/Complex/HTML Page2.htm">
```

Following the actual URL is the description of the link that a visitor sees in the Web browser. In the example above, the Hyperlink dialog box simply repeats the URL, like this:

```
http://dell/Complex/HTML Page2.htm</A>
```

But you'll want to edit this source code to something different, something more meaningful to humans, like this:

```
Click here to go to Page2</A>
```

You can repeat Steps 12 through 18 and create a hyperlink from Page2 to Page1. Then make sure to choose File⇔Save All to save your work.

Viewing links graphically

A Web site with more than a single public page must include ways for visitors to get from page to page, which usually involves *links*. Users click links, or hyperlinks as they're sometimes called, and they are transported to a different page of the site. This different page is the target of the link.

After your Web site becomes fairly complex, you'll want to see how it's organized and perhaps reorganize it. Visual InterDev includes a powerful site organizing utility. To see how it works, follow these steps:

1. **Start Visual InterDev by clicking its icon on your desktop.**

    The New Project dialog box opens. If it doesn't open, choose File⇨New.

2. **Click the Recent tab in the New Project dialog box.**

    You see a list of the most recent projects that you've worked on in Visual InterDev.

3. **Double-click the project you created in the section, "Playing with links," earlier in this chapter.**

    The project that you named Complex in the "Playing with links" section is loaded into Visual InterDev. It has two pages, HTML Page1.Htm and HTML Page2.Htm. These pages are linked to each other. If you don't have the project named *Complex,* create it by following the steps in the section titled "Playing with links."

4. **Right-click HTML Page1.Htm in the Project Explorer.**

    The context menu pops out for HTML Page1. If the Project Explorer isn't visible, choose View⇨Project Explorer.

5. **Click View Links in the context menu.**

    The Link View window opens, illustrating the link relationships between Page1 and Page2, as shown in Figure 18-3.

As shown in Figure 18-3, a hyperlink is illustrated with a line between two pages. On one end of the line is a small ball. That ball is the hyperlink. On the other end of the line is an arrow that points to the page that opens if a visitor clicks the hyperlink. Figure 18-3 shows that Page1 has a link to Page2, and Page2 has a link to Page1. Page1's icon is larger than the other icons because it was Page1 that you requested a Link View of.

Expanding and collapsing links

A complicated Web site can contain many dozens, even hundreds, of pages. Clearly, some way of simplifying such a complex site is necessary, or you would need a monitor the size of a movie screen to see the relationships.

Visual InterDev's Link View offers two tools to simplify what you see in a complex Web. Notice that two of the icons in Figure 18-3 have small + symbols attached to them. This symbol means the same thing that a + (plus sign) means in Windows Explorer: Click the + to see additional details. (The + also changes to a - (minus sign), indicating that you can collapse the contents back again.)

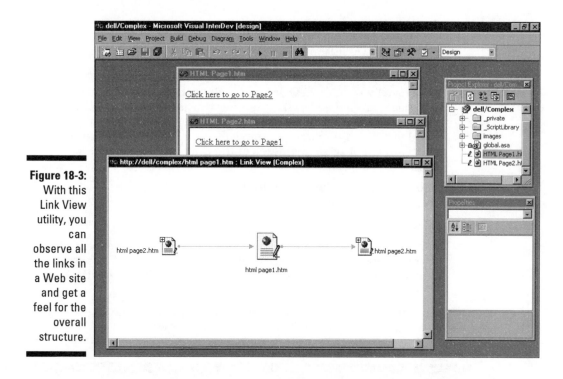

Figure 18-3:
With this
Link View
utility, you
can
observe all
the links in
a Web site
and get a
feel for the
overall
structure.

The second way to simplify a Link View is to use the Zoom feature. Just
right-click somewhere in the background of the Link View window (not on an
icon). Then select Zoom from the context menu that pops out. You can
choose zooms ranging from 200% down to 10%. You also can choose Fit to
have Visual InterDev size the diagram so that it exactly fits the window. Also,
if you want to center the diagram, choose Center View from the context
menu.

Checking Out a Big Site in Link View

How about playing around with a really huge, complicated Web site? You can
imagine how big Microsoft's site is — probably thousands of pages. Want to
see it in Link View? To see a Link View diagram of Microsoft's Web site,
follow these steps:

1. **Log on to the Internet by using Internet Explorer.**

   Keep your browser open while you perform the following steps.

2. **Start Visual InterDev by clicking its icon on your desktop.**

   You can open an existing Web if you wish, or just leave Visual InterDev
   empty.

3. **Choose Tools⇨View Links on WWW.**

   The View Links on WWW dialog box opens.

4. **Leave the Only Show Pages check box checked.**

   You'll usually want to view only those links that a visitor actually uses to navigate around a Web site (in other words, ordinary HTML pages). But be aware that many other kinds of support documents are contained in a Web site. Here's a sample of some of the other kinds of pages you might see if you deselect the Only Show Pages check box: Audio files, Excel spreadsheets, Images, or Style sheets.

5. **In the Address text box, type in the Microsoft URL:**
   www.microsoft.com.

6. **Click the OK button.**

   The dialog box closes, and Visual InterDev contacts Microsoft's site. After it's contacted, the primary hyperlinked pages are displayed, as shown in Figure 18-4. The window shows only the links from the home page.

   You can expand most of the pages surrounding the home page in Figure 18-4 to display wheels of linked pages of their own.

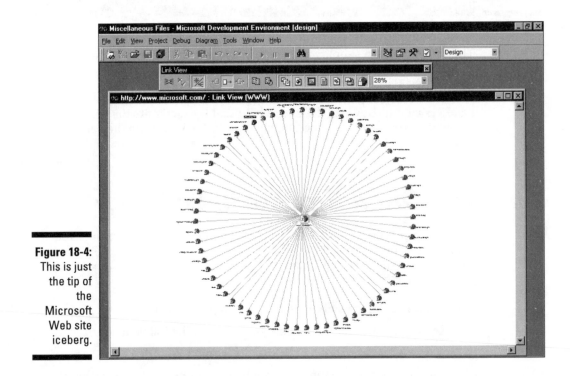

Figure 18-4:
This is just the tip of the Microsoft Web site iceberg.

7. Choose View➪Toolbars➪Link View.

The Link View toolbar appears. (Refer to Figure 18-4.) It allows you to select various kinds of pages in addition to standard HTML pages. You can also adjust the Zoom and toggle the orientation between a wheel view (shown in Figure 18-4) and a fan (radial) view.

You can change the style (orientation) of the Link View by clicking the third icon from the left on the Link View toolbar. When you use the fan view, you can see the links going into pages or links going out from pages, but not both at the same time.

8. Click the drop-down list at the far right end of the Link View toolbar and choose 150%.

The Microsoft diagram expands so that you can see just the home page and the links radiating out from it, as shown in Figure 18-5.

9. Slide the scrollbars on the Link View window until you locate an .Htm page that looks interesting.

10. Click the + icon on the interesting .Htm page to expand it.

After searching out all the links in the interesting page, a whole new wheel appears in your Link View.

11. Click the + icon on several more .Htm pages in the Link View.

Many pages include entire wheels of links, as shown in Figure 18-6.

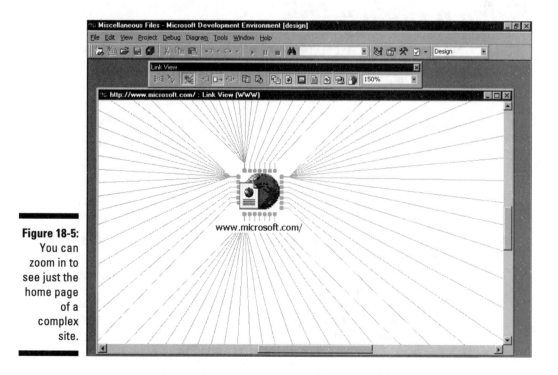

Figure 18-5:
You can zoom in to see just the home page of a complex site.

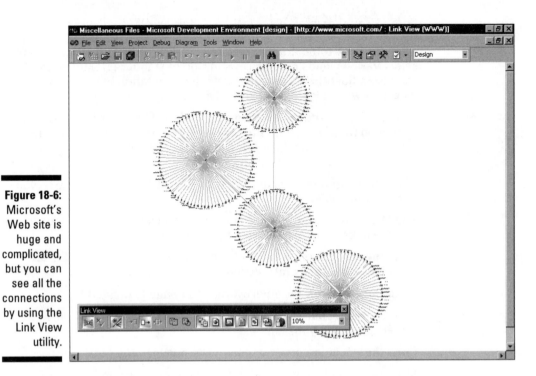

Figure 18-6:
Microsoft's
Web site is
huge and
complicated,
but you can
see all the
connections
by using the
Link View
utility.

Fixing a Broken Link

Nothing is forever. Hyperlinks can break, meaning that they are no longer accurate. The page they point to doesn't exist any more. Perhaps it was deleted. Perhaps it was renamed. In any case, the link isn't right and should be repaired. To see how to fix a broken link, follow these steps:

1. **Start Visual InterDev by clicking its icon on your desktop.**

   The New Project dialog box opens. If it doesn't appear, choose File⇨New.

2. **Click the Recent tab in the New Project dialog box.**

   You see a list of the most recent projects that you've worked on in Visual InterDev.

3. **Double-click the project you created in the section "Playing with links," earlier in this chapter.**

   The project you named Complex in the "Playing with links" section is loaded into Visual InterDev. It has two pages, HTML Page1.Htm and HTML Page2.Htm. These pages are linked to each other. If you don't have the project named *Complex,* create it by following the steps in the section titled "Playing with links."

4. **Right-click HTML Page2.htm in the Project Explorer and choose Delete from the context menu that appears.**

   The Delete File dialog box opens, asking if you really want to do this and warning you that the action can't be undone.

5. **Click the Yes button.**

   The dialog box closes, and HTML Page2.htm disappears from the Project Explorer and is gone from Visual InterDev. However, if you look at the source code in HTML Page1.htm, you see that the link to HTML Page2 still exists:

   ```
   <A HREF="http://dell/Complex/HTML Page2.htm">Click here
        to go to Page2</A>.
   ```

6. **Right-click HTML Page1.htm in the Project Explorer and choose View Links from the context menu that appears.**

   You see the Link View. It shows a red, broken page2 icon. A red, cracked icon indicates a link to something that no longer exists, as shown in Figure 18-7. (Trust me when I tell you the icon is red.)

Figure 18-7:
When a link is no longer valid (a broken link), Visual InterDev's Link View shows you by breaking the target page's icon and coloring it red.

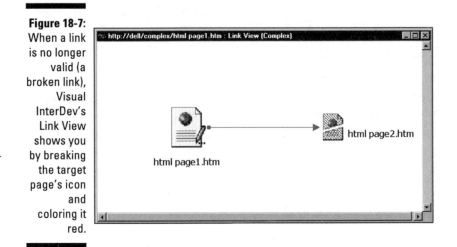

7. **Hold your mouse pointer over the Page2 icon.**

   A small tip box opens, telling you "object not found in project."

8. **Click the name of this project, *Complex,* in the Project Explorer. The name of the project is in boldface.**

   You select the name of the project. The name changes to white text on a black background.

9. **Choose File⇨Save All.**

   The entire project is saved to disk. This action officially deletes Page2 from the project.

10. **Choose View⇨Broken Links Report.**

    A new window, named the Broken Links Report, opens and provides the following information about the project named Complex:

    - **Unused files in project:** html page1.htm.

    - **Broken links in project:** html page2.htm: broken link from html page1.htm.

    - **Broken external links:** Broken links report complete. All items have been added to the task list.

11. **The report lets you know that the hyperlink in HTML Page1 to HTML Page2 is incorrect. So click the Source tab in HTML Page1's window.**

    The HTML source code is displayed.

12. **Delete the hyperlink line in the source code.**

    The hyperlink line is:

    ```
    <A HREF="http://dell/Complex/HTML Page2.htm">Click here
            to go to Page2</A>
    ```

13. **Choose File⇨Save All.**

    Page1's edited source code becomes official.

14. **Right-click the background of the Link Diagram window and choose Refresh from the context menu that appears.**

    The broken link between HTML Page1 and HTML Page2 disappears from the Link View. HTML Page2 also disappears from the Link View.

Automatic Link Repairs

Visual InterDev has a feature that keeps track of any files you rename or move. It then ensures that your Link Diagram remains accurate, in spite of such broken links. Nevertheless, this feature does not change the source code in pages containing the broken hyperlinks. You still have to do that by hand. (Note that FrontPage's PageNavBar Webbot *does* automatically repair the source code.)

You can request that Visual InterDev's automatic link repair feature work two ways: It can notify you of problem links, or it can automatically repair them for you in the Link Diagram. It's your choice.

To turn on Visual InterDev's automatic link repairing feature, choose Tools⇨Options⇨Projects⇨Web Projects. The Options dialog box that appears gives you many options for repairing links.

The following list explains the most important link repair options that are available in the Options dialog box:

- **The Repair Links In Referring Files option button:** Any time you move or rename a file (or folder) in the current project, Visual InterDev automatically notices these changes. Visual InterDev then ensures that any links to a moved or renamed file remain accurate in the Link Diagram. ("Referring files," the term used in the button name, means the file containing the hyperlink.) Note that this feature doesn't solve the problem of deleted files. Nor does this feature deal with external links (hyperlinks pointing to pages on the Internet that are not part of your Visual InterDev application). Such links, if broken, are illustrated by red, broken icons in Link View and are also listed in the broken links report described in Step 12 in the section earlier in this chapter titled "Fixing a Broken Link."

  Remember, too, that even with automatic link repair you still have to edit the source code's hyperlink to reflect the renamed or moved target page. Likewise, you may also need to change the source code to reword the text describing the hyperlink to visitors. If the name of the target page has changed, you may have to reword the visible description of the link.

- **The Don't Repair Links In Referring Files option button:** When you choose this option button, no automated link repairs take place. You must make any necessary repairs to broken links by hand.

- **The Ask Me Each Time option button:** If you choose this option, a dialog box always first asks your permission before any repairs are made to moved or renamed pages.

Part VII
The Part of Tens

The 5th Wave   By Rich Tennant

I told you dynamic HTML was impressive.

In this part . . .

This is called The Part of Tens, which may sound like an obscure ritual performed in a dark room by advanced Masons.

No such luck. The Part of Tens is just a tradition in ...*For Dummies* books — a chapter or two that include ten items. In this part, you get a chapter that includes ten topics that I wanted to put in the book but couldn't fit into one of the normal chapters. Although these topics didn't fit into the main portion of the book, you'll find some useful stuff here.

Chapter 19

Ten Visual Studio 6 Topics That Didn't Fit Anywhere Else

*E*ven if you've read just a chapter or two of this book, you undoubtedly noticed how tight and logical the organization of topics is. But don't get too overwhelmed with admiration, because I have a confession to make: As thoughtfully designed as this book's table of contents is, several topics that you may find useful didn't fit well into the earlier chapters. These extra topics may be valuable to various readers, so I've collected them here in this Part of Tens chapter.

This chapter's sections cover ten subjects that may interest you. Jump down along the headlines, and I bet you'll discover at least a few subjects worthy of your inspection.

Find the Latest Visual Studio 6 News

To see what's up, what's new, samples, breaking news, and the hottest aftermarket products, visit the official Visual Studio Web 6 site at:

```
http://msdn.microsoft.com/vstudio/
```

For specific information and updates about the individual tools in the Visual Studio 6 suite, check the following Web sites regularly:

- **The Visual InterDev page:** premium.microsoft.com/msdn/library/ devprods/vs6/davinci/html/vistartpage.htm
- **The Visual Basic page:** premium.microsoft.com/MSDN/Library/ devprods/vs6/vb/html/vbstartpage.htm
- **The Visual C++ page:** premium.microsoft.com/MSDN/Library/ devprods/vs6/vc++/vcedit/vcstartpage.htm
- **The Visual FoxPro page:** premium.microsoft.com/MSDN/Library/ devprods/vs6/vfoxpro/html/vfpstartpage.htm
- **The Visual J++ page:** premium.microsoft.com/MSDN/Library/ devprods/vs6/vj/vjstartpage.htm
- **The FrontPage page:** www.microsoft.com/frontpage/?RLD=29

Download the Latest Visual Studio 6 Service Pack

Microsoft releases Service Packs as a way of curing bugs or, sometimes, adding features to its applications. Visual Studio 6 Service Pack 1 is now available for downloading, and you should update your Visual Studio 6 by incorporating this Service Pack. It fixes what Microsoft calls "binary compatibility issues with certain runtime redistributables in Visual Studio 6.0. Microsoft recommends that developers install the Service Pack prior to releasing their applications, so that they redistribute the latest runtime files." In English, this translates to, "This Service Pack fixes some bugs."

If you're a Visual Studio 6 Enterprise Edition customer and you've mailed in your fulfillment vouchers, the Service Pack is sent to you through the mail. You also automatically get the Service Pack if you belong to either MSDN Professional or MSDN Universal. But, if you need to download the Service Pack, you can find it at:

```
msdn.microsoft.com/vstudio/sp
```

You may want to check this Web site from time to time to see whether additional Service Packs are made available in the future.

Read Some Good Periodicals

Several publishers put out journals covering the applications and technologies in Visual Studio 6. These magazines and newsletters provide up-to-date advice, source code examples, tutorials, and other aids for the harried developer:

- The Cobb Group (www.zdjournals.com/publicat.htm) publishes a variety of monthlies.

- Pinnacle Publishing (www.pinpub.com/home.htm) is another good source of monthlies.

- Fawcette Technical Publications (www.windx.com) has a particularly useful site that is updated frequently.

Start Making Intellisense

Try turning on Intellisense statement completion and syntax displays. (Even C++ has it now.) Intellisense features help you by making it unnecessary to memorize complex object models (all those properties and their many settings), by offering suggestions and lists for you to select, and by displaying the parameters of your functions. Two of the most useful Intellisense features are Auto List Members and Auto Quick Info. Auto List Members is covered in Chapter 12, but here's the lowdown on Auto Quick Info.

Auto Quick Info tells you the parameters and variable type, if one is specified (such as an Integer), that a function or sub requires. This is useful because you don't have to remember the variable types or parameters required by a function or sub. Often, functions and subs are defined in modules other than the one you're currently working in — so you can't just look in the code window to see what parameters are required. With Auto Quick Info, the answer pops up right in front of you. To see how this works, follow these steps:

1. **Start Visual Basic by clicking its icon on your desktop.**

   The New Project dialog box opens. If it doesn't open, choose File➪ New Project.

2. **Double-click the Standard EXE icon in the New Project dialog box.**

   A blank form appears, and Visual Basic is ready for you to create a Windows application.

3. **Choose Tools⇨Options.**

   The Options dialog box opens.

4. **On the Editor tab of the Options dialog box, click to place a check mark in the Auto Quick Info check box.**

5. **Click the OK button.**

   The dialog box closes and the Auto Quick Info feature is now active.

6. **Double-click Form1.**

   The Form1 Programming Editor opens, with the Form Load event displayed.

7. **Move your insertion cursor (the blinking vertical line) to the top of the code window at the start of the line** `Private Sub Form_Load()`, **and then press the Enter key two times.**

   You've made some space in the General Declarations section of the code window, where you can type in a new function.

8. **Move your insertion cursor to the top of the code window and type the following:**

   ```
   Private Function Adder(iFnum As Integer, iSnum As
           Integer) As Integer
   Adder

   End Function
   ```

   As soon as you type `Adder` the second time (on a line of its own, as shown in this code example above), Visual Basic assumes that you want to know the Quick Info about the Adder function. Visual Basic displays the complete definition of the Adder function, including all parameters and variable types.

Take a Crash Course in Visual Studio 6

Microsoft frequently offers certification courses, developer conferences, and specialized training sessions. If, after reading this book, you're still a bit hazy about the more esoteric and complex capabilities of Visual Studio 6 (such as managing distributed applications, mastering middle-tier technologies, and working with scalable COM objects), you may want to take a crash course.

Call 1-800-509-8344 or 303-813-4245 for information about any upcoming Visual Studio 6 conferences or sessions, or look at the home Web site for Visual Studio 6 training at www.microsoft.com/vstraining.

Understand Online, Offline, Master, and Local Modes

You need to consider several issues when you're working on a Web site in Visual InterDev as part of a team of people. The concepts you need to understand are local, master, offline, refreshing, synchronizing, comparing, and releasing.

You can work in Visual InterDev using two primary modes: local mode or master mode. The distinction between these modes is similar to the difference between a draft copy and a final copy of a document. When you work in local mode, you're working on a draft copy. It's not the "official" copy (the copy that's located on the server). However, if you work in master mode, you do work with the official copy.

Working in local mode is a good idea if you are part of a development team. If you make changes to a file at the same time someone else makes changes to that same file, that causes the dreaded *version problem*. Which version of the file do you use if you and someone else have both made improvements to it? How can the two files be reconciled? Does someone have to go through and copy all of their changes by hand into the other latest version? The answer is yes. If you and someone else has simultaneously made changes to the same file (the same Web page), one of you has to use the Merge feature (discussed at the end of this section).

Of course, if you're a lone toiler on this Web site, you can choose master mode with no problem. (In master mode, changes saved to the hard drive are saved both to your local workstation as well as to the "official" version on the server.)

Select the project's filename in the Project Explorer, and then choose Project⇨Web Project⇨Working Mode to specify which mode (master or local) you want to work in.

When you work in master mode or local mode, you are working online. However, you have a third possibility: working *offline,* meaning that you're not connected in any way to a Web server. The primary difference between working online and offline relates to link diagrams (described in Chapter 18). If you're working online, your link diagram displays the links for all relevant files — those located in your local Web project, in the master Web application, and any other URLs in your project's pages. But, when you work offline, only those files located on your local Web project are displayed.

The following list explains the several ways that you can manipulate local and master files:

- **Refreshing:** If you want to see the latest official list of files in a project (from the master Web server), you *refresh* your project. This lets you see if someone else has added new files to the project. To do this, click the name of the project that you want to refresh in the Project Explorer; then choose Project➪Web Project➪Refresh Project View.

- **Synchronizing:** If you want to view the latest versions of master files (the "official" versions of files that are stored on the master Web server) on your local workstation, you *synchronize* the files. Notice that this provides you with read-only copies; you cannot edit these copies. To synchronize, click the name of the project where the files are that you want to update in Project Explorer; then choose Project➪ Web Project➪Synchronize Files.

- **Comparing local files to master files:** If you simply want to compare a local file to the official master copy of that file (on the server), right-click the filename in Project Explorer and select Compare To Master Web from the context menu that appears.

- **Releasing:** When you work in Local mode, you may want to update the master Web files with the changes that you've made to your local files. Suppose that you're finished working for the day and you've saved your work to your local workstation (using File➪Save All). Now, you want to also *release* the local working copies of these files and update the master Web server so its files, too, include your changes. To do this, select the files that you want to send to the master Web server in Project Explorer. Then choose Project➪Web Files➪Release Working Copy. The selected files are now saved on the master Web server and replace existing versions there — becoming the official, current versions. However, it's possible that one of your team members has also been working on one or more of these files at the same time as you were. If they updated the master copy of a file (including their changes) since you "checked out" your copy, a Merge dialog box is displayed showing you the differences between the versions. At this point, you have to agree to or reject each change.

Use the Wizard of Wizards

You've probably used some of the many wizards available in Visual Studio 6 and you're probably quite grateful they're there. Wizards can really save a lot of time and hand-programming.

But what if you want to write your *own* wizard? Is there a wizard that can help you create a new wizard?

Perhaps you're in charge of a group of workers. They have to do some programming or designing using Visual Studio 6, and they have to do that task repeatedly. You want to write your own wizard to step your staff through that job to make life easier for them. Or, you may even want to create wizards to assist in tasks that you frequently perform.

Does any wizard exist that helps you to create your own wizards? You bet it does! You still have to write the underlying programming to make your wizard do its thing, of course, but the Wizard Wizard (Microsoft calls it the Wizard Manager) does a lot of the dirty work for you. The Wizard Wizard creates the sequential forms, the Next buttons, and all the other elements that any wizard contains. In other words, your wizard looks and behaves like the wizards from Microsoft.

To start the Wizard Wizard, start Visual Basic and then double-click the VB Wizard Manager icon in the New Project dialog box. (If the New Project dialog box doesn't open, choose File➪New Project.) A message now notifies you that a wizard form wasn't found. The message asks whether you want to create a new wizard project. Click Yes. The Wizard Manager message box closes and a Save New Wizard As dialog box opens. Click Save. The dialog box closes and your wizard project is saved to the hard drive using the default filename: MyWizard.Vbp. The Wizard Manager window appears, and the wizard template files are listed in the Project Explorer.

Explore the Microsoft Developer Network Library CDs

The Microsoft Developer Network (MSDN) library comes included with Visual Studio 6. The MSDN Library CDs feature 1.1 gigabytes of reference information, application documentation, sample source code, and the latest edition of the Microsoft Developer Knowledge Base.

So, when you press F1 while in a Visual Studio 6 application, don't limit yourself to the Search and Index tabs of the help system. Click the Contents tab and look around to familiarize yourself with the books, magazines, conference papers, and other documentation that may be useful to you. Some of the information is for reference, some is tutorial, and a lot is useful when you've got a problem to solve or a topic you want to understand.

Join the Microsoft Developer Network Online

The Microsoft Developer Network is more than the collected books, periodicals, and help systems that you find on the CDs included with the Visual Studio 6 package. MSDN is also a set of Web pages and search engines that are frequently updated on the Internet by Microsoft.

You can join MSDN Online for free, and thereafter you get access to the MSDN Library Online; you can optionally subscribe to the MSDN Flash (announcements and tips that are sent to you via e-mail or subscriptions that automatically arrive on your Active Desktop) and other benefits. To register, go to www.microsoft.com/msdn.

You can also subscribe to MSDN via regular mail. (You get packages of CDs quarterly and a monthly newsletter.) You can choose from three levels of subscriptions, ranging in price from $99 to $2499. If you're interested in this program, go to msdn.microsoft.com/developer/join/subscriptions.htm.

Create Instant Windows Programs

Visual Basic includes a special wizard that helps you get a Windows application quickly sketched in (and then you later fill in the programming that makes it do some useful job). This wizard, called the VB Application Wizard, helps you create applications that have a family resemblance — that share the traditional Windows user-interface design, such as gunmetal gray backgrounds. The wizard also jump-starts beginners, giving them a useful template to customize.

To try the VB Application Wizard, follow these steps:

1. **Start Visual Basic by clicking its icon on your desktop.**

   The New Project dialog box opens. If it doesn't open, choose File➪ New Project.

2. **Double-click the VB Application Wizard icon in the New Project dialog box.**

   The first page of the wizard appears.

3. **Click the Next button.**

   Visual Basic asks what kind of interface you want — Multiple (like a word processor window that can hold smaller windows) or Single (only one window, with no child windows inside it). A third option is the Explorer-style window (like Windows Explorer and Internet Explorer).

4. **Click Single Document Interface (SDI).**

5. **Click the Next button.**

   The menus page appears. Choose whatever menus you want to include in your application.

6. **Click the Next button.**

   The Toolbar page appears. Here you specify which standard Toolbar options you want to make available to your application's users. Usually these are options such as Save, Copy, Bold, Italic, and so on, which are the contents of the Standard toolbar in most Microsoft applications.

7. **Click the Next button twice.**

   You've skipped the Resources page (for foreign language applications) and are at the Internet Connectivity page. The Internet Connectivity page allows users of your applications to easily go online. Offering this gateway is wise. People today like to be able to get onto the Internet from practically *anywhere* in their computer, including your application.

8. **Click the Next button.**

   You can choose to add a template or four traditional features to your application on this page:

   - **Splash Screen:** A graphic or logo that is displayed when your application is first started.

   - **ID and password window:** Filters who gets into your application.

   - **Options dialog box:** Enables users to customize your application.

   - **Standard Windows About message box:** Is displayed if users choose Help⇨About.

9. **Click the Next button.**

   You're now offered the option of attaching a database to your application.

10. **Click the Next button and then click Finish.**

    A warning message box opens, telling you that creating your new application could take a few minutes.

11. **Click the OK button.**

    Visual Basic rapidly builds your application template to your specifications.

    Another message box opens, telling you that Visual Basic has created the application. This is fairly redundant information, so you may want to click the check box labeled: Don't Show This Dialog In The Future.

12. **Click the OK button.**

    You see your template, in all its glory, ready for you to add the programming that makes the buttons, menus, and other features actually do their jobs.

Appendix

About the CD

• •

*T*he *Visual Studio 6 For Dummies* CD-ROM has an HTML interface that walks you through all the available programs on the CD and shows you where to find them. Here's some of what you can find on the *Visual Studio 6 For Dummies* CD-ROM:

- ✔ All the programming code from the book. (And I mean *all*.) Some readers prefer to copy and paste even single-line code examples to avoid typos and save a little time. So, even if an example is only a single line of source code, you can find it on the CD.

- ✔ Demos of some of the best Visual Studio add-on products from Lead Technologies, VideoSoft, Desaware, and Crescent.

System Requirements

Make sure that your computer meets the minimum system requirements outlined in the following list. If your computer doesn't match up to most of these requirements, you may have problems in using the contents of the CD.

- ✔ A PC with a Pentium 90 or faster processor.

- ✔ Microsoft Windows 95 or later, or Windows NT 4 or later.

- ✔ At least 24MB of total RAM installed on your computer if you use Windows 95/98. Windows NT 4/5 users need 32MB. For best performance, I recommend that a computer equipped with Windows 95/98 or Windows NT 4/5 have at least 48MB of RAM installed.

- ✔ At least 60MB of hard drive space available to install all the software from this CD. (You'll need less space if you don't install every program.)

- ✔ A CD-ROM drive that is double-speed (2x) or faster.

- ✔ Recommended: A video system capable of displaying at least 256 colors — SuperVGA or higher recommended.

- ✔ Recommended: A modem with a speed of at least 14,400 bps.

If you need more information on the basics, check out *PCs For Dummies,* 6th Edition, by Dan Gookin; *Macs For Dummies,* 6th Edition by David Pogue; *Windows 95 For Dummies* or *Windows 98 For Dummies,* both by Andy Rathbone; or *Windows 3.11 For Dummies,* 3rd Edition, by Andy Rathbone (all published by IDG Books Worldwide, Inc.).

Accessing the HTML Interface File

To access the HTML interface file on the CD, follow these steps:

1. **Insert the CD into your computer's CD-ROM drive.**

2. **Open your Web browser.**

   Visual Studio includes the latest version of Internet Explorer. Most of the examples in this book are geared toward this Web browser.

3. **Choose File⇨Open in Internet Explorer.**

4. **In the dialog box that appears, type** D:\DEFAULT.HTM **and click OK.**

   Replace the letter *D* with the correct letter for your CD-ROM drive, if it is not *D.* This action displays the file that will walk you through the contents of the CD.

5. **To navigate within the interface, simply click on any topic of interest to take you to an explanation of the files on the CD and how to use or install them.**

   After you are done with the interface, close your browser as usual.

To run some of the programs, you may need to keep the CD inside your CD-ROM drive. This is a good thing. Otherwise, you may have to install a very large chunk of the program to your hard drive space, which could keep you from installing other software. (For example, the MSDN Help system for Visual Studio is so huge that it isn't saved to your hard drive. Instead, when you use Help, you have to put the CD in your CD-ROM drive.)

Copying the Source Code

The CD contains a folder named Source, and in it are separate subfolders for each chapter, containing any source code (even single-line examples) included in that chapter. Each folder is named after its chapter: Chap1, Chap2 . . . Chap19.

Each folder contains a single .Txt file that includes all the source code examples in that chapter. The .Txt files can be read by Windows Notepad or any other text editor or word processor. However, you may find it easiest to simply double-click the .Txt file on the CD to load it into Notepad. Then you can press F3 and type in a search term unique to the code example that you want to work with. Notepad locates the code containing that search term. Then drag your mouse across the code example to select it. Press Ctrl+C to copy the sample. Now go to the editor in Visual InterDev, Visual J++, Visual Basic, or whichever Visual Studio tool you're working in. Click the location in the editor where you want to paste the code. Then press Ctrl+V to paste the code into the editor.

What You Get on the CD

The following list describes the software included on the *Visual Studio 6 For Dummies* CD:

Leadtools imaging software: Leadtools is a feature-rich collection of imaging and graphics manipulation tools that you can add to your Visual Studio projects. Leadtools includes more than 600 functions, properties, and methods. For example, you get scanning support, color conversion, special effects, display, annotation, image processing (with more than 50 filters), image compression, extensive graphics format import/export filters, common dialogs, Internet/intranet imaging, database imaging, printing, OCR, multimedia, and FlashPix extension support. If you need to do *anything* with graphics, you'll probably find the necessary tools available in the Leadtools suite. Contact them at www.leadtools.com.

To install this program in Windows 95/98 or Windows NT 4/5, open the LEADTOOL folder and then run the Setup.Exe program.

VideoSoft's VS-OCX: If you've ever written a Windows application in Visual Basic, you know the nasty secret: Although Visual Basic programs are easy to create and can look great, they are *resolution dependent.* If you create a Visual Basic application in 800x600 resolution and then try to use it in 1024x768 resolution, the forms and all the controls are tiny. Perhaps worse than that, resizing a Visual Basic application's window doesn't resize the controls on it. If you make the window smaller, the command buttons, textboxes, and other controls don't get smaller. They just become covered up. VS-OCX to the rescue! This excellent product automatically resizes all the controls on a form, makes forms resolution-independent, and includes a couple of bonus components, such as a special tabs component and a parsing engine. You can contact VideoSoft at www.videosoft.com.

To install this program in Windows 95/98 or Windows NT 4/5, open the VIDSOFT folder and then open the VS_OCX subfolder. Run the Setup.Exe program.

VSFlexGrid Pro from VideoSoft: If you connect a database to a Visual Basic project, you have plenty of uses for the VSFlexGrid Pro component. It's simultaneously powerful and lightweight (as well as being fast and completely dependency-free, so that you won't have DLL versioning problems down the road). The component supports ADO 2.0, OLE DB, and DAO; includes data input masking; is fully data bound with read/write capability; has Outlook-style sorting and Excel-compatible tab- and comma-delimited text files; has automatic auditing to track changes in data; and has in-cell editing and many additional useful features. VSFlexGrid Pro supports up to 2 billion database rows, which should be enough. Contact VideoSoft at www.videosoft.com.

To install this program in Windows 95/98 or Windows NT 4/5, open the VIDSOFT folder and then open the VSFlexGrid Pro subfolder, named VSFLEX. Run the Setup.Exe program.

VSSpell from VideoSoft: If you want to add spell-checking or thesaurus features to your Visual Basic applications, VSSpell is just what you're looking for. Containing over 50,000 entries, the VSSpell spelling engine component can generate custom dictionaries and is also compatible with dictionaries created by Microsoft Word. The thesaurus component comes with more than 30,000 entries and it permits you to create and manage custom thesaurus files. Contact VideoSoft at www.videosoft.com.

To install this program in Windows 95/98 or Windows NT 4/5, open the VIDSOFT folder and then open the VSSpell subfolder. Run the Setup.Exe program.

VSDirect from VideoSoft: Microsoft's DirectX technology can speed up various kinds of multimedia features in a PC. VideoSoft offers three components to simplify a Visual Basic programmer's access to DirectX functions. The vsDirectDraw component accesses features that improve the speed of animation. The vsDirectSound component provides a gateway to hardware/software sound playback and mixing functions. The vsDirectPlay component offers features that can connect game players using a modem or network. Contact VideoSoft at www.videosoft.com.

To install this program in Windows 95/98 or Windows NT 4/5, open the VIDSOFT folder and then open the VSDirect subfolder. Run the Setup.Exe program.

Desaware's Gallimaufry controls: Desaware calls its Gallimaufry controls an eclectic collection of controls, which is true. For Visual Basic, these components even include their own source code so that you can see how they were constructed (which can be a great way to learn how to build your own components and also allows you to modify the Gallimaufry controls themselves). The components include an animated banner, a common dialog, a Multiple Document Interface taskbar, a cool *perspective list* component (which allows you to display text animated to look like the credits in Star Wars), and more. Contact Desaware at www.desaware.com.

To install this program in Windows 95/98 or Windows NT 4/5, open the DESAWARE folder and then open the Gallimaufry subfolder, named GALLIMAU. Run the Setup.Exe program.

VersionStamper from Desaware: If you've had version problems with your Visual Basic projects (such as OCX, DLL, and VBX files floating around everywhere), you'll appreciate VersionStamper. It's an ActiveX control that allows you to create self-updating applications. No longer will you have to worry that your Visual Basic application won't run because the wrong support files are in the user's SYSTEM directory. The VersionStamper component also includes support for Internet and intranet applications. Contact Desaware at www.desaware.com.

To install this program in Windows 95/98 or Windows NT 4/5, open the DESAWARE folder and then open the VERSTAMP subfolder. Run the Setup.Exe program.

SpyWorks from Desaware: Have you ever had C++ envy? I haven't. I've been able to do anything I want to do in Visual Basic (except create applications that are resolution-independent, which is solved by VideoSoft's VS-OCX as described earlier in this appendix). But if you want to go down to lower-level programming than the typical Visual Basic user gets into, you might want to try SpyWorks. Desaware calls it the "ultimate 'you CAN do it in VB' low-level programming toolkit," and that's a good description. You can use the tools in this package to intercept Windows messages globally, create custom interfaces for your components, and use subclassing and export DLL functions. Contact Desaware at www.desaware.com.

To install this program in Windows 95/98 or Windows NT 4/5, open the DESAWARE folder and then open the SPYWORKS subfolder. Run the Setup.Exe program.

Crescent's QuickPak VB/J++: The QuickPak set of programming tools has been popular for many years. Visual Basic programmers have relied on its many tested functions and enhancements to the look of the user interface to amplify their own programming abilities. Now QuickPak VB/J++ embraces J++ in addition to Visual Basic. It contains a collection of ActiveX components and features, including improved array manipulation methods, access to an undocumented API for accessing the low-level Internet Core Messaging Protocol, memory and utility productivity enhancing routines, functions that manage Microsoft's Internet Information Server and Personal/Peer Web Server, file management, and functions that can Ping a TCP/IP server. Contact Crescent at `crescent.progress.com`.

To install this program in Windows 95/98 or NT 4/5, open the CRESCENT folder and then run the VBJ11DEM.Exe program.

If You've Got Problems (Of the CD Kind)

I tried my best to ensure that the examples in this book and the demo software on the CD will work on most computers with the minimum system requirements. Alas, your computer may differ, and some programs may not work properly for some reason.

The two likeliest problems are that you don't have enough memory (RAM) for the programs you want to use, or you have other programs running that are affecting installation or running of a program. If you get error messages like `Not enough memory` or `Setup cannot continue`, try one or more of these methods and then try using the software again:

- Turn off any anti-virus software that you have on your computer. Installers sometimes mimic virus activity and may make your computer incorrectly believe that it is being infected by a virus.

- Close all running programs. The more programs you're running, the less memory is available to other programs. Installers also typically update files and programs. So if you keep other programs running, installation may not work properly.

- Have your local computer store add more RAM to your computer. This is, admittedly, a drastic and somewhat expensive step. However, adding more memory can really help the speed of your computer and allow more programs to run at the same time. Memory prices have fallen quite a bit in the past few years, and software applications have grown quite a bit in size. Even 128MB of RAM isn't uncommon these days.

If you still have trouble with installing the items from the CD, please call the IDG Books Worldwide Customer Service phone number: 800-762-2974 (outside the U.S.: 317-596-5430).

Index

● *Y* ●

● *Z* ●

IDG Books Worldwide, Inc., End-User License Agreement

READ THIS. You should carefully read these terms and conditions before opening the software packet(s) included with this book ("Book"). This is a license agreement ("Agreement") between you and IDG Books Worldwide, Inc. ("IDGB"). By opening the accompanying software packet(s), you acknowledge that you have read and accept the following terms and conditions. If you do not agree and do not want to be bound by such terms and conditions, promptly return the Book and the unopened software packet(s) to the place you obtained them for a full refund.

1. **License Grant.** IDGB grants to you (either an individual or entity) a nonexclusive license to use one copy of the enclosed software program(s) (collectively, the "Software") solely for your own personal or business purposes on a single computer (whether a standard computer or a workstation component of a multiuser network). The Software is in use on a computer when it is loaded into temporary memory (RAM) or installed into permanent memory (hard disk, CD-ROM, or other storage device). IDGB reserves all rights not expressly granted herein.

2. **Ownership.** IDGB is the owner of all right, title, and interest, including copyright, in and to the compilation of the Software recorded on the disk(s) or CD-ROM ("Software Media"). Copyright to the individual programs recorded on the Software Media is owned by the author or other authorized copyright owner of each program. Ownership of the Software and all proprietary rights relating thereto remain with IDGB and its licensers.

3. **Restrictions on Use and Transfer.**

   (a) You may only (i) make one copy of the Software for backup or archival purposes, or (ii) transfer the Software to a single hard disk, provided that you keep the original for backup or archival purposes. You may not (i) rent or lease the Software, (ii) copy or reproduce the Software through a LAN or other network system or through any computer subscriber system or bulletin-board system, or (iii) modify, adapt, or create derivative works based on the Software.

   (b) You may not reverse engineer, decompile, or disassemble the Software. You may transfer the Software and user documentation on a permanent basis, provided that the transferee agrees to accept the terms and conditions of this Agreement and you retain no copies. If the Software is an update or has been updated, any transfer must include the most recent update and all prior versions.

4. **Restrictions on Use of Individual Programs.** You must follow the individual requirements and restrictions detailed for each individual program in the Appendix of this Book. These limitations are also contained in the individual license agreements recorded on the Software Media. These limitations may include a requirement that after using the program for a specified period of time, the user must pay a registration fee or discontinue use. By opening the Software packet(s), you will be agreeing to abide by the licenses and restrictions for these individual programs that are detailed in the Appendix and on the Software Media. None of the material on this Software Media or listed in this Book may ever be redistributed, in original or modified form, for commercial purposes.

5. **Limited Warranty.**

   (a) IDGB warrants that the Software and Software Media are free from defects in materials and workmanship under normal use for a period of sixty (60) days from the date of purchase of this Book. If IDGB receives notification within the warranty period of defects in materials or workmanship, IDGB will replace the defective Software Media.

   (b) **IDGB AND THE AUTHOR OF THE BOOK DISCLAIM ALL OTHER WARRANTIES, EXPRESS OR IMPLIED, INCLUDING WITHOUT LIMITATION IMPLIED WARRANTIES OF MER-CHANTABILITY AND FITNESS FOR A PARTICULAR PURPOSE, WITH RESPECT TO THE SOFTWARE, THE PROGRAMS, THE SOURCE CODE CONTAINED THEREIN, AND/OR THE TECHNIQUES DESCRIBED IN THIS BOOK. IDGB DOES NOT WARRANT THAT THE FUNCTIONS CONTAINED IN THE SOFTWARE WILL MEET YOUR REQUIREMENTS OR THAT THE OPERATION OF THE SOFTWARE WILL BE ERROR FREE.**

   (c) This limited warranty gives you specific legal rights, and you may have other rights that vary from jurisdiction to jurisdiction.

6. **Remedies.**

   (a) IDGB's entire liability and your exclusive remedy for defects in materials and workmanship shall be limited to replacement of the Software Media, which may be returned to IDGB with a copy of your receipt at the following address: Software Media Fulfillment Department, Attn.: *Visual Studio 6 For Dummies,* IDG Books Worldwide, Inc., 7260 Shadeland Station, Ste. 100, Indianapolis, IN 46256, or call 800-762-2974. Please allow three to four weeks for delivery. This Limited Warranty is void if failure of the Software Media has resulted from accident, abuse, or misapplication. Any replacement Software Media will be warranted for the remainder of the original warranty period or thirty (30) days, whichever is longer.

   (b) In no event shall IDGB or the author be liable for any damages whatsoever (including without limitation damages for loss of business profits, business interruption, loss of business information, or any other pecuniary loss) arising from the use of or inability to use the Book or the Software, even if IDGB has been advised of the possibility of such damages.

   (c) Because some jurisdictions do not allow the exclusion or limitation of liability for conse-quential or incidental damages, the above limitation or exclusion may not apply to you.

7. **U.S. Government Restricted Rights.** Use, duplication, or disclosure of the Software by the U.S. Government is subject to restrictions stated in paragraph (c)(1)(ii) of the Rights in Technical Data and Computer Software clause of DFARS 252.227-7013, and in subparagraphs (a) through (d) of the Commercial Computer–Restricted Rights clause at FAR 52.227-19, and in similar clauses in the NASA FAR supplement, when applicable.

8. **General.** This Agreement constitutes the entire understanding of the parties and revokes and supersedes all prior agreements, oral or written, between them and may not be modified or amended except in a writing signed by both parties hereto that specifically refers to this Agreement. This Agreement shall take precedence over any other documents that may be in conflict herewith. If any one or more provisions contained in this Agreement are held by any court or tribunal to be invalid, illegal, or otherwise unenforceable, each and every other provision shall remain in full force and effect.

Installation Instructions

To access the HTML interface file on the CD, follow these steps:

1. **Insert the CD into your computer's CD-ROM drive.**

2. **Open your Web browser.**

   Visual Studio includes the latest version of Internet Explorer. Most of the examples in this book are geared toward this Web browser.

3. **Choose File⇨Open in Internet Explorer.**

4. **In the dialog box that appears, type** D:\DEFAULT.HTM **and click OK.**

   Replace the letter *D* with the correct letter for your CD-ROM drive, if it is not *D*. This action displays the file that will walk you through the contents of the CD.

5. **To navigate within the interface, simply click on any topic of interest to take you to an explanation of the files on the CD and how to use or install them.**

   After you're done with the interface, simply close your browser as usual.

For more information, see the "About the CD" appendix.

Discover Dummies™ Online!

The *Dummies* Web Site is your fun and friendly online resource for the latest information about *...For Dummies®* books on all your favorite topics. From cars to computers, wine to Windows, and investing to the Internet, we've got a shelf full of *...For Dummies* books waiting for you!

Ten Fun and Useful Things You Can Do at www.dummies.com

1. Register this book and win!
2. Find and buy the *...For Dummies* books you want online.
3. Get ten great *Dummies Tips™* every week.
4. Chat with your favorite *...For Dummies* authors.
5. Subscribe free to *The Dummies Dispatch™* newsletter.
6. Enter our sweepstakes and win cool stuff.
7. Send a free cartoon postcard to a friend.
8. Download free software.
9. Sample a book before you buy.
10. Talk to us. Make comments, ask questions, and get answers!

Jump online to these ten fun and useful things at
http://www.dummies.com/10useful

For other technology titles from IDG Books Worldwide, go to
www.idgbooks.com

Not online yet? It's easy to get started with *The Internet For Dummies®,* 5th Edition, or *Dummies 101®: The Internet For Windows® 98,* available at local retailers everywhere.

Find other *...For Dummies* books on these topics:

Business • Careers • Databases • Food & Beverages • Games • Gardening • Graphics • Hardware
Health & Fitness • Internet and the World Wide Web • Networking • Office Suites
Operating Systems • Personal Finance • Pets • Programming • Recreation • Sports
Spreadsheets • Teacher Resources • Test Prep • Word Processing

IDG BOOKS WORLDWIDE BOOK REGISTRATION

Register This Book and Win!

We want to hear from you!

Visit **http://my2cents.dummies.com** to register this book and tell us how you liked it!

- ✔ Get entered in our monthly prize giveaway.

- ✔ Give us feedback about this book — tell us what you like best, what you like least, or maybe what you'd like to ask the author and us to change!

- ✔ Let us know any other ...*For Dummies*® topics that interest you.

Your feedback helps us determine what books to publish, tells us what coverage to add as we revise our books, and lets us know whether we're meeting your needs as a ...*For Dummies* reader. You're our most valuable resource, and what you have to say is important to us!

Not on the Web yet? It's easy to get started with *Dummies 101*®: *The Internet For Windows*® *98* or *The Internet For Dummies*,® 5th Edition, at local retailers everywhere.

Or let us know what you think by sending us a letter at the following address:

...*For Dummies* Book Registration
Dummies Press
7260 Shadeland Station, Suite 100
Indianapolis, IN 46256-3945
Fax 317-596-5498

BESTSELLING BOOK SERIES FROM IDG